D0926828

One Hundred Years of Children's Books in America

Decade by Decade

CHILDREN'S BOOKS BY MARJORIE N. ALLEN

The Remarkable Ride of Israel Bissell as Related by Molly the Crow
(with Alice Schick, illustrated by Joel Schick)

Farley, Are You for Real?
(with Carl Allen, illustrated by Joel Schick)

The Marble Cake Cat
(with Carl Allen, illustrated by Marylin Hafner)

One, Two, Three—AhChoo!
(illustrated by Dick Gackenbach)

Changes
(photographs and concept by Shelley Rotner)

One Hundred Years of Children's Books in America

Decade by Decade

MARJORIE N. ALLEN

Foreword by
JANE YOLEN

Facts On File, Inc.
AN INFOBASE HOLDINGS COMPANY

One Hundred Years of Children's Books in America: Decade by Decade

Facts On File, Inc.
11 Penn Plaza
New York, NY 10001

Library of Congress Cataloging-in-Publication Data

Allen, Marjorie N.
One hundred years of children's books in America: decade by decade / Marjorie N. Allen.
p. cm.
Includes bibliographical references and index.
ISBN 0-8160-3044-8 (alk. paper)
1. Children's literature, American—History and criticism. 2. Children's literature, American—Bibliography. 3. Children—United States—Books and reading.—I. Title.
PS490.a38—1996
810.9'9282—dc20 95-34104

Facts On File books are available at special discounts when purchased in bulk quantities for businesses, associations, institutions or sales promotions. Please call our Special Sales Department in New York at 212/967-8800 or 800/322-8755.

Text design by Catherine Rincon Hyman
Jacket design by Vertigo Design

This book is printed on acid-free paper.

Printed in the United States of America

MP FOF 10 9 8 7 6 5 4 3 2 1

TO MY HUSBAND,

DAVID,

WITH LOVE

Those books . . . first encountered in childhood do more to shape the imagination and its style than all the later calculated readings of the acknowledged masters.

—Gore Vidal, *United States: Essays 1952–1992*

CONTENTS

ACKNOWLEDGMENTS

The paths that led to writing this book had their origins in 1972 when my mentor, Helen Buckley Simkewicz, reintroduced me to the magical world of children's literature, a world I had left behind at the age of 12. Helen's enthusiasm, her writing and teaching talents, and her wonderful collection of children's books kindled in me an Olympian flame fueled over the years by many people—Jane Yolen and the Society of Children's Book Writers and Illustrators, Joan German Grapes and the American Society of Journalists and Authors, Rachael Hungerford, Judith Storie, Elinor Rothman and the Ada Comstock Scholars Program at Smith College, Katherine Paterson, Maurice Sendak, and Deborah Schneider, agent exemplar. The overwhelming chore of researching a hundred plus years of children's literature was pared considerably by the Berkshire Athenaeum's collection of children's books, carefully preserved and thoughtfully chosen over the years, and by the cooperation of the staff in both the children's and reference departments. Equally helpful were Steve Satullo, Christine Erb, and the staff of the Either/Or Bookstore in Pittsfield, carrying on the tradition of excellence established in Bertha Mahony's Bookstore for Boys and Girls in Boston. Karen Nelson Hoyle, curator of the Kerlan Collection of Children's Literature at the University of Minnesota, and Carolyn Davis, library assistant, offered invaluable assistance during my visit there when I was awarded the Ezra Jack Keats scholarship in 1991. I also wish to thank Caroline Sutton and Derek Burke, my extremely perceptive editors at Facts On File, and my husband, Dave, my children, John, Carl, and Dena, their mates, and my grandchildren, Meghan, Matthew, Sean, and Taylor, who have always supported me in my need to explore worlds of the imagination.

FOREWORD: The Facts and Fictions of Peter Rabbit

Children's literature is—like it or not—a didactic literature. That is to say that children's books, whether good, bad, or perfectly horrible, teach the young readers something, filling up the interstices of their lives. A child will warm to stories, *Peter Rabbit* or the *Baby-sitters Club*, and having warmed, will become molded by that story. Tales are simply part of a child's cultural baggage. As author Michael Martone said at a recent writer's conference: "Your stories are fictions, but they are also the facts of your time."

He was talking about adults writing stories for other adults. But he would have been even more accurate talking about children's books. The books of childhood get read and reread over the years. They carry the facts of a particular time, made into fiction, into the life of the reading child. The book becomes the child's life source, becomes—in that peculiar metamorphism of art—the child herself.

As a youngster I read compulsively, and read again my favorites: *Babar*, *The Story of Ferdinand*, *Mary Poppins*. I read them with my whole heart. Did I take in messages of imperialism, pacifism, or kneejerk racism as I read? Certainly not consciously. But the unconscious mind builds its own great storehouse of musty wares. We dine off those plates for the rest of our lives.

However, we must not judge children's books solely on certain hidden messages that our evolving cultures often consign to the scrap bin of history. Rather, we need to learn to read, critique, and discuss these books in a manner that includes a longer historical view, a critical vocabulary, and an understanding of the book's structure. Isn't it odd then how the literature itself has developed more thoroughly and radically and with more depth than the manner of our reading it? There are plenty of books out there that talk about *using* books with children: using them in the classroom, using them as therapy, using them as adjuncts to learning science, history, math. But until this book, there has not been a single volume that puts the literature of childhood in its historical context, the facts along with the fictions.

Perhaps it is Marjorie Allen's own particular background: a published children's book writer with years as a book reviewer and commentator on the publishing scene. This gives her a certain perch from which to view the literary world, both from within and without. Here she sets children's books squarely within the decade-by-decade history of the past century, discussing individual key books in some depth and additional books in encapsulated reviews. It is a long-needed book in the field, one that adds depth and breadth to our understanding of the books and authors who write down the facts of their own time in the fiction of their devising.

—Jane Yolen

INTRODUCTION: Patterns in History

It is, in the end, not the parents, the teachers, the preachers,
not even the authors, but the children themselves
who determine what their literature is to be.

—Henry Steele Commager
Introduction to the first edition of
A Critical History of Children's Literature

Reading for Pleasure

Although storytellers have existed throughout the world since the beginning of time, the children's book industry in the United States is a phenomenon of the 20th century. As published books became more and more accessible to the general public, oral storytelling gave way to the printed word, and reading became a private affair.

But with the advent of whole-language philosophy in the 1980s, which, by way of trade books, brought storytelling back into the classroom as part of the curriculum, the publication of children's books has developed into a multimillion-dollar business. Whole-language philosophy is an attitude, not a method. It is relating the act of reading to one's immediate environment, i.e., the "off" and "on" buttons for the television set, the numbers on the telephone dial, the days and dates on a calendar. It is a child hearing a story read aloud in the classroom, then looking at the printed page and recognizing some of the words in the context of story. It is a parent and child sharing a story, and the child recognizing words and phrases on the page as they're being read aloud by the parent. It is, in effect, connecting print with meaning.[1]

Exploring a hundred years of contemporary children's literature decade by decade from a socio-historical viewpoint—in other words, connecting print with meaning—creates a focus on certain authors and illustrators whose books reflect the decade in which they were written and continue year after year to influence new readers. This chronological history of the children's book industry in our country will say as much about the development of the United States since the Civil War as it does about the books chosen for discussion.

When early settlers emigrated from England to find religious freedom, they gathered in an area they called "New England," and in the name of freedom took over the leadership of the country, imposing their tenets on American society. The Puritan ideal became so much a part of this society that its influence continues to restrict American attitudes to this day. Some early titles under discussion in this study show, in retrospect, a lack of sensitivity that is due in great part to the predominant view of American society at that time as being exclusively Anglo-Saxon and Protestant. Other early titles represent a more unbiased vision and an expanded viewpoint. A growing comprehension on the part of the American people as to the diversity of cultures and beliefs in this country has created an effort by children's book authors and illustrators in the latter part of this century to celebrate that diversity by creating a more representative body of American children's literature. As this century draws to a close, it is time to present an overview of the children's books best remembered in this country and to reflect on what has made them last.

The people who run the country and who make decisions and offer new ideas don't suddenly appear in place, fully grown and competent. They all were children once, and children are influenced by the books they read. Rose Kennedy, mother of John F. Kennedy, took the time to make an evolving list of books she wanted her children to read, even though young Jack preferred a story called *Billy Whiskers* (1902),[2] which was not on his mother's list and which she considered quite silly.[3] The book, the first of a series, introduced one dilemma after another as a willful goat did exactly as it pleased, sometimes creating chaos, sometimes inadvertently accomplishing good deeds. Often coarse in its delivery,[4] the story was far from an example of propriety on the part of the author, but it contained nonstop action and excitement at a time when the best books for children stayed within certain boundaries of behavior. Kennedy was equally enthralled by the stories of King Arthur.

Since the children's book industry in America is so new—it didn't begin to exist as a business until the third decade of the 20th century—members of the generations who remember the earliest books are still around to buy them for grandchildren and great-grandchildren. Certain titles by American authors remain popular. In the bookstore, a customer makes a request: "Do you have *Hitty: Her First Hundred Years?* I want to buy it for my granddaughter; I loved that book when I was her age." Another says, "I always buy a copy of *Goodnight Moon* for new parents. My children couldn't get enough of it when they were little." At the library, certain titles become dog-eared from constant use: *The Secret Garden*, *Danny and the Dinosaur*, *Millions of Cats*, *Where the Wild Things Are*, *Horton Hatches the Egg*, *The Snowy Day*. Almost everyone remembers a childhood book—from *Winnie the Pooh* to *Nancy Drew*—and there is pleasure in remembering.

History in the Making

Today's children take for granted the existence of children's books in libraries and bookstores. As the industry moves toward its second hundred years, people who remember a time when there were no children's rooms in libraries and no children's book departments in publishing companies will be gone. Because of that, *One Hundred Years of Children's Books in America* becomes an effort to keep the connection unbroken. Even now, when we are reading books about children's literature written and edited by renowned librarians and critics from the past, it is evident that much of the history of the genre would have been lost forever if these historians hadn't put their experiences with children's books into print.[5] The Kerlan Collection at the University of Minnesota in Minneapolis is one of the many research collections of children's literature in this country (see Appendix A) that offer a unique view of children's books through manuscripts, letters, and sketches, and visiting such a collection constitutes a living journey through the past. Only with these direct connections to children's book authors and illustrators could this overview of American children's books as an integral part of America's social history have been written.

The viewpoint in this book is historical as well as critical, which means that some books under discussion may be suspect in the literary world: for instance, *Nancy Drew* and the *Hardy Boys*, as well as Dorothy Kunhardt's *Pat the Bunny* and Ann Martin's more recent *Baby-sitter* series. Some of the titles are as easy to read and as compelling today as they were when first published: *Hans Brinker; or, the Silver Skates* by Mary Mapes Dodge, Marjorie Bianco's *The Velveteen Rabbit*, and *Caddie Woodlawn* by Carol Ryrie Brink. Some authors and illustrators, in light of growing social awareness in this country, have been criticized for books written in a less enlightened social environment: Helen Bannerman, author/illustrator of *Little Black Sambo*, and Hugh Lofting, author/illustrator of the *Doctor Dolittle* series, to name only two. Why are some books immortal and why do others overcome, or succumb to, the flaws caused by changes in social attitudes? These issues will be discussed in subsequent chapters.

The children's book industry began to evolve in this country in the early 1900s, and almost a hundred years later its product output continues to increase at a phenomenal rate. In 1919, 433 children's books were published in the United States (mostly European imports); in 1929, the number more than doubled to 931 (mostly American);[6] in 1961, it almost doubled again with 1,700; and in the 1990s it has tripled, with 5,000 to 6,000 children's books a year being published in this country.[7] In 1990, there were 40,000 trade titles in print.[8] Just four years later, there were more than 70,000 trade children's book titles (not textbooks) available to libraries and bookstores,[9] an indication of how quickly the industry has grown in this decade alone.

Recording America's Past

In an effort to make selective decisions regarding the myriad of titles published over the years, many bibliographies have been published and updated periodically since the mid-20th century. *One Hundred Years of Children's Books in America*, with a combination of text and annotated bibliography covering each decade from just after the Civil War through the present time, offers a full-scale chronological study of the children's book industry. What kinds of children's books were being written just before the stock market crash of 1929 or during the social revolution of the 1960s? And how did those books reflect the times? What makes a book part of the social history of a country?

The text focuses on American authors and illustrators whose books remain in print and European contributors who have found a permanent place in American literature, but both the text and the annotated bibliographies do occasionally include some out-of-print books. They are mentioned because they act as links in the genre's development. In books cited from the 19th century through 1919, the original country of publication is listed. From that time on, since this is a book about children's books in America, only American publishers are listed, even though a book may originally have been published outside of the United States.

The children's book industry has expanded over the years, reaching into every facet of American society—not just with contemporary fiction and fantasy but with biographies and reference books, with historical fiction, science fiction, and easy-reader chapter books for middle readers, with picture books and poetry for preschoolers. Everyone has at some time been touched or influenced by a children's book. As stated by historian R. Gordon Kelly, "Children's books are an accessible, readily available feature in an elusive enterprise—the creation, maintenance, and modification of meaning in society. We have hardly begun to examine children's books in America from this perspective and to locate them in the cultural contexts in which they were written, read, and selectively preserved and made available to successive generations of American children."[10]

Choosing Titles

Though the choices are meant to be perspicacious and without personal prejudice, prejudice will surface. Another author exploring the same theme would be writing an entirely different book. In the words of award-winning author Katherine Paterson, "No one knows exactly how someone else feels. But I do know how I feel, and I try to stay true to those feelings."[11] The books chosen for discussion are those that have a direct connection to the decade in which they were written—sometimes veering from the mainstream or even going directly against the current, and sometimes simply reflecting the social attitudes of the time.

The differences between the business of writing and the profession of writing are the degrees of emotional involvement, craftsmanship, and commitment. An old Japanese folktale speaks of a woman who weaves beautiful fabrics, unlike anything ever seen, but she is actually a crane who creates her unique tapestries by plucking out her feathers one by one and weaving them with her life's blood into the cloth.[12] A true classic could not have been written by anyone else at any other time; its fabric contains the author's life-blood. The best books of any decade are so much a part of their creators that they never go out of style. And the best writers would continue writing regardless of how much they earned. Wanda Gág, author of *Millions of Cats* (1928), confirmed that statement with these words: "I am simply not interested in illustration as such, or in illustrating as a job for which I can get a certain amount of money. It has to be a story that takes hold of me way down deep—something inevitable."[13] Pulitzer prize-winning author Alison Lurie points to the ethical standards exhibited by children's book authors when she says, "Opinions and attitudes that are not currently in style in the adult world often find expression in the children's books of the time."[14]

When Gág's *Millions of Cats* was first published, it proffered opinions and attitudes not in style in the adult world of the Twenties. Certainly, the public at that time didn't see her book as a reflection of society's ills, but in retrospect that is exactly what it was—a story about greed and vanity getting out of hand. Children's books expand the universe, whether they're read by children or adults. The most memorable children's books of the last 150 years offer an overview of history from prehistoric times to the present in a highly accessible format, and somewhere in the collection might well be the one book that will spark a lifelong love of literature in the most reluctant reader.

Overview

The 19th century was a golden age of children's books in Great Britain, with an expanding body of literature being published specifically for children and some of the most highly respected artists of the day contributing their talents to the genre. Sir John Tenniel considered himself a success in the adult world as an artist for *Punch* magazine but gained far more recognition as the illustrator of *Alice's Adventures in Wonderland*. From the time John Newbery, publisher and bookseller, decided to create books just for children in 18th-century England until the end of the 19th century, when English industry produced children's books of the highest quality, the body of children's literature that became available from England earned a growing respect throughout the literary world.

In America, technology took longer to develop, with the major industrial growth taking place after the Civil War. Perhaps because printing technology lagged behind that of England and perhaps because children were looked upon as small adults, children's books in 19th-century America were not appreciated as a potential art form. There were no economical and attractive picture books in color published for American children. In fact, there were no American picture storybooks at all, and very few were imported from England until the early 20th century. However, because of fast economic growth and a high rate of production, the 20th century has become a golden age of children's books in America. In the 21st century the study and examination of children's literature will call for a global survey, for it is through the viewpoint of the child, uncluttered by sociopolitical trappings, that the universality of the human condition suddenly becomes clear.

The chapters have been divided by decades, except for the first chapter, which basically covers the years from the end of the Civil War to the end of the 19th century, and the second chapter, which includes the first 20 years of the 20th century. Each chapter is half text and half annotated bibliography, with the text attempting to show the tie between America's social development and the books children read, followed by the annotated bibliography. The third decade, 1920 to 1929, represents the first real decade of children's books in the marketplace, while throughout society fun and games prevailed. The fourth, 1930 to 1939, deals with the Great Depression. The fifth decade, 1940 to 1949, spans World War II and its aftermath. The sixth, 1950 to 1959, leads to an expanding technology. The seventh, 1960 to 1969, covers social revolution. In the eighth decade, 1970 to 1979, the focus is on big business. The ninth decade, 1980–1989, heralds a development of social and ecological awareness. In the final decade, 1990–2000, worldwide reconstruction has become paramount.

Approximately 600 books are discussed in these pages. Considering that 900-plus children's books were published in 1929 alone and 5,000 in 1990, finding 60 worth discussion in a 10-year publishing span would seem to be an easy task. Not so. Only the most extraordinary books survive, and most of the books published in any given year are not extraordinary. In 1959, 1,647 new children's books were published, but at that time fewer than one-third were considered worthy of media review, let alone predicted as books that would become lasting contributions to the genre.[15] When a new genre has surfaced in a particular era—such as the picture book format[16] in the 1920s or the so-called problem novel of the 1970s[17]—the titles chosen are those that reflect literary worth and/or historical relevance, with innovation a key factor.

It is difficult to define an age group for "children's" books. So much depends on a reader's interest level, experience, and access to books. Since this study looks at the children's book industry, I shall accede to the publishers themselves and include only titles that have been published under a children's book imprint, which includes the "young adult" category. To quote critic John Rowe Townsend: "The only practical definition of a children's book today—absurd as it sounds—is 'a book which appears on the children's list of a publisher.'"[18]

In the first half of this volume, each chapter lists 30 to 50 titles in the annotated bibliography. All are available to the general public either in bookstores or libraries; occasionally a book is out of print. As the industry continues to increase its output, both the number of cited books and the proportionate number of out-of-print books increases. In the case of a collection of books by the same author, e.g., the *Oz* books and the *Doctor Dolittle* books, the titles chosen are those that reflect the best or most relevant efforts of these authors. For the predictable series book over the years, one or, at best, two titles in a given series have been selected to outline the basic premise. Whenever a book was too difficult to locate, it wasn't included. In the second half of the volume, 75 to 100 books per chapter are annotated. For books published from the 1940s on, locating available titles became easier than choosing which of them to include. The number of books left out might very well equal the number of books cited here.

Some authors have been more prolific than others: Margaret Wise Brown wrote close to a hundred books for children in her career, and Jane Yolen has written well over a hundred and has yet to reach her zenith. But it is Brown's simple picture books showing the familiar world of the very young and Yolen's classical fairy tales and poetic text that stand out in the history of children's books. The second half of the century was also a time when the genre became divided into categories, subcategories, and more subcategories, creating an increasingly complicated network of titles, especially in the picture-book field. With the overwhelming number of picture books being printed today, only those in which text and illustrations merge harmoniously to create a third level of excellence, in which an innovative format creates a new concept, or in which content has generated controversy merit discussion in this study. The illustrations selected for inclusion are limited to one per chapter and are intended only to reveal the attitudes of a given decade in terms of social awareness.

The final decade covered in this book hasn't ended yet, and some of the best books have yet to be written. But certain authors and illustrators already stand above the rest in the 1990s through craftsmanship and originality. Both Katherine Paterson and Virginia Hamilton continue to write beautifully developed works that reflect society's imperfections; Lois Ehlert keeps producing her outstanding original collages; Chris Van Allsburg, who never stops taking chances, has already created classic material, even though, in his more recent books, he is apt to be somewhat didactic in his approach; and the classic fairy tale is giving way to the fractured fairy tale with *The True Story of the Three Little Pigs by A. Wolf*, created by Jon Scieszka and illustrator Lane Smith.

Children's books, like the children who read them, have long been ignored by the general public, but the spotlight has recently been turned on these books, and the time has come to incorporate children's literature into the social history of 20th-century America. Let the celebration begin!

NOTES

1. As defined by Kenneth Goodman in *Reading: A Conversation with Kenneth Goodman*. Chicago: Scott, Foresman, 1976, ed. Ghia Brenner, pp. 1–13.
2. Frances Trego Montgomery. *Billy Whiskers: The Autobiography of a Goat*, illtd. W. H. Fry. Akron, Ohio: Saalfield Publishing Co., 1902; New York: Dover, 1969.
3. Judie Mills. *John F. Kennedy*. p. 17.
4. Little care was taken to show respect for people of other nationalities: "The first thing he came to was a flower and fruit stand, the owner of which, *a greasy, black-looking Italian* [my italics], was talking to a fat blue-coated policeman." Montgomery, op. cit., p. 40.
5. The contributions to the history of children's books made by Gale Research Company in its Something About the Author series and by Horn Book's volumes on Newbery Medal and Caldecott Medal books are invaluable.
6. Ruth Hill Viguers. "Golden Years and Time of Tumult: 1920–1967," *A Critical History of Children's Literature*. ed. Cornelia Meigs, p. 397.
7. Writer's Digest. *Children's Writer's and Illustrator's Market*. Cincinnati, Ohio: 1993, p. 1.
8. Betsy Hearne. *Choosing Books for Children*, p. 9.
9. R. R. Bowker, eds of. "Introduction," *Children's Books in Print*, 1992., p. 1.
10. M. Thomas Inge, ed. *Handbook of American Popular Culture*, vol. 1, p. 50.
11. Katherine Paterson. *The Spying Heart*, p. 108.
12. Sumiko Yagawa. *The Crane Wife*, tr. Katherine Paterson; illtd. Suekichi Akaba. New York: Morrow, 1981.
13. As told to her friend, Alma Scott. *Wanda Gág*, p. 185.

14. Alison Lurie. *Don't Tell the Grownups: Why Kids Love the Books They Do*, p. 9.
15. Zena Sutherland. "Current Reviewing of Children's Books," *A Critical Approach to Children's Literature*, ed. Sara Innis Fenwick. p. 110.
16. Consisting of a brief text and a full-page illustration on each double spread.
17. Identified as novels for "young adults," in which issues eclipsed character development.
18. John Rowe Townsend. *A Sounding of Storytellers: Essays on Contemporary Writers for Children*, p. 10.

One Hundred Years of Children's Books in America

Decade by Decade

Frontispiece illustration by A. B. Frost from Uncle Remus and his friends, old plantation stories, songs, and ballads with sketches of negro character *by Joel Chandler Harris (Houghton Mifflin, 1900). Courtesy of the Kerlan Collection, Walter Library, University of Minnesota, Minneapolis, Minnesota. The drawings of A. B. Frost cut straight through the difficult dialect and multiple levels of meaning in Harris' collection of folktales to focus on character. Uncle Remus, though bent and crippled by a life of servitude, retains his dignity as he looks directly at his audience from the center of the page.*

1

EMERGING MOTIFS 19TH CENTURY

One of the most striking things about children's books is how widely they are known by adults. Probably almost everyone in America . . . is familiar with *Cinderella* and *Alice's Adventures in Wonderland*; not one in ten will have read James Joyce.

—Alison Lurie
Don't Tell the Grown-Ups: Why Kids Love the Books They Do

All Work, No Play

In the 1800s, children were viewed as small adults, useful in the workplace. For the working class, education was the exception rather than the rule, with most children attending school for no more than 14 weeks each year[1] and then either being sent off to the factories or becoming full-time farm workers. By 1890, almost 2 million children were formally employed, with thousands more working the city streets.[2] Until the 20th century, there was no middle class in American society, only the rich and the poor. The rich had the option of sending their children to private schools and colleges, while the poor struggled to make ends meet; for them, education was not a priority.

After the Civil War, there was an increase in formal education for the masses, with the belief that learning would make the American dream (see p. 26)—poor man to rich man—come true. Schooling became available to everyone, but few could afford to take advantage of the opportunity. By the early 1900s it became mandatory, and the public education system eventually developed a curriculum that was considered standard for the country. But for most people in the late 1800s, taking time to become literate was taking time away from the work front.

The Other Side of the Cloth

In the last decade of the 19th century, literature published specifically for children didn't exist as a business in America. In the 1890s, children able to read were forced either to recite religious tracts by rote in Sunday schools or to read the dreary text in McGuffey's Readers. Some managed to stash dog-eared copies of dime novels—forerunners of the series book—and pass them around until they disintegrated. When something that appealed to children was widely accessible, such as the poem *A Visit from St. Nicholas* ("'Twas the night before Christmas . . .") by Clement Clarke Moore,[3] its popularity led to its becoming a classic, honored over time for its child appeal.

Nathaniel Hawthorne's *A Wonder Book for Girls and Boys* (1852) was one of the earliest American books written specifically to entertain children, and his versions of the Greek and Roman myths were avidly consumed by those few children in America able to read and whose families were wealthy enough to own books. Mythology, like fairy tales, developed through oral storytelling in the early days of civilization. The

Greek and Roman gods were created in the minds of men to explain natural phenomena, and the stories that developed became the basis for classic literature in the Western world. Filled with action, excitement, and suspense, these myths were bound to appeal to young people.

Despite medical advances, many children didn't survive past infancy, and parents, especially among the poor, were apt to distance themselves emotionally from their offspring.[4] Literature occupied only a small corner of American culture—there wasn't much time for it—but its importance was realized by a determined few, and by the third decade of the 20th century, children's literature, intended to entertain rather than merely teach, had firmly taken root as a separate genre.

Even though all books in the 1800s were published in the United States for a general adult market, some seemed to appeal to children as much as, if not more than, to adults. The best of these, over a period of a hundred years, have been labeled "children's literature." Many were imported from England, where they had been published specifically as children's books, and were purchased mainly by wealthy families.

In England, where industry had flourished in the 18th century and created a middle class much earlier than in the United States, children's literature had become a well-established genre by the time Lewis Carroll wrote *Alice's Adventures in Wonderland* (1865). English bookseller and publisher John Newbery had initiated a children's book industry in England in 1744 with books expressly intended to entertain child readers. Although a limited supply of Mother Goose rhymes were published in New England in 1785 by American publisher Isaiah Thomas, they were merely copies of those published in England. Nineteenth-century America was far behind her former mother country in industrial development, still in the process of learning to handle newly gained independence. Children reading Mother Goose verses quickly picked up the rhythms and the unusual language of these rhymes and took them for their own, even though several were originally based on British political commentary written for adults, not for children. Maurice Sendak says, "The powerful rhythms of the verses combined with their great strengths and resonance account largely for their appeal to the child's inborn musical fancy."[5]

> Tom, Tom, the piper's son,
> Stole a pig and away he run;
> The pig was eat,
> And Tom was beat,
> And Tom went howling down the street.[6]

In the United States, where the rich diversity of cultures could have given America its own broad spectrum of children's rhymes, songs, and stories and encouraged more interaction between ethnic groups early on, there was no effort to plumb the literary riches available in our newly emerging country. Books were simply imported from Britain. Following the Civil War, North and South joined to become a republic, but the concept of a single and unique nation was so new that, in the literary world at least, dependence on Britain's literature remained. In addition, the large number of immigrants coming into this newly settled land brought their storytellers with them. Just about the only early nursery rhyme credited to an American author was "Mary Had a Little Lamb," but no one can agree on which American author should get the credit. Industrialist Henry Ford was convinced that the first 12 lines were written in 1815 by 12-year-old John Roulstone of Sterling, Massachusetts, and the second 12 lines by Sarah Josepha Hale, editor of *Godey's Lady's Book*.[7] On the other hand, Hale herself takes credit for the whole poem; as to the "impression that some part of this particular poem was written by another person," she claims "there is no foundation for it, whatever."[8]

Britain's "Golden Age" of Children's Literature

By the late 1800s, Lewis Carroll's *Alice's Adventures in Wonderland* (1865) had been imported to America from Britain. Carroll allowed the reader to plunge with Alice down the rabbit hole and see Wonderland as Alice saw it—with no effort at guidance, unlike many of the stories considered morally acceptable in both England and America at that time. Sir John Tenniel's illustrations remain as much a part of the charm of Carroll's *Alice* as the story's language. It is impossible to hear the words "Cheshire-Cat" and not see that animal's broad grin as Tenniel created it. Both the disagreeable Duchess and the equally disagreeable baby were brought to life by Tenniel, and the punctilious rabbit remains enchanting. Both *Alice* and its sequel, *Through the Looking Glass* (1871), appealed to a child's unquestioning acceptance of the fantastic, but underlying the fantasy were satire and experimental forays into the world of mathematics. Because of the many levels of meaning in these books, one of the greatest controversies in the history of children's literature has been whether or not they should carry the label of children's book. The question then becomes, "What is a children's book as distinguished from an adult book?"

Children's books as a rule are a specialty genre; they stay in a separate area, are reviewed in separate sections of the media, and become as segregated from the general public as the children for whom they are written. When a children's book does somehow move into the spotlight and ultimately garners a high degree of respect, the question immediately arises as to whether or not it really is a children's book. This does not happen outside of this country; for some reason, American critics have trouble accepting anything with child appeal as academically legitimate. Richard Adams's *Watership Down* was published in England in 1972 and was awarded a Carnegie Medal as the best children's book of the year; in America, it was lauded in *Newsweek*[9] by a columnist who did not identify it as a children's book at all, and suddenly it was not only an adult best seller in this country but also labeled an immediate adult classic by the academic community.

When *Alice* was first published in England, children there weren't much interested in it. Even the reviewers dismissed it as unremarkable. But by the time *Through the Looking Glass* was published, critical acclaim for *Alice* had grown considerably and continues to this day. It is the epitome of European fairy tale and myth, in which the reader becomes absorbed into an imaginary world of shape-changers and magical potions, with origins that can be traced back through the centuries to storytellers among the common folk. Carroll, like the storytellers of old, dramatized his story by telling it aloud to his child audience. When he wrote the story for publication, it contained an underlying element of social commentary in the guise of entertaining fantasy. What he didn't do that marked so much of the Victorian literature of England was to preach, although he used an upper-class Victorian setting as a jumping-off place for his fantasy.

World Cultures Through Fairy Tales

The Blue Fairy Book (1889) was edited by collector Andrew Lang and was the first of several volumes edited by him and known as the "color" fairy tales, which introduced folk and fairy to children in England at the end of the 19th century. The stories contained in this and subsequent "color" collections are "older than reading and writing, far older than printing"[10] and have their origins in all of the ancient cultures of Europe and Asia. The first collection was so popular that it quickly was followed by "red," "green," and "yellow" *Fairy Books*. The books were available on a small scale in America by subscription, but it wasn't until 1921 that American children in general were introduced to these collections, which include now-familiar titles—"Cinderella," "Little Red Riding Hood," "Sleeping Beauty," and "Beauty and the Beast," versions translated from the French of Charles Perrault—as well as stories by the Brothers Grimm (Germany) and Hans Christian Andersen (Denmark). Since then, with the development of children's picture storybooks, a genre that didn't fully emerge until the 1930s, there have been many renditions, but Lang's "color" versions continue to be found in the library stacks under "fairy tale collections."

Because of the emphasis on Victorian and Puritan values in the books that parents were encouraging their children to read at the time, the romance, adventure, and roguish independence found in the fairy tales sparked the imaginations of the children who had access to them, and they asked for more. Even so, the stories represented Old World cultures rather than the evolving combination of old and new that accurately reflected American culture. Even today, if the question is asked of an American, "What are your origins?" the answer probably will be to name a country outside of the United States rather than simply to answer, "I'm an American."

Italy's *The Adventures of Pinocchio* by Carlo "Collodi" Lorenzini (1880), translated and published in England in 1892, was embraced by American children long before Walt Disney created an American version. Maurice Sendak, who prefers the animated version, compares the Disney story to the Collodi original: Disney's *Pinocchio*, he says, is "rooted in melancholy, and in this respect it is true to the original Italian tale. But that is where any significant resemblance between Disney and Collodi ends . . . While Collodi's *Pinocchio* is an undeniably engaging narrative that moves with tremendous energy—despite its shaky, loose construction—it is also a cruel and frightening tale."[11]

It is quite true that Collodi's puppet character lacks the charm of Disney's creation—Pinocchio deserves everything that happens to him in the Italian version—but the difference between the two represents the difference between American idealism and European recognition of man's imperfections. Children have a dark side that adults in this country prefer to ignore, but Geppetto forgave Pinocchio and accepted him, faults and all. Disney's animated version reflects American culture and attitudes with a Pinocchio whose basic goodness overcomes his childish curiosity.

American Realism

The English fantasy imports created a market in America for books that directly appealed to children and opened the door for American authors who preferred storytelling to moralizing; such authors include Mary Mapes Dodge, who adhered to the New England proclivity for realistic fiction as opposed to fantasy. But even with real characters in a real setting, children discovered that reading could be a pleasure rather than a chore. Dodge's *Hans Brinker; or, The Silver Skates* was published in the United States in 1865, the same year as *Alice* in England, and became a milestone of entertaining realistic fiction for children in America, offering strong characterizations and riveting suspense while playing down the strict morality that pervaded the religious tracts of Puritan America and Victorian England. For more than a century, *Hans Brinker* has never been out of print.

Although the book was praised as a carefully detailed study of life in Holland, it is character and story that hold the attention of the reader rather than the travelogue sections. The reader cannot help being caught up in the lives of the characters and hoping for a resolution to the labyrinth of problems that keep developing as the story progresses. The social relevance of the book, however, is its descriptive attention to the culture of another country. Published the year the Civil War ended, it focused on a real-life setting far removed from war-torn America. The story offered an orderly way of life in the midst of the upheaval that existed in the newly formed United States. It also presented a viewpoint unusual at that time in books that might be read by children. The Brinkers were not only very poor, but the father of Hans and Gretchen was also brain damaged because of an accident, and his children loved him anyway. In 19th-century literature, defective adults were usually evil or unworthy of compassion.

Dodge not only introduced American children to the kind of reading that made them want more books to read, she also became the editor of a magazine published exclusively for children, *St. Nicholas*, and from 1873 until her death in 1905 she showcased the authors and illustrators[12] who would carve out a permanent niche in literature for children in this country. *St. Nicholas* provided imaginative reading for young people without the didactism that had marked earlier stories for children in America; it published contributions by Frank R. Stockton, who assisted Dodge in the editing of the magazine, Emily Dickinson, Louisa May Alcott, Howard Pyle, Rudyard Kipling, Frances Hodgson Burnett, Joel Chandler Harris, Mark Twain, and Jack London. The magazine remained popular until 1940.

Louisa May Alcott would be considered a writer of young-adult novels today, but such categories didn't exist in the 1800s. In 19th-century America, the books that appealed to children were categorized as either folk and fairy, realistic fiction, biographies, or poetry.

Alcott reluctantly wrote *Little Women* (1868) at the urging of her editor, Thomas Niles of Roberts Brothers, who wanted her to create a story for girls to compete with Lee and Shepard's very popular "Oliver Optic" series for boys. She had already proved herself marketable in adult publishing by writing, under a pseudonym, a whole series of Gothic tales dealing with the unlikely subjects of murder, adultery, drug addiction, and insanity.[13] The only way she could meet Niles's expectations for a children's book was to write about her own upbringing and to base her characters on herself and her sisters. Niles was not overly impressed with her manuscript but decided to try it out on a young niece. It was so enthusiastically received that he offered it to some other young girls, who were equally excited about it.[14] On publication, the book was an immediate best seller, and Louisa, after years of financial struggle, was able to take care of her family's needs.

The members of the March family in *Little Women* had one thing that Louisa didn't have—the stability of a family homestead. Louisa had moved 27 times in 25 years, as her father searched for a way of life that more often than not turned out to be unorthodox and without profit. Her father's many failed business ventures left the family almost indigent, until Louisa became a successful writer and helped to keep her family "fed, clothed, sheltered, and out of debt, a financial feat that she accomplished much more successfully than either of her parents."[15]

In *Little Women*, Alcott wrote about real life instead of the folk, fairy, or fantasy tales so popular in England, and she managed successfully to enter into the lives of her own family members and make adventurous storybook characters out of them, concentrating on the emotional ties rather than the continuing struggles within her family.

Samuel Langhorne Clemens, under the pen name "Mark Twain," offered a purely American small-town setting with a cast of small-town American characters, and children who didn't always do "the right thing," in *The Adventures of Tom Sawyer* (1876). This approach contradicted the commonly accepted view of children as young innocents, paragons engaged at all times in proper behavior under the real threat of early death, a view that marked the educational and religious publications for children. Twain, in fact, wrote *Tom Sawyer* as an act of defiance against those publications, which he despised.[16] In the 1800s, books published specifically for children in America consisted of tedious religious tomes promising hell and damnation to those who veered from righteous paths. Even the exceptions such as *Little Women* and Frances Hodgson Burnett's *Little Lord Fauntleroy* (1886) reflected the strict morality and upper-class sentiments of the time. Tom Sawyer was a character who blatantly defied tradition and avoided retribution—it's no wonder he became a hero for the young. He also represented small-town America, living as he did on the Mississippi River banks. Alcott and Burnett, although they created memorable characters who stretched the social limits of acceptable behavior, retained a formal English-type setting.

The Adventures of Tom Sawyer quickly gained popularity as a children's book and was considered acceptable reading material for the children of that time, regardless of Clemens' claim that he considered it unsuitable for children and resented its being labeled a "boys' book." On its publication, he made the comment, "*Tom Sawyer* is not a boys' book at all—it will be read only by adults."[17] Twain was noted, however, for his ambiguity, often saying one thing while meaning just the opposite. The book also introduced Huck Finn and his disreputable father, socially undesirable but nonetheless appealing, and ultimately led to Clemens' writing of *The Adventures of Huckleberry Finn* (1885), set in the Slave South of pre-Civil War days and issued during the twentieth anniversary of the end of the Civil War.[18] The story was a social satire, clearly less intended for children than *Tom Sawyer*, even though the publisher insisted on calling it a sequel, thereby bringing down the wrath of the reviewers who said it was "immoral." The objections continue today, but because Twain attempted to attack American slavery and made his feelings against it apparent in *Huckleberry Finn*—something not done at that time—the present label for the book is not "immoral" but, according to some educators, "racist." Nevertheless, all of Twain's books remain on recommended reading lists for students 12 and up.

Little Lord Fauntleroy (1886), by Frances Hodgson Burnett, duplicated the format of the English children's novel but presented the contrast between England and America through the viewpoint of an American child who travels to England after it is discovered he is the grandson of an earl. Frances Hodgson was born in England in 1849 but migrated with her family to Tennessee in 1865 and married her first husband, Swan Burnett, in Tennessee in 1873. She was a child who started life with all the amenities but was introduced to poverty at the age of four when her father died. A year before her marriage, the 23-year-old Frances, by now a published author who claimed she wrote only for the money,[19] returned to England, the setting for her children's books. From that time on she traveled back and forth across the Atlantic 33 times.[20] Although Burnett published more than 20 children's books, only a few have retained their popularity—*Little Lord Fauntleroy* (1886), *A Little Princess* (1905), and *The Secret Garden* (1911) are her best known titles.

Fauntleroy is considered "almost as important as social history as it is in the history of children's literature."[21] It was the first American children's book to separate American culture from English culture and offer a comparison of the two. The "Fauntleroy" image of velvet and curls contrasted sharply with the "Tom Sawyer" image of patches and dirt, the difference between them representative of the contrast between England and America at that time. Young Cedric's candor and lack of concern for an individual's social status combined with the down-to-earth character of Cedric's blacksmith friend, Dick, offered a view of the working class not usually seen in books of the time. And the American dream became a reality when Cedric was accepted into the nobility and he and his mother enjoyed financial security for the rest of their lives.

American Folklore

The American South was the setting for Joel Chandler Harris's collections of *Uncle Remus* stories, the first of which was called *Uncle Remus: His Songs and His Sayings* (1880), illustrated by F. S. Church and J. H. Moser. The stories were an effort to capture in print a unique language—the language, as it had developed in America, of the black slave population. But Harris, who was white and not a professional folklorist, was so careful to preserve the dialect as he heard it that the general reader, especially a child reader, couldn't understand the stories.

Nevertheless, Brer[22] Rabbit and Brer Fox were discovered by the children of educated families and appreciated despite the language barrier. Like the folk and fairy tales of Europe, these stories have been published in many different versions and have become firmly established as true American folklore, being authentically rewritten in recent years by black authors who grew up hearing the oral tales within their families.

The origins of these tales can be traced in part to Africa, but the stories told orally by the blacks in this country, stories that Harris captured in print, clearly reflected the slave population's fight for identity in a society that denied their humanity and considered them chattel.

Uncle Remus was the storyteller, but the stories were about animals, and white children introduced to these stories accepted the characters entirely at face value, never seeing them as the metaphors they obviously were. But then, their parents didn't either. The drawings of A. B. Frost in the 1892 edition of *Uncle Remus* cut through the difficult dialect and multiple levels of meaning in Harris's collection of folktales to focus on character. In the frontispiece of the Frost edition, Uncle Remus, though bent and crippled by a life of servitude, retains his dignity as he looks directly at his audience from the center of the page (see illustration p. xxviii).

Coming of Age

Stephen Crane wrote *The Red Badge of Courage* (1895) 30 years after the Civil War ended and never had any kind of battle experience, but his story offered a personal view of wartime that reflected its futile nature as no other book has. He was a poet and a short-story writer, and was 25 years old when he wrote *Red Badge*. In the story, he captured the painful passage from youth to maturity in a way that spoke directly to a young adult population. Although his body of work has never been categorized as "children's" literature, *Red Badge* continues to be required reading in secondary schools. Crane was the only 19th-century author to offer a lasting retrospective for young people on the Civil War. Much of the history of the United States exists within the framework of memory, and it takes time to offer an objective viewpoint of events that have occurred within a writer's lifetime.

By the end of the 19th century, the "religious" emphasis in the children's books of the day had started to give way to a more regional viewpoint as immigrants poured into the country and established various ethnic communities in cities and states. Attitudes began to reflect the cultures of Europe and Asia as well as the beliefs of the founding fathers. The country began to grow and develop at an astounding rate, and so did the children's book industry.

CHRONOLOGICAL BIBLIOGRAPHY 19th Century

Almost all of the titles listed below are available in several editions. See Bowker's *Books in Print*.

Hawthorne, Nathaniel. *A Wonder Book for Girls and Boys*. Boston: Houghton Mifflin, 1852, 1951. (Folk/Myth)

This collection of Greek myths was put together by Hawthorne while he was in residence in the Berkshire Hills of Massachusetts, and he wrote them in a style he considered appealing to children. In the story of Pandora, called "The Paradise of Children," he hinted at the inherent equality of the sexes long before civil rights became an accepted cause when he said, "The fingers of little girls, it has always appeared to me, are the fittest to twine flower-wreaths; but boys could do it, in those days, rather better than they can now." Hawthorne's simple, rhythmic storytelling and sense of humor was representative of the American storyteller, direct and to the point, rather than following the classical interpretations, which Hawthorne considered cold and "as repellant [sic] as the touch of marble."[23]

———. *Tanglewood Tales for Girls and Boys*. Boston: Houghton Mifflin, 1853, 1951. (Folk/Myth)

Hawthorne continued his renderings of Greek myth after moving from the Berkshires to Concord and wrote them as if they were brought to him from Tanglewood by the hypothetical narrator of his first collection, a college student by the name of Eustace Bright. The stories were written in the same light, liberated style of the first volume.

Kingsley, Charles. *The Water Babies: A Fairy Tale for a Land-Baby*. London: Macmillan, 1863; New York: Crown, 1986. (Fantasy/Fairy)

Kingsley wrote *Water Babies* for his youngest child to teach him "what a fine thing it is to love truth, mercy, justice, courage, and all things noble and of good report."[24] But although Kingsley made an effort to instruct, he just as often forgot the instructions in the joy of writing about a subject that mattered a great deal to him—nature and its wonders. Reading Kingsley's words in this rhythmic passage, "[Tom] was sitting on a water-lily leaf, he and his friend the dragon-fly, watching the gnats dance," illustrates not only his fascination with the outdoors but also his love of words. Kingsley was a naturalist as well as a writer, and he combined these two loves to create a fantasy world firmly rooted in fact.

Carroll, Lewis (pseud. of Charles Dodgson). *Alice's Adventures in Wonderland*, illtd. John Tenniel. London: Macmillan, 1865; New York: St. Martin's Press, 1977. (Fantasy)

Alice manages to make her way through Wonderland after falling down a rabbit hole by confronting and dealing directly with all the obstacles she faces. She employs logic in the face of nonsense, and it is almost disappointing that the whole adventure turns out to be a dream. Alice overcomes the often convoluted reasoning of the adult world with the straightforward logic of childhood. The Mad Hatter, the Cheshire-Cat, the Duchess, the White Rabbit, Caterpillar, and other characters in the book have become familiar to children worldwide, while the book and its author continue to be the subject of academic discussion.

Dodge, Mary Mapes. *Hans Brinker; or, The Silver Skates*, illtd. F. O. C. Darley and Thomas Nast. New York: James O'Kane, 1865; New York: BDD (Dell), 1985. (Realistic Fiction)

Hans Brinker and his sister skate on the canals of Holland along with the other children in their community, but because they live in poverty, their skates are makeshift. Hans dreams of winning the silver skates in the big race, a dream that becomes more intense as the story continues and seems destined never to come true as one thing after another goes wrong, not the least of which is a leak in the dike, which Hans plugs with his finger until help arrives.

Alcott, Louisa May. *Little Women*. Boston: Little, Brown, 1868 (first half), 1869 (second half); New York: Scholastic, 1986. (Realistic Fiction)

The March family chronicles were based largely on Alcott's own family with all its faults and failures. The four sisters—Meg, Jo, Beth, and Amy—are sharply drawn characters from the very first page of this classic novel. Jo, tomboy and nonconformist, is the protagonist, and the personalities of her three sisters, plus mother, father, and the boy next door, Laurie Lawrence, revolve around and contribute to Jo's personal growth throughout the novel.

———. *Little Men*. Boston: Little, Brown, 1871; New York: Scholastic, 1987. (Realistic Fiction)

This sequel to *Little Women* presents a matronly Jo, married and with children of her own, who runs a school for her own children and those less fortunate, a school that encourages independence and free thinking as opposed to rigid discipline. With a group of adventurous children getting into scrapes but never in real danger, the book has an old-fashioned moralistic flavor that probably does not much appeal to children today and makes it easy to understand why Alcott protested against *Huckleberry Finn* as fare for "pure-minded lads and lasses."

Carroll, Lewis (pseud. of Charles Dodgson). *Through the Looking Glass*. London: Macmillan, 1871; New York: Macmillan, 1993. (Fantasy)

Alice continues her adventures by climbing through the looking glass in the drawing room and becoming first a pawn in a continuing chess game and finally Queen Alice. Her matter-of-fact attitude toward threats and nonsense keeps her intact in the face of danger, and once more the adventure is revealed to be a dream sequence. Tweedledum and Tweedledee, the Walrus, Humpty Dumpty, and the Red and White Queens are memorable characters in a complicated series of mathematical explorations.

Twain, Mark (pseud. of Samuel Clemens). *The Adventures of Tom Sawyer*, illtd. True W. Williams. New York: Harper, 1876; New York: Scholastic, 1993. (Realistic Fiction)

This adventure story presented Tom Sawyer as a less-than-perfect character at a time in American social history when children and the books written for them reflected the moral ideal. Tom is tricky and somewhat lazy but always likable, and his attempts to impress young Becky take the two of them into danger and a confrontation with the sinister Injun Joe.

Sewell, Anna. *Black Beauty: His Grooms and Companions*. London: Jarrrold and Sons, 1877; New York: Random House, 1989. (Realistic Fiction/Animal)

In England, where fantasy and fairy tales were predominant, this author wrote her only book, a work of realistic fiction that was also the first to make a case for the horse population of the time. Sewell wrote the book from the viewpoint of Black Beauty, a horse who experiences all varieties of treatment, good and bad, and in so doing allows readers to empathize with the way in which a horse is treated by humans. It is true that, as librarian May Hill Arbuthnot complained, *Black Beauty* is "full of human proprieties" and occasionally the main character sounds more like a "genteel lady than a horse,"[25] but the story was and still is an emotional success, offering a clear portrait of Victorian England's working class as well as its gentry.

Collodi, Carlo (pseud. of Carlo Lorenzini). *The Adventures of Pinocchio*, first published in Italy in 1880. London: F. Fisher Unwin, 1892; New York: Puffin, 1985. (Fantasy)

Children in Victorian England and Puritan America were supposed to behave in an adult manner, striving to please their parents at all times. Into this strict atmosphere came a story about an imperfect puppet called Pinocchio, who defies all the rules of proper behavior and completely ignores anything his father, Geppetto, expects of him. This defiance had great appeal for children who harbored a secret desire to break free from the bonds of good behavior and do something totally unacceptable. Children knew they weren't perfect, never had been, and never would be, no matter how many rules their parents set up. But they hoped their parents would continue to love them as Geppetto loved Pinocchio. The Disney version of this book presents a more pristine Pinocchio whose shortcomings are not inherent but due to the influence of others.

Harris, Joel Chandler. *Uncle Remus: His Songs and Sayings*, illtd. Frederick S. Church and James H. Moser. New York: Appleton, 1880; illtd. A. B. Frost, 1892; New York: Viking Penguin, 1982. (Folk/Myth)

Although over the years many versions of these American folktales have been published, it was Harris who originally collected them and put them into print, and it is the illustrations of A. B. Frost that are best remembered. Brer Rabbit represented the slave population, far more clever than the white masters ever realized, and by the same token he represented children, also more clever than any adult ever realized. In the story of Brer Fox and the Tar-Baby, Brer Rabbit outsmarts Brer Fox by setting a trap, and the apparently easy prey within Brer Fox's reach turns out to be not only inedible but highly confining as well, a sticky tar baby that won't release Brer Fox.

Sidney, Margaret (pseud. of Harriet Mulford Stone Lothrop). *Five Little Peppers and How They Grew*. New York: Lothrop, 1881; New York: Scholastic, 1989. (Realistic Fiction)

First published as a series of short magazine stories about the Pepper family, the stories were so popular they were put together in book form. Polly, Ben, Joey, Davie, and Phronsie, and their mother, Mamsie, became familiar characters to many generations of children in this and the 11 books that followed. Only the original has survived, probably for the sake of nostalgia, because Sidney's writing style was old-fashioned and overly complicated. The predictable story is bogged down by detail.

Stockton, Frank. *The Bee-man of Orn.* New York: Scribner, 1881; New York: Harper, 1987. (Fantasy/Fairy)

Both common sense and humor mark the fairy tales of Frank Stockton, who described his work as "the world of fancy invaded by the real [and] the world we live in as seen through spectacles of more or less fantastic colors."[26] In *The Bee-man of Orn*, one of his most popular tales, the Bee-man is told by a sorcerer that, because of his unusual occupation, he must have been transformed from something else at one time. The Bee-man, who has been content with his life, becomes curious and begins a quest to discover his former identity. After several disappointments and dangerous confrontations, he finds the answer, which ultimately takes him back where he started—as the Bee-man of Orn.

Twain, Mark (pseud. of Samuel Clemens). *The Prince and the Pauper.* New York: Harper, 1882; New York: Puffin, 1983. (Realistic Fiction)

In an attempt to move out of the children's book field, Twain deliberately directed his next book toward an adult audience, criticizing law, family, and religion.[27] Because the protagonists in the story were children and *Tom Sawyer* had been so successful, this book, too, was publicized as a children's book, followed by no effort on the part of the public to determine whether it really was suitable for children. In the story, set in England, two boys meet and discover they are look-alikes, but when they decide to trade places and social status, they discover that the grass isn't greener on the other side of the fence after all. The English society that Twain presented in this book definitely has its brutish aspects.

Pyle, Howard. *The Merry Adventures of Robin Hood.* New York: Scribner, 1883; New York: Macmillan, 1977. (Folk/Myth)

Robin Hood, who stole from the rich to give to the poor in medieval England, has become a hero to children worldwide through myth, story, film, and cartoon. America author-illustrator Howard Pyle vivified this hero in both words and pictures and introduced him to American children in the costume and mood of the period.

Spyri, Joanna. *Heidi*, first published in German in 1880. Boston: DeWolfe Fiske, 1884; New York: Dutton, 1992. (Realistic Fiction)

Heidi, like Lewis Carroll's Alice, is a character who meets life head-on with curiosity and courage, and when she is separated from her beloved grandfather and has to live in town, she manages to touch the lives of all around her, especially the invalid Clara. Clara finds she is able to walk when she visits Heidi's rejuvenating mountains. Spyri brings the Swiss mountain setting of this book to the reader in a way that makes the country unforgettable, as Mary Mapes Dodge did with the Dutch background in *Hans Brinker*. The realism of Spyri's fiction, at a time when folk and fairy dominated European children's literature, was refreshing.

Stevenson, Robert Louis. *A Child's Garden of Verses*, illtd. Jesse Willcox Smith. London: Longmans, 1885; New York: Crown, 1985. (Poetry)

This collection was the first written directly from the child's viewpoint, and many children introduced to these poems when very young grew up to appreciate the music and rhythm of the English language. Stevenson wrote these verses at a time in English literature when stories were often told by adult narrators who interjected their own commentary into the fiction, but here Stevenson bypassed the narrator and spoke as the child inside himself:

> I have a little shadow that goes in and out with me,
> And what can be the use of him is more than I can see.

In this collection are memories for countless generations of children.

Twain, Mark (pseud. of Samuel Clemens). *The Adventures of Huckleberry Finn*. New York: Harper, 1885; New York: Random House, 1985. (Realistic Fiction)

This story was written as the autobiography of "a poor-white-trash boy" in Huck Finn's own dialect and, although intended as a sequel to Tom Sawyer, Twain became so involved in the social inequities of the time that the book evolved into a political statement. Nevertheless, the publisher offered it as "another boy's book," incurring the wrath of reviewers and leading the Concord Library to ban it as "immoral," "coarse," and "the veriest trash."[28]

Pyle, Howard. *Pepper & Salt*. New York: Harper, 1886; New York: Dover, 1990. (Fantasy/Poetry)

This collection of short stories and poems is more than just an artist's showcase. Pyle added the spice of humor to stories based on old European folktales and, at intervals, inserted short, illustrated poems among the stories. The poems are clever but are handwritten in old-fashioned script, which makes them difficult to read. The stories are a combination of folk and fairy; in one, "Farmer Griggs and the Boggart," Pyle introduces the mischievous boggart, an imp who does "a little good and much harm." Once Farmer Griggs invites the boggart into his home, it's almost impossible to get rid of him. The Griggses even move out of their house with all their belongings in an effort to lose the creature, but the boggart, who is invisible, hides in their churn and travels along with them. Finally, the local wise man suggests a solution to their problem and the boggart leaves. Pyle tells his readers he wishes he could get rid of his boggart so easily (for he has one in his own house), but, "alackaday! There are no wise men left to us."

Burnett, Frances Hodgson. *Little Lord Fauntleroy*, illtd. Frederick S. Church. New York: Scribner, 1886; New York: Bantam, 1987. (Realistic Fiction)

Young Cedric, an American child who is so loved by his mother that he considers himself fortunate in the face of poverty, is offered the title of an earl and is brought to his grandfather's English estate. But the price of wealth and royal status means separation from his mother, and Cedric is relieved when another family member claims his title. It is at this point that America and England, working class and aristocracy, confront each other and eventually come to an understanding for the sake of Cedric.

Twain, Mark (pseud. of Samuel Clemens). *A Connecticut Yankee in King Arthur's Court*. New York: Harper, 1889; New York: Bantam, 1983. (Fantasy)

Although there is humor in Hank Morgan's clashes with medieval superstition when he is transported back in time, the book is actually intended as a satire that calls for adult experience to be understood. Regardless of its appearance on some children's-book lists as part of Mark Twain's body of work, it is not a children's book.

Lang, Andrew, ed. *The Blue Fairy Book*. London: Longmans, 1889; New York: Dover, 1965. (Fantasy/Fairy)

The "color" fairy stories collected by Lang became America's connection to the storytellers of old. "Cinderella," "Hansel and Gretel," and "Little Red Riding Hood" were only a few of the classic tales translated from Charles Perrault's French collections and introduced in this first book. Following just one of these stories through myriad interpretations from decade to decade would offer a microcosm of changing attitudes in America.

———. *The Red Fairy Book*. London: Longmans, 1890; Cutchogue, N.Y.: Buccaneer, 1987. (Fantasy/Fairy)

The most familiar selections in this collection are "Little Snow Drop" (now "Snow White") and "Rapunzel," both translations from the brothers Grimm collection, and an early English folktale, "Jack and the Beanstalk."

———. *The Green Fairy Book*. London: Longmans, 1892; New York: Dover, 1965. (Fantasy/Fairy)

In this third collection by Lang, "Three Little Pigs" and "The Three Bears" made their debut in print. With the exception of these two stories, most of the selections were from the brothers Grimm. Also represented were Russia, Italy, Scotland, and China.

Grinnell, George Bird. *Blackfoot Lodge Tales*. New York: Scribner, 1892; Lincoln: University of Nebraska Press, 1962. (Folk/Myth/Blackfoot tribe)

In an effort to bring to the attention of the American people the need for respect in dealings with Native tribes, Grinnell collected stories told by the Blackfoot people as well as information about their culture. This collection is the only lasting 19th-century publication for young people about the Native peoples of North America.

Lang, Andrew, ed. *The Yellow Fairy Book*. London: Longmans, 1894; New York: Puffin, 1988. (Fairy/Fantasy)

Andrew Lang, though a serious collector of folklore, intended his fairy tale collections to entertain children. The purists in the Folk Lore Society objected to some of his choices for the collections, considering them frivolous, and Lang addressed these objections in his introduction to this fourth collection. "If the children are pleased," he comments in his preface, "and they are so kind as to say they are pleased, the Editor does not care much for what other people may say." Lang included in this collection Native American folklore, originally published in America by the Smithsonian Bureau of Ethnology. He referred to these selections as "Red Indian Stories." Many of the stories of Hans Christian Andersen were included in this book: "The Princess and the Pea," "Thumbelina," "The Nightingale," and "The Steadfast Tin-soldier."

Kipling, Rudyard. *The Jungle Book*. London: Macmillan, 1894; New York: Viking, 1990. (Fantasy)

While living in Vermont, English author Kipling wrote *Jungle Book*, which introduced unforgettable characters to American children:

Mowgli, the boy raised by wolves, Baloo the bear, Kaa the snake, and Bagheera the black panther. These stories are more representative of British colonialism than of American culture, but with the Law of the Jungle at the heart of the story, the animal world became depicted in Kipling's natural, musical style in a way that offered insight into nature, a subject not usually addressed in 19th-century children's books.

———. *The Second Jungle Book*. London: Macmillan, 1895; New York: Viking, 1990. (Fantasy)

In this second volume, Kipling offered a collection of stories, the most familiar of which is "Rikki-Tikki-Tavi," the story of a young mongoose and his battle with the terrible snakes, Nag and Nagaina. The setting of these stories moved from India to Alaska and back to India, and they were written from the viewpoint of the animals under discussion.

Crane, Stephen. *The Red Badge of Courage*. New York: Appleton, 1895; in *Great Short Works of Stephen Crane* (New York: Harper, 1968; Random, 1990). (Realistic Fiction/Historical/Civil War)

Henry Fleming, referred to by Crane throughout this short novel as the "youth," joins the army and sets out to do his part in the American Civil War. At first, he is an observer, but gradually he begins to participate in the fighting, feeling a sense of accomplishment when helping to turn back the first charge and later dismay when the charges continue. He becomes overwhelmed by the danger and turns and runs, convinced everyone else must be retreating as well. When he discovers the others have gone on fighting, he is ashamed—the wounded have the "red badge of courage," and he has run away from the fighting. However, Henry fulfills his rite of passage, facing his doubts and overcoming them, and in the end, Crane ceases to refer to him as the "youth." Henry, writes Crane, "was a man."

Thompson, Ernest Seton. *Wild Animals I Have Known*. New York: Scribner, 1898; New York: Viking, 1986. (Informational/Animal)

Thompson took up the cause of nature long before it was the popular thing to do. He was a naturalist who respected animals enough to try to introduce them to the public, and he did not perpetuate the stereotype that all wolves were the enemy and all dogs a friend to man. The stories he told of individual animals were those he had heard from others or had experienced himself, with some storytelling added for color. Thompson's writing style is simple and easy to read and his plea for animal rights continues to be relevant.

NOTES

1. Otto L. Bettmann. *The Good Old Days—They Were Terrible*, p. 78.
2. Ibid., p. 79.
3. Appeared in the *Troy* (New York) *Sentinel* on December 23, 1823.
4. From Philippe Aries' *Centuries of Childhood*, as noted by Sheila Egoff in *Thursday's Child*, p. 3.
5. Maurice Sendak. *Caldecott and Co.: Notes on Books and Pictures*, pp. 13, 14.
6. Raymond Briggs. *The Mother Goose Treasury*. New York: Dell (BDD), 1986, p. 22.
7. Mr. and Mrs. Henry Ford. *The Story of Mary and Her Little Lamb*. Dearborn, Michigan: Ford, 1928.
8. Sarah Josepha Hale. *Mary Had a Little Lamb*, illtd. Tomie de Paola. New York: Holiday House, 1984, quote from end note.
9. Peter Prescott. *Newsweek*, March 18, 1974, p. 114.
10. Andrew Lang. *The Green Fairy Book*. New York: Random House Looking Glass Library, 1960, p. 7.
11. Sendak, op. cit., p. 112.
12. Burton C. Frye, ed. *A St. Nicholas Anthology: The Early Years*. New York: Meredith Press, 1969.
13. Madeleine Stern, ed. *Behind a Mask: The Unknown Thrillers of Louisa May Alcott*. New York: Morrow, 1975; Madeleine Stern, ed. *Plots and Counterplots: More Unknown Thrillers by Louisa May Alcott*. New York: Morrow, 1976.
14. Norma Johnston. *Louisa May: The World and Works of Louisa May Alcott*, p. 174.
15. Jane M. Bingham, ed. *Writers for Children: Critical Studies of Major Authors Since the Seventeenth Century*. New York: Scribner, 1988, p. 1.
16. Ibid., p. 575.
17. Ibid., p. 574.
18. Ibid., p. 578.
19. Ibid., p. 103.
20. Ibid.
21. Ibid., p. 104.
22. Since "Brer," not "Br'er," is the preferred spelling in most contemporary references to and rewritings of the *Uncle Remus* stories, that is the spelling selected here.
23. Nathaniel Hawthorne. *A Wonder Book for Girls and Boys*. Boston: Houghton Mifflin, 1951, p. 10.
24. Quote attributed to Charles Kingsley's daughter, Rose G. Kingsley, from the editor's introduction to *The Water Babies*. New York: Dodd, Mead, 1910, p. viii.
25. May Hill Arbuthnot. *Children and Books*, 3rd ed., p. 401.
26. Quote attributed to Frank Stockton from the editor's introduction to *The Storyteller's Pack: A Frank R. Stockton Reader*. New York: Scribner, 1968, p. xviii.
27. Bingham, op. cit., p. 578.
28. Ibid.

Illustrations from The Story of Little Black Sambo *by Helen Bannerman. The first, by the author, is from the 1905 Harper edition; the second is by John R. Neill and is taken from the 1908 Stokes edition. Both illustrations are courtesy of the Kerlan Collection, Walter Library, University of Minnesota, Minneapolis, Minnesota. The illustrations in* Little Black Sambo *ultimately became so synonymous with racism that the book was, and still is, banned from libraries.*

2

THE EVOLUTION 1900–1919

The story of American life often resembles a Hollywood narrative, a miraculous metamorphosis in which people of humble origins, using simple implements, ascend to a "city on a hill."

—Ruth Sidel
On Her Own: Growing Up in the Shadow of the American Dream

The Burgeoning Marketplace

In the first half of the 1900s, industrial advances brought about corporate growth and called for increased transportation and communication, along with satellite businesses and an expanding need for merchants, all of which led to the establishment of a middle class in America. The middle class worked set hours, had time off, and didn't have to depend on its children to bring food into the house. With new advances in medicine, the child mortality rate was dropping. Instead of holding back affection because children so often died in infancy, parents began to allow themselves the pleasure of watching their children grow.[1]

The year 1900 was the beginning of a meteoric century of progress. It was the year of the first billion-dollar corporation in America. McKinley was reelected president of the United States, only to be assassinated in 1901 and succeeded by his vice president, Theodore Roosevelt, one of our more colorful presidents. Carrie Nation began her fight for temperance, and the women's suffrage movement began to materialize. Child labor laws were passed, and children could no longer spend long hours in the workplace. In 1900, 4,000 automobiles were produced in America; in 1910, 187,000 American automobiles were produced.[2]

The industrial revolution also brought with it the ability to manufacture large numbers of books, accessible to the general public. As the United States grew in stature, so did literature in the mainstream. Books became big business in America, while the books written specifically for children moved away from general publishing and became a separate genre. As laws were passed to keep children out of the workplace and in the schools, a protective attitude developed toward them, and the curriculum in schools reflected that attitude. Textbooks avoided contentious issues and presented American society as predominantly white and Protestant. Until the late 1970s, publishers listed a group of taboos in children's books and sent the list to prospective authors—no mention of death, birth, religion, sex, divorce, or drugs. But the books that lasted were the ones that found a way around the taboos and respected the child's ability to deal with reality and accept it.

There was a great deal of activity in the children's literature field during the early 1900s, as librarians, booksellers, and publishers joined to bring the body of work already in existence, much of it from England, to the attention of, and within the means of, the average person. Prior to the 20th century, books had been sold mostly by subscription to a limited audience. Now, with the advent of young people's magazines—*The Riverside Magazine*, *Wide Awake*, *Our Young Folks*, *St. Nicholas*, and *Harper's Young People*, as well as with a growing number of children's bookstores and children's rooms in libraries—the expanded market for children's books in the United States came to the attention of publishers in both America and England. Deluxe limited editions of English titles were being sold out immediately, and British publishing firms, such as Macmillan, Oxford University Press, Frederick Warne, and John Lane, established branches in New York City.[3] Although large numbers of books could now be published in America at reasonable prices, the print quality of the books lagged behind that of England, and attractive, economically produced color illustrations were to be found only in the books produced in England. But even with the reading public's preference for the better-made English books, the demand exceeded supply, and American publishers found children's books to be a worthwhile investment.

Historian of Oz

Fairy tales and fantasy continued to be popular imports from England, but most American authors avoided imaginary worlds in their stories for children. One important exception was L. Frank Baum. He introduced a fantasy world with its roots in middle America and a practical heroine who put family unity above wealth and power and depended on her own ingenuity to survive. The timing of this Utopian adventure was exactly right, and *The Wonderful Wizard of Oz* was published in 1900 to rave reviews, with children discovering it before the newly established library block decided it wasn't literature and stopped offering it in libraries. Like many of the children's books that have survived over the years, word-of-mouth recommendations created a continuing public demand for this and the additional Oz books.

Unlike the fairy tales from England, *The Wonderful Wizard of Oz* represented the search for the American dream that has always symbolized the United States. As sociologist Ruth Sidel states, "the American dream has been an essential component of American ideology since the first settlers crossed the Atlantic."[4] And what is the American dream? When Horatio Alger wrote books for children in the 19th century in which a child, poor and ragged, comes to the attention of a wealthy benefactor who gives him his chance to make good, the phrase "American dream" was born. Alger's heroes, through hard work, perseverance, and luck, always reached their goals of financial security, no matter where they began on the social ladder, and the "Horatio Alger hero" became synonymous with the American dream of success. The difference between Alger and Baum was the goal—for Alger's characters it was financial, for Baum's characters it was emotional. In *The Wonderful Wizard of Oz*, no one needed money. The Scarecrow wanted to be noted for his intelligence, the Cowardly Lion for his bravery, the Tin Woodman for his compassion, and Dorothy wanted to go home.

Baum was in his forties before he realized success from his writing, a pastime that had engaged him since childhood. He enjoyed telling stories to his four children and was a loving father. His first book, *Mother Goose in Prose* (1897), introduced illustrator Maxfield Parrish and was a critical but not a commercial success. He had trouble finding a publisher for *Oz* at first and was ready to finance it himself when it was accepted by publisher George M. Hill in Chicago. Even with a publisher, he and illustrator W. W. Denslow had to pay printing costs, which were high due to the author and illustrator's insistence on quality production. The inclusion of 24 color plates, at a time in American publishing when illustrations were mostly black-and-white, helped focus attention on the book.

Baum had no intention of writing any more books about Oz; he was having success with *The Wizard of Oz* (1902), his stage version of the book, and was writing other stories for children far removed from the land of Oz. He disliked routine, preferring to veer off in different directions, trying one thing and then another, and was especially fond of theatrical productions. Because of his penchant for change, he never sustained financial success for very long. He was from a well-to-do family, and his father supported his efforts at a career. He tried newspaper work, managing a store, selling on the road, running a print shop, acting, and, through it all, continued to write. Accumulating money was never that important to him; he spent what he earned and then some—at one point declaring bankruptcy—and his wife, Maud, finally insisted on taking over their financialaffairs.

Although Baum finally gave in to demand from his child readers and wrote *The Marvelous Land of Oz* (1904), he refused to make Dorothy a character in that book, saying that her story had been told. He did, however, find a place for her in later stories. The new book focused on the Scarecrow and Tin Woodman, the popular stars of his stage play, and the boy Tip took over Dorothy's role. With John Neill's lively illustrations giving life to Jack the Pumpkinhead, Mombi the witch, the Saw-Horse, and the Woggle-Bug, Baum had embarked on a continuing series whether he liked it or not. Social issues were also a focus of his stories. His mother-in-law was an advocate of women's rights, and this was reflected in *Land of Oz*, with General Jinjur and her army of women soldiers capturing Oz by using knitting needles as weapons and turning over the cleaning and baby-sitting chores to the men:

> As they passed the rows of houses they saw through the open doors that men were sweeping and dusting and washing dishes, while the women sat around in groups, gossiping and laughing.
>
> "What has happened?" the Scarecrow asked a sad-looking man with a bushy beard, who wore an apron and was wheeling a baby-carriage along the sidewalk.
>
> "Why, we've had a revolution, your Majesty—as you ought to know very well," replied the man; "and since you went away the women have been running things to suit themselves. I'm glad you have decided to come back and restore order, for doing housework and minding the children is wearing out the strength of every man in the Emerald City."[5]

The third book in the series was *Ozma of Oz*, published in 1907, and Baum acceded to his readers' continued demands by bringing Dorothy back, this time by way of a shipwreck. The consecutive publication of Oz books (14 in all) continued until a year after Baum's death. The popular series was then continued by Ruth Plumly Thompson, who wrote 18 more Oz books in collaboration with illustrator John Neill.

The Library Block

Librarians dismissed Baum's work out of hand, and his books, for several reasons, were deliberately not part of library collections, even though children loved them. It was a time in society when educating children was a priority, and new fairy tales were deemed unacceptable, especially non-traditional fairy tales. European imports were almost all fantasy so it was felt that no more were needed, and realistic fiction was considered by many leading American educators to be more suitable for impressionable minds.

Also, Baum was very prolific and librarians were suspicious of the literary value of any series of books. Edward Stratemeyer (creator of the "fifty-cent juvenile"[6]) was producing an endless supply of adventure stories under the copyright of the Stratemeyer syndicate—for example, the Rover Boys, Tom Swift, and, just before his death in 1930, the perennial Nancy Drew. All the books for these series were written by a battery of hired writers and based on Stratemeyer's outlines. Stratemeyer had read with passion the works of Horatio Alger and Oliver Optic (pseudonym for William Taylor Adams) when he was a boy,[7] and this passion, along with his business acumen, established the series book as a permanent facet of the children's book genre, even without library circulation.

A handful of children's librarians were very powerful during the first half of the 20th century—notably, Anne Carroll Moore, who developed a children's department at the New York Public Library in 1906, Bertha Mahony Miller, Cornelia Meigs, and Ruth Hill Viguers, who was editor of *The Horn Book* magazine. These women made powerful decisions about library acquisitions and what constituted good children's literature. Not only were the Stratemeyer books absent from library collections until the last few decades, but Viguers also made a lasting pronouncement against Baum in 1953:

> Had L. Frank Baum possessed stylistic genius along with his lively imagination, he might have succeeded in being the first American to write great fantasy for children. But, inventive though it was, *The [Wonderful] Wizard of Oz* was told in such lifeless prose that rereading it in adulthood is a disappointment.[8]

But of more significance, as Baum stated in his introduction to *The Wonderful Wizard of Oz*, the book is a "modernized fairy tale, in which the wonderment and joy are retained and the heartaches and nightmares are left out." Representative of the American spirit, it remains "a New World fairy tale, appealing not only to children but to those special adults and even nations young in spirit."[9] Gore Vidal sanctions the Oz books with this statement: "Although Baum's books were dismissed as trash by at least two generations of librarians and literary historians, the land of Oz has managed to fascinate each new generation and, lately, Baum himself has become an O.K. subject, if not for the literary critic, for the social historian."[10]

Age of Innocence

By 1901, the children's book market was beginning to reflect childhood's so-called innocence, with emphasis on sentimentality and a child's joy of living. Children were compartmentalized, and child characters in books rarely faced any real adversity. In England, E. Nesbit had introduced the Bastable children in 1899 with *The Story of the Treasure Seekers* and followed it with two more in the series, *The Would-be-goods* (1901) and *The New Treasure Seekers* (1904). The Bastables were middle-class children whose innocence led them into one predicament after the other, predicaments that were easily resolved, though usually through the intervention of an understanding grownup. But it was in fantasy that Nesbit made her most important contributions to the children's book genre, with *The Five Children and It* (1902), *The Phoenix and the Carpet* (1904), and *The Story of the Amulet* (1906). Even though the five children were never in danger as they experimented with magic and traveled through time, the stories were so imaginatively logical and humorous that they have continued to capture the interest of both children and adults through the years.

In *Rebecca of Sunnybrook Farm* (1903), Kate Douglas Wiggin presented a lively heroine, so creative, so full of imagination that she brightened every page of the book. She defied the propriety expected of young women in the early 1900s, but even her unprecedented behavior never caused any real problems and in fact was more apt to bring about good fortune. Just as Jo was the pivot around which the characters in

Little Women revolved, so Rebecca became the light that brightened everyone's life.

Historian J. C. Furnas calls Rebecca the prototype of the American Cinderella story. She was a female "Horatio Alger," a child of poverty who went from rags to riches. There are touches of sentimentality in the book, with sadness quickly turning to joy. *Rebecca* was one of the few American books published at the turn of the century that took place in a standard New England setting and allowed young readers to recognize the everyday details of life in a small American town rather than the curious settings of fairy tales and English novels.

The writing style of Jack London was in stark contrast to the security enjoyed by the characters in most novels for children. In *The Call of the Wild* (1903) he presented an allegory of survival in which savagery battled with civilization through the struggles of a dog, Buck. Not specifically intended for children, this story appealed greatly to a child's adventurous spirit and love of animals. Though London wrote 50 books in 20 years, only *The Call of the Wild* and *White Fang* (1906) appealed to young people. He died at the age of 40 after living a life that matched the drama of his books.

Innovations Abroad

An English country setting, quaint and timeless, became the focus of Beatrix Potter's series of animal fantasies, with format and subject matter taking English children's literature in a new direction. *The Tale of Peter Rabbit* was published in England in 1900 by Potter herself and simultaneously in London and New York in 1902 by Frederick Warne. It didn't take long for this and the rest of her innovative small books for children, a total of 23, to become well established in the United States. Being a child was "in," and Peter's mischievous antics were accepted in America as typical childhood behavior. American authors created safe settings for their lively characters, but Potter kept hers on the edge of danger:

> Flopsy, Mopsy, and Cottontail, who were good little bunnies, went down the lane to gather blackberries: But Peter, who was very naughty, ran straight away to Mister McGregor's garden, and squeezed under the gate![11]

Beatrix Potter was brought up in a Victorian household and did not defy her parents or show signs of rebellion. She did, however, possess an iron will and an adventurous spirit, which had its outlet in her stories and led her to insist on being independent later in life. While growing up, she was very interested in drawing, especially sketching flora and fauna in meticulous detail, perhaps because she had trouble drawing people. Eventually, her artistic talent was combined with storytelling, and the result, unrealized until she was in her mid-30s, was a continuing supply of charming little storybooks, just right for children to hold in their hands.

Potter had tried to market *Peter Rabbit* on her own, only to have the manuscript rejected by Frederick Warne and by six other publishers. She decided to publish it herself and had definite ideas about how it should look—small, five inches by four inches, with one or two simple sentences on a page and a picture on each double spread. Not only did her limited supply sell out, she also decided to send a copy of the finished book with its black-and-white illustrations to Warne. This time, his company agreed to publish it—with colored plates.[12]

Potter's talking animals took on human attributes but never contradicted their animal natures. They flirted with danger and survived only through the author's good graces. In real life, they never would have made it. Peter Rabbit was almost caught by Mister McGregor but managed to escape, and Squirrel Nutkin should have been a meal for Old Brown, the owl, but lost only his tail. It was this gamble that created suspense, and it was Potter's respect for her child audience that has kept these books popular through the years. They were prototypes for the picture storybook format in children's book publishing, a format that was uncommon in Great Britain at the turn of the century and practically nonexistent in America until the 1930s.[13]

The Many Faces of Sambo

Scottish author Helen Bannerman wrote and illustrated a book called *The Story of Little Black Sambo* (1900) that fit very well into the small picturebook format.[14] Published first in England, then in America in 1905, the book received public and critical acclaim and remained popular for several years. Ultimately, however, it became so synonymous with racism that it was, and at this writing still is, banned from libraries.

This picture storybook, set in India and about a little boy outwitting a tiger, has been the subject of controversy during the second half of this century because the protagonist, Sambo, is "black," and the illustrations reflect a demeaning stereotype.

The author was a good writer but an untrained illustrator. She wrote the story for her own children while on her way back to India after bringing the children from India to be educated in Scotland. The book became very popular with American children and went through so many reprints after its initial publication that J.B. Lippincott copyrighted its own version 20 years after *Sambo* had been introduced to America without a copyright. Even though the earliest American edition of *The Story of Little Black Sambo* (1905), sponsored by L. Frank Baum, was supposedly a replica of the original [see illustration page 22] the illustrations were obviously copied by someone else and showed subtle changes that implied Sambo was African rather than East Indian. Many subsequent editions in the United States presented the work of different illustrators—with John Neill's pictures blatantly caricaturing Southern blacks and creating the stereotype heretofore blamed on Bannerman [see Illustration page 22].

For some reason, in almost a hundred years, no one has been able to illustrate *The Story of Little Black Sambo* in a way that is non-offensive, yet complementary to the text. An attempt in the 1960s offered illustrations of stereotypical, high-caste East Indians who have no association with the text. In an effort to visually create a Sambo that suits everybody, the charm of this story has been weakened.

The *Just So Stories* (1902) also had an East Indian setting, and one of the picture captions indicated that either Rudyard Kipling had read *The Story of Little Black Sambo* or that the name Sambo was already synonymous with Africa instead of India. In "How the Leopard Got His Spots," Kipling's own illustration for the story (in which an Ethiopian chooses to be black and a Leopard chooses spots when the two discover that, away from their home territory, they no longer blend into the background) was captioned as follows: "This is the picture of the Leopard and the Ethiopian . . . The Ethiopian was really a negro, and so his name was Sambo."[15] The difference between this Sambo and Bannerman's was the degree of artistic ability. Kipling's Sambo was a well-proportioned, finely featured young man, while Bannerman's Sambo lacked character and was the subject of many unfortunate interpretations.

Kipling's text, with its imaginative use of language, has been admired over the years—the stories originally appeared in *St. Nicholas* magazine—but his illustrations deserve equal time. They used expressive, creative, and highly unusual examples of modern design long before modern design was popular.

A Connection to Place

Kenneth Grahame's *Wind in the Willows* (1908) introduced some of the most memorable characters in the history of children's literature—Toad, Ratty, Mole, Otter, and Badger—more human than animal and each with a strong sense of place. The river, the meadow, and the Wild Wood were as much characters in the book as the animals. A "willing suspension of disbelief"[16] allows the reader to accept toads in women's clothing, a mole and a rat drinking mulled ale, and field mice singing carols. It further allows animals to interact with people, own motor cars, and have sufficient cash to live a life of luxury.

Grahame wrote two highly acclaimed collections of adult essays before he wrote *Wind in the Willows*. Like many authors of the time in England, his children's book was made up of stories originally told to his son, Alistair. This was the last significant thing he wrote—at one level a children's book, at another level a study of human needs and desires. The strong connection to place and the sense of belonging to a timeless environment made *Wind in the Willows* a portrait of the English countryside that spawned it, its history reaching back through the centuries. This timeless quality also tied it to Beatrix Potter's "country of the mind,"[17] the power of place in her stories that created a solid background for her animal characters.[18]

Frances Hodgson Burnett, who lived in America but spent most of her life traveling back and forth from America to England, created an English country estate as the setting for *The Secret Garden* (1911), with a main character quite different from Cedric in *Fauntleroy* and very different from Wiggin's Rebecca. Where those characters were candid and trusting, products of a loving American home, Mary Lennox was willful and disagreeable, a product of parental neglect in India:

> By the time [Mary] was six years old she was as tyrannical and selfish a little pig as ever lived. The young English governess who came to teach her to read and write disliked her so much that she gave up her place in three months.[19]

The story, despite Mary's unpleasant personality, has a magical appeal, and the characters of Mary, Dickon, and Colin are memorable in their development. Mary and Colin, like the flowers in the secret garden, blossom under loving care, which they have never before experienced in their 10 short years of life. The English moor becomes a place of beauty, a rejuvenating setting, and Dickon a magical Pan.

Although magic is often mentioned throughout the text with a capital "M," it is faith in miracles and the miracle of nature itself that make wishes come true for Mary, Colin, and Dickon, rather than any fantasy or fairy. But since this, like *Fauntleroy*, was not fantasy but realistic fiction, Burnett expressed in *The Secret Garden* the same prejudices that shadowed *The Story of Little Black Sambo*. Mary's housemaid, Martha, is interested in Mary's lifestyle in India, where the little girl lived until her parents died of cholera, and when Mary says that India is different from England, Martha agrees: "I dare say it's because there's such a lot of blacks there instead o' respectable white people. When I heard you was comin' from India I thought you was a black too." And Mary replies: "You thought I was a native! You dared! You don't know anything about natives! They are not people—they are servants who must salaam to you."[20]

Despite this one-sided look at the people of India, *The Secret Garden* has great appeal for contemporary children and, since its copyright ran out, has been issued in many different editions. The dysfunctional family so common now in modern society was very much represented in this book. The story also focused on the importance of environmental concerns long before those concerns gained prominence as a political issue.

In the second decade of the century Dorothy Canfield Fisher wrote *Understood Betsy* (1917), which reflected in its setting, among other things, the growth of the public school system in America. The book introduced Betsy as living in a medium-sized city in a medium-sized state and attending a school with 600 students. This group approach to education had already become the accepted standard. But when Betsy is sent by her spinster aunts to stay with relatives in the country, she attends a one-room schoolhouse. Away from the rigid structure of city life, Betsy blossoms and grows, progressing under the Montessori method of free thought introduced by educator Maria Montessori in Italy in 1907. Many of the details set forth in *Understood Betsy* contrast city living with small-town farm life and offer a clear picture of life in America at the beginning of the 20th century. Fisher not only lived most of her life in

Vermont, the setting for *Betsy*, but also was active in education and wrote books advocating the Montessori method.[21]

The lack of a solid connection to place may have made American children's literature seem more shallow than its English counterpart and may have encouraged most American authors to stay with realistic fiction. The history that is part of English fantasy and gives to it so many levels of meaning has yet to accumulate in America. Early 20th-century children's books in the United States instead offered contrasts—between rich and poor, city and country, West and East—and it was this concentration on lifestyles and regional differences that became more and more associated with American children's literature as the industry continued to grow in the 1920s.

A Separate Market

In 1916, Bertha Mahony Miller, then Bertha Mahony, opened a bookstore in Boston. It was called The Bookshop for Boys and Girls, and Miss Mahony not only made good children's books available to the general public, she made them visible as well. New York librarian May Massee said: "The children brought their parents and the parents brought their children and the uncles and the cousins and the aunts came too, as well as any fortunate educator, or author, or artist, or bookseller, or editor or anyone else who had any interest in children's books."[22] Mahony credited Frederic G. Melcher of the Stewart Company's bookshop in Indianapolis with the success of her shop.[23] Melcher, who became editor of *Publishers Weekly* and served in that capacity for several years, was an enthusiastic advocate of children's books. It concerned him that their sale was limited to Christmastime, so in 1919 he established Children's Book Week, an October celebration recognized throughout the country and currently sponsored by the Children's Book Council in New York City.

Also in 1919, Macmillan Publishing Company in New York created the first children's book department and thus established a separate literary genre. The first list of department head Louise Seaman mostly included previously published English and American titles. With Melcher's 1922 establishment of the Newbery Medal, which has become the most prestigious award in the children's book field, and with Ann Carroll Moore's children's book-review column, "Three Owls," appearing in the

New York Herald Tribune by 1924—followed by Ann Eaton's page in *The New York Times* in 1930—the children's book industry as we know it today was established.

The Newbery Medal was named for 18th-century bookseller, John Newbery. In 1744, he was the first to make a business of children's books—at his shop, the Bible and Sun, in London's St. Paul's Churchyard—and the first to encourage children to read for pleasure as well as for learning.[24] A special committee of children's librarians was formed to select the most distinguished contribution to American literature for children in 1921, and the first Newbery Medal was given to Hendrik Willem Van Loon in 1922 for *The Story of Mankind*. Van Loon's eminently readable world history did much to connect the United States with the rest of the world, and the American children's books of the 1920s reflected this connection.

CHRONOLOGICAL BIBLIOGRAPHY 1900–1919

All of the titles listed below, if not otherwise noted, are available in several editions. See Bowker's *Books in Print*.

Baum, L. Frank. *The Wonderful Wizard of Oz*, illtd. W. W. Denslow. Chicago: George M. Hill, 1900; New York: New American Library, 1984. (Fantasy)

Characterization and imagination highlight the first book in a fantasy series initially set in the heart of America, as the child Dorothy, not so meek and mild, and her little dog, Toto, travel from Kansas to Oz by means of a tornado. Like bright flames that never quite die, Dorothy, the Scarecrow, Tin Woodman, and the Cowardly Lion have continued to entertain new generations of children. Unlike fairy tales, the magic of Oz has its practical aspects—as soon as the farmer paints an ear on the Scarecrow's head, he can hear; the Wizard, in his capacity as pundit, stuffs the Scarecrow's head with a mixture of bran, pins, and needles and tells him he now has *bran-new* brains. There was of course real magic in Oz for those who lived there: Animals and scarecrows could speak, a man could be made entirely of tin and still live because no one died in Oz, and bad witches melted away.

Bannerman, Helen. *The Story of Little Black Sambo*, illtd. Helen Bannerman. London: Grant Richards, 1900; New York: HarperCollins (reproduction of 1905 Harper edition), 1993. (Fantasy/Picture Book)

Sambo is a self-assured young East Indian child who lives in the jungle with his caring parents and decides to go for a walk in the new clothes his mother has made for him. He is dressed in purple pants and crimson shoes and is carrying a green umbrella. "And then wasn't Little Black Sambo grand?" Bannerman writes. And so he was, at least until confronted by fierce tigers who demand his clothes. But Sambo uses his wits to outsmart the tigers, not only reclaiming his clothes but turning the tigers into butter, which he uses on the stack of delicious pancakes his mother has made for him, eating every last one.

Potter, Beatrix. *The Tale of Peter Rabbit*. London: self-published, 1900; London: Frederick Warne, 1902; New York: Frederick Warne, 1902, 1987. (Fantasy/Picture Book/Animal)

While Peter's siblings behave nicely, Peter takes his chances in Mister McGregor's garden, filling himself up with vegetables and almost meeting his father's fate of being put in a pie. He survives but loses his jacket and shoes to the farmer's scarecrow and, while Flopsy, Mopsy, and Cottontail enjoy blackberries and milk, Peter feels ill and is dosed with camomile tea.

———. *The Tale of Squirrel Nutkin*. London: Frederick Warne, 1901; New York: Frederick Warne, 1902, 1987. (Fantasy/Picture Book/Animal)

While Squirrel Nutkin's brother and cousins show proper respect for their elders, Nutkin teases Old Brown the owl with silly riddles and very nearly becomes Brown's dinner, escaping only by the skin of his tail.

Washington, Booker T. *Up From Slavery*. New York: Doubleday, 1901; Cutchogue, N.Y.: Buccaneer, 1990. (Informational/Biography)

This autobiography of a man who knew firsthand the indignity of slavery also presented a man who took advantage of the opportunities that existed in this country for those able to reach out for them. Because of his efforts, at a time in America's social history when the Negro race was looked down upon, and because of the help he received from people who took time to know the individual, regardless of race, color, or creed, Washington was able to achieve success and to assist in the education of many fellow citizens who otherwise would have remained illiterate. Washington's autobiography negated the common view of all African Americans as slow learners. His achievements created a foundation that continues to be built upon, and the story of his life, though originally published for adults, speaks to young people.

Eastman, Charles A. *Indian Boyhood.* New York: McClure, Phillips, 1902; New York: Dover, 1971. (Informational/Biography)

Eastman, a Sioux Indian who was a Dartmouth graduate and a licensed physician, wrote an autobiography in which he recalled his childhood impression of pre-Civil War white settlers as heartless because they kept slaves, something Indians did not do. In writing about his life after childhood, however, Eastman referred to his own people, the Sioux, as "savages," as if he were merely an observer of Indian culture, not part of it. Though it was the only book written by an American Indian at the time, it did very little to define Indian culture.[25]

Kipling, Rudyard. *Just So Stories*, illtd. author. New York: Doubleday, 1902; New York: Puffin Books, 1987. (Short Story/Fantasy Collection/Animal)

Some of the best-loved stories for children are contained in this collection, including "The Elephant's Child," a story in which a young elephant, curious to know what a crocodile eats, gets too close to the crocodile. The crocodile decides to eat the elephant and grabs his little round nose. In an effort to get away, the elephant's nose stretches and stretches as he runs along the bank of "the great grey-green greasy Limpopo River." The rhythm of the language throughout this collection calls for the stories to be read aloud, and some of the word combinations create a whole new meaning, for example, "catty-shaped" (shaped like a common house cat) and "patchy-blatchy" or "speckly-spickly" shadows (patches of dappled light and darkness in spots, blotches, and stripes).

Nesbit, Edith. *Five Children and It.* London: T. Fisher Unwin, 1902; New York: Puffin, 1985. Also, *The Phoenix and the Carpet* (London: T. Fisher Unwin, 1904; New York: Puffin, 1985) and *The Story of the Amulet* (London: T. Fisher Unwin, 1906; New York: Puffin, 1986). (Fantasy)

The five children are Robert, Anthea, Jane, Cyril, and two-year-old Lamb, and they are spending the summer in the country. The "it" turns out to be a Psammead or sand-fairy capable of granting their wishes. "I wish we were as beautiful as the day," Anthea impulsively says, and so they are. But Lamb has a temper tantrum because they are all suddenly strangers to him, and when they arrive back at the house, Martha, the nursemaid, won't let them in because she doesn't know who they are. Fortunately, the wishes last only till sundown, and once the spell is over, the children are free to make a new wish the following day. No matter how hard they try, however, each wish they make creates complications, the worst moment being when they try to talk the Lamb, whom they have wished grown up, into leaving the young lady he has just met before he turns back into a baby at sundown. In *The Phoenix and the Carpet*, the children continue their fantastical adventures, traveling through time on a magic carpet, and in *The Story of the Amulet*, the Psammead sends the children back in time to ancient Egypt to find the second half of an amulet. It is Cyril who suggests that they travel into the future, to the time after they have found the amulet. Then they will know where it is, and they can then go back and get it.

London, Jack. *The Call of the Wild*. New York: Macmillan, 1903. (Realistic Fiction/Animal)

A pet dog, Buck, is kidnapped from his home in California and taken to the Klondike, where he becomes a sled dog. Cruel treatment by humans sends him into the wild, where eventually he becomes a leader of a pack of wolves. Though originally not published as a children's book, both this story and *White Fang* (1905) were adapted as motion pictures directed at children and are categorized as young adult novels appealing to children 10 and up.

Wiggin, Kate Douglas. *Rebecca of Sunnybrook Farm*. Boston: Houghton Mifflin, 1903; New York: Outlet, 1993. (Realistic Fiction)

Rebecca, outspoken and enthusiastic, is sent to live with her two aunts when her widowed mother, burdened with several other children, has trouble getting by. Rebecca becomes the reflection of independent thinking and brings to her spinster relations, and to everyone else within her sphere, the riches of compassion and warm emotion. Rebecca never loses her sense of self-worth.

Potter, Beatrix. *The Tale of Two Bad Mice*. London: Frederick Warne, 1904; New York: Frederick Warne, 1904, 1987. (Fantasy/Picture Book/Animal)

Two mice, Hunca Munca and Tom Thumb, invade the home of the dolls, Lucinda and Jane, while the two dolls are on an outing. The mice are extremely destructive when they discover all the food to be artificial. But all's well that ends well, and the two bad mice do reform their ways by mending the damage they have caused.

Baum, L. Frank. *The Marvelous Land of Oz*, illtd. John R. Neill. Chicago: Reilly and Britton, 1904; New York: Puffin, 1985. (Fantasy)

Many authors would have capitalized on *The Wonderful Wizard of Oz* by simply retelling Dorothy's story, but Baum respected his young audience. Although he made the Scarecrow and Tin Woodman part of his second book, he created an additional cast of imaginative characters: the boy Tip, Jack Pumpkinhead, the Sawhorse, and Mr. H.M. Wogglebug, T.E. (Highly Magnified and Thoroughly Educated).

Burnett, Frances Hodgson. *A Little Princess*. Philadelphia: J.B. Lippincott, 1905; New York: Dell Yearling, 1975. (Realistic Fiction)

Wealthy Captain Crewe leaves his beloved young daughter, Sara, with Miss Minchin at a private school in England and goes off to India, and Miss Minchin has no choice but to treat Sara like royalty. But when Sara's father dies a pauper, Sara is left penniless, and Miss Minchin shows her true nature. She no longer has to cater to Sara, who becomes a Cinderella figure and the brunt of Miss Minchin's resentment, which has been building over the years. But just as Burnett's Fauntleroy regains security and wealth, so, too, does Sara, in keeping with the writing fashion of the time that ultimately made "good" children recipients of good fortune.

Potter, Beatrix. *The Tale of Mr. Jeremy Fisher*. London: Frederick Warne, 1906; New York: Frederick Warne, 1987. (Fantasy/Picture Book/Animal)

Jeremy Fisher is a frog who one day decides to go fishing in a pond. First it rains, but he is wearing his rubber macintosh and galoshes. Then he is annoyed by a water beetle and threatened by a rat. Finally, he is swallowed by a trout who fortunately doesn't like the taste of macintosh and spits him out.

Baum, L. Frank. *Ozma of Oz*,. illtd. John R. Neill. Chicago: Reilly and Britton, 1907; New York: Puffin, 1992. (Fantasy)

Dorothy, as courageous and independent as ever, returns in this adventure, but not to Oz. Also, Dorothy's speech patterns have become uncharacteristically babyish, even though her actions contradict her manner of speaking. Dorothy and her pet hen, Billina, are shipwrecked and end up in the fairy land of Ev, where they have to save the Queen of Ev from the Nome King. They are helped by Tik-Tok (the earliest self-sufficient robot), the Princess Ozma (Tip transformed), and Dorothy's old friends Scarecrow, Cowardly Lion, and Tin Woodman.

Grahame, Kenneth. *Wind in the Willows*. illtd. Ernest H. Shepard. London: Macmillan, 1908; New York: Macmillan, 1991. (Fantasy/Animal)

Mole meets Rat and a true friendship is born as Mole is introduced to Rat's beloved river. The two visit Toad, boastful and reckless, who has a new obsession—a motor car, which he promptly crashes, only to buy another and another until his mania causes him to break the law and go to prison. Curiosity takes Mole into the Wild Wood in search of Badger, about whom Rat has told him intriguing stories. He becomes lost in a storm, and Ratty searches him out and finally locates Badger's underground home, saving them both. Mole finds a kindred soul in Badger, and when Toad escapes from prison, they all set out to save Toad's ancestral home, Toad Hall, from the stoats and the weasels who have taken it over. This is a story of deep friendship and connection to place, creating in Grahame's fictional world strong feelings of security and dependability.

Montgomery, Lucy Maud. *Anne of Green Gables*, illtd. M. A. and W. A. Claus. Boston: L.C. Page, 1908; New York: Bantam Classic. (Realistic Fiction)

When an elderly couple applies to an orphan asylum for a boy, they get a redheaded, freckle-faced girl instead. The girl, Anne, is fresh, original, and unconventional, an appealing character who ultimately finds love and security. This book was the first in a series of popular books about Anne by Canadian author Montgomery.[26]

Burgess, Thornton. *Old Mother West Wind*. Boston: Little, Brown, 1910; Cutchogue, N.Y.: Buccaneer, 1992. (Fantasy/Short Story Collection/Animals)

This collection of animal stories about Grandfather Frog, Reddy Fox, Peter Rabbit, Jimmy Skunk, Johnny Chuck, and others is tied together by Old Mother West Wind and her Merry Little Breezes. Grandfather Frog tells the story of how he lost his tail, and the familiar race between the turtle and the hare is made more interesting in this collection by the addition of a fox and a mink along with the hare, as Spotty the Turtle puts one over on the other three and wins the race. The simple, clear text has not lost its appeal for beginning readers after all these years.

Potter, Beatrix. *The Tale of Mrs. Tittlemouse*. London: Frederick Warne, 1910; New York: Frederick Warne, 1910, 1987. (Fantasy/Picture Book/Animal)

Mrs. Tittlemouse, writes Beatrix Potter, "was a most terribly tidy particular little mouse." She spends all her time tidying up after beetles and spiders and bees who make their way into her passages, and finds Mr. Jackson, an overweight and uncouth toad, the most disagreeable of all her visitors. Even so, after spring cleaning, she invites them all, even Mr. Jackson, in for a party.

Smith, E. Boyd. *The Farm Book*. Boston: Houghton Mifflin, 1910, 1990. (Informational/Picture Book)

Although *Chicken World* (1910) received more critical acclaim than Smith's other books, it is *The Farm Book*, *The Seashore Book* (1912), and *The Railroad Book* (1913) that have remained in print. Even though the text in *The Farm Book* is extensive and informational, its illustrations stand out, picturing old-time farm life and introducing the picture-book format to informational books for American children. There was something to see on every page in the full-size color illustrations detailing the panorama of a New England farm.

Barrie, James M. *Peter and Wendy* [Peter Pan], illtd. F. D. Bedford. London: Hodderadd Stoughton, 1911; New York: Scribner, 1911; New York: Outlet, 1990. (Fantasy)

First presented as a play in 1904 and based on the introduction of Peter in two earlier books by Barrie—*Tommy and Grizel* (1900) and *The Little White Bird* (1902)—Barrie made the play into a book, *Peter and Wendy*. This story of the boy who never wanted to grow up has never lost favor and continues to delight audiences as a book, play, and movie. At a time in American history when childhood was looked upon as a state of bliss, it is no wonder this story enjoyed everlasting popularity. *Peter Pan* is an expression of eternal youth and represents the eternal boy in Barrie himself, "the boy who loved tales of pirates and tales of wonder and magic, the boy who refused to grow up and lose the joy and wonder of the Never Never Land."[27]

Burnett, Frances Hodgson. *The Secret Garden*. Philadelphia: J.B. Lippincott, 1911; New York: Random House, 1993. (Realistic Fiction)

Mary Lennox didn't know how it felt to be part of a loving family for the first 10 years of her life, but when her parents, who always had left her care to others, die in a cholera epidemic in India, Mary is sent to live with her reclusive uncle in England. Here she meets caring people who are not in the least intimidated by her willful ways, and soon Mistress Mary stops being quite so contrary and starts watching her garden grow, in the process assuring a fuller life for herself and those around her.

Webster, Jean. *Daddy Long-Legs*. New York: Meredith Press, 1912; New York: Knopf, 1993. (Realistic Fiction)

At a time when first-person books were not being written, Webster wrote this novel as a series of letters by 17-year-old Jerusha Abbott to her benefactor, who has offered to finance her college education and take her from the orphanage where she has spent her childhood. The letters cover the four years of her education, and the reader watches her grow into a self-assured young woman, ready to meet the Trustee whose shadow loomed long and tall the day she discovered she was going away to school and whom she has named "Daddy Long-Legs." If *Little Women* can be considered a 19th-century young adult novel, *Daddy Long-Legs* takes the young adult reader into the early 20th century, with its emphasis on education and women's rights in a story that maintains its suspense to the very end.

Baum, L. Frank. *The Patchwork Girl of Oz*. Chicago: Reilly and Britton, 1913; New York: Dover, 1990. (Fantasy)

Ojo, a Munchkin boy, lives with his uncle in the blue section of Oz. With the powder of life he activates Scraps, the Patchwork Girl, who speaks in rhyme and, with an excess supply of brains, finds the greatest pleasure in living. With the Crooked Magician (not dishonest, just crookedly shaped), the Patchwork Girl, and the Glass Cat, young Ojo sets out on a scavenger hunt for materials to save his uncle, Unc Nunkie, and the magician's wife from permanently being turned to stone. Any author who creates a series takes the chance of not always living up to expectations. Although reviewers liked *The Patchwork Girl*, it was a poor repeat of *The Land of Oz*, with Ojo taking Tip's role, the Crooked Magician once more using the powder of life, and the Patchwork Girl becoming ambulatory as was Jack Pumpkinhead in the earlier book. There were also gratuitous characters, for example, the phonograph player and the Tottenhots, portrayed in John R. Neill's illustrations as half-naked savages. It was Baum who created the name "Tottenhots," an obvious play on words; the

Hottentots have been delineated as people of South Africa akin to both the Bushman and the Bantu.[28]

Porter, Eleanor. *Pollyanna*. Boston: L.C. Page, 1913; New York: Puffin, 1988. (Realistic Fiction)

The Pollyanna character has become a stereotype for unrealistic optimism, but the story itself has a double edge. Pollyanna may be looking for the good side of everything, but the reader is well aware that all is not well in the life of this child and waits with suspense for the resolution, which doesn't occur until the very end. This is a well-written story, and the fully rounded portrayal of Pollyanna creates a sympathetic character. The story captures and holds the attention of the reader even though the Pollyanna image of everlasting optimism has become a cliche.

Fisher, Dorothy Canfield. *Understood Betsy*, illtd. Ada C. Williamson. New York: Henry Holt, 1917; New York: Dell, 1993. (Realistic Fiction)

Fictional young orphans in the early 1900s were apt to be subsidized by wealthy patrons, but Elizabeth Ann is taken in by two frugal spinster relatives who are not at all wealthy. Betsy is brought up to be totally dependent on them, and the turning point comes when Aunt Harriet has a stroke and Aunt Frances turns her attention away from young Betsy and focuses on her sister's needs. Betsy has been told time and again by her Aunt Frances that no one understands her as well as her aunt, but now Aunt Frances doesn't have time for Betsy. The decision is made by the two aunts to send Betsy to the Putneys' farm in Vermont—even though Aunt Frances has always referred to them as "those horrid Putney cousins"—and Betsy is apprehensive. At the farm, everyone takes it for granted she can take care of herself, and slowly she discovers that being independent has its rewards.

Gruelle, Johnny. *Raggedy Ann Stories*. Chicago: P.F. Volland, 1918; New York: Outlet, 1991. (Fantasy/Toys)

Raggedy Ann is the leader in the nursery, Marcella represents a mother figure, and the various adventures the toys have are closely tied to the way in which children play with toys. In the first few selections, there is an inconsistency in viewpoint from one story to the next, and throughout the book, transitions are awkward. But the chapters in which Raggedy Ann runs her fingers through her yarn hair, a sign that she is thinking, are the best, for that's when the reader is most drawn to Raggedy Ann as a character. In one story, she rescues Fido from the dogcatcher, in another she saves a small mouse from being eaten by the cat, and, finally, she falls in the river and needs rescuing herself.

Baum, L. Frank. *The Magic of Oz*. Chicago: Reilly and Britton, 1919; New York: Ballantine, 1985. (Fantasy)

This book and *Glinda of Oz* were written as backups in case Baum's illness prevented him from writing after a gallbladder operation. Because he also had a weak heart, he did end up removing them from the safe-deposit box where he had stored them and spending quite a bit of time revising them throughout 1918 and 1919. *Magic* appeared in bookstores soon after Baum's death in 1919, and *Glinda* was published a year later. In *The Magic of Oz*, Baum brings back the characters who have appeared in all of his other books, not just those set in Oz. Although magic is outlawed in Oz by its ruler, Ozma, a boy called Kiki Aru inadvertently learns his father's secret of transformation and joins with the ex-Nome King to capture Oz by magic means. In the meantime, the girl Trot and Cap'n Bill of Merryland become trapped on an island when they try to remove the Magic Flower as a birthday present for Ozma. With a large cast of characters, all familiar to Oz fans, each of these two predicaments is addressed and finally resolved, culminating in a large birthday celebration.

———. *Glinda of Oz*. Chicago: Reilly and Britton, 1920; New York: Ballantine, 1985. (Fantasy)

This story reflected wartime, not surprisingly since World War I was being fought at the time Baum wrote the book. It was one of the few children's books that made any reference to the fact that America was involved in a war. In the story, the Flatheads and the Skeezers are warring nations, but of course no one dies in Oz, and Dorothy and Ozma attempt to bring peace to these two lands.

NOTES

1. Time Life eds. *This Fabulous Century*: 1900–1910, vol. 1.
2. J. C. Furnas. *The Americans: A Social History of the United States, 1587–1914*, p. 809.
3. Susan E. Meyer. *A Treasury of the Great Children's Book Illustrators*, p. 39.

4. Ruth Sidel. *On Her Own: Growing Up in the Shadow of the American Dream*, p. 4.
5. L. Frank Baum. *The Marvelous Land of Oz*. New York: Dover, 1969, p. 170.
6. Books for boys and girls between the ages of 10 and 16 with many sequels and no character development, as defined in Sheila Egoff's *Only Connect: Readings on Children's Literature*, p. 42.
7. Ibid., p. 54.
8. Ruth Hill Viguers. "1920–1967: Golden Years and Time of Tumult," in *A Critical History of Children's Literature*. ed. Cornelia Meigs, p. 412.
9. Selma G. Lanes. "Introduction," *The Wonderful Wizard of Oz*. New York: New American Library, 1984, p. xiii.
10. Gore Vidal. *United States: Essays 1952–1992*, p. 1096.
11. Beatrix Potter. *The Tale of Peter Rabbit*. New York: Frederick Warne, 1987, p. 18.
12. Margaret Lane. *The Magic Years of Beatrix Potter*, pp. 97–100.
13. Except for American artists E. Boyd Smith and Wanda Gág, who introduced an American version of the picture storybook before photo-offset technology allowed for ease of production and created an expanded market for picture books.
14. The first American edition in 1905 was a reproduction of the original in a "Dumpy Book" format (4.5" by 5.5") with full-color pictures on every double spread.
15. Rudyard Kipling. *Just So Stories*. New York: Puffin, 1987, p. 44.
16. "That willing suspension of disbelief for the moment, which constitutes poetic faith." Samuel Coleridge, *Bartlett's Familiar Quotations*, ed. Emily Morison Beck. Boston: Little Brown, 1980, p. 437:15.
17. Eleanor Cameron in *The Green and Burning Tree* (p. 176): "When one thinks of Beatrix Potter and her country of the mind, the word that compellingly rises is the word 'release,' and this word is precisely what the discovery and use of the writer's own country of the mind afford him; it is what happens to him when he discovers it. He is released as an artist."
18. Ibid., p. 178.
19. Francis Burnett. *The Secret Garden*. Philadelphia: Lippincott, 1962, p. 8.
20. Ibid., pp. 28–29.
21. *Yesterday's Authors of Books for Children*, vol. 1, p. 122.
22. Bertha E. Mahony, et al. *Illustrators of Children's Books: 1744–1945*. Boston: Horn Book, 1947, p. 232.
23. As stated in Bertha Mahony Miller's introduction to *Newbery Medal Books: 1922–1955*, p. 2.
24. Cornelia Meigs. "Roots in the Past Up to 1840," *A Critical History of Children's Literature*, ed. Meigs, p. 58.
25. Anne Commire, Op. cit., *YABC*, p. 113.
26. Montgomery's publisher asked for a sequel (*Anne of Avonlea*, 1909), which Lucy was reluctant to write. She was critical of her efforts, considering herself a prisoner of her own creation. "If the thing takes," she said, "they'll want me to write her through college. The idea makes me sick . . ." Demands for "Anne"

stories weighed her down, and after six books she refused to write any more. (*Yesterday's Authors of Books for Children*, vol. 1, p. 187)

27. Elizabeth Nesbitt. "A Rightful Heritage: 1890–1920," in *A Critical History of Children's Literature*, ed. Cornelia Meigs, p. 345.
28. As defined in *Webster's Ninth New Collegiate Dictionary*. Springfield, Mass.: Merriam-Webster, 1983.

Illustration by author Johnny Gruelle from Eddie Elephant *(P.F. Volland, 1921). Little Cocoa-boy and the two oxen are the only unclothed characters in the book, the implication being that "animals" wearing clothes are superior to those without.*

3

THE COMMON FOLK 1920–1929

I know I talk too much, I write too much,
I force too many of my drawings
and ideas upon my friends.

—Wanda Gág
Growing Pains

Fun and Games

By the 1920s the United States was riding high, as enthusiastically involved in the business of living as the young Wanda Gág who spoke the words quoted on the preceding page. The country had fought in the First World War and won, the economy was up, and the American dream seemed a reality for the common man. Those people involved in having fun were doing so almost to the point of frenzy. The population of the United States had been growing fast—between 1900 and 1910, nine million immigrants entered the country[1], and even with an immigration quota law passed in 1921 and a basic immigration law passed in 1924 the yearly quota remained at almost 200,000.[2] Fast-developing modes of transportation allowed for quick communication and a wider knowledge of United States terrain.

At the beginning of the century, children began to be seen as a separate entity and by the Twenties were the object of experimental study, as influenced by Darwin's controversial theory of evolution, by Sigmund Freud's dream theories, and by John Dewey's psychological research regarding children and education. In the laboratory schools of Dewey and Maria Montessori, emphasis was on the "whole child," forerunner of the "whole language" approach to reading that would finally bring children's literature into the literary mainstream. According to Dewey, "Every act may carry within itself a consoling and supporting consciousness of the whole to which it belongs and which in some sense belongs to it."[3] And Maria Montessori "developed a process of education that [was] attuned to the child's inner drives, that promote[d] the beneficial interaction of the child and his surroundings, and that [led] to the child's mastery of himself and his environment."[4]

The Reading Public

In the world of books, two separate trends were developing. In keeping with the times, the Stratemeyer syndicate had been pouring into the marketplace the "series" book, for example, Bobbsey Twins and Tom Swift and, later in the decade, the Hardy Boys and Nancy Drew—written by hired writers who were required to follow a specific outline. The resulting storylines followed a common pattern that was comfortably predictable for the children reading them. These books were inexpensive and readily accessible to the general population. They also reflected American affluence, with characters who not only had everything they wanted but also could do anything they wanted. In the meantime, the new genre called children's literature was growing, with the help of editors Louise Seaman and May Massee, heading the newly established children's book departments at Macmillan and Doubleday, and with the added influence of several highly respected librarians, among them Anne Carroll Moore, Anne Thaxter Eaton, Bertha Mahony Miller, and Alice Jordan, all of whom reviewed children's books for the media.

In 1924, the first issue of *The Horn Book Magazine* was published by the Bookshop for Boys and Girls in Boston.[5] It was and still is a magazine devoted exclusively to books of interest to children. The children's rooms in community libraries contained critically acclaimed titles, but it wasn't always easy for families to visit the library, especially those families who lived outside the cities on farms or in small villages. In order to have books in the home, they had to be purchased. The mass market books were much cheaper than the recommended trade titles, and in many homes, quantity edged out quality.

The lasting works of the 1920s reflected, for the most part, a melting pot of cultures and a simpler lifestyle—both in the cities and on farms—offering a contrast to the English upper-class settings of past children's literature. The sprigged calico of *Hitty: Her First Hundred Years* (1929) was a far cry from *Little Lord Fauntleroy*'s velvet and lace (1886). Wanda Gág's unpretentious couple with their Old World clothing and tiny hut in *Millions of Cats* (1928) would be lost in the English estate that harbored *The Secret Garden* (1911).

In and Out of the Nursery

Although most of the memorable children's books of the 1920s were independent of England and offered diverse backgrounds, the English nursery was still part of the children's book scene. And the book that was given the greatest popular approval by the American public in the 1920s wasn't an American book at all, nor was it a storybook. It was a book of poems written by British author and journalist A. A. Milne, called *When We Were Very Young* (1924). Milne was a craftsman who believed that poetry should have a rhythmic flow: "Every piece of poetry has a music of its own which it is humming to itself as it goes along, and every line, every word in it has to keep time to this music."[6] The public agreed. The collection became a best-seller almost immediately in England and was quickly published in the United States. The books that followed—*Winnie the Pooh* (1926), *Now We Are Six* (1927), and *The House at Pooh Corner* (1928)—joined with the first to receive worldwide acclaim. *Now We Are Six* was even more popular in America than in England. With these four books, Milne was established for all time as a renowned writer for children. But he was also a journalist, a columnist, and a playwright, and it was in these fields that Milne yearned for prominence. He actually resented being recognized first and foremost in the children's book field, and undoubtedly it would please him to know that the resurgence of interest in his books that developed in the 1980s can be credited to an adult audience. Children love the characters, but their parents love the characterizations.

When Milne's first children's book was written, his son, Christopher, was three years old, and by the time *The House at Pooh Corner* was published, Christopher was around seven. Even though the stories were about him and about his favorite toys—Pooh Bear, Eeyore, Piglet, as well as Kanga and Roo—Christopher Milne was relatively unaffected by being the embodiment of the stories during those years. It was during his adolescence and after that he found himself trying to deal with forever being locked into childhood by his father's stories and poems—and did so by writing a book about his childhood called *The Enchanted Places*.[7]

In contrast to Milne, Johnny Gruelle, American author of the Raggedy Ann and Andy series, was looking not for literary recognition but mainly to make a living in the newly emerging children's book field. For him, writing children's stories became a money-making proposition, although his first book, *Raggedy Ann Stories* (1918), was born of emotional need, a memento to his daughter, Marcella, who had died two years earlier from an infection caused by a contaminated vaccination needle.[8] The dilapidated rag doll that ultimately generated the Raggedy stories, which Marcella never saw published, was discovered by her in the family attic. The doll had belonged to Gruelle's mother. With the publication of *The Original Adventures of Raggedy Andy* (1920) and the manufacture and sale of the dolls themselves, Gruelle discovered a continuing source of income. From then on, he kept a supply of stories on hand at all times, selling them whenever he needed money. The dolls, first made and marketed by the Gruelle family themselves, then manufactured on the assembly line, have become as necessary for children to own as the classic teddy bear. But the Raggedy stories that continue to be produced today, written or adapted by a staff of writers, have no real connection to the original.

In the classic *The Velveteen Rabbit* (1926), American author Margery Williams Bianco also wrote about a group of toys, including a most memorable stuffed rabbit comfortably ensconced in an English-style nursery. The characterizations were so well developed that even today the reader can't help being drawn into the rabbit's adventures as it yearns to be real. Bianco was always deeply involved in her subject matter. "To engage children's interest in anything," she said, "you have to be keenly interested in that thing yourself."[9]

According to Bianco's daughter, illustrator Pamela Bianco, her mother often discussed Pamela's nursery toys as if they were real. *The Velveteen Rabbit* was Bianco's first children's book, with earlier books being published on adult lists, but it wasn't labeled a classic until much later. And it was the only one of her children's books that gained such a status, even though *Winterbound* was a 1937 Newbery runner-up.

At every reading of *The Velveteen Rabbit* the reader's emotions are tapped when the toy rabbit finds that he has become real, that even though the child has outgrown him, he has an existence that will continue for all eternity. The dreams of a stuffed rabbit become the dreams of all of us as we face our own mortality. "Death should be treated naturally," Bianco asserted. "You don't have to educate children about death. Speak of it as a natural occurrence and they will do the same."[10] Margery Bianco's book confronted death at a time in American history when children were beginning to be shielded from these truths; by the 1930s, books began reflecting only the bright side of life and avoiding the subject of death. Bianco's direct approach to a subject about which all children express curiosity has kept this book in print and made it an exemplary contribution to literature.

Colonial Viewpoint

Regardless of the efforts of L. Frank Baum to focus on America as a setting for American children's books, most writers rejected that setting, relying instead on the culture most familiar to them. The settings were not only based on books they had read as children but also reflected a way of life that relied on customs brought from countries outside the United States.

Hugh Lofting was born in England but moved to America, and his Doctor Dolittle books not only sold well here but also received critical acclaim. *The Story of Doctor Dolittle* (1920) has been considered his best.

Lofting combined an English country setting with the simple needs of the provincial American farm family and created a character who cared nothing for money. He made him so distinctive and so real that if Doctor John Dolittle suddenly showed up in the community today, no one would be surprised. Even though the setting was English rather than American, Lofting never allowed the doctor to put on airs; he kept him humble.

The idea for the Doctor Dolittle stories came during World War I. Lofting, who was serving in the British army, was concerned that while wounded soldiers were treated and cured, wounded horses were shot.[11] He began writing to his children about a doctor who learns the language of animals. On a trip back to America with his family in 1919, he met novelist Cecil Roberts aboard ship and showed him the manuscript pages for *The Story of Doctor Dolittle*. Roberts referred him to his publisher, Frederick A. Stokes, and the manuscript was accepted.

Doctor Dolittle understands animals better than people—people are apt to disappoint him. In *The Story of Doctor Dolittle*, once the doctor learns to speak the language of animals, he gives people up almost entirely. He becomes renowned in the animal world and is summoned to Africa to save the monkeys from an epidemic. The King and Queen of Jolliginki try to prevent the doctor from completing his task, but he gains the support of their son, Bumpo, an avid reader with a broader view of society than his parents, who have rejected all white people. Bumpo's great desire to be white implies that to be white is to be superior.[12]

Lofting was an advocate of internationalism and had traveled extensively, including trips to Africa. He prided himself on his understanding and would no doubt have been stunned by an accusation of racism on his part. Though rebuked by the Council on Interracial Books for Children in 1968 for his "grotesque caricatures" of Africans,[13] none of Lofting's drawings flattered any of the characters they portrayed. Doctor Dolittle looked more like W. C. Fields than Rex Harrison, who played the good doctor in the movie version, which included material from both *The Story of Doctor Dolittle* and the Newbery Medal book, *The Voyages of Doctor Dolittle* (1922). Lofting went on to write nine more Doctor Dolittle books, all of which celebrated his creativity in words and pictures, but none ever matched his first effort in terms of originality and logical fantasy. He resented the condescending attitude of the public toward children's literature and commented that for years it shocked him to find his writings among "Juveniles"; he felt there should be a "category of 'Seniles' to offset the epithet."[14] The controversy over both pictures and text in the Doctor Dolittle series became so heated in the 1970s that the books went out of print and were not reprinted until 1988, and then only because Lofting's son Christopher edited the series, removing references to Prince Bumpo wanting to be white and other references and illustrations that might be considered derogatory.

Defining Society

The subconscious acceptance of white superiority was reflected in many children's books published between 1900 and 1940, for example, in Kipling's text in *Just So Stories* (1902), in John R. Neill's illustrations for *Little Black Sambo* (1908), in the text of *The Secret Garden* (1911), in Baum's *Patchwork Girl of Oz* (1913), and in the original Nancy Drew mysteries (1930), which placed non-Anglo-Americans in subservient roles only. It was during these early years of the 20th century that demeaning stereotypes became commonplace in all aspects of society: in the toy industry, with Nicodemus dolls; in the minstrel shows, with Rastus and Sambo jokes told by white performers in blackface; in the movies, with Buckwheat of Our Gang fame, and the perpetually frightened black chauffeur in many Charlie Chan movies.

In Johnny Gruelle's *Eddie Elephant* (1921), the featured characters are animals in brightly colored clothing, and the only human in the story is a child by the name of "Cocoa-boy," who at one point is ridiculed by the animals:

> "I wish I had something nice in my pocket to give you for helping us!" said the little Cocoa-boy. Eddie Elephant and the oxen laughed at this, for, you see, the little Cocoa-boy only had his brown skin for clothes.

As it turns out, little Cocoa-boy and the two oxen are the only unclothed characters in this book, the implication being that "animals" in clothes are superior to those without. [See illustration page 48.]

Another example of a book written with little respect for the African-American race is *Epaminondas and his Auntie* (1907) by Sara Cone

Bryant. The whole basis for this story is Epaminondas' stupidity. When his aunt gives him a piece of cake to bring to his Mammy, he scrunches it up too tight and ends up with a fistful of crumbs. His mother explains that he should have wrapped it in leaves and put it on his head under his hat. Next time, when Auntie gives him butter, he wraps it in leaves and puts it on his head under his hat. Of course, it melts.

This premise is repeated, with Epaminondas almost drowning a puppy to keep him cool and dragging a loaf of bread through the dirt at the end of a string. Epaminondas just never learns. When his Mammy goes to visit Auntie after baking six mince pies, she says to him, "You be careful how you step on those pies!" And he "*was* careful . . . He stepped–right–in–the–middle–of– every–one." The story itself can be traced to European storytelling. Isaac Bashevis Singer included a version of it in his collection, *Zlateh the Goat and Other Stories* (1966) (see p. 190). The difference is that the protagonist in Singer's story, "The Mixed-Up Feet and the Silly Bridegroom," is an adult, not a child, and he is no more foolish than anyone else in the village of Chelm, where common sense seems to be a quality only the children possess.

Social awareness and a growing respect for the wide mix of cultures in the United States began to develop during the second half of this century. And in the field of American children's literature, each decade from the 1940s on has reflected a higher level of cultural understanding and acceptance.

Around the World

With the number of immigrants making their homes in America, it was inevitable that the British setting would give way to a broader world view. But even as the authors and illustrators of the Twenties moved away from the English nursery, they, for the most part, still avoided the American home setting. Many children's books were set in foreign lands, but the fact that the population of America itself was largely multicultural was not acknowledged in society.

Padraic Colum, born in Ireland, exhibited the tendency to look to faraway lands for children's book settings. He went back to the earliest storytellers to compile his popular collections of myths and folktales, still in print today. For American children, Colum expanded the world of literature to include the oral tradition of ancient storytelling, but, although he lived in the United States and became a citizen here, he never included in his collections the mythology of Native Americans. *The Children of Odin*, published in 1920, was a collection of Norse folklore, and *The Golden Fleece and the Heroes Who Lived Before Achilles* (1922) told of Greek gods and goddesses.

Charles Finger, on the other hand, was born in the United States but chose to study the folklore of South American tribal cultures and to document their myths. To Americans, South America was far removed from the United States, a distant land with little relationship to American society. Finger's well-crafted and creative text in *Tales from Silver Lands* (1924) was honored with the 1925 Newbery Medal.

In his books for children, Dhan Gopal Mukerji, who chose to settle in America from India, devoted himself to educating Americans about the culture of India. He said, "The West believes in time . . . and, consequently, in cause and effect, then in good and evil. But the East begins by denying the fundamental reality of time . . . This is the essential difference between the East and the West."[15] Mukerji was awarded a Newbery Medal in 1928 for *Gay-Neck: The Story of a Pigeon* (1927), his third book published in the United States.

Arthur Chrisman, an American who chose to study an Eastern culture, wrote a collection of stories called *Shen of the Sea* (1925), a tongue-in-cheek combination of Eastern and Western sensibilities, which employed Western humor in the retelling of Eastern folktales. His variations on Chinese storytelling are apt to be offensive to Chinese Americans, who may consider them demeaning and disrespectful. Chrisman studied Chinese history and became friendly with Chinese immigrant families living in California but lacked the sensitivity to see that he was corrupting the traditional values of an ancient culture by applying Western standards. Since award-winning children's books are used as examples of literary excellence in the classroom, it is important for teachers to be aware of any shortcomings that might depreciate their value.

Seeing Is Believing

Wanda Gág, child of immigrant parents, managed to incorporate into an original folktale all of the qualities now typical of the American picture storybook—text and illustrations on every double spread and equally balanced; a developing story line, with action and suspense; simple language with strong characterizations. Even though the style and background were European, the content was very much a reflection of the attitudes of the Twenties in America.

Millions of Cats (1928) was published when the country was still in a state of euphoria, just before the stock market crash of 1929, and has never been out of print. The black-and-white block print drawings showed Old World people engaged in an Old World, European lifestyle, with the text carefully hand-printed and in perfect balance with the illustrations that appear on every page.

In many folktales, an old man and an old woman, poor and lonely, are common characters, and this book follows that tradition. The old woman asks the old man to find her a cat, and he sets out to find one. He comes upon a hill covered with cats, but he can't choose just one, so he comes home with "Hundreds of cats,/Thousands of cats,/Millions and billions and trillions of cats" who drink all the water in the pond and eat all the grass on the hill. They can't keep all these cats, so the old man leaves the choice to the cats themselves. "Which one of you is the prettiest?" he asks. The battle that follows, with each cat thinking itself prettier than the next, leaves the old man and the old woman without a cat—almost. One small, scrawny cat, who never claimed to be pretty at all, is hiding under a bush. And so the old woman finally has a cat, and the old couple, who offer it loving care, see their cat as beautiful.

Egotism and preoccupation with self became the downfall of all those thousands and millions and trillions of cats. The "fat cat" attitude of the rich and powerful in the United States at the time Gág was writing her book makes one wonder if her theme was coincidental, intuitive, or intentional. The theme could be related to the stock market crash of 1929, which occurred shortly after the publication of Gág's book, when hundreds of people, thousands of people, millions and millions and millions of people discovered that "pride goeth before a fall." The first decades of the 20th century in America had been a time of soaring industrial growth and advancing technology. In the "Roaring Twenties" everyone was having fun. Toys, games, and comic strips were all the rage. By the third decade, America was riding high—too high. Perhaps Wanda Gág, children's book author and illustrator, knew more about America than all the politicians and bankers when she wrote *Millions of Cats*.

The American Way

Rachel Field, born and raised in America, was one of the few authors in the Twenties to recognize and celebrate her American background, in *Hitty: Her First Hundred Years* (1929), the story of a doll whose adventures send her up and down the Eastern Seaboard and even out to sea. It would seem logical that American children's book authors would look to their own land for subject matter, but very few books in the Twenties had an American setting. *Hitty* is one of the finest contributions to children's literature in any decade. The real doll that became the subject of the book was already a hundred years old when Field and illustrator Dorothy Lathrop discovered her. Now, heading toward another century in her life, the doll makes her home at the village library in Stockbridge, Massachusetts, where she is on display by appointment, when she's not visiting other museums and libraries.

Unlike Milne's stuffed animals or Gruelle's Raggedy dolls, where the toy's owner is the parent figure, Hitty never loses her dignity and never indulges in childlike mischief—she leaves that to the children who own her at various times in her life. Just 6½ inches high, made of mountain ash, and wearing a perpetual smile, Hitty could probably continue her memoirs throughout the 20th century and even into the 21st, for dolls last longer than people, but neither Rachel Field nor Dorothy Lathrop is still around to offer her unique viewpoint.

Reality Prevails

Books for children in the Twenties were a decided contrast to the standard fairy tales and family stories of the early 1900s. Will James offered children a very real view of the historical American West in the Newbery-winning *Smoky: A Cow Horse* (1926), and Carl Sandburg presented a view of urban America disguised as a sophisticated metaphorical fairy tale in his *Rootabaga Stories* (1922). In the children's version of his time-honored Abraham Lincoln biography called *Abe Lincoln Grows Up* (1928), Sandburg's style became the blueprint for aspiring biographers who wanted to capture the interest of child readers. Hendrik Van Loon, originally from Holland and winner of the first Newbery Medal in 1922, also sustained the interest of children with *The Story of Mankind* (1921), tying American history into world history and showing just how young the United States was in the overall scheme of things. Van Loon's illustrations and direct style of writing showed respect for his child audience. When he explained that no pyramid has ever been pushed out of shape by the weight of the stones that press on all sides of it and that hieroglyphics have logical meaning, for example, a picture of a bee is either an insect called a bee, the verb "to be" or the letter "b," his enthusiasm colored his text. And in a country where the Bible had always been accepted as a heavenly revelation, he offered children the story of Moses as history rather than as a religious miracle.

The Twenties ended in the Great Depression, following the stock market crash of '29, and the American public, instead of meeting the problem head-on in their books for children, continued to perpetuate the American dream. Poverty, unemployment, and hunger were not mentioned in the children's books of the 1930s.

CHRONOLOGICAL BIBLIOGRAPHY 1920–1929

Lofting, Hugh. *The Story of Doctor Dolittle*. Philadelphia: J.B. Lippincott, 1920; New York: BDD (Dell Yearling), 1988 (rev. ed.). (Fantasy)

Doctor Dolittle of Puddleby-on-Marsh cares more for animals than for people and finally gives up his people practice to become an animal doctor exclusively. When his parrot, Polynesia, teaches him how to speak the language of animals, he becomes world renowned and travels to Africa to save the monkeys from a deadly epidemic. After some perilous adventures, Doctor Dolittle and his group manage to reach the monkey colony, and the Doctor saves the monkeys by vaccinating them. The annoying problem of money again comes up with debts to be paid back at home, but the unexpected arrival of a pushmi-pullyu, a highly unusual animal with a head at each end, saves the day. It agrees to accompany the Doctor home and make public appearances for a fee.

Gruelle, Johnny. *The Original Adventures of Raggedy Andy*. Chicago: P.F. Volland, 1920; New York: Outlet, 1991. (Fantasy/Toys)

This book was written as a companion piece to *Raggedy Ann Stories* (1918), but, although Gruelle includes Raggedy Ann in these new adventures, it is Raggedy Andy who makes all the important decisions. This collection was better crafted than the first, moving smoothly from one story to the next as Andy first is introduced to the reader, then to the nursery toys, and gradually becomes the featured character. Raggedy Ann's diminished role is disappointing.

Colum, Padraic. *The Children of Odin*. New York: Macmillan, 1920, 1984. (Folk/Myth/Norway)

Irish author Colum, who immigrated to the United States in 1914, was a full-time writer by the age of 20, and although he was well-known for his folktales and mythology, he preferred to be known as a storyteller. *Odin* is a collection of Norse folklore, telling tales of Norwegian heroes from the dwellers in Asgard to the death of Sigurd.

Stratemeyer Syndicate. Series books, beginning: The Bobbsey Twins (1904), Tom Swift (1910), Hardy Boys (1927), Nancy Drew (1930). New York: Simon and Schuster. (Realistic Fiction/Series)

The appeal of these series books lies in their adventurous nature and their adherence to the American dream. Edward Stratemeyer created the outline, and various authors, writing under pseudonyms that have become familiar to readers—Laura Lee Hope (Bobbsey Twins), Victor Appleton (Tom Swift), Franklin W. Dixon (Hardy Boys), and Carolyn Keene (Nancy Drew)—filled in the details. The Bobbsey Twins presents two sets of twins in the same family who solve one dilemma after another, although the twins are never at risk; Tom Swift introduces science fiction in a series of fantastic tales; and Nancy Drew and the Hardy Boys are self-appointed young detectives who, in the finest James Bond tradition, are also never at risk.

Gruelle, Johnny. *Eddie Elephant*. Chicago: P.F. Volland, 1921. (Fantasy/Picture Book/Animal)

Eddie Elephant dresses up in his nice new clothes and goes to visit Gran'ma Elephant. He goes through the jungle and helps little Cocoa-boy and two oxen get a cart unstuck from the mud. Then he saves the monkeys from the men who were trying to take them away in a boat. Grandpa Monkey shows him a secret garden of lollipops and gives him a tricycle, which he promptly gives away to someone less fortunate than he. This makes him feel "all tingly with happiness inside!"

Van Loon, Hendrik Willem. *The Story of Mankind*. New York: Liveright, 1921, 1985. NEWBERY MEDAL. (Informational/Historical)

This was not the homogenized textbook approach to history. Van Loon's excitement, his personal concerns, and his analytical but always fresh approach to the events that shaped civilization combined to create an outline of world history that encouraged children to question the universe and not simply accept the status quo. He offered a different view of world events, whether looking at religion as history or bringing the reader into the scene he was describing, thereby creating a new understanding of ancient times and places. The book is 500 pages in length, somewhat daunting for today's children, who prefer instant books, but it's a book that can be read at intervals, according to a child's present interests.

Colum, Padraic. *The Golden Fleece and the Heroes Who Lived Before Achilles*. New York: Macmillan, 1922, 1983. (Folk/Myth/Greece)

This collection of myths was a Newbery runner-up; Colum received two more runner-up awards but never a Newbery during his long career. He told his stories with an Irish lilt and an easy rhythm, which keeps these familiar tales of Greek gods and goddesses ever fresh and new, as appealing to the children of today as they were in the Twenties. Willy Pogan's flowing pen-and-ink drawings capture the essence of the characters—the strength of Heracles, the unsightly Harpies, sad Demeter and her daughter, Persephone, who divided the seasons, the intractable Prometheus, and the terrible Medea.

Lofting, Hugh. *The Voyages of Doctor Dolittle*. Philadelphia: J.B. Lippincott, 1922; New York: BDD (Dell Yearling), 1988 (rev. ed.). NEWBERY MEDAL. (Fantasy)

This sequel to *The Story of Doctor Dolittle* seems a bit labored at the beginning. The spontaneity that made the first book so successful is missing here, perhaps because Lofting tried to write the book from a child's viewpoint (Tommy Stubbins) rather than letting Doctor Dolittle tell the story as he did in the first book. Perhaps the problem here occurred because of several incidents that don't actually move the story along, but instead create loose ends that need tying up before the real adventures can begin. A scene in which stowaways aboard the ship are discovered early in the trip and are put ashore never to appear again seems irrelevant. Far more satisfying are the hermit's trial, the bullfight, the search for Long Arrow, and the discovery of the Great Snail. Some parts of *Voyages* surpass the original, but, overall, Lofting's first Doctor Dolittle book was more cohesive.

Mukerji, Dhan Gopal. *Kari, the Elephant*, illtd. J. E. Allen. New York: Dutton, 1922. (Fantasy/Animal)

Mukerji created an elephant character, opinionated and clever, but, unlike Gruelle's Eddie Elephant, still a wild animal with an animal's instincts. In the process, he tells us a great deal about life in the jungle and Indian culture and beliefs.

Sandburg, Carl. *Rootabaga Stories*, illtd. Maud and Miska Petersham. New York: Harcourt, 1922; San Diego: Harcourt, 1990. illus. Michael Hague (*Rootabaga Stories: Part One*). (Fantasy)

Sandburg's America in the 1920s included trains and prairies, liver and onions, cream puffs, skyscrapers, and cornfields. His own children asked questions; he answered them: Where do trains go? If potatoes have eyes, are they able to see? Are dreams real? Do wishes come true? These collections of stories are poetic language experiments, "filled with words that sputter and splash and roll and pop,"[16] fun to read to those children who will listen. Sandburg was credited with creating "a new field in American fairy-tale conception," set for the first time in the "American middle west."[17]

Sandburg, Carl. *Rootabaga Pigeons*, illtd. Maud and Miska Petersham. New York: Harcourt, 1923; San Diego: Harcourt, 1990, illus. Michael Hague (*Rootabaga Stories: Part Two*). (Fantasy)

More stories about the Village of Liver and Onions, the Potato Face Blind Man, and others.

Hawes, Charles Boardman. *The Dark Frigate*. Boston: Little, Brown, 1923, 1971. NEWBERY MEDAL. (Realistic Fiction/Historical)

Winner of the 1924 Newbery award, this book is a story of pirates and the sea, a shipwreck, and a sailor, Philip Marsham, who unwittingly becomes involved in circumstances that contradict his own values. Hawes' uncompromising writing style and attention to detail move this story along quickly and have kept it interesting for the contemporary young adult reader.

Clark, Margery. *The Poppy Seed Cakes*, illtd. Maud and Miska Petersham. New York: Doubleday, 1924. (Realistic Fiction)

The Andrewshek, Erminka, and Auntie Katushka stories contained in this book have a rhythm and refrain that help establish character, and each story culminates in a satisfactory way. For instance, Andrewshek, like almost all youngsters, has the best of intentions and really means to do as he has said, but there are just too many interesting things to do and sometimes he forgets. Even so, he manages to avoid complete disaster in the long run. Margery Clark was a pseudonym for Mary E. Clark and Margery C. Quigley, both of whom ultimately moved away from trade publishing and concentrated on the more homogenized area of textbooks.

Finger, Charles J. *Tales from Silver Lands*, illtd. Paul Honoré. New York: Doubleday, 1924; New York: Scholastic, 1989. NEWBERY MEDAL. (Folk/Myth)

This collection of folk tales from the South American Indians, recorded by the author in his travels across the continent of South America, was awarded the 1925 Newbery Medal. The language in these stories flows in unbroken rhythm, and the South American myths, often parallel to the myths and tales of other cultures and other Indian tribes, reflect the vista of the southern continent's rain forests, mountains, lakes, rivers, and islands. An interesting study in the culture of a unique people, these stories would lend themselves well to a picture-book format, though, at present, the myths are available only as a short story collection.

Milne, A. A. *When We Were Very Young*, illtd. Ernest H. Shepard. New York: Dutton, 1924, 1992. (Poetry)

Simplicity, rhythm, and careful craftsmanship join to create a musical composition that makes it a pleasure to recite Milne's poetry out loud. Milne, conscientious writer that he was, deliberately set about to create this kind of music. This collection of poems speaks to the child in all of us, and especially to the child that once was A. A. Milne (hence the "we" in the titles of his two poetry collections) and continues to bring pleasure, when read aloud, to the adult reading them and to the child who listens. British author Milne, not a demonstrative person, personified his love for his only son in all of the children's books he wrote.

Mukerji, Dhan Gopal. *Hari, the Jungle Lad*, illtd. Morgan Stinemetz. New York: Dutton, 1924. (Realistic Fiction/India)

Two years after *Kari, the Elephant*, Mukerji wrote another jungle story, this time about a young boy living in the jungle. The author created breathtaking suspense in the scenes where villagers are threatened by the wild animals—tigers and leopards, snakes and crocodiles. Although the speech patterns are somewhat formal as Mukerji tries to express the color of the Indian language in English terminology, his timing, which creates suspense, is impeccable.

Chrisman, Arthur Bowie. *Shen of the Sea*, illtd. Else Hasselriis. New York: Dutton, 1925, 1968. NEWBERY MEDAL. (Folk/Myth)

When Chrisman's book was published, very little was known in this country about Chinese culture. This collection of folktales, in which block printing—a Chinese innovation—is said to have been invented by a recalcitrant child throwing jam-covered blocks against a wall, and in which chopsticks presumably come into use after a king is threatened by a knife, spoon, and fork, does little to enlighten Westerners.

Thompson, Blanche J., ed. *Silver Pennies*. New York: Macmillan, 1925; Cutchogue, N.Y.: Buccaneer, 1991. (Poetry)

When this collection of poetry was published for children, it comprised selections from the works of some of the best poets of that time in both the United States and England: Vachel Lindsay, Sara Teasdale, Walter de la Mare, Robert Frost, Rose Fyleman, and Carl Sandburg, to name a few. The poems in this first children's anthology ever published are those that appeal to children, and appeared at a time when poetry was enjoying a renaissance. The selections begin in Fairyland and move into the real world—a microcosm of the trend toward realism in American children's book collections.

Bianco, Margery Williams. *The Velveteen Rabbit*, illtd. William Nicholson. New York: Doubleday, 1926; San Diego: Harcourt, 1987. (Fantasy/Animal)

This story arouses empathy in all who read it, when a stuffed rabbit, whose presence is quickly forgotten in the excitement of Christmas morn—"For at least two hours the Boy loved him"—discovers that becoming real requires long-term affection from a child. The rabbit eventually receives this affection and is secure in his conviction that he has become real until he meets real rabbits when left outside one day. Then the Boy becomes ill, and the faded, shapeless, and well-loved rabbit, considered contaminated with germs, is consigned to the bonfire. But love creates its own miracles, and the velveteen rabbit's dream of being real finally does come true.

James, Will. *Smoky: A Cow Horse*. New York: Scribner, 1926; New York: Macmillan, 1993. NEWBERY MEDAL. (Realistic Fiction/Animal)

Sometimes natural talent rises beyond the rudiments of a formal education. As with Abraham Lincoln, Will James was self-taught. He was an honest-to-goodness cowboy who wrote and illustrated his popular children's books straight from his own personal experiences. His editor, the great Maxwell Perkins, crafted the text without losing James' voice,[18] and *Smoky* was awarded the Newbery Medal in 1927. The story is Smoky's: We see him as a young colt fighting for his life in the wild and as a one-man cowhorse who loses his kind master and rebels when mistreated by others, eventually becoming a bucking bronco in the rodeo. Here is adventure with a satisfying conclusion, a story that combines humor with a strong sense of character and place—a book reflecting an America that has all but disappeared.

Milne, A. A. *Winnie the Pooh*, illtd. Ernest H. Shepard. New York: Dutton, 1926; New York: Puffin, 1992. (Fantasy/Toys)

Young Christopher Robin, Pooh Bear, and the rest of the toys in the Milne nursery have become the most widely quoted characters in the history of American children's literature, even though the story collections originated in England. Melancholy Eeyore, clever Piglet, and Pooh, who refers to himself as a "Bear of No Brain at All," exhibit characteristics we all encounter in ourselves, such as lack of self-worth, unforeseen misunderstandings between friends, and guilt without real basis.

Mukerji, Dhan Gopal. *Gay-Neck: The Story of a Pigeon*, illtd. Boris Artzybasheff. New York: Dutton, 1927, 1968. NEWBERY MEDAL. (Realistic Fiction/Animal)

Mukerji's first two books, discussed previously, were a passionate effort to educate his adopted country of America in the ways of East Indian culture. In *Gay-Neck*, he transferred that passion into the telling of his relationship with a remarkable carrier pigeon who survived by her wits from infancy through her experiences in World War I. This Newbery Medal-winning book still deserves the accolade.

Milne, A. A. *Now We Are Six*, illtd. Ernest H. Shepard. New York: Dutton, 1927; New York: Puffin, 1992. (Poetry)

This book contains more verses than *When We Were Very Young* but of less consistent quality. A few quotable standouts make the collection worthy:

> Christopher Robin
> Had wheezles
> And sneezles,
> They bundled him
> Into
> His bed.
> They gave him what goes
> With a cold in the nose,

And some more for a cold
In the head.

Nicholson, William. *Clever Bill*. New York: Doubleday, 1927. (Fantasy/Picture Book/Toys)

A red-coated toy soldier is left behind when his young owner goes off on a train trip, and this story follows his race to catch up to her. Nicholson was an English illustrator, and like E. H. Shepard and Helen Bannerman, experimented with the newly developing picture-book format. American librarians had trouble accepting this type of book because it was so different from anything published before for children. "Quality is there if quantity is lacking" was the succinct comment of Marcia Dalphin in a review of Nicholson's book.[19]

Paine, Albert B. *Girl in White Armor, the True Story of Joan of Arc*, adapted from adult biography. New York: Macmillan, 1927. (Informational/Biographical)

In the wake of Hendrik Van Loon's *Story of Mankind*, nonfiction works and biographies for children began to enjoy unusual popularity. This book, adapted for children, is still somewhat overwhelming in its text and has very few illustrations. A more accessible choice for today's children would be *Joan of Arc*, a 1980 picture-book based on 19th-century illustrations and text by Maurice Boutet de Monvel, a French artist. Saint Joan, called by God to save France by leading the people into battle but burned at the stake as a heretic, has always been representative of heroism and dedication to an ideal. She remains of continuing interest to new generations of children as well as providing a role model for girls.

Beskow, Elsa. *Pelle's New Suit*. New York: Harper, 1928; Mount Rainier, Md.: Gryphon House, 1979. (Picture Book/Informational)

Translated from the Swedish, this colorful book presented realism—specifically the steps taken in creating cloth from the wool of a sheep—in a most appealing way, with a young Swedish boy, Pelle, interacting at each stage of the process. The book showed American authors and illustrators that nonfiction didn't have to be tedious, a point also made by Hendrik Van Loon.

Gág, Wanda. *Millions of Cats*. New York: Coward, 1928; New York: Putnam, 1977. (Picture Book/Folk/Myth)

Fortunately, the format of this book has not been tampered with over the years, since the layouts reflect the contemporary design of the American picture book. Gág's book, with its humble theme, has pictures on every double spread and the text is printed as part of the book design. When an old man brings home millions of cats and says he will keep the prettiest, only one stays out of the beauty contest because she doesn't think herself pretty. The rest, through pride and vanity, annihilate each other.

Kelly, Eric P. *The Trumpeter of Krakow*, illtd. Angela Pruszynska. New York: Macmillan, 1928, 1992. NEWBERY MEDAL. (Realistic Fiction/Historical/Poland)

The Newbery award was given in 1929 to this riveting adventure set in medieval Poland. A young boy adapts an ancient ritual to his present dilemma during a period in history when Poland has just overcome partition and is developing into a powerful free state. The story reads as well today as it did when it was first published.

Lofting, Hugh. *Doctor Dolittle in the Moon*. Philadelphia: Lippincott, 1928; New York: BDD (Dell Yearling), 1988, rev. ed. (Fantasy)

This book, at the time it was written, was sheer fantasy. There are prophetic moments—when the travelers discover they can defy gravity and when the landscape of the moon is described as being filled with craters and volcano-like protuberances—but the idea of fruits and vegetables growing on the barren moon now defies the suspension of disbelief, especially since the story revolves around that premise. Altogether, Lofting wrote 11 titles in the Doctor Dolittle series.

Milne, A. A. *The House at Pooh Corner*, illtd. Ernest H. Shepard. New York: Dutton, 1928, 1991. (Fantasy/Toys)

Though less spontaneous than *Winnie the Pooh*, the charm of the characters is not diminished, and the book has its very special moments. Pooh finds a note intended for Piglet, and, though he can't read, recognizes the letter "P" as being part of his name. He thinks the note is for him, and, when he is told differently, says, "Oh, are those 'P's' Piglets? I thought they were Poohs." This is also the Pooh book in which the game of Poohsticks is invented: Participants drop sticks off one side of the bridge and run to the other side to see whose stick comes through first.

Sandburg, Carl. *Abe Lincoln Grows Up*, illtd. James Daugherty. New York: Harcourt, 1928; San Diego: Harcourt, 1985. (Informational/Biographical)

This book is composed of the first 27 chapters of Sandburg's biography of Abraham Lincoln, *Abraham Lincoln: The Prairie Years*. Sandburg's original intent was to write a book for children about Abraham Lincoln, but once he had written the boyhood chapters, he continued the story of Lincoln's life through two volumes. *Abe Lincoln Grows Up* begins by covering Lincoln's genealogy starting with his grandparents, continues with his boyhood, and ends with Lincoln leaving home to seek his fortune. The book has a sense of immediacy as the reader becomes involved in the scenes and the action, and the freshness of the language moves the reader through Abe's story with delight. Sandburg has gone one step beyond the portrayal of Lincoln the person by tying the life of the child Abe to the land itself with its hardships and joys and to the people who touched his life. Homey details add much—a yellow petticoat and a linsey-woolsey shirt for the infant Abe, his bed of dry leaves in the corner of the pole shed when he was eight years old—as do examples of the speech and politics of the day through various stages of Abe's life. James Daugherty's lively illustrations are in keeping with the enthusiastic text.

Field, Rachel. *Hitty: Her First Hundred Years*, illtd. Dorothy P. Lathrop. New York: Macmillan, 1929, 1969. NEWBERY MEDAL. (Fantasy/Historical/Toys)

Hitty, a small wooden doll, travels through a hundred years of American history as she voyages on a whaling ship, enters high society in Philadelphia, becomes an artist's model, and acts as a showcase for an aspiring dress designer. She spends time in a Quaker home and is introduced to poet John Greenleaf Whittier; she sees an end to the Civil War, eventually travels south, and is owned by a child who is very poor and another child who travels with her father and has no place to call home. Ultimately, Hitty returns to her native state of Maine and the very house where she began her adventures, but when the old lady who lived there dies, she is moved once more, this time to an antiques shop in New York City shortly after the turn of the century. (Hitty currently receives visitors by appointment at the village library in Stockbridge, Massachusetts.)

Gág, Wanda. *Funny Thing*. New York: Coward, 1929; New York: Putnam, 1991. (Picture Book/Fantasy)

Bobo is an old man who lives in the mountains, and one day along comes a Funny Thing, a creature who insists he is an "aminal" who likes to eat dolls. "And very good they are—dolls," says he. But wise

Bobo, sensing how vain the Funny Thing is, gives him an appealing alternative to eating dolls, and everyone is happy.

Salten, Felix. *Bambi*, illtd. Kurt Wiese. New York: Simon & Schuster, 1928, 1991. (Realistic Fiction/Animal)

This story, written from an animal viewpoint, was the blueprint for the Disney animated film *Bambi*, which followed Salten's text very closely. The book, written long before environmental concerns became an issue, brings the very heart of the natural world into play and makes the reader understand its beauty and its cruelty, as well as its relationship to the human creature. The rite of passage experienced by Bambi, a young deer, in a setting where the most dangerous predator is man, offers an uncompromising and riveting allegory with a most fitting conclusion.

NOTES

1. Edmund H. Harvey, Jr., ed. *Our Glorious Century*, p. 15.
2. Carolyn Horne, et al., eds. *Barron's Student's Concise Encyclopedia*. New York: Barron's, 1988, p. H42.
3. John J. McDermott, ed. *The Philosophy of Dewey: The Lived Experience*, vol. 2, p. 723.
4. R. C. Orem, ed. *Montessori: Her Method and the Movement, What You Need to Know*, p. 15.
5. Ruth Hill Viguers. "Golden Years and Time of Tumult: 1920–1967," *A Critical History of Children's Literature*, ed. Cornelia Meigs, p. 395.
6. Ann Thwaite. *A. A. Milne: The Man Behind Winnie the Pooh*, pp. 248–249.
7. In this book, Christopher Milne discussed his relationship with his father, who, according to Christopher, didn't show much affection for his only son except through the children's books he wrote.
8. Anne Commire, ed. *Something About the Author: Vol. 35*, p. 109.
9. Ibid., p. 33.
10. Ibid., p. 35.
11. Anne Commire, ed. *Something About the Author: Vol. 15*, p. 182.
12. This refers to the original book, not the reprint published in 1988, in which all references to color were removed.
13. Isabelle Suhl. "The 'Real' Doctor Dolittle," in *Interracial Books for Children*, vol. 2, 1968, p. 6.
14. Anne Commire, ed. *Something About the Author: Vol. 15*, p. 183.
15. Anne Commire, ed. *Something About the Author: Vol. 40*, p. 155.

16. Ruth Hill Viguers. "Golden Years and Time of Tumult: 1920–1967," *A Critical History of Children's Literature*, ed. Cornelia Meigs, p. 452.
17. According to comments made regarding Sandburg's collection in the 1922 issue of *Literary Review*.
18. Referred to by James himself as "Englishing Will James." *Newbery Medal Books: 1922–1955*, Bertha Mahony Miller and Elinor Whitney Field, eds., p. 47.
19. Marcia Dalphin. *New York Herald Tribune*, Sept. 15, 1927, p. 7.

Illustration by author Laura Armer from Waterless Mountain *(McKay, 1931); reprinted by permission of Rollin Armer. For the first time in American children's books, Native American culture and storytelling are presented as specific to a particular tribe, the Navaho in the Southwest, through the viewpoint of a particular child.*

4

THE "POLLYANNA" SYNDROME 1930–1939

Sure I remember the Nineteen Thirties,
the terrible, troubled, triumphant, surging Thirties.
I can't think of any decade in history when
so much happened in so many directions.

—John Steinbeck
Esquire, June 1960

Building Blocks

Like a wooden wagon whose wheels are falling apart, sending slats in all directions, the United States almost lost control in the 1930s. It seemed that the American dream that had been so clearly reachable was nothing more than a myth after all. Not only had the stock market crashed in 1929, but also in 1933 the United States banking system collapsed. Industrial output had been cut in half, unemployment was rampant, and for those still in the work force, hourly wages had dropped drastically. The struggle continued throughout the decade, but by 1939, with the help of Franklin Delano Roosevelt's New Deal and its ambitious government programs, America began to recover.

For most children, however, the Depression didn't exist, even though their parents might be struggling to get by. For the children, it was a magic time of radio and movie heroes, the funny papers, and Jack Armstrong, the All-American Boy, expounding on the benefits of eating Wheaties. Clean living brings rewards, said the media, and for children the American dream remained intact. They joined Little Orphan Annie's Secret Society on radio, read Big Little Books about Flash Gordon, and became Tom Mix Ralston Straight Shooters. Little girls dreamed of owning a Shirley Temple doll with hair that felt and looked real.

Pollyanna, in Eleanor H. Porter's 1913 book of the same name, was a little girl who remained consistently optimistic through all kinds of travail (see p. 44). As Americans struggled through the Depression, the theme of almost all children's books being published was one of hope and belief in the future, carrying on the myth of the American dream. The market was expanding, however, and for the first time children's books were being published that represented cultural diversity within the United States itself. In the Thirties, the American dream had come to mean different things to different people. To the formerly affluent, it meant regaining their money and status. To those continuing in poverty, it meant ultimately acquiring status and money. To the so-called "minorities," which included newly arrived immigrants, American blacks, and Native Americans, it meant shared opportunity and respect. In the original Stratemeyer series books, major roles were assigned only to characters of Anglo-Saxon descent, with other figures in the books given either subservient roles or undesirable character traits. The books were widely popular with young people, and 70 million Nancy Drew books alone were sold between 1930 and 1980.[1] In the mid-1950s, Harriet

Stratemeyer Adams, who took over the syndicate when her father died, began to delete all racist references from revised editions of the series.[2]

The Thirties also were marked by a focus on education in an effort to guide future generations toward a well-balanced economy. It had suddenly occurred to America that the children who might grow up to become leaders needed a solid educational background, not only in reading, writing, and arithmetic, but also in science and the arts. In the 1930s, "the largest cities had the best school systems and the nation as a whole felt a legitimate pride in its unique creation: the free public high school."[3] At the same time, early education became important, and the kindergarten introduced children to the social factors that would help them in their school adjustment. According to educator and historian W. F. Connell, the 1930s were, in spite of the Depression, "education's golden years."[4]

Regardless of a depressed economy, children's books continued to be a fast-growing industry, as the development of photo-offset technology allowed for increased publication of children's picture books. For the first time, books were being written for the youngest child, the preschooler who hadn't learned to read yet. The nonreader could enjoy the pictures while listening to the stories. By 1938 the Caldecott Award had been established by children's book advocate Frederic Melcher to honor the most distinguished picture-book illustrator of the year, and the first to receive the medal was Dorothy P. Lathrop for *Animals of the Bible* (1937). Lathrop, illustrator of the Newbery-winning *Hitty: Her First Hundred Years*, was one of the first artists in the 1930s to write her own text (*The Fairy Circus*, 1932) rather than only illustrate the text of others.

The Caldecott Medal was named for Randolph Caldecott, a master illustrator of nursery rhymes for children in 19th-century England. Maurice Sendak calls him "illustrator, songwriter, choreographer, stage manager, decorator, theater person," and considers him the originator of the modern picture book and an artist of "unexpected depth."[5]

And the Wheel Keeps Turning

When Melcher initiated the Caldecott and Newbery medals, he did so mainly to publicize children's literature and to sustain interest in children's books throughout the year. But he also wanted to stimulate a competitive edge within the industry and in so doing create a higher standard for children's literature.[6]

By the 1930s, after a decade of Newbery books, the Newbery Medal had become an accepted method of determining excellence in the field of children's literature, as librarians representing different sections of the United States formed a committee each year to choose one book as the most distinguished in a given year. The system did raise questions, however. Should the award be given in years when there was a lack of outstanding books? Should an author be awarded a Newbery for an inferior book because an earlier book by that author had earned critical acclaim?

Over time, the lasting merit of some of the winning books has been questioned. But the main purpose of the award, in addition to recognizing good literature, always has been the publicizing of children's literature, and the only criterion for selection was and still is the critical judgment of each year's committee.

Almost all of the Newbery and Caldecott winners have remained in print on the strength of their award status, while, unfortunately, many Newbery and Caldecott runners-up [see Appendix B] have gone out of print, to be found only in library collections. Though the committee can choose only one book each year as a medal winner, it often designates several others as runners-up or "Honor Books" for that year. Some years there are many; some years there are none.

Although this country was slow to recognize and accept cultural, racial, and religious differences as part of the American scene, some of the award-winning books in the 1930s addressed those differences. One such book was *The Cat Who Went to Heaven* (1930), the 1931 Newbery award-winner by Elizabeth Coatsworth, which presented an understanding of Eastern thought unusual for a Westerner to capture. Coatsworth lived in the Far East for a year. In this book, she combined the life story of Buddha with the story of a poor Japanese artist commissioned by the priests of a Buddhist temple to make a painting of the Lord Buddha's last days. The artist chose to draw animals blessed by the Buddha that depicted Lord Buddha's special qualities—the elephant for dignity, the horse for courage, the buffalo for self-respect, the dog for fidelity, the deer for generosity, the monkey for forgiveness, and the tiger for strength. By including his own small and insignificant cat, the artist jeopardized acceptance of the painting by the priests, who did not consider the cat to be an animal blessed by the Buddha. But Lord Buddha's compassion extended to all, no matter how insignificant, and the priests had to accept this truth when, during the night, the picture underwent a miraculous change. Lynd Ward's original wash paintings for this book added dimension to the story, but in the 1958 edition it was his animal paintings, each meticulously rendered on a Japanese rice-paper background and printed in two colors, that gave dramatic impact to the text.

Elizabeth Foreman Lewis, who had lived in China and had studied Chinese language and culture, wrote the 1933 Newbery book, *Young Fu of the Upper Yangtze* (1932), in which family values and loyalties were expressed through the experiences of a young boy serving as a coppersmith's apprentice in Chungking. The story's background was contemporary with the time of its publication and showed China as an unsettled country with a weak central government and a large percentage of the population living in poverty. The advent of communism has significantly dated this story, which demonstrated a way of life that no longer exists and a time when a poor man had the freedom to make choices and could even buy his own business if he could work hard and find a way to become educated.

The Newbery committee recognized the Native American by awarding a Newbery Medal in 1932 to Laura Adams Armer for *Waterless Mountain* (1931). The book was told from the viewpoint of a young Navaho boy and acknowledged the specific qualities that set the Navaho apart from other Native American tribes. Armer lived among the people she was writing about, first as an artist, then as an author. The book was written in a simple, poetic style that offered a dreamlike but accurate study of life on an Indian reservation and the way in which that life contrasted with the harsh realities of the Navaho's existence in a white man's world.

Recognizing Diversity

Arna Bontemps was an active member of the "Harlem Renaissance," a group of men committed in the 1920s and 1930s to educating whites about African-American culture. Remembering clearly the lack of any black history in his school textbooks, he chose to write for children. Bontemps and his friend, poet Langston Hughes, collaborated on *Popo and Fifina: Children of Haiti* (1932). Hughes had visited Haiti, made friends there, and wanted to show how the poor people of Haiti lived. These people were mostly of African descent as were Hughes and Bontemps. Bontemps' gentle nature softened Hughes's more passionate attitude toward injustices in Haiti, and the story was written without directly contrasting rich and poor. As noted in the book's afterword, "both men understood the usual requirement that children's books avoid controversy, and both men needed money badly."[7] It was, however, very evident that the people of Haiti were barely able to make a living, and though poverty-stricken, made the best of their existence in loving, close-knit family units. The message was subtle but clear. Both Bontemps' *You Can't Pet a Possum* (1934) and *Sad-Faced Boy* (1937) reflected the author's respect for members of his race and were stories based on children in his Alabama neighborhood.

Bontemps was a strong influence on the children in the African-American community who themselves grew up to become influential writers of children's literature in a more enlightened age—Virginia Hamilton, Mildred Taylor, Ashley Bryan, Walter Dean Myers, Rosa Guy—clearing a path "for acceptance of black themes in the wider world of children's literature."[8]

Westward Ho

Although the 1933 Newbery was awarded to Elizabeth Lewis for *Young Fu*, Rachel Field, a former Newbery recipient, was a runner-up for *Calico Bush* (1932), representing the country's emerging interest in books about America's regional development. In America, western settlements were not yet tied to the past, being newly established, and one family might have lived in several different locations, looking for just the right homestead before settling in. The stories of these westward journeys became the subject of many children's books in the 1930s as second- and third-generation Americans looked back on their family's struggles.

Monica Shannon was awarded the 1934 Newbery Medal for *Dobry* (1933), and this story of a Bulgarian peasant boy who wanted to be a sculptor portrayed the European tradition of loyalty to the land, as did Kate Seredy's award-winning *The White Stag* (1937), which took place in Hungary. In many European countries, the land had been passed down from generation to generation through several centuries, tying families closely to their homesteads.

Laura Ingalls Wilder initiated her series with *Little House in the Big Woods* (1932) and was able to capitalize on her fortunate timing by continuing her series throughout the decade. Her Little House books, which followed a family's search for the good life in America as they traveled from one region to another, dominated the Thirties in popularity, and interest in the series continues to this day. Although Wilder was never awarded a Newbery Medal, her books were runners-up in 1938, 1940, 1941, 1942, and 1944, and a successful television series, loosely based on the books, which ran from 1974 to 1980, helped keep the collection in print and assure its popularity over the years. With the help of her daughter, journalist and biographer Rose Wilder Lane, Laura Ingalls Wilder presented a comforting picture of a pioneer family settling in the West. Originally, she recorded the details in a first-person autobiographical "narrative of her life from her childhood in the forests of Wisconsin to the prairies of Kansas and Dakota," but her daughter, acting as editor and ghostwriter, developed the story line into an easy-to-read narrative told in the third person.[9]

Nevertheless, the story was Laura's and covered her childhood as she nostalgically remembered it, cushioning the recollection of hardships with the warmth of close-knit family relationships. Her daughter's efforts in rewriting her mother's memoirs were never acknowledged by Laura Ingalls Wilder, who took full credit for the popularity of the series.[10]

In terms of excitement and suspense, *Caddie Woodlawn* (1935) by Carol Ryrie Brink certainly earned its Newbery Medal. Brink based the book on stories her grandmother had told her about life in pioneer Wisconsin. She was also aware of the importance of preserving American history. "Before I began writing *Caddie Woodlawn,*" she said, "I had not thought very much about the duty we owe our children in regard to the past . . . I talked with a number of old pioneers when I was forming my background for the story, and the more I talked with them the more convinced I became that we are about to lose a most precious contact with something that has vanished."[11] This was Brink's second children's book, and, although she went on to write 23 more books for both children and adults, this is the only one of her books that has retained its popularity.

In 1936, the year *Caddie Woodlawn* was awarded the Newbery, there were three Little House books on the market. But the enthusiasm that made Brink's book stand out was perhaps not so evident in Wilder's book, since Rose Wilder Lane not only resented the time she had to spend on them but also believed that writing for children trivialized her talents.[12]

Expanding the Market

Fortunately, Lane's condescending attitude toward children's books was not shared by all, as the genre was expanding in all directions, with frontier adventure stories, biographies, and stories from other cultures appearing not only in books for those who were able to read well but also in picture books. Almost completely missing from the marketplace, however, was fantasy, even in England. But two English authors in this decade did create such unusual characters and worlds of magic that their books continue to influence, if not dominate, all fantasy written since.

For the child reader who had been raised on fairy tales and wondered why there weren't any new ones, two British authors wrote books that found their way to America and filled the void. Pamela L. Travers's *Mary Poppins* (1934) was a dream come true, and the sophisticated style of *The Hobbit* (1937) by J. R. R. Tolkien created new worlds for the imagination.

Mary Poppins—"never stepping out of character, equal to any emergency; to the outer eye, stern and opinionated, but to the children, secret and magical"[13]—represented the kind of discipline that made children feel secure and gave them the freedom, within secure boundaries, to reach for the stars. Mary Shepard's illustrations in company with Travers's words brought the Mary Poppins portrait to life. P. L. Travers was born in Australia and lived in England. She, like so many recognized children's book authors from the past, claimed she was not writing for children, but her books spoke clearly to the child in all of us and surely were connected to the child in her.

Anyone who reads Tolkien's description of a hobbit—"They are (or were) a little people, about half our height, and smaller than the bearded dwarves . . . they are inclined to be fat in the stomach; [and] wear no shoes, because their feet grow natural leathery soles and thick brown hair"[14] is presented with a vivid portrait of what a hobbit looks like without seeing an artist's interpretation. Eleanor Cameron, author and critic, says, "Words are as fantastical as wishes or charms. If we never learn to understand and to use them with subtlety and precision, we live at only half our mental height and width and breadth."[15]

When *The Hobbit* and *Mary Poppins* were published, children's books were divided into clear-cut categories—fairy tales, folk and myth, realistic fiction, nonfiction or informational books, and a fairly new category, picture books. But many of the children's books published in the 1930s didn't fit easily into these categories. The growing number of picture books alone called for further categorization, and "fairy tales" became too broad a category to explain the work of Tolkien, Travers, and Dr. Seuss.

Expanding Genres

With this need for separate categories and subcategories, publishers began cataloging books according to recommended age groups, with all picture books assigned to the youngest age category regardless of the author's intention. This practice has narrowed children's choices over the years, since children's books are divided by age categories in most libraries and bookstores, and once a limit has been set, it is difficult to expand it. The age category for *Peter Pan* and *The Wonderful Wizard of Oz* has been labeled 9–11, Beatrix Potter's *The Tale of Peter Rabbit* 3–6, and A. A. Milne's *Winnie the Pooh* 5–8.[16]

While American children's books in the 1930s continued to lean toward the realistic and Travers and Tolkien portrayed fantasy in new ways, the picture-book industry began its magical infiltration into the world of the very young. In the early development of picture books directed at preschoolers, illustrations were done more often than not by the author, and the illustrated manuscript was delivered directly to the publisher, who published the book as presented. Artist Wanda Gág was the first to introduce the picture-book prototype[17] to American publishing in 1928 with *Millions of Cats*. The idea of reaching children with both pictures and words before they were able to read was such a new and intriguing idea that many writers for children jumped on the bandwagon, without concern for how well they could draw.

Involving the Child

An example of a picture book published as presented and created by a writer who chose to make her own pictures is Dorothy Kunhardt's *Junket Is Nice* (1933).[18] Mrs. Kunhardt decided to supplement the family income during the Depression years by writing and illustrating a picture book. The book was hand-printed on sheets of cardboard, and the drawings colored with a child's paint set, using a wide array of colors. As soon as it was completed, she took it directly to the offices of Harcourt, Brace and Company. A reading by editor Elizabeth Hamilton led to Mrs. Kunhardt's bringing her manuscript to Mr. Harcourt himself.

Mr. Harcourt liked the book but felt it would cost too much to reproduce all the colors. He asked Mrs. Kunhardt if she would redo the manuscript and bring it back within a couple of days. A hand-printed, hand-drawn manuscript could hardly be redone in a day, but Mrs. Kunhardt was not one to let a golden opportunity slip through her fingers. She took the manuscript home, filled the bathtub with cold water and unceremoniously dumped the entire manuscript into the tub for an overnight soaking. The water swelled the cardboard to at least three times its normal size, and the water colors faded. She hung the wet pages by clothespins until they had dried, and the book was returned to Mr. Harcourt in February 1933. The reds and blacks were accented, the pages photographed, and in October 1933 *Junket Is Nice*, the story of an old man eating Junket pudding and asking his readers to guess what he was thinking, was in print and went on to sell more than a million copies.[19]

As the picture-book genre became more and more popular in the 1930s, the role of the children's book illustrator became increasingly important to the success of the book. Publishers began to insist on a professional approach and gave the artist an equal place of importance with the writer, as evidenced by the establishment of the Caldecott Medal in 1938. Up until this time, children's book illustrators either were not acknowledged or, in the case of the more popular illustrators such as John Tenniel, E. H. Shepard, W. W. Denslow, John Neill, Dorothy Lathrop, and the Petershams, were simply paid outright and often gave up all rights to their works.

The Petershams, Maud and Miska, who in the 1920s had illustrated the work of others, chose to write and illustrate their own texts in the 1930s in a series of integrated and informational picture books describing the various industries that had emerged in America in the early 20th century. Unlike other informational books of the time, the brief text of the books was accompanied, on every facing page, by detailed illustrations in black and white and in color and appealed to children just learning to read. In *The Story Book of Clothes* (1933), each kind of material used in making clothing was described in combination with illustrations showcasing the culture that spawned it: fur in Alaska, bark in the Far West, tapa cloth in the Pacific islands, grass and silk in the Far East, wool and flax in Europe, and cotton in the United States. This format was also used in *The Story Book of Houses* (1933) and was continued in 1935 in a series of books on coal, iron and steel, oil, trains, and gold. *The Story Book of Sugar* (1936) gave a history of sugar use and manufacture. These books did not survive the 1940s, during which World War II created shortages that necessitated rationing and substitutes for many of the materials so carefully explained in the Petersham books.

A Hint of the Future

The popularity of Wanda Gág's *Snippy and Snappy* (1931) and *ABC Bunny* (1933) and of Marjorie Flack's *Angus and the Ducks* (1931), *Angus and the Cat* (1932), and *The Story About Ping* (1933) did much to bring recognition of the picture-storybook format to an emerging market.[20] Louis Lenski's *The Little Auto* (1934) and *The Little Airplane* (1938), Hardie Gramatky's *Little Toot* (1939), and Virginia Lee Burton's classic *Mike Mulligan and His Steam Shovel* (1939) explored growing American technology. Dr. Seuss (Theodor Geisel) put a crack in the shining armor of American idealism with *And to Think That I Saw It on Mulberry Street* (1937) and *The 500 Hats of Bartholomew Cubbins* (1938) by combining tongue-in-cheek humor with a whimsical text to begin a career unmatched in the history of children's literature. *Mulberry Street* was one of the first children's picture books to portray a parent who was less than the ideal, and *500 Hats* presented Bartholomew Cubbins as "the small and modest individual" who triumphs and (in the best Horatio Alger fashion) even surpasses his larger, more powerful, and pompous adversary "by dint of simply carrying on as best he can."[21]

Mulberry Street was turned down by 27 publishers before it was accepted by Vanguard, and then only because the children's editor there was an old college friend who was willing to take a chance on something totally without precedent in American picture books. It was, after all, a fantasy (not always popular in America), in verse (no longer popular in America), and didn't "teach" anything. But the book not only sold well, it also was accepted by the library block and became the first in Seuss's long line of innovative and highly imaginative textual and artistic experiments in the picture-book genre. Humor and novelty were qualities appreciated by the American publishing community.

James Daugherty started out by illustrating the books of others and finally wrote his own picture storybook, *Andy and the Lion* (1938), in which his vigorous style of illustrating fit surprisingly well within the structured framework of the picture book. Andy was a typical American boy, full of curiosity and willing to act when the need arose, regardless of apparent danger. He became a blend of the comic-book hero so popular in the 1930s and the Greek slave featured in Aesop's "Androcles and the Lion."

Daugherty made biographies of famous Americans part of the picture-book scene with *Daniel Boone* (1939). His illustrations seemed larger than life, with action in every scene. Unfortunately, with Daniel Boone as the hero, there had to be villains in Daugherty's biography, and the villains were Native Americans whose violent actions in the book seemed part of their inherent makeup. Daugherty had illustrated Stewart Edward White's *Daniel Boone: Wilderness Scout* (1920) a decade earlier, and White devoted an entire chapter to closely analyzing the characteristics of the Native American, who was seen by the majority of settlers as "fiend incarnate" and by others as "noble redman."[22]

> The major traits [of the Indian] were cruelty, love of liquor, a capacity for hatred and revenge . . . and improvidence. Their minor faults were an inability to do long-continued team work, a touchy pride, ungovernable rages.
>
> A deep ingrained racial cruelty is one of the Indian characteristics; and was a powerful factor, when the scales of Eternal Justice were poised, in bringing about his elimination from the land.[23]

Although Daugherty's text was less judgmental than White's, it nonetheless measured the Native American culture against white standards, unlike Laura Armer's *Waterless Mountain*, which was more difficult to read but far more empathetic to the inner voice of Native Americans. *Daniel Boone* is one of the few Newbery Medal books no longer listed as being in print, but *Andy and the Lion* continues to be popular.

Another picture-book biography, and the winner of the Caldecott Medal in 1940, was *Abraham Lincoln* (1939), by Ingri and Edgar Parin D'Aulaire. The D'Aulaires were from Norway and came to the United States as adults, but Edgar's mother was American, and he grew up listening to stories of American heroes. For Ingri and Edgar, America was a magical place, just as snowbound Norway might be to American children, and they incorporated this sense of wonder into their biographies of George Washington (1936) and Abraham Lincoln (1939).

Completely new in the presentation of biographies was Robert Lawson's *Ben and Me* (1939), humorously portraying a mouse called Amos, whose inventive ideas were picked up by Benjamin Franklin. It was also in this decade that *Invincible Louisa* (1933), by Cornelia Meigs, was written. The book, a biography of Louisa May Alcott, reflected the indomitable spirit of the author of *Little Women* and was awarded a Newbery Medal in 1934.

From exotic lands to the streets of New York, from Buddha to the Bible, from the pioneers who struggled to tame a wild country to the individuals who contributed toward its shaping, the children's books of the 1930s told a story of a vast land and a people who would never give up. America was accumulating its own folk material and showing the diversity of a country that boasted a multitude of nationalities and a broad social scale.

CHRONOLOGICAL BIBLIOGRAPHY 1930–1939

Coatsworth, Elizabeth. *The Cat Who Went to Heaven*, illtd. Lynd Ward. New York: Macmillan, 1930, 1990. NEWBERY MEDAL. (Folk/Myth/Buddhism)

This is a simple treatment of the life and death of Buddha in which the worth of all living creatures and the common connection among them are portrayed by an artist and his cat.

Keene, Carolyn (pseud. of Stratemeyer Synd.). *The Secret of the Old Clock*. New York: Grosset & Dunlap, 1930; Bedford, Mass.: Applewood, 1991 (rev.). (Realistic Fiction/Series/Mystery)

The first Nancy Drew mystery appealed greatly to children, especially because Nancy was never afraid to become involved in a case and to carry it through to its end. With her best friend, Helen, and her blue roadster, this liberated young woman began her role as detective. Her attorney father was always willing to help her out, and she always solved the case—Horatio Alger's American dream personified.

Piper, Watty (pseud. of Mabel Caroline Bragg). *The Little Engine That Could*. New York: Platt and Munk, 1930; New York: Putnam, 1990. (Fantasy/Picture Book)

Ms. Bragg was a teacher and author from Milford, Massachusetts, who worked for Platt and Munk Publishers. She wrote this story under the house name of Watty Piper. But because the text was just one of many she wrote for the company, and in spite of the fact that the story has become a staple of children's literature, she never received personal credit or monetary compensation outside of her regular salary. This is a story about an animated train engine trying to make it up a mountain, using a repetitive phrase: "I think I can, I think I can." Perseverance wins the day, and the little engine finally reaches the top of the mountain.

Flack, Marjorie. *Angus and the Ducks*. New York: Doubleday, 1930. (Picture Book/Animals)

According to Barbara Bader, "Marjorie Flack drew, but not very well; she wrote, but she wasn't a writer; what she had was a feel for stories—situations, for the most part—that would tell well in words and pictures and a knack for dramatizing them: a true picture-book sense."[24] This deceptively simple story clearly indicates Flack's ability to create suspense through language, format, and design as Angus, a small dog who was exceptionally curious and whose "head was very large and so were his feet," sneaks out of the house one day and has an unexpected encounter with two ducks after which, "for exactly THREE minutes/by the clock, Angus was/NOT curious about anything at all."

Armer, Laura. *Waterless Mountain*, illtd. Sidney Armer and Laura Armer. New York: McKay, 1931; New York: Knopf, 1993. NEWBERY MEDAL. (Realistic Fiction/Native American/Navajo)

For the first time in American children's books, Native American culture and storytelling were presented as specific to a particular tribe, the Navaho in the Southwest, through the viewpoint of a particular Navaho child (see illustration page 72). Books about the American Indian written for children prior to this tended to present all Native Americans as part of a single culture. Drawing on Navaho legends and personal experience, Armer wrote a story of Younger Brother's journey into young adulthood. His vision of the earth is experienced by the reader, who is made aware of the boy's attachment to the natural world and of the corrupting influence of the white man in the Navaho's domain. This contrast of the old with the new offers the reader a direct connection with an ancient culture and with the lack of respect shown by the white man toward that culture.

Field, Rachel. *Calico Bush*. New York: Macmillan, 1931, 1990. (Realistic Fiction/Historical)

Twelve-year-old Marguerite Ledoux is as different from the Puritan family with whom she is placed as her name would imply. As Bound-Out Girl to the Sargents and their five small blond children, her dark hair and French accent keep her separate from them, and she is unbearably lonely. Her *Grandmere* and *Oncle Pierre* have recently died, leaving her no choice but to travel with a family that has chosen to settle on the coast of Maine. For the next six years she is to be bound to this family. Her first year in Maine, divided into four seasons in the book, offers a clear portrait of the hardships of pioneer living in the 1600s and portrays Marguerite's strength of character in the face of danger and tragedy. Field made no compromises and didn't avoid the conflicts young Maggie had to face and resolve as her French-Catholic upbringing clashed with Puritan beliefs.

Gág, Wanda. *Snippy and Snappy*. New York: Coward, 1931. (Picture Book/Animal)

Again, Gág combines text and pictures to create the story of a quest, this time for sheer adventure, as two small mice venture into the unknown world while unrolling a ball of yarn: "They rolled it up; they rolled it down,/They rolled it up and up and down./They rolled it up and DOWN and down,/They rolled it UP AND DOWN." Over hills and through valleys they journey until finally they reach a house and find the cheese they are seeking. But the cheese is locked in a mousetrap, and the two little mice find they aren't as independent as they think. Although not written in rhyme, Gág's word choices in both this book and in *Millions of Cats* established a rhythmic, musical refrain with no missing beats, creating a primer for would-be picture-book authors.

Bontemps, Arna, and Hughes, Langston. *Popo and Fifina: Children of Haiti*, illtd. E. Simms Campbell. New York: Macmillan, 1932; New York: Oxford University Press, 1993. (Realistic Fiction/Haiti)

Not all blacks in America have come directly from Africa, as these two poets show in a story about two children who live in Haiti. This story is presented through the eyes of Popo and Fifina, two small children who move from one end of their island to the other when their father decides to become a fisherman. The day-to-day existence of a poor family is described, with only a single reference to the then-current U.S. Marine presence in Haiti and another to the contrast between native religion and Catholicism. The book instead focuses on the lack of opportunity for a child in Haiti to get an education, to learn how to read and write, to rise out of poverty.

Flack, Marjorie. *Angus and the Cat*. New York: Doubleday, 1931, 1989. Also, *Angus Lost*. New York: Doubleday, 1932, 1989. (Picture Book/Animal)

The little dog Angus knows the cat is hiding somewhere, but he can't find it; the child reading the book knows exactly where "that cat" is at all times. In *Angus Lost*, Angus once more ventures into the unknown, and only by following the milk wagon as the milkman makes his rounds does he find his way back home.

Lewis, Elizabeth. *Young Fu of the Upper Yangtze*, illtd. Kurt Wiese. New York: Holt, Rinehart and Winston, 1932; New York: BDD (Dell), 1990. NEWBERY MEDAL. (Realistic Fiction/Historical/China)

In Young Fu's rites of passage, Lewis shows the universality of youth, no matter which culture is being presented, in this engrossing study of pre-Communist China. Young Fu is an apprentice to a coppersmith, and his future looks bright. But, in a moment of folly after Young Fu's mother entrusts him with a portion of their savings, he not only lets his mother down but also keeps his actions from her until he is forced to admit his wrongdoings.

Wilder, Laura Ingalls. *Little House in the Big Woods*. New York: Harper, 1932, 1993. (Realistic Fiction/Historical/Regional)

Young Laura is the focus of this family story, which offers homey details about life in the Wisconsin woods in the 1800s and which carries the family through the seasons. The plainness and resourcefulness of the Wilders was comforting for children in the 1930s, as the United States struggled through the Depression. Wilder offered an idealized portrait of pioneer life.

Gág, Wanda. *ABC Bunny*. New York: Coward, 1933, 1978. (Picture Book/Concept[25])

While most of the early picture books were published in a format wider than they were long and fit nicely in a child's hands, this book was bigger all around. Also, alphabet books had always been made up of lists, but in *ABC Bunny* Gág created a storyline from the alphabet—"A for Apple, big and red/B for Bunny snug a-bed/C for Crash! D for Dash!/E for Elsewhere in a flash"—as bunny is awakened by a falling apple and hurries from the scene, meeting various other alphabet animals as he looks for a way back home. Although Gág used a rhyming scheme, the book has more to do with concept than with poetry.

Kunhardt, Dorothy. *Junket Is Nice*. New York: Harcourt, 1933; Lenox, Mass.: Bookstore Press, 1979 (as *Pudding Is Nice*). (Picture Book/Concept)

"Once there was an old old man with a red beard and red slippers" begins this picture book that almost immediately involves the child reader in a quest to discover what the old man is thinking while he is eating his pudding. The premise carries the book and appeals to the very young child who can empathize with the matter-of-fact little boy on his bike who finally comes up with the logical answer.

Meigs, Cornelia. *Invincible Louisa: The Story of the Author of "Little Women."* Boston: Little, Brown, 1933, 1968. NEWBERY MEDAL. (Informational/Biographical)

The interest in biographies that marked the 1920s continued into the 1930s, and Meigs offered the first inside look at the development, from childhood, of a well-known writer whose work was greatly popular with young people. *Little Women* (1868) was based on Louisa May Alcott's own family; although Louisa's father never stayed very long in any one teaching post, always hoping to find acceptance for his unconventional ideas about education, Louisa gave the fictional March family the secure setting she dreamed about, one that became a reality for the Alcotts through the financial success of *Little Women*. The biography offers a deeper understanding of Louisa's strength of character, which is also reflected in her writing, especially in her depiction of Jo March. *Little Women* was published in two parts, the first half ending with Meg's engagement, and the second half (1869) with Amy's wedding and Beth's death. Although Louisa never married, she was the prototype for Jo, who did marry and had sons who were the protagonists in *Little Men* (1871).

Petersham, Maud and Miska. *The Story Book of Clothes*. Chicago: John C. Winston, 1933. Also, *The Story Book of Houses*. Chicago: John C. Winston, 1933. (Picture Books/Informational)

These books introduced children to information that was made more readable by the colorful illustrations and a square format that made it easier to pore over the book. From cave dwellers to skyscrapers, from animal skins to rayon, the Petershams described industrial development in simple text and pictures.

Wilder, Laura Ingalls. *Farmer Boy*. New York: Harper, 1933, 1993. (Realistic Fiction/Historical/Regional)

In the second book of the Little House series, Wilder describes farm life in central New York State as she writes about the childhood of her husband, Almanzo, again with all the homey details that offer comfort and delight for the children reading the book.

Coatsworth, Elizabeth. *Away Goes Sally*. New York: Macmillan, 1934. (Realistic Fiction/Historical/Regional)

While the Newbery committee was highlighting books about other cultures, Coatsworth focused on 19th-century New England with the charming story of a little girl whose uncle builds the first mobile home and moves the family, including Sally, her three aunts, and two uncles, from their farm in settled Massachusetts to the Maine woods. "I will never leave my own fire nor sleep in any but my own bed," initially protests Aunt Nannie. Uncle Joseph later accommodates her by building a little house on wheels in which the family travels to Maine.

Lenski, Lois. *The Little Auto*. New York: H.Z. Walck, 1934; New York: McKay, 1980. (Picture Book/Concept)

Automobiles are a phenomenon of the 20th century, and out of that phenomenon Lenski created a little man and his little auto. Mr. Small, who drives the little auto, looks like a toy wooden doll, and the automobile, red and shiny, is a miniature copy of the real thing. Reproductions of cars and trucks have been popular toys for a long time—perhaps the Mr. Small books introduced the idea to the toy industry.

Shannon, Monica. *Dobry*, illtd. Atanas Katchamakoff. New York: Viking, 1934; New York: Puffin, 1993. NEWBERY MEDAL. (Realistic Fiction/Historical/Bulgaria)

A young peasant boy from Bulgaria longs to become a sculptor rather than till the fields of his ancestors as his mother wishes. Dobry's character is well-rounded, making him likable and interesting, and his grandfather's forays into old folktales throughout the book create a sense of ageless connection to the past and to the land.

Travers, P. L. *Mary Poppins*, illtd. Mary Shepard. New York: Harcourt, 1934; New York: BDD (Dell), 1991. (Fantasy)

Each chapter is a new adventure for the Banks children, Jane and Michael, once Mary Poppins, nursemaid extraordinaire, makes her appearance. In the first chapter, their new nursemaid slides up the banisters and into their lives, giving them medicine that tastes very much like strawberry ice and lime-juice cordial. In another chapter, the magical merriment that surrounds the Banks children's airborne adventure begins when laughter carries them to the ceiling in Uncle Wigg's house. "Spit-spot, to bed you go," says Mary Poppins at the beginning of yet another chapter, but later she wakes up the two children and takes them on a nighttime trip to the zoo, where they are able to talk to the animals who wander around freely while the zoo keepers are confined in cages. More adventures follow with Mary Poppins disappearing at the end of the book as suddenly as she appeared.

Brink, Carol Ryrie. *Caddie Woodlawn*, illtd. Kate Seredy. New York: Macmillan, 1935, 1990. NEWBERY MEDAL. (Realistic Fiction/Historical/Regional)

Caddie is a tomboy and apt to make a few wrong decisions at times, but her bravery keeps her community safe and her family's friendship with the local Indian tribe intact. One act of bravery involves Caddie traveling through the woods to warn her father's friend, Indian John, that a group of white men are planning to kill him and his people and that to survive they must leave their land. Brink also stresses the need for conservation in a land that seems to be filled with neverending bounty, especially when she writes about Caddie's concern over the thoughtless killing of passenger pigeons: "This was not hunting—it was a kind of wholesale slaughter . . . Something of sadness filled her young heart, as if she knew that they were a doomed race. The pigeons, like the Indians, were fighting a losing battle with the white man."

Gág, Wanda. *Gone Is Gone*. New York: Coward, 1935. (Folk/Myth/Picture Book)

In this story based on Grimm, the troubles of a man who tries to take over the housework and care of his children reflect the type of humor that made General Jinjur's capture of Oz so delightful in *Ozma of Oz*. Deliberate humor in a picture book became acceptable, though not always successful, in the 1930s, but Gág made it work by presenting the unexpected at the child's level of experience. Children of the Thirties took it for granted that mothers were homemakers and fathers were not.

Travers, P. L. *Mary Poppins Comes Back*, illtd. Mary Shepard. New York: Harcourt, 1935; New York: BDD (Dell), 1991. (Fantasy)

When, at the end of the first book of the series, Mary Poppins left the Banks family as abruptly as she arrived, the children were devastated. But in this book, she comes back on the end of Michael's kite and brings with her a whole new set of adventures.

Petersham, Maud and Miska. *The Story Book of Trains* (1935). Also, *The Story Book of Coal* (1935), *The Story Book of Iron and Steel* (1935), *The Story Book of Gold* (1935), *The Story Book of Oil* (1935). New York: Harcourt. (Informational/Picture Books)

All of these books described industries that, in the 1990s, have regained economic status, and updated versions of these out-of-print books would hold their own, even with the morass of informational books available now. The books are historically valuable, describing their subject matter in concise language that is easy for young people to understand. The design of the books also complements the text.

Leaf, Munro. *The Story of Ferdinand*, illtd. Robert Lawson. New York: Viking, 1936; New York: Puffin, 1991. (Picture Book/Animal)

Ferdinand is a bull who is expected to fight the Picadores in the arena, but his is a gentle nature, and he prefers to sit under a tree and smell the flowers. At the time the book was written, a civil war was being fought in Spain, and some critics considered the book "subversive" and "fascist," labels that much annoyed the author, who said the story was "innocent fun."[26] Lawson's expressive pen-and-ink drawings are a perfect complement to the text.

Petersham, Maud and Miska. *The Story Book of Sugar*. New York: Harcourt, 1936. (Informational/Picture Book)

This was the last book in the series. It tells the story of sugar from prehistoric days, when the only sweetener was honey, to Alexander the Great's importing sugar cane from India, to sugar's travels as a trade item, and to its finally reaching America. The processes of making sugar from sugar cane, from beets, and from maple sap are described. The Petershams called sugar a health food and a staple that was plentiful and cheap. But World War II was just ahead, at which time sugar became extremely rare. This was one of the factors leading to present-day sugar substitutes.

Sawyer, Ruth. *Roller Skates*, illtd. Valenti Angelo. New York: Viking, 1936; New York: Puffin, 1986. NEWBERY MEDAL. (Realistic Fiction/Historical/Regional/Urban)

At a time when pioneer life was being portrayed by many children's book authors, Sawyer wrote a story of city life on the streets of New York. In it, she created an enthusiastic child who enjoys her relationships with the people she meets as she roller-skates around the ethnically diverse neighborhoods of a safe New York City in the late 19th century and as she stays with other people when her parents travel abroad. Lucinda meets the Irish, the Italians, and the Turks. Though from a wealthy family, she is introduced to abject poverty in the persons of a young couple, and has to deal with death when their infant daughter dies from pneumonia. Many authors of the time would have allowed the infant to survive, but Sawyer followed through with integrity.

Bontemps, Arna. *Sad-Faced Boy*, illtd. Virginia Burton. Boston: Houghton Mifflin, 1937. (Realistic Fiction/Black American)

Bontemps was one of the very few published African-American children's writers, at a time in history when the contributions of people of color to the development of America had been virtually ignored. His *Sad-Faced Boy* "told of three Alabama Negro boys who beat their way to New York City and had some amusing and surprising adventures there."[27]

Fish, Helen Dean, ed. *Animals of the Bible*, illtd. Dorothy P. Lathrop. Philadelphia: Lippincott, 1937; New York: Harper. CALDECOTT MEDAL. (Picture Book/Animal)

Until this decade, books dealing with religion were either didactic and unappealing to children—with the exception of John Bunyan's *Pilgrim's Progress* (1678) and Charles Kingsley's *Water Babies* (1863)—or were renditions of the King James version of the Bible by writers and theologians. Lathrop presented the Bible from a viewpoint guaranteed to interest children by including the flora and fauna of biblical times, carefully researched and enriched by her love of animals. The illustrations by Lathrop were based on specific verses from the Bible selected by Helen Dean Fish.

Flack, Marjorie. *The Restless Robin*. New York: Doubleday, 1937. (Picture Book/Informational)

Not only did Flack write a science book for very young children in a picture-book format, she also created a storyline that built to a climax and was resolved as a robin flies from Georgia to New Hampshire in the spring to find a mate and raise a family throughout the summer. One of the baby robins is restless and falls out of the nest before he is ready to fly, requiring the assistance of two young children to save him. This was a book intended to teach, but it was presented in a way that made learning fun. Flack definitely had an eye for what would appeal to children.

Seuss, Dr. (pseud. of Theodor Seuss Geisel). *And to Think That I Saw It on Mulberry Street*. New York: Vanguard, 1937; New York: Random House (Books for Young Readers), 1989. (Fantasy/Picture Book)

Well-adjusted children in well-adjusted families were the rule in almost all children's books, and although Seuss's early books were considered a new kind of nonsense because of the lilting rhythm of the verses and the cartoonish drawings, they were actually lasting examples of families struggling to connect. In *Mulberry Street*, Marco is trying very hard to live up to his father's unrealistic expectations by finding something interesting to talk about each day when he comes home from school. His father wants vicarious excitement but he also wants truth. Poor Marco has made up a delicious adventure, but he is so afraid his father won't believe his story that when his father asks him: "Was there nothing to look at . . . no people to greet?" Marco answers, "Nothing . . . /But a plain horse and wagon on Mulberry Street." On that note, all the wonderful pictures that his imagination had conjured are replaced by the same dull scene that began the book.

Atwater, Richard and Florence. *Mr. Popper's Penguins*. Boston: Little, Brown, 1938; New York: Dell, 1986. (Chapter Book/Humor)

Mr. Popper paints houses, but his main interest in life is penguins. Shortly after writing to Captain Cook at the South Pole, Popper receives a penguin of his own. Owning a penguin can be disastrous, however, and Mr. Popper finds himself in debt and, worse yet, with a penguin who has suddenly become ill. He appeals to an aquarium for help, and they send him a female penguin who is also in failing health. The two penguins revive each other, and the result is a family of penguins. In order to pay for their upkeep, Mr. Popper, his wife and children, and his 12 penguins take to the road to offer penguin performances in movie theaters across the country. At the time this book was written, live stage shows were still part of movie-theater programs, and it was taken for granted that a married woman would be subjugated by her husband. Mrs. Popper suffers without complaint her husband's costly obsession with penguins, taking their two children out of school and traveling across the country, and cheerily sends him off to the Arctic at the end of the book.

Bishop, Clare Huchet. *The Five Chinese Brothers*, illtd. Kurt Wiese. New York: Coward, 1938; New York: Putnam, 1989. (Original Folk/Myth/Picture Book)

This story was the product of Bishop's oral storytelling talents. She came to the United States from France, where she had been a librarian and storyteller. *The Five Chinese Brothers* was one of the stories she developed herself, and she told it at the New York Public Library. It was so well-received that she decided to write it down, and it became her first published children's book. The five brothers all look alike, but each has an individual trait that sets him apart from his brothers. When No. 1 brother, through no fault of his own, is sentenced to death, each of his brothers makes use of his particular talent to save No. 1 brother's life.

Daugherty, James. *Andy and the Lion*. New York: Viking, 1938; New York: Puffin, 1989. (Contemporary Folk/Myth/Picture Book)

Written in a style sure to create suspense and illustrated with scenes that carry the action quickly from one page to the next, the story of Andy's confrontation with a lion, his good deed, and his reward make this one of the best and most innovative picture books of the 1930s. Open-ended sentences carry the reader from one page to the next: "It was a lion! At this moment/Andy thought he'd better be going and/the lion thought so too. They ran and ran around the rock."

Handforth, Thomas. *Mei Lei*. New York: Doubleday, 1938, 1955. CALDECOTT MEDAL. (Picture Book/Fantasy)

Mei Lei told the story of a little girl who lived in pre-communist China, but neither the book's pictures nor story has held up, even though the book was a Caldecott winner and is still in print. Barbara Bader said, "I have always found it harsh and clumsy, with an obvious story line and more thuds in the telling—the whole no more Chinese than Hindustani."[28] The Caldecott acceptance speech and autobiographical paper by Handforth[29] demonstrated that, though he had spent a great deal of time in the Orient, he saw Asian culture through Western eyes. The story, in which Mei Lei takes her three lucky pennies to the fair and bribes her brother with marbles so that she can realize her dreams, clearly portrays Western values and mores rather than presenting an understanding of Chinese culture. The illustrations move the story abruptly from reality to fantasy without a logical transition.

Leaf, Munro. *Wee Gillis*, illtd. Robert Lawson. New York: Viking, 1938, 1967. (Picture Book/Humor/Scotland)

Wee Gillis is a young Scot who journeys through both the Highlands and the Lowlands of Scotland but can't decide which he prefers. During his visit to the Lowlands, he brings home the longhorn cattle every evening and learns to call very loudly through the mists so the cows will hear him and return to him. During his visit to the Highlands, he learns to hold his breath for a very long time so he won't frighten the stags away as he stalks them. The answer to Wee Gillis's dilemma comes when a man makes a set of bagpipes but finds he can't play them because he made them too big. Wee Gillis's uncles try, but they can't play them either. Wee Gillis is then invited to try, and the successful result makes him welcome wherever he goes, up or down. The black and white illustrations by Lawson showing the character and setting of Scotland are a far better celebration of the illustrator's Scottish background than are the illustrations in his award-winning *They Were Strong and Good* (1940).

Lenski, Lois. *The Little Airplane*. New York: H.Z. Walck, 1938; New York: McKay, 1980. (Picture Book/Concept)

In this machine-oriented decade, the newly developed airplane was explained in simple terms through the description of Pilot Small's flight.

Seuss, Dr. (pseud. of Theodor Seuss Geisel). *The 500 Hats of Bartholomew Cubbins*. New York: Vanguard, 1938; New York: Random House, 1989. (Fantasy/Picture Book)

The first Seuss book was written in rhyme. This one was straight text, if "The Kingdom of Didd was ruled by King Derwin" or "'Screebees!' screamed Sir Snipps" can be considered straight text. Bartholomew tries to remove his hat in deference to the king, but no matter how many times he takes his hat off, another one takes its place. With bow and arrow, executioner's ax, and a promised push over the castle turret, members of the king's entourage try to remove Bartholomew's hat, to no avail, until finally the last hat appears. Bartholomew sells the 500th hat to the king and returns home, his fortune made.

Tolkien, J. R. R. *The Hobbit*. Boston: Houghton Mifflin, 1938, 1988. (Fantasy)

This book takes the reader into an imaginary land created by Tolkien and tackles issues of good and evil, the corrupting influence of absolute power, and the inner battle necessary to overcome that influence. In *The Hobbit*, Tolkien established the guidelines for defining a book as "serious" (complex) fantasy, a category that hadn't existed before, as opposed to "light" (simple) fantasy.

Bemelmans, Ludwig. *Madeline*. New York: Simon & Schuster, 1939; New York: Viking, 1993. (Realistic Fiction/Picture Book)

Designed in cartoonish double spreads with minimum text, the book highlights the charm of Madeline, who emerges as an individual in a group of 12 little girls who all look alike. Sketches of familiar Paris landmarks create a travelogue, and the Catholic school setting was a first in children's books. The book is written in rhyme, and the storyline is slight. The reason that Madeline emerges as an individual is simply because she has her appendix out and is left with a satisfying scar that is the envy of her 11 classmates.

Brown, Margaret Wise. *The Noisy Book*, illtd. Leonard Weisgard. New York: William R. Scott, 1939; New York: Harper Trophy, 1993. (Picture Book/Animal/Concept)

This was the beginning of many Brown/Weisgard collaborations and the beginning of Brown's extremely prolific career as a picture-book author. A student of Lucy Mitchell at Mitchell's Bank Street school in New York City, Brown believed in offering the small child a familiar setting and did this better than any other author of her time. In *The Noisy Book*, she encouraged children to participate in the plight of a small dog who had a cinder in his eye and had to have his eyes bandaged temporarily. Children listening to the story had the opportunity to answer questions: "Then the sun began to shine. Could Muffin hear that?" or "It began to snow. But could Muffin hear that?" This concept of allowing the child to take part in the book by answering questions was a continuation of Dorothy Kunhardt's similar device in *Junket Is Nice* (1933) (see p. 88). The bright, colorful Weisgard illustrations balanced the text in an avant-garde style not seen before in children's books.

Burton, Virginia Lee. *Mike Mulligan and His Steam Shovel*. Boston: Houghton Mifflin, 1939, 1993. (Fantasy/Picture Book)

This unpretentious story had more depth than was immediately obvious, as it tackled fast-growing technology in America, gave a small steam shovel and its owner proper values, and created illustrations that took the reader through an entire day from sunup to sundown just by moving the face of the sun in each spread. The settings—city, country, rivers, or ocean—were obviously American, and showed rowboats and sailboats next to ocean liners, mountain-climbing hikers next to a train, and trucks, buses, and automobiles on the road with horse-drawn carriages. The story builds in suspense—will Mike Mulligan's steam shovel, Mary Anne, be able to dig the cellar in time?—and an unexpected problem that develops at the end is solved by a child who is watching the proceedings.

Daugherty, James H. *Daniel Boone*. New York: Viking, 1939. NEWBERY MEDAL. (Picture Book/Biographical)

In comparison with other biographies written in later years about Boone, this text, though it seemed at first to be as lively as the illustrations, actually presents a rather unimaginative story line in an edited-down version of Stewart Edward White's 1920 Boone biography, which had been illustrated by Daugherty. White's evaluation of the Native American as a race incapable of redemption is evident in Daugherty's version.

D'Aulaire, Ingri and Parin. *Abraham Lincoln*. New York: Doubleday, 1939, 1987. CALDECOTT MEDAL. (Picture Book/Biography)

This story of Lincoln's childhood was presented from the viewpoint of the authors, who had recently emigrated from Norway. The pictures for this book and for the D'Aulaires' earlier biography of George Washington (1936) seem bigger than life and somewhat conceptual in style.

Gramatky, Hardie. *Little Toot*. New York: Putnam, 1939, 1992. (Picture Book/Fantasy)

Similar in concept to *Mike Mulligan*, this personified tugboat connected America with the rest of the world through its presence in an active sea lane, perhaps the St. Lawrence River, and, after behaving childishly, redeemed itself by saving a huge ocean liner from being dashed on the rocks during a storm.

Haywood, Carolyn. *"B" Is for Betsy*. New York: Harcourt, 1939; San Diego: Harcourt, 1990. (Realistic Fiction)

This was the first book of a series that children have continued to read because the books reflect an atmosphere that is most important to them when they first learn how to read—the school setting. It doesn't, however, address a child's fears or the misunderstandings that occur when a child first becomes part of a society outside the home. The resolutions presented are too pat, reflecting the effort in the first half of the 20th century to protect children from grown-up concerns. The Betsy books relate more to the way children see themselves than the Dick and Jane textbooks do, but they still avoid the variations that make American culture so diverse.

Lawson, Robert. *Ben and Me*. Boston: Little, Brown, 1939, 1988. (Fantasy/Biographical)

This was Lawson's first effort at writing and illustrating a book of his own, and he presented history in a way that encouraged a child—or an adult—to look further into the life of a famous figure, in this case, Benjamin Franklin. The "me" in the title was a mouse called Amos who took credit for Franklin's creative genius. Not quite a picture book, not quite a novel, but more like the present-day chapter books for early readers, this nonsense fantasy continues to appeal to today's children.

NOTES

1. Jane See White. "Nancy Still Hot on the Trail," *The Minneapolis Star* (Associated Press), March 3, 1980.
2. Karen Plunkett-Powell. *The Nancy Drew Scrapbook: 60 Years of America's Teenage Sleuth*. New York: St. Martin's Press, 1993, p. 83.
3. Jaques Barzun. *Begin Here: The Forgotten Conditions of Teaching and Learning*, p. 5.
4. W. F. Connell. *A History of Education in the Twentieth Century World*, p. 153.
5. Maurice Sendak. *Caldecott and Co.*, p. 24.
6. Bertha Mahony Miller and Elinor Whitney Field. "Frederic G. Melcher—A Twentieth Century John Newbery," *Newbery Medal Books: 1922–1955*, p. 4.

7. Arnold Rampersad, professor at Princeton University, from the Afterword to *Popo and Fifina*. New York: Oxford University Press, 1993, p. 103.
8. Jane M. Bingham. *Writers for Children*, p. 82.
9. William Holtz. *The Ghost in the Little House*, pp. 220–221.
10. Ibid.
11. Quote attributed to Carol Ryrie Brink by Ethel Blake in "Caddie Woodlawn: The Newbery Medal Book," *Journal of the National Education Association of the United States*, November 1936, vol. 25, No. 8., p. 261.
12. Holtz, op. cit., p. 230.
13. Ruth Hill Viguers. "Golden Years and Time of Tumult," *A Critical History of Children's Literature*, ed. Cornelia Meigs, p. 474.
14. J. R. R. Tolkein. *The Hobbit: Or There and Back Again*, rev. ed. New York: Ballantine, 1972, p. 16.
15. From an Eleanor Cameron essay on fantasy called "The Unforgettable Glimpse," in *The Green and Burning Tree*, p. 29.
16. Betsy Hearne. *Choosing Books for Children*, pp. 192–197.
17. A picture book is intended to be read aloud to younger children as well as to be enjoyed by children who can read.
18. Reprinted in 1979 as *Pudding Is Nice* by Bookstore Press, Lenox, Massachusetts, because the manufacturers of Junket rennet custard considered the original title an infringement of their trademark unless "Junket" was clearly identified as a trademark every time it was mentioned in the book.
19. Based on a personal interview with Dorothy Kunhardt at her New York City apartment in 1979.
20. In the picture-book format of the 1930s, the text on each page was short and to the point, with illustrations creating action and character development on each double spread. Most picture books contained somewhere between 48 and 64 pages of text and pictures, with the designer's choice of text and picture placement an important part of creating suspense.
21. Ruth K. MacDonald. *Dr. Seuss*, p. 38.
22. Stewart Edward White. *Daniel Boone: Wilderness Scout*. (copyrighted by the Boy Scouts of America in 1921). New York: Doubleday, 1922, p. 75.
23. Ibid., pp. 82, 83.
24. Barbara Bader. *American Picturebooks from Noah's Ark to the Beast Within*, p. 61.
25. A conceptual picture book is one in which the idea is more important than any of the characters and leads to a patterned presentation that can then be used in subsequent books.
26. Bader, op. cit., p. 146.
27. Ruth Hill Viguers. "Experiences to Share," *A Critical History of Children's Literature*, ed. Cornelia Meigs, p. 590.
28. Bader, op. cit., p. 57.
29. As reproduced in Bertha Mahony Miller and Elinor Whitney Field's *Caldecott Medal Books 1938–1955*.

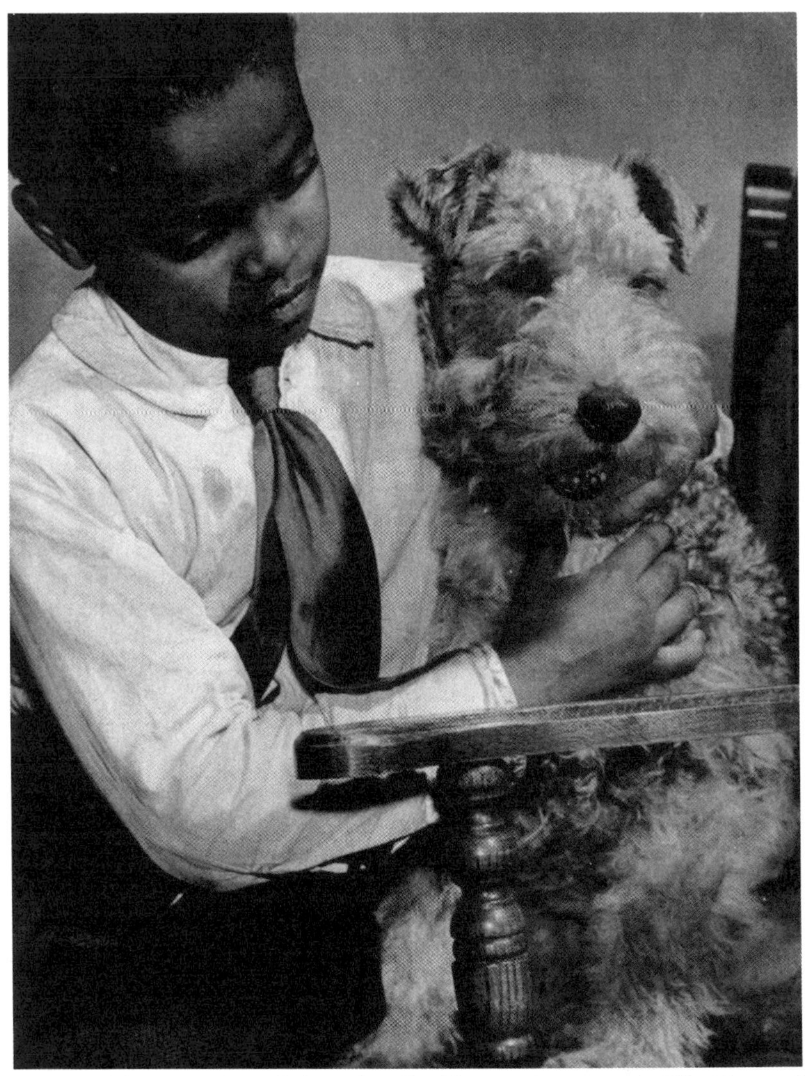

Photograph by Alexandra and Alexander Alland from My Dog Rinty *by Ellen Tarry and Marie Hall Ets (Viking, 1946); reprinted by permission of Ellen Tarry. The use of photographs guaranteed that black Americans would be shown as real people rather than as the caricatures that marked earlier books.*

5

BOMBS, BABIES, AND MARGARET WISE BROWN 1940–1949

The problem, once of not enough books for children, became suddenly the problem of too many, with the combined voice of critics making too small a sound to be heard very widely above the roar of the 1940s.

—Ruth Hill Viguers
A Critical History of Children's Literature

Hooray for the Red, White, and Blue

By the 1940s, the majority of the population in the United States was living in relative comfort in an urban middle-class social setting, even though poverty had not been eliminated and was still evident in many areas. The economic depression and social upheaval of the 1930s had left scars on the face of America.[1]

Into this newly stabilized economic structure came the threat of European war, and the last thing anybody in America wanted was to become involved with outside problems. The country turned inward and joined in a common cause to concern itself with local problems and virtually ignore the rest of the world. The children's books in the second half of the 1930s had already reflected a growing focus on America, with pioneer stories of the building of this country outnumbering stories set among other cultures. As the European threat grew, so, too, did the American resolve to stay out of it. But on December 7, 1941, Japan shocked the world and commanded America's attention by bombing Pearl Harbor on the island of Oahu in the Hawaiian Islands. Not only did the United States have to pay attention now, it also had little choice but to participate in a second world war, this time against Japan and Germany.

Already joined in a common cause to rejuvenate the economy, America turned her full strength as a nation to protecting her freedom, and Japan and Germany never had a chance against the onslaught of American zeal.

Children in the 1940s continued to be immersed in the American dream and filled with patriotic fervor, and the act of identifying silhouettes of enemy planes became as exciting as any picture book. During the war years, when America had to ration gas, meat, butter, and sugar, it would seem that fewer children's books would be published, but that was not the case. In the 1940s children's books were considered important to modern education and were accepted as a branch of current literature.[2] With growing library and school markets, as well as the ability to mass produce inexpensive books, children's books became big business. The market was split between trade books purchased by libraries, schools, and book shops and the books published for the mass market, inexpensive and as much a commodity in supermarkets as the weekly groceries.

The Gold in Golden Books

Although librarians avoided series books and stocked the children's books recommended by the library establishment, the Nancy Drew and Hardy Boys series along with Simon & Schuster's new line of Golden Books were readily accessible to the general public in supermarkets and department stores. *The Poky Little Puppy* (1942) cost 25 cents and was one of the first 12 Little Golden Books produced. It was a book children wanted to hear read aloud again and again, but the daunting text, with its predictable repetition of certain phrases, caused many parents to dread the next request by their children for a bedtime reading. Of the 42 pages in the book, only 14 were illustrated, as opposed to Margaret Wise Brown's *The Noisy Book* (1939), a trade book[3] with 48 pages, 32 of which were illustrated. As of 1953, nearly 300 million Little Golden Books had been sold, with *The Poky Little Puppy* accounting for more than three million copies in a 10-year period.[4]

The mass-market books were cheap, colorful, and filled a need during wartime when fewer toys were being produced. Western Printing, joint owner of Golden Books, was able to manufacture large quantities of the books with its large paper allocation. Since parents during the Forties were being encouraged to read aloud to their children, picking up a few inexpensive Golden Books on a trip to the market became a viable option.

One Simon & Schuster book that took the place of a toy and became the prototype for a whole new line of children's books was Dorothy Kunhardt's *Pat the Bunny* (1940), which eventually was published for the mass market under the Golden Press imprint. It encouraged not only a child's mental participation but his or her physical participation as well. *Pat the Bunny* paved the way for all future tactile books, and the model for Mrs. Kunhardt's cover illustration was a white knitted bunny that belonged to her daughter Nancy. The cardboard mockup of the book was manufactured by Dorothy at home, where she utilized scraps of bunting and cloth, cotton balls, and sandpaper to create her "touch-and-feel" innovation.[5] *Pat the Bunny* was followed by *The Telephone Book* (1942), which encouraged a child to pick up the cardboard telephone receiver and say "hello," and then on subsequent pages to mail a letter, open a bureau drawer, and bathe a baby.

Although librarians considered any mass-market book suspect in terms of literary merit, some of the authors and illustrators who contributed their talents to Golden Books were able to cross the library barrier and gain the respect of children's literature advocates. Lucy Sprague Mitchell, a pioneer in progressive education, was asked to do a group of Bank Street Books, focusing on the real-life experiences of young children, for the Golden Book line, and the contributors she enlisted included Margaret Wise Brown, Leonard Weisgard, Edith and Clement Hurd, and Garth Williams, names that have become hallmarks in the picture-book field.

Mitchell was the founder of the Bureau of Educational Experiments, a center for childhood development research located at 69 Bank Street in New York City and now known as Bank Street College. In the 1920s, Mitchell was known for her *Here and Now Storybook*, in which everyday things, commonplace to adults but brand new to very young children, became the material of her stories rather than the fairies, elves, and magical beings of the European fairy tales. This attitude toward children's books was in direct contrast to New York librarian Anne Carroll Moore's vision of childhood as a "fixed state of innocence to be shielded from, rather than shaped by, historical change and environmental factors,"[6] and Moore was exceptionally critical of the impact of progressive education on children's literature.

Running the Gauntlet

Margaret Wise Brown, as a student of Lucy Mitchell at the Bank Street school, found the perfect outlet for her unique talents. She was able to respond with childlike wonder to the circumstances of everyday life and to describe this wonder in the simplest, most effective way. But because she was an apprentice of library mogul Anne Carroll Moore's nemesis, because she was prolific, and because she was an author of the mass-market Little Golden Books, she had three strikes against her in the library-oriented children's literature field. It is a sign of her exceptional ability that she was able to overcome this and gain positive recognition among the well-known and powerful librarians and critics of the Forties: Bertha Mahony Miller, Louise Seaman Bechtel, and even Anne Carroll Moore.

The Noisy Book was followed by *The Country Noisy Book* (1940), *The Seashore Noisy Book* (1941), and *The Indoor Noisy Book* (1942), all illustrated by Leonard Weisgard, and then by *The Winter Noisy Book* (1947), illustrated by Charles Shaw. *The Runaway Bunny* (1942), illustrated by Clement Hurd, was published the same year as her third Noisy book, and *A Child's Good Night Book* (1943), illustrated by Remy Charlip, followed. These two books, as well as the Noisy series, have also continued in popularity, but *Goodnight Moon* (1947), illustrated by Clement Hurd, has become one of the top sellers of all time, even though when it was first published the *Horn Book* ignored it and the New York Public Library didn't include it on its list of recommended titles.[7]

Brown was affiliated with several publishers as author and as editor, beginning with William R. Scott, Inc., and moving on to E.P. Dutton, Harper, Simon & Schuster, Doubleday, and Random House. She wrote several books with Clement Hurd's wife, Edith Thatcher Hurd, and wrote under the pseudonym of Golden MacDonald at Doubleday, where Leonard Weisgard was awarded a Caldecott Medal in 1947 for the illustrations in her book, *The Little Island* (1946). The island featured in the book was based on a very real coastal island in Maine that Brown had named "Starfish Island." The text and pictures were a celebration of nature's bounty, and also reflected her reaction to the destruction caused by the atomic bomb at the end of World War II.

Brown was always ready to try something new. When she happened to see a collection of animal photographs by zoo and wildlife photographer Ylla (Camilla Koffler) on her editor's desk at Harper, she offered to write the text for the collection.[8] The result was a book called *They All Saw It* (1944), in which the animals in the photos, with their almost human expressions, reacted to the mysterious "it" that they all saw:

> What in the world was it?
> The rooster rolled his yellow eye.
> When the little cat saw it
> he jumped in the air.
> The polar bear was asleep
> so he didn't see it.[9]

The deceptively simple and rhythmic text builds in suspense, with the surprise being revealed on the last page of the book.

The Many Faces of America

Brown also felt strongly about the need to reflect in children's books the personal experience of black children. Until the Forties, history had been idealized as predominantly white. An interview by Brown with Augusta

Baker, children's librarian at the Harlem branch of the New York Public Library, revealed that there were very few black writers for children, noting that Harlem children "read what other city youngsters read: *Peter Rabbit*, *Peter Pan*, *The Wind in the Willows* and Andrew Lang's color fairy-tale collections—the 'classics,' most of them imported from England."[10] The one book that offered American folktales as traditional black literature was Harris's *Uncle Remus* (see p. 15), but the Gulla dialect was so meticulously rendered in the text that children couldn't make sense of it, and Baker acknowledged that the book remained on the shelf. Margaret Wise Brown decided to modify the dialect, while continuing to capture the rhythm, cadence, and timing of the stories, and to eliminate the seven-year-old "little white boy" to whom the old slave storyteller told his tales.[11] The result was *Brer Rabbit* (1941), and Brown considered this book to be her contribution to the cause of racial equality. It is unfortunately out of print at the present time.

The Forties became a decade of social awareness when, for the first time, books were published that actually acknowledged and attempted to deal with problems in society caused by unemployment and discrimination. *Blue Willow* (1940), by Doris Gates, was awarded the 1941 Newbery Medal for its portrayal of the hardships faced by migrant workers, in this case a family that had known better times before the Depression. Gates was one of the first to acknowledge in a children's book that a depression had existed in the United States and that all Americans were not Anglo-Saxon. A character in the book, Janey, had a new friend, Lupe Romero, who was Mexican-American. In *The Hundred Dresses* (1944), Eleanor Estes allowed readers to observe a young girl's near emotional destruction by her peers, simply because she was different. Ellen Tarry and Marie Hall Ets, with *My Dog Rinty* (1946), made an effort to fill the gap created by a notable lack of black history and the heretofore demeaning portrayal of blacks in the children's book field by writing a book, with a setting in Harlem, about a very ordinary little boy who happened to be black. And Florence Crannell Means confronted the unconscionable manner in which Americans of Japanese descent were treated during World War II in *The Moved-Outers* (1945).

One glaring omission from children's books in this decade of enlightenment was any acknowledgment of the Jewish population in America. Anti-Semitism had long been an invasive reality in the United States and throughout the world, especially in Nazi Germany, where Adolf Hitler was responsible for ordering the annihilation of six million Jews during World War II, simply because of what he called their "race."[12]

The subject of Jewish persecution, which goes back many centuries, was never addressed in children's books until the taboos[13] were lifted in the Seventies. Wanda Petronski, the character victimized in *The Hundred Dresses* for being different from her peers, was representative of various ethnic minorities, including those of Jewish descent, though she herself happened to be Polish Catholic.

Branching Out

Even with the taboos that still existed in the children's book industry, the Forties introduced inventive genres in books for older children, with William Pene Du Bois moving between fantasy and science fiction in his award-winning *Twenty-One Balloons* (1947). Robert Heinlein introduced science fiction to young readers with *Rocket Ship Galileo* (1947) and with *Red Planet* (1949), a futuristic novel about the planet of Mars, populated by native Martians and colonists from Earth. When Heinlein wrote *Stranger in a Strange Land* (1961), which went on to attract a cult following among young adults, he utilized and built upon some of the elements of Martian life he had introduced in *Red Planet*. Heinlein was a prolific writer and, at a time when science fiction was being published mostly in short-story form, he wrote several science-fiction novels for children.

Also in the Forties, humor became an important element in children's books, beginning with the poignant humor of *Horton Hatches the Egg* (1940) by Dr. Seuss, in which Horton the elephant agrees to act as the foster parent of an egg belonging to Mayzie, the lazy bird. Through all kinds of travail, Horton continues to nurture the egg—"I meant what I said/And I said what I meant/An elephant's faithful/One hundred per cent." The result is an elephant bird whose loyalties remain not with the bird Mayzie, who abandoned him, but with Horton the elephant, who loves him.

Seuss in the Thirties created books with a subdued moral tone, with Seuss the entertainer taking precedence over Seuss the moralist. In the Forties, the moral of the story became more evident, but humor, suspense, and action in both text and illustrations cushioned any direct righteous impact. Even though Theodor Seuss Geisel insisted that he wrote children's books to entertain himself, his strong feelings about the way things ought to be found their way into his text. At the end of *Horton*, when the egg hatches into an elephant-bird and creates a happy ending, the text reads, "And it should be, it *should* be, it SHOULD be like that!"

His early books before World War II dealt with personal relationships—between Marco and his father in *And to Think That I Saw It on Mulberry Street* (1937), between Bartholomew and the king in *500 Hats* (1938), and between Horton and his personal convictions in *Horton Hatches the Egg*. But after a hiatus from children's books while he served his country during the war, he came back to his profession with a broader view, and this worldly concern was reflected in his postwar picture books. *Yertle the Turtle and Other Stories* (1950) was a deliberate parable of the life of Adolf Hitler.[14] After World War II, Seuss was stationed in Japan, and his concern for the needs of this small island nation was reflected in *Horton Hears a Who* (1954).

Most younger American children saw Asia as a magical land with no connection to any kind of reality, certainly not as a continent composed of an actual group of nations. The common belief among children was that if one could dig a deep enough hole, China was on the other end of it. And as far as many of these children were concerned, the Japanese simply disappeared as soon as the war was over. Given this mystical perspective, the Japanese folk tales of Yoshiko Uchida in *The Dancing Kettle* (1949) were a welcome diversion, but perhaps not as educational as the author might have wished. Uchida was born and brought up in California, and the stories reflect the American "happy-ending" approach to the fairy tale rather than the pathos that so often marked native Japanese writing; further, they avoided any real adversity. Uchida was uprooted during the war and was sent to an internment camp, but this hardship is not addressed in her writing until long after the end of World War II.

Many of the authors and illustrators introduced in the Thirties continued to be popular and productive through the Forties and into the Fifties. Some made an indelible imprint with a style so recognizable that each new book was immediately distinguished on publication as the work of a particular creator. Dr. Seuss was one such creator; the team of Leonard Weisgard and Margaret Wise Brown was another.

Although some of the most original and exciting work ever produced in the children's book field was to make its appearance in the Fifties, "mediocrity" became the label for the majority of children's books in this growing market. The Forties had brought forth such an avalanche of books that anything published in the Fifties had to be extremely innovative or noticeably controversial in order to gain major attention. In the meantime, if a book did fairly well in the marketplace, ordinary or not, it stayed in print.

CHRONOLOGICAL BIBLIOGRAPHY 1940–1949

Brown, Margaret Wise. *The Country Noisy Book*, illtd. Leonard Weisgard. New York: Harper, 1940, 1994. (Picture Book/Concept)

The small dog Muffin, introduced in Brown's *Noisy Book* (1939), is once more confronted with sounds he doesn't understand—he travels to the country in a box and, once out of the box, everything is brand new. It is the child listener who is given the opportunity to identify sounds for Muffin—quack, quack, etc.

Gates, Doris. *Blue Willow*. New York, Viking, 1940; New York: Puffin, 1976. (Realistic Fiction/Migrant)

Janey Larkin's real mother died when Janey was very small, and all she has left of her is a blue willow plate, a delicate piece of china with a house, willow trees, and a small curved bridge painted on its face. To her, the plate represents security from her past and of a place in the future when her father, a migrant worker, won't have to move from place to place along with the crops. The story presents a portrait of what it is like to be poor and insecure. When Janey's stepmother becomes ill and can't be moved and her father is out of work, Janey has to give up her precious plate to pay the rent. But, because of her attachment to the plate and her desire to see it just one more time before she and her family move on, her dream of security becomes unexpectedly real.

Kunhardt, Dorothy. *Pat the Bunny*. New York: Simon & Schuster, 1940; New York: Golden Press, 1970. (Picture Book/Concept)

The tactile nature of this small book (4 inches by 5¼ inches) has been thrilling preschoolers for more than half a century. Whatever Paul and Judy can do on the pages, the child can do—pat the bunny, play peek-a-boo, smell the flowers, look in the mirror, and wave bye-bye at the end.

Knight, Eric. *Lassie Come-Home*. New York: Henry Holt, 1940; New York: Dell Yearling, 1992. (Realistic Fiction/Animal)

The character of Lassie was first introduced by English author Eric Knight, who moved to Philadelphia when he was 15 years old and later became a newspaperman there. After his marriage, he moved to the hills of Pennsylvania, a setting that reminded him of Yorkshire, and it was in Pennsylvania that he wrote *Lassie Come-*

Home, set in England. Lassie was a thoroughbred collie, intelligent and well-behaved. Every day she met young Joe Carraclough at school, but one day she didn't, having been sold by Joe's father to the duke of Rudling when hopeless poverty forced Mr. Carraclough into the sale. But Lassie was a one-man dog, and no matter how hard the duke tried to retrain her, she kept finding a way to get back home—even when he sent her off to Scotland. Lassie traveled a good thousand miles in her quest to return from Scotland to England's Yorkshire hills and her beloved Joe, a miracle of perseverance. This is not simply a story about a dog; it is a story about relationships, about loyalty and perseverance and love. Though made into a movie in 1942 and later into a popular television series, only by reading the original story can the true emotional impact be experienced. Just three years after *Lassie* was published, Eric Knight died in a plane crash en route to Africa while serving in the American army. *Lassie Come-Home* was his only children's book and is a fitting tribute to his memory.

Lawson, Robert. *They Were Strong and Good*. New York: Viking, 1940. CALDECOTT MEDAL. (Informational/Picture Book/Biographical)

The Forties became a decade of discovery in children's books, with stories of regional life in America portraying children from varied backgrounds at different economic levels, thereby expanding a child's understanding of the wide scope of American life. Lawson made the connection between America's present and past with the story of his own parents and grandparents, but unfortunately he kept within the limits of his Scottish, Dutch, and English background, adding to his scenes pictures of stereotypical black slaves and showing demeaning behavior by Native Americans. In retrospect, this book is not the best indicator of the tapestry of American culture. It is, however, representative of the attitude of Anglo-Saxons toward people of color in the first half of this century.

Lovelace, Maud Hart. *Betsy-Tacy*, illtd. Lois Lenski. New York: Thomas H. Crowell, 1940. Also, *Betsy-Tacy and Tib* (1941), *Over the Big Hill* (1942), *Down Town* (1943). New editions of Lovelace by Harper Trophy in 1994. (Realistic Fiction/Series)

Many five-year-olds are just beginning to explore social skills with their peers, and *Betsy-Tacy* was the first children's book to examine this very important step in a child's life. Lovelace used a familiar Midwest location as the setting for her book about two little girls, Betsy, from English stock, and Tacy, from a large Irish family, who find themselves to be kindred souls and develop the kind of friendship that children yearn for as they become older. With imagination and the direct logic of childhood, they see themselves flying to magic lands. At one point they must deal with the unexpected death of Tacy's baby sister, Bee, and do so by putting a purple Easter egg in the nest of the first spring robin. They are convinced the bird will take the egg to Bee, and she will know that they care. As this series continues, the duo becomes a trio, when Tib (German) joins them, and the girls continue their friendship, growing older and dealing with more complex problems in their lives in each new book.

McCloskey, Robert. *Lentil.* New York: Viking, 1940; New York: Puffin, 1978. (Realistic Fiction/Picture Book/Humor)

Lentil is a modern-day Tom Sawyer, who lives in a small Ohio town. In this, McCloskey's first book, Lentil unwittingly becomes the town's hero just because he can't sing or whistle, which has led him to save money to buy a harmonica. The plot also involves old Sneetch, the town grouch, who has no use for the town's leading citizen, Colonel Carter. When the town makes ready to welcome the colonel back home with flags and banners and a full band, Sneetch starts sucking a lemon just as the band is about to play, and Lentil, unaffected by the old man's actions, plays his harmonica and saves the day.

Seuss, Dr. (pseud. of Theodor Seuss Geisel). *Horton Hatches the Egg.* New York: Random House, 1940, 1991. (Fantasy/Picture Book/Humor)

When Mayzie the lazy bird talks Horton the elephant into watching out for the egg in her nest so she can travel to Florida and enjoy the sun, Horton takes his responsibility very seriously. Nothing deters him from his obligation, even when he is transported across the sea, still in the tree, and is sold to a circus. "They dug up his tree and they put it inside,/With Horton so sad that he practically cried." His loyalty is rewarded when the egg hatches into an elephant-bird with ears and a tail and a trunk like his. The easy rhythm of Seuss's poetry has become his trademark, with no one yet matching his carefully developed beat.

Sperry, Armstrong. *Call It Courage.* New York: Macmillan, 1940; New York: Aladdin, 1990. NEWBERY MEDAL. (Realistic Fiction/South Pacific)

The South Pacific and its tribal culture became the setting for this award-winning character study. When Mafatu was an infant, he and his mother were thrown from their canoe into the sea during a storm. His mother was able to save him at the expense of her own life, and Mafatu's memory of that time makes him fear the sea. Mafatu, "stout heart," is unable to live up to his name until at the age of 12 he makes a vow to himself to conquer his fear or die.

Wilder, Laura Ingalls. *The Long Winter*. New York: Harper, 1940, 1994. *Little Town on the Prairie*. New York: Harper, 1941, 1994. *These Happy Golden Years*. New York: Harper, 1943, 1994. (Realistic Fiction/Historical/Regional)

These three Little House books cover the years the Ingalls family spent in De Smet, South Dakota, during which time the children completed their education, and Laura spent a year teaching school, and then married Almanzo Wilder. The popularity of Wilder's books are due in great part to the security represented by a closely knit family relationship in the face of difficulties.

Brown, Margaret Wise. *Brer Rabbit: Stories from Uncle Remus*, illtd. Victor Dowling. New York: Harper, 1941. (Folk/Myth/Picture Book/Black American)

Brown applied her talent for communicating with small children to a rewrite of Joel Chandler Harris's Uncle Remus stories. Her intention was to make them easier to read without losing their charm. She, like Beatrix Potter, respected her audience and spoke of children wanting "words better arranged than their own, and a few gorgeous big grownup words to bite on."[15]

———. *The Seashore Noisy Book*, illtd. Leonard Weisgard. New York: Scott, 1941; New York: Harper, 1994. (Picture Book/Concept)

In yet another "noisy" book, Muffin is on a sailboat, and around him the fog is so thick that he cannot see. This somewhat farfetched concept is used by Brown to set up the litany of sounds that the little dog hears, or doesn't hear, in this now-familiar format.

Edmonds, Walter V. *The Matchlock Gun*, illtd. Paul Lantz. New York: Dodd, Mead, 1941; New York: Putnam. NEWBERY MEDAL. (Realistic Fiction/Historical/Regional)

This was Edmonds's first book for children, and it relates a single incident that occurred during the French and Indian Wars in the Hudson Valley near Albany, New York. Edmonds is best known as the author of *Drums Along the Mohawk*, which also takes place in New York State. In *The Matchlock Gun*, he includes a foreword that elaborates on the Dutch lullaby mentioned in the story and implies that the real hero in the story is little Trudy, Edward's sister, though the text never backs up this claim. The story is written in 10 short chapters as a picture storybook, with dramatic illustrations and suspenseful immediacy in the telling as young Edward finds himself responsible for setting off the old matchlock gun against marauders while his father is away.

Enright, Elizabeth. *The Saturdays*. New York: Henry Holt, 1941, 1988. (Realistic Fiction/Regional/Urban)

The story takes place in New York City, with trips to Central Park, Broadway, and along Fifth Avenue at a more peaceful time in America's past. The Melendy children, Mona, Miranda, Rush, and Oliver, each have an adventure as they pool their allowances and take turns using it to do something special on a Saturday. When Oliver, the youngest, decides he would like to go to the circus and does so all by himself without telling anyone, the children decide they had better spend their Saturdays together after all. Enright was awarded a Newbery Medal in 1939 for *Thimble Summer* (1938), a story of a Wisconsin farm girl. Other books about the Melendys are *The Four-Story Mistake* (1942) and *Then There Were Five* (1944).

Estes, Eleanor. *The Moffats*. New York: Harcourt, 1941; San Diego: Harcourt, 1989. (Realistic Fiction/Historical/Family)

The four Moffats, Sylvie, Joe, Jane, and Rufus, represent small-town America, just as the Melendy children represent urban living. Their mother, having been widowed when Rufus was an infant, earns a living for her family as a seamstress. But, although the Moffats have trouble making ends meet and are faced throughout the book with the impending sale of their house, a fact that creates continuing suspense, the family is close-knit and enthusiastically involved in the activities of the community. These are the days of trolleys and trains, scarlet fever and whooping cough, cobblestone streets and horse-drawn wagons delivering milk and groceries, along with airplanes, automobiles, and machine-made clothing. The series continues with the focus on Jane in *The Middle Moffat* (1942) and on Rufus in *Rufus M.* (1943).

Holling, Holling C. *Paddle to the Sea*. Boston: Houghton Mifflin, 1941, 1969. (Picture Book/Historical/Regional)

A great deal of text, perhaps more than necessary, accompanies the realistic full-page paintings of various scenes in the telling of this story. The appeal is in the focus on a tiny wooden canoe with a miniature Indian figure holding a paddle. With diagrams and sketches on each text page and full-color illustrations on the page opposite, Holling starts the Indian figure on a journey across the Great Lakes, up the St. Lawrence River and out to the sea. "Please put me back in water. I am Paddle To The Sea" are the words carved on the bottom of the small canoe, and the vastness of the settings compared to the smallness of the canoe and its occupant creates continuous suspense as the canoe faces all kinds of adversity on its long journey.

McCloskey, Robert. *Make Way for Ducklings*. New York: Viking, 1941; New York: Puffin, 1976. CALDECOTT MEDAL. (Picture Book/Animal/Regional)

This simple story of two mallard ducks trying to find a safe home for themselves and their growing family in the metropolis of Boston is a perfect combination of background, character development, and design. Familiar Boston landmarks—the Public Garden with its swan boats, iron gates, monuments, and bridge over the pond; the Beacon Hill section of Boston with the State House, Louisburg Square, and rows of town houses; and the mighty Charles River—create a connection to place not seen often enough in American books for children. The ducklings, each one different from the next, their parents, Mr. and Mrs. Mallard, and Michael the policeman become live performers in a stirring drama, as Michael leads the eight ducklings into the park by way of the Corner Book Shop, Charles Street, and Beacon Street to settle on the tiny island in the park.

O'Hara, Mary. *My Friend Flicka*. New York: Harper, 1941, 1988. (Realistic Fiction/Animal)

Not originally published as a children's book, this story has been embraced by children who enjoy reading about a boy who disappoints his father again and again until his loyalty to a renegade colt leads both the boy, Ken McLaughlin, and the horse, Flicka, through many levels of adversity into maturity. At a time when most children's books were aimed at preschoolers and early readers, this sophisticated and emotional study of family relationships respected the adolescent enough to offer a complicated rite of passage in the life of a 10-year-old boy, a dreamer who avoided confronting reality until the summer his father finally allowed him to have a colt of his very own. By skipping some of the expository passages that slow the story down, today's readers can become totally involved in the struggle faced by young Ken McLaughlin and admire his parents, Nell and Rob, in their efforts to do what is best for their children in the harsh setting of Wyoming ranch country.

Rey, H. A. *Curious George*. Boston: Houghton Mifflin, 1941, 1973. (Picture Book/Fantasy/Animal)

The focus is on the monkey in this adventurous romp. George, like Collodi's Pinocchio (see p. 15), represents a mischievous little boy who does all the exciting things children aren't allowed to do, although the Man in the Yellow Hat, like a responsible parent, is always hovering in the background, ready to step in if necessary. George uses the telephone indiscriminately, floats across the city by hanging on to a bunch of balloons, and recklessly calls out the fire department. Rey brought the manuscript from Lisbon in 1940 and immediately found a publisher. His simple, cartoon-like drawings, with a free-spirited character that fits in anywhere, have been capturing the interest of children through several generations. The stories were written with the help of Rey's wife, Margret, who since his death has taken over the series.

Brown, Margaret Wise. *The Runaway Bunny*, illtd. Clement Hurd. New York: Harper, 1942, 1977. (Fantasy/Picture Book/Animal)

"I am running away," the little bunny tells his mother in that tentative bid for independence children everywhere make at a certain time in their lives, even though neither bunny nor child really wants to be alone just yet. His mother says, "If you run away, I will run after you for you are my little bunny." And when the bunny tells her he'll become a fish, she says she'll become the stream. She'll be a mountain for his rock, a gardener for his crocus, a tree for his bird, the wind for his sailboat, and when he finally becomes a little boy again, she says she'll be his mother. This simple story offers warmth and security to the preschool child.

———. *The Indoor Noisy Book*, illtd. Leonard Weisgard. New York: Scott, 1942; New York: Harper, 1994. (Picture Book/Concept)

When the little dog Muffin has a cold and must stay in the house, he hears a broom, some spoons, a telephone, a vacuum cleaner, and even a pin dropping. But what does custard sound like? This is one more question-and-answer "noisy" book for the very young.

Burton, Virginia Lee. *The Little House*. Boston: Houghton Mifflin, 1942, 1978. CALDECOTT MEDAL. (Fantasy/Picture Book)

This story of an anthropomorphic house has outgrown its status as an award-winning book. The storyline is plodding, and some of the pictures are near-repeats of the ones just before. The idea holds up, showing the ravages of progress on a natural landscape, as the little house becomes surrounded by skyscrapers and subways, but the book is too long for the slight premise it illustrates.

Gray, Elizabeth Janet. *Adam of the Road*, illtd. Robert Lawson. New York: Viking, 1942; New York: Puffin, 1987. NEWBERY MEDAL. (Realistic Fiction/Medieval/Historical/England)

This well-researched novel takes the reader back to 13th-century England with its castles, inns, and the busy excitement of the town fair as experienced by young Adam Quartermain, who is learning to be a minstrel like his father. The unfamiliar settings are easily absorbed as the reader becomes involved with Adam and his quest to find both his father and his dog. In a decade focusing on American history by region, this broader view was refreshing.

Hamilton, Edith. *Mythology*. New York: Dutton, 1942, 1989. (Folk/Myth)

This collection of Greek and Norse myths was true to its sources and appealed to the purist who wanted to read the myths as faithfully translated but appreciated Hamilton's easy-to-read style. She is a master of the myth, and, at the time this book was published, there were only a few collections of these stories for children. Today there are a wide variety of appealing presentations for children of different ages, but Hamilton's book remains a model.

Brown, Margaret Wise. *A Child's Good Night Book*, illtd. Remy Charlip. New York: Scott, 1943; New York: Harper, 1992. (Picture Book/Concept)

Charlip's elementary illustrations, looking as if colored with crayons in soft shades of green and brown, orange and pink, are a tranquil accompaniment to Brown's sleep-inducing text. The sun goes down, the lights go on, the birds and the fish and the sheep and the monkeys all go to sleep. And so do sailboats, cars, trucks and kangaroos, pussy cats, bunnies, bees and squirrels and, finally, children.

Chase, Richard. *The Jack Tales: Folk Tales from the Southern Appalachians Collected and Retold*, illtd. Berkley Williams, Jr. Boston: Houghton Mifflin, 1943, 1993. (Folk/Myth/Regional)

In an effort to put into print the folktales of the American South as told by the mountain folk of North Carolina, Chase collected several of the so-called "Jack" tales from Mr. R. M. Ward (Uncle *Mon*-roe), a farmer from Beech Mountain in the southern Appalachians, and captured the flavor of the storyteller in his collection. The story of "Jack and the Bean Tree" is the American folk version of England's "Jack and the Beanstalk." In black versions of the Jack tales, the hero is often called John, i.e., John de Conquer.

Forbes, Esther. *Johnny Tremain*, illtd. Lynd Ward. Boston: Houghton Mifflin, 1943; New York: Dell Yearling, 1987. NEWBERY MEDAL. (Realistic Fiction/Historical/American Revolution)

When author Forbes was working on her Pulitzer prize-winning book, *Paul Revere and the World He Lived In* (1942), she became interested in the apprentice boys of Boston and their part in the Revolutionary War. She invented a character, Johnny Tremain, and made up a story of what might have happened to him in the Boston of Revolutionary War days. She made such good use of her research material from *Paul Revere* that she was able to write a book that uncompromisingly imbued that time with emotional force. An example of character development at its best, this Revolutionary War story has lasted throughout the years. Though it has become required reading in most schools, once a student begins reading it, the suspense, adventure, and interest in what happens to arrogant Johnny Tremain, when an injury brings his career to an end, keep the student reading to the very end. The references to real historic figures as characters in the book, who have the same faults and flaws as ordinary people, further engage the interest of the reader.

Lenski, Lois. *Bayou Suzette*. Philadelphia: Lippincott, 1943; Cutchogue, N.Y.: Buccaneer, 1991. (Realistic Fiction/Regional)

Lenski, highly regarded for her Mr. Small picture books and her illustrations in the books of others, felt strongly about the lack of books regarding children from different social levels in various regions of the country. This story of a child who lived in the Louisiana bayou was the first of many regional books she wrote in the 1940s.

McCloskey, Robert. *Homer Price*. New York: Viking, 1943; New York: Puffin, 1976. (Realistic Fiction/Humor)

In a Norman Rockwell setting, McCloskey introduces 11-year-old Homer Price, his skunk, Aroma, and his best friend, Freddy, in a series of adventures, chapter by chapter, as Aroma helps catch bank robbers, Freddy is disillusioned by his comic-book hero, Super-Duper, and Homer finds himself with a runaway doughnut machine.

The characters are exaggerated and the dilemmas easily resolved in a book that showcases McCloskey's comic flair, especially in the illustrations.

Saint Exupery, Antoine de. *The Little Prince*. New York: Harcourt, 1943; San Diego: Harcourt, 1993. (Fantasy)

While American authors were careful to present to children a world free from deep concerns, French author Saint Exupery had no such compunctions. This allegory on life and death as seen through the mind and heart of a child, the little prince, is a thoughtful treatise, perhaps more suitable for adults who have forgotten what's important in life rather than for children, who always know.

> "Only the children know what they are looking for," said the little prince. "They waste their time over a rag doll and it becomes important to them; and if anybody takes it away from them, they cry . . ." "They are lucky," the switchman said.[16]

Sauer, Julia. *Fog Magic*. New York: Viking, 1943; New York: Puffin, 1986. (Fantasy/Time Travel/Historical/Regional)

In a country inclined to dismiss the fantastic and encourage the practical, Sauer made fantasy palatable by placing it in a down-East Maine setting and introducing one child in a community of hard-working, practical fishermen. The child, Greta, is not only inclined to embrace the fog but also allows it to take her back in time to explore an old mystery. The time fantasy was a new genre in American children's books, introduced by English authors H.G. Wells and Edith Nesbit in the early part of the 20th century and embraced by American authors. Unlike Tolkien's Middle Earth, the fantasy world discovered by Greta Addington was simply her own familiar world in an earlier time.

Thurber, James. *Many Moons*, illtd. Louis Slobodkin. New York: Harcourt, 1943, 1990 (illtd. Marc Simont). CALDECOTT MEDAL. (Fantasy/Fairy/Picture Book)

This story not only celebrates language—"One day Lenore fell ill of a surfeit of raspberry tarts" and "'I have sent as far as Samarkand and Araby and Zanzibar . . .' said the Lord High Chamberlain"—but it also captures the simple logic of a child's mind. Princess Lenore wants the moon, and if she gets it she'll be well, she tells her father, the king. But no one knows how to go about getting the moon except the court jester. He has the good sense to ask Lenore what she thinks the moon looks like and is able to put Lenore's idea of the moon, no bigger than her thumbnail, on a chain she can hang around her neck. Slobodkin's illustrations earned the 1944 Caldecott Medal, but here is a case where text deserves as much recognition as pictures. Though written in the classic format of the fairy tale, *New Yorker* cartoonist Thurber brings to *Many Moons* the American penchant for humor.

Brown, Margaret Wise. *They All Saw It*, photog. Ylla (pseud. of Camilla Koffler). New York: Harper, 1944. (Picture Book/Photographs/Concept/Animal)

Ylla's dramatic presentation of animals in this collection of photographs, tied together in picture book format by Margaret Wise Brown's imaginative text, was an indicator of what could be done with photographs as works of art in a children's book, an innovation that has yet to be utilized in its fullest potential.

Estes, Eleanor. *The Hundred Dresses*, illtd. Louis Slobodkin. New York: Harcourt, 1944; San Diego: Harcourt, 1974. (Realistic Fiction/Social Behavior)

With past featured characters in 20th-century children's books being almost exclusively white middle-class Protestants, the introduction of Wanda Petronski—poor, Polish, and Catholic—has a subtle impact on the child reader who sees Wanda through the eyes of her middle-class schoolmates and observes the destruction that can be caused by misunderstanding through ignorance and thoughtlessness. Slobodkin's ethereal pastel sketches for the book complement the low-keyed but powerful theme.

Field, Rachel. *Prayer for a Child*, illtd. Elizabeth Orton Jones. New York: Macmillan, 1944, 1984. CALDECOTT MEDAL. (Poetry/Picture Book/Concept)

Field's simple poem avoided the particulars that would limit it to a specific religion, and Jones's pictures were able to rise above the cliched poetry—"Bless this milk and bless this bread/Bless this soft and waiting bed/Where I presently shall be/Wrapped in sweet security"—by adding details such as the tiny wooden dolls, the spice rack with labels such as "kava," "houska," "hrack," and "cuka," and the tiled fireplace. Like Margaret Wise Brown's *Goodnight Moon*, the book offers security; unlike *Goodnight Moon*, it speaks more with the voice of the parent than with the voice of the child.

Lawson, Robert. *Rabbit Hill*. New York: Viking, 1944. NEWBERY MEDAL. (Fantasy/Animal)

Strong characterizations and appealing illustrations captivate the reader and make believable this animal story about a family of rabbits and their interactions with other animals, as well as with the new Folks who have moved to the house on Rabbit Hill. Mother Rabbit is a perpetual worrier, Father Rabbit is a tedious talker, and little Georgie is self-confident and adventurous, well-loved by everybody for his exuberance. When he is the victim of a hit-and-run driver, the entire animal community is in mourning. But Georgie is taken in by the new Folks and nursed back to health. Their kindness is highly appreciated by the animals, leaving the handyman to wonder why the new owners' garden stays intact when all the previous owners of Rabbit Hill had been driven out by animal vandalism: "I just can't understand it," he says. "Here's these new folks with their garden and not a sign of a fence around it, no traps, no poison, no nothing, and not a thing touched, not a thing. Must just be Beginner's Luck."

Lenski, Lois. *Strawberry Girl*. Philadelphia: Lippincott, 1945; Cutchogue, N.Y.: Buccaneer, 1991. NEWBERY MEDAL. (Realistic Fiction/Regional)

This award-winner, a continuation of Lenski's effort to present a spectrum of social settings in different regions of the United States, is the story of a girl who lives in rural Florida and helps her poverty-stricken family by suggesting that they sell the strawberries she helped plant and cultivate near their home. Lenski continued her series with *Boom Town Boy* (1948), about the Oklahoma oil fields, and *Cotton in My Sack* (1949), about Arkansas cotton pickers.

Means, Florence Crannell. *The Moved-Outers*. Boston: Houghton Mifflin, 1945; New York: Walker, 1992. (Realistic Fiction/Historical/World War II/Japanese American)

Even though Means tried a little too hard to convince readers that the Japanese-American Ohara family fit comfortably into the white neighborhood in which they lived, *The Moved-Outers* was the only book at the time to acknowledge what happened to Japanese families during World War II. At the beginning of World War II, there was no effort to determine the loyalty of the second- and third-generation Japanese, born in America, who were living in California and had established businesses there. Uprooted from everything they knew, treated as prisoners, unable at first to join their former neighbors in the fight for the country they called their own, the Oharas were one of many families whose lives were forever disrupted by an ignorant few. They were sent to live in American internment camps until the war was over and perhaps would never be able to regain the security they had known before.

Petersham, Maud and Miska. *The Rooster Crows: A Book of American Rhymes and Jingles*. New York: Macmillan, 1945, 1987. CALDECOTT MEDAL. (Poetry/Picture Book)

The appeal of this book lies in its early American flavor, with its still-quoted childhood rhymes and jingles supplementing Mother Goose. "Bye, baby bunting. Father's gone a-hunting" and "Trot, trot to Boston/To buy a loaf of bread" are pictured by the Petershams as examples of 18th-century American rocking rhymes to entertain the very young. And "Lazy Mary, will you get up,/Will you get up, will you get up?" is 20th-century humor for the school-age child.

White, E. B. *Stuart Little*. New York: Harper, 1945, 1974. (Fantasy)

When this book was accepted for publication, Anne Carroll Moore tried to suppress it because she considered a story about an American mother giving birth to a mouse to be indecent.[17] But Ursula Nordstrom, children's book editor at Harper, paid no attention, and the book has become a standard library title. White respected his audience, whether child or adult, and his command of language proffers a textbook for writers. "When Mrs. Frederick C. Little's second son arrived, everybody noticed he looked very much like a mouse . . . Before he was many days old he was not only looking like a mouse but acting like one, too—wearing a gray hat and carrying a small cane." It is this type of matter-of-fact and humorous logic that allows White's impossible premise to succeed and takes away any discomfort about a mouse child in a human family.

Bailey, Carolyn Sherwin. *Miss Hickory*, illtd. Ruth Gannett. New York: Viking, 1946; New York: Puffin, 1977. NEWBERY MEDAL. (Fantasy/Toys)

Rachael Field's Hitty was very much a doll whose fate was in the hands of whichever person owned her at a given time, but Bailey's Miss Hickory exists as part of the natural world, created from a twig and a hickory nut and dressed in leaves, moss, and apple blossoms. Although the doll appears throughout the book, the focus shifts from chapter to chapter, at one time describing the groundhog's reaction at seeing his shadow, and at another time presenting the squirrel as a character unable to prepare himself for winter. Miss Hickory, rather than being a pivotal character, is too often relegated to the background, and this causes the story to flounder. Because Ruth Gannett's lithographs of Miss Hickory in the different outfits the doll creates for herself are so lively and because Bailey's character descriptions are so rich—"In spite of her stiff twig body and nut head, Miss Hickory was intensely feminine"—the somewhat minor role given Miss Hickory in the story is disappointing in an award-winning book.

De Angeli, Marguerite. *Bright April*. New York: Doubleday, 1946. (Picture Book/Realistic Fiction/Black American)

In keeping with the effort of children's book authors in the 1940s to educate their readers about the commonality of all mankind, this family story of a young middle-class black girl negated the stereotypical view of blacks in America and offered a personal glimpse of a comfortable home and the familiar daily routine the family followed.

MacDonald, Golden (pseud. of Margaret Wise Brown). *The Little Island*, illtd. Leonard Weisgard. New York: Doubleday, 1946; New York: Dell, 1993. CALDECOTT MEDAL. (Picture Book/Regional)

It's not surprising that Leonard Weisgard was awarded a Caldecott Medal. His illustrations had been delighting audiences for quite some time in Brown's *Noisy* books and some of her other titles. Weisgard illustrated nearly one-fourth of Brown's approximately 100 books,[18] but this book about Brown's special island in Maine, written by Brown under a pseudonym, seems less innovative than other collaborations between the two. The text is inconsistent, with unnecessary dialogue between a kitten and a fish that intrudes on the natural poetry of the island itself, as portrayed in Weisgard's illustrations, with rock formations and wildflowers acting as a haven for seabirds and seals.

Tarry, Ellen, and Ets, Marie Hall. *My Dog Rinty*, photog. Alexander and Alexandra Alland. New York: Viking, 1946. (Realistic Fiction/Black American/Urban)

The use of photographs guaranteed that black Americans would be shown as real people rather than as the caricatures that marked earlier books (see illustration p. 100). In this story of a little boy, David, and his dog, the setting is Harlem, the neighborhood consists of close-knit family units, and Rinty's penchant for catching rats offsets his bad habits and convinces the neighbors that David should be allowed to keep his dog. Tarry and Ets were willing to split a two-and-a-half-cent royalty on the first 10,000 copies of this book so that its price would make the book accessible to all economic levels.[19] The "story lady" pictured in the book is Augusta Baker, acclaimed Harlem children's librarian.

Brown, Margaret Wise. *Goodnight Moon*, illtd. Clement Hurd. New York: Harper, 1947, 1977. (Picture Book/Concept)

This book speaks to preschoolers in the same way Maurice Sendak's *Where the Wild Things Are* (1963) captures the imaginations of nursery-school and elementary-grade children. Clement Hurd had done the illustrations for Brown's *Runaway Bunny* before World War II interrupted his promising career. Just before Hurd got out of the service, Brown asked her publisher, Harper, to send him the spiral notebook in which she had written the text of *Goodnight Moon*. The collaboration that followed produced a book that has been recommended from one generation to the next, accelerating in sales until, by 1990, four million copies had been sold. The simple concept, in which a small bunny says good night to the familiar objects in his bedroom, offers the very young child a way to accept the mystery of the night by reciting a litany of ordinary, everyday things.

———. *The Winter Noisy Book*, illtd. Charles Shaw. New York: Scott, 1947; New York: Harper, 1994. (Picture Book/Concept)

Again, design takes precedence over story line as Muffin watches fall turn to winter and experiences his first snowfall.

Henry, Marguerite. *Misty of Chincoteague*, illtd. Wesley Dennis. New York: Macmillan, 1947, 1991. (Realistic Fiction/Animal)

This story has become a favorite of many generations of horse lovers. It tells of two children, Paul and Maureen Beebe, who dream of capturing one particular wild pony from a herd of wild ponies on the island of Assateague. No one has ever been able to capture the pony they call Phantom and make her swim to Chincoteague at roundup time, but she recently has had a foal, and that makes her vulnerable. Paul joins the roundup on Assateague, and because Phantom has to protect her colt she allows Paul to lead her to the water. The two horses swim across to Chincoteague Island with the rest of the herd, and Paul and Maureen set about to gain Phantom's trust. After many months of working hard and saving their money, the two children have enough to buy both Phantom and her colt, which they have named Misty, but only if someone else doesn't buy the horses first.

Pene du Bois, William. *The Twenty-one Balloons*. New York: Lothrop, 1947; New York: Dell, 1982. NEWBERY MEDAL. (Fantasy/Science Fiction)

By combining facts with ingenuity, Pene du Bois created a believable adventure that triggers the imagination. After a long career as a math teacher in the San Francisco school system, William Waterman Sherman dreams of spending a year floating above the Earth in a balloon. But a sea gull puts an end to his plans, and the professor finds himself on the island of Krakatoa where the inhabitants have created a highly inventive and satisfying society—until the island's volcano shows signs of erupting and everyone must find a way to leave the island.

Tresselt, Alvin. *White Snow Bright Snow*, illtd. Roger Duvoisin. New York: Lothrop, 1947; New York: Morrow, 1988. CALDECOTT MEDAL. (Picture Book/Concept)

With the small homey details that children recognize, the text describes a heavy snowstorm, how it affects the postman, the farmer and a policeman, and how much pleasure the children find playing in the snow. Duvoisin uses primary colors on a gray background that gradually becomes paler until the center spread is all white snow with accents of red and yellow. By the end of the book, the gray has disappeared and green dominates as spring arrives. The illustrations are a carefully developed rendering of an uncomplicated text.

Gannett, Ruth Stiles. *My Father's Dragon*, illtd. Ruth Chrisman Gannett. New York: Random House, 1948. (Fantasy/Chapter Book/Humor)

The unnamed narrator tells highly imaginative stories about her father, Elmer Elevator, who, in this first book of Gannett's series, runs away to Wild Island to rescue a dragon, which has a long tail, yellow and blue stripes, and gold wings. Elmer, assisted by his cat, goes about this adventure in a very matter-of-fact way, eating tangerines on the island of Tangerina and outsmarting a circle of tigers, a rhinoceros, and a lion on his way to free the dragon. The story brings to mind *Little Black Sambo* (1905), who dealt with a similar circle of tigers, and *Doctor Dolittle* (1920), who also overcame obstacles with ease. Other dragon titles include *Elmer and the Dragon* and *The Dragons of Blueland*.

Godden, Rumer. *The Doll's House*. New York: Viking, 1948. (Fantasy/Toys)

When a family of dolls—Mr. Plantagenet, his wife, Birdie, their children, Tottie and Apple, and their dog, Darner—are rejuvenated, refurbished, and reunited with the doll house they remember from generations earlier, they become, with the help of their young owners, Emily and Charlotte, joyful tenants until the unexpected arrival of the immoral Marchpane, a doll concerned only with her own gratification. Marchpane's selfishness leads to tragedy in the Plantagenet family, and because Godden imbues her characters with so much individuality, the story becomes sharply defined and impossible to forget. The doll Tottie, tiny and made of wood, could be the English counterpart of Rachel Field's Hitty, also tiny and made of wood (see p. 69).

Henry, Marguerite. *King of the Wind*, illtd. Wesley Dennis. New York: Macmillan, 1948, 1991. NEWBERY MEDAL. (Realistic Fiction/Animal)

This story, which takes the reader from Canada to Morocco and then to France and England, connects past with present by introducing the reader to Man o' War, American Triple Crown champion, and then going back in time to tell the story of the Godolphin Arabian, ancestor of Man o' War, and the young Moroccan boy who loved and believed in him through all manner of misfortune.

De Angeli, Marguerite. *The Door in the Wall*. New York: Doubleday, 1949; New York: Dell, 1990. NEWBERY MEDAL. (Realistic Fiction/Historical/Medieval England/Physical Adjustment)

Because Robin is the son of a nobleman, certain things are expected of him, and he is determined to make his parents proud of him. While his father is at war and his mother attends the queen, Robin plans to fulfill his parents' expectations. He is, however, struck by illness the day after his parents leave and loses the use of his legs. The setting is medieval England, and De Angeli describes the many obstacles Robin must surmount, both physical and mental, as he attempts to overcome his disability and deal with his dependency on others. This book, though set in the Middle Ages, was written in a decade in which infantile paralysis (poliomyelitis) was a constant threat and for which there was no cure. Dr. Jonas Salk did not develop the polio vaccine until the 1950s. Even though the problems Robin faces are too easily resolved, the book was one of the few to acknowledge physical impairment in the often idealized world of children's books.

Heinlein, Robert. *Red Planet*. New York: Scribner, 1949; New York: Ballantine, 1986. (Science Fiction)

Heinlein's story takes place on the planet Mars and features a boy named Jim Marlowe, one of the early colonists there. Jim befriends a Martian, whom he has named Willis and who is shaped like a puff ball and able to mimic, in the voice of the speaker, any conversation he hears. But Willis, it turns out, is more important to the puzzle that is Mars than the colonists originally understood.

Uchida, Yoshiko. *The Dancing Kettle and Other Japanese Folk Tales*. New York: Harcourt, 1949; New York: Creative Arts, 1986.

These retellings of folk tales familiar to Japanese children are intended to entertain American children; therefore, Uchida wraps up each story with a "happily ever after" ending and avoids any real adversity within the stories. In the Japanese version of "Urashima Taro and the Princess of the Sea," Taro dies and the tortoise that had taken him to the princess never returns, while in Uchida's version, Taro still lives at the age of 300, and even though he can never again visit the Palace of the Sea, "knows, perhaps [that] one day the old tortoise [will come] back to the beach once more to help his old friend." The stories, though not quite the same as those familiar to Japanese children, are indeed entertaining and easy to read.

NOTES

1. Cabel Phillips. *Decade of Triumph and Trouble: The 1940s*, p. 10.
2. Ruth Hill Viguers. "Golden Years and Time of Tumult: 1920–1967," *A Critical History of Children's Literature*, ed. Cornelia Meigs, p. 405.
3. Books published for the library and bookstore market as opposed to the less expensive mass-market series books.
4. Barbara Bader. *American Picturebooks: From Noah's Ark to the Beast Within*, p. 277.
5. Interview with Dorothy Kunhardt in 1979.
6. Leonard S. Marcus. *Margaret Wise Brown: Awakened by the Moon*, p. 57.
7. Ibid., p. 215.
8. Ibid., p. 179.
9. Barbara Bader, op. cit., p. 109. Please note that the entire text of the out-of-print *They All Saw It* is reproduced in Bader's book.
10. Ibid., p. 80.
11. Ibid., pp. 81–82.
12. Milton Meltzer. *Never to Forget: The Jews of the Holocaust*, p. xv.
13. No mention of death, birth, religion, sex, divorce, or drugs was allowed in children's books.

14. C. Robert Jennings. "Dr. Seuss: 'What Am I Doing Here?'" *Life*, October 23, 1965, p. 106.
15. Viguers, op. cit., p. 638.
16. Antoine de Saint Exupery. *The Little Prince*. San Diego: Harcourt, 1971, p. 89.
17. Marcus, op. cit., p. 186.
18. Viguers, op. cit., p. 638.
19. Letter from Ellen Tarry dated January 31, 1994.

Artwork by Norman Rockwell titled "Problem We All Live With"; printed by permission of the Norman Rockwell Family Trust (copyright © 1964 the Norman Rockwell Family Trust). Artist Norman Rockwell immortalized the school integration effort with a painting that portrayed a small black child, flanked by two large guards, bravely entering a Little Rock School.

6

WEAVING THE GOLDEN WEB 1950–1959

Americans have never believed that childhood was merely a preparation for life; they have insisted, rather, that it was life itself.

—Henry Steele Commager
Introduction to the first edition of
A Critical History of Children's Literature

Horn of Plenty

Complacency settled over the United States following World War II. The economy was solid, and most of America's youth took for granted the security of the family unit, with Dr. Spock urging mothers to stay home with their young children. Spock, a New York pediatrician, wrote *The Common Sense Book of Baby and Child Care* (1946). The book sold 750,000 copies in its first year and became a bible for parents throughout the baby boomer years (1946 to 1964).[1] Instead of advocating the rigid discipline long recommended by behaviorist John B. Watson as the proper way to raise children,[2] Benjamin Spock offered a happy medium that relied more on a mother's instinct than on rules of behavior. The American Dream encompassed a small house in the suburbs, a washing machine, refrigerator, automobile, and, wonder of wonders, a television set. In 1948 there were fewer than 17,000 television sets in the United States. By the end of the Fifties, Americans owned about 50 million.[3]

The 1950s were known as the "Bland Decade," but the label was deceptive. The rumblings of change were beginning to be heard and in retrospect should have been a warning of what was to come in the Sixties. But the young people who were to become advocates of social change in the next decade seemed to be concentrating on Little League and the Girl Scouts and ignoring the fact that the United States was once again involved in a war, this time in far away Korea. South Korea was fighting for independence against communist North Korea, and America entered the fight.

In 1952, Gen. Dwight D. Eisenhower was elected president, and the phrase "I like Ike" became as popular nationwide as Ike himself. Ike's running mate was Richard Nixon, who became a temporary embarrassment to the Republican Party when his political integrity was questioned during the campaign but managed to convince the nation of his sincerity before the election. Doris Day, Pat Boone, and disc jockey Dick Clark were entertainment's squeaky clean representatives of the American ideal, while a less-than-restrained Elvis Presley shocked television viewers when he performed on Ed Sullivan's television show, "Toast of the Town."

Presley, called the king of rock'n'roll, became the idol of teenagers, but their parents considered him a dire threat to the status quo. In the meantime, Rosa Parks, a black seamstress from Montgomery, Alabama, was arrested on December 1, 1955, when she refused to move to the back of the bus. And the 1954 Supreme Court ruling that public schools must be integrated was tested in 1957 when nine black students were enrolled at a previously all-white school in Little Rock, Arkansas. Artist Norman Rockwell immortalized the school integration effort with a painting he called "Problem We All Live With," which portrayed a small black child, flanked by two very large guards, bravely entering a Little Rock school (see illustration p. 128). Children's book author Dorothy Sterling wrote *Mary Jane* (1959), a story about the problems experienced by one girl who chose to attend a formerly all-white school and who, little by little, managed to break down barriers among her peers.

The Red Threat

Throughout the 1950s, the winds of change increased in intensity. The growing fear of the Soviet Union, which had its own atomic bomb, led to paranoia with regard to communism. In Indianapolis, an attempt was made "to remove *Robin Hood* from the library shelves because of the claim that the book's hero acted like a Communist, and the name of the Cincinnati baseball team was changed from 'Reds' to 'Redlegs.'"[4] Sen. Joseph McCarthy took his campaign against communism to the small screen with televised congressional hearings and later exposed himself as an unscrupulous zealot when pitted against lawyer Joseph Welch and television commentator Edward R. Murrow. The American public discovered for the first time that the television camera had a way of revealing true character, good and bad. Nevertheless, McCarthy's unsupported charges against public servants as well as scientists, teachers, actors, television personalities, writers, and even clergymen created enough doubt in the minds of the people to damage the reputations of those accused, in some cases keeping them from ever achieving their career goals.

Harnessing the Informational Flood

When the Soviets launched Sputnik, the first space capsule, on October 4, 1957, the focus in America turned to science and technology, and improvement of American education became a primary concern. America's status as a No. 1 power was at stake. The result was what Ruth Hill Viguers called "an informational flood,"[5] one, she said, that almost eclipsed the children's story as an art form. Manufacturing products for children became highly lucrative, and good business demanded more attractive textbooks and more informative trade books, with the result that children's books became less a branch of literature and more a gainful product.[6] The basal reader, which tested reading comprehension at the expense of reading for pleasure, became the core of the school curriculum, and trade books, no longer used as part of the curriculum, were relegated to the public libraries, which became their main purchasers.

Mid-century Perspective

Because of the phenomenal growth of the children's book industry since the beginning of the 20th century and the lack of any comprehensive studies regarding the genre, there was a need at mid-century to initiate a critical analysis of available children's books and put them in some kind of perspective for future readers and educators. The result was a broad study called *A Critical History of Children's Literature*, written in four sections, each by a well-known expert in the field of children's literature, first published by Macmillan in 1953 (and revised in 1969).

The project was developed by Macmillan children's book editor Doris Patee, with Cornelia Meigs exploring the roots of the industry, Anne Thaxter Eaton gathering the works that marked its early development, Elizabeth Nesbitt analyzing the material produced in the beginning years of this growing enterprise, and Ruth Hill Viguers exploring the titles that between 1920 and 1967 constituted a fully established genre in the American economic base. If it weren't for this exceptional effort, edited overall by Cornelia Meigs, it would be extremely difficult to trace the children's book industry back to its beginnings. Although this survey contains information about a great many books now out of print, a surprisingly high percentage of the cited titles from the past continue to be available and relevant.

The controversy that has arisen in the last half of this century over the insensitivity shown by some early children's book authors and illustrators toward people of color is not reflected in *A Critical History* because it was not a social issue when these four experts gathered their information.

Creating the Web

In the 1950s, while education in this country focused on the factual and informative, the trade-book market turned to fantasy and some of the most notable fantasies since the 19th century were propagated by both English and American authors. Narnia could be reached through the back of the wardrobe in English author C. S. Lewis's *The Lion, the Witch and the Wardrobe* (1950), the first of seven books about this fascinating allegorical world. *The Magician's Nephew* (1955), which Lewis suggests should be read first, introduces readers to the history of Narnia and the reason it became enchanted. A young boy, Digory, and his friend Polly are transported to an in-between world that leads to other worlds, one of which is Narnia. Digory's mother has cancer, and the boy hopes to find a cure in one of these magical worlds. Lewis's own mother died from cancer when Lewis was nine years old. Unable to save her, he allows Digory to save his mother when the two children meet the great Aslan in the newly emerging country of Narnia.

Mary Norton catered to children's captivation with the very small in *The Borrowers* (1952), introducing a series of books about a family of tiny people living under the floorboards at Firbank Hall in the English countryside. J. R. R. Tolkien followed *The Hobbit* with an ambitious trilogy called *The Lord of the Rings*, continuing the saga of Middle Earth with *The Fellowship of the Ring* (1954), *The Two Towers* (1955), and *The Return of the King* (1956). Lucy Boston formulated her series of time fantasies, beginning with *The Children of Green Knowe* (1954) and *Treasure of Green Knowe* (1958).

In America, heretofore not noted for producing fantasy books, E. B. White, coauthor of *Elements of Style*, the essayist's bible, wrote *Charlotte's Web* (1952), a fantasy that took its place with the finest in the field, and American author Edward Eager emulated his English idol, E. Nesbit, with *Half Magic* (1954) and *Knight's Castle* (1956). Eleanor Cameron combined science and fantasy in *The Wonderful Flight to the Mushroom Planet* (1954) and *Stowaway to the Mushroom Planet* (1956).

Combining humor with science fiction, Ellen MacGregor introduced a delightful new heroine in *Miss Pickerell Goes to Mars* (1951); *Miss Pickerell and the Geiger Counter* (1952); *Miss Pickerell Goes Undersea* (1953); and *Miss Pickerell Goes to the Arctic* (1953). The indomitable Miss Pickerell, to whom neither age nor the fact that she is a female makes any difference at all, rockets into space, travels beneath the sea, meets the atomic energy challenge, and faces the cold Arctic regions in a series of four adventures. Unfortunately, Ellen MacGregor died in 1954 after writing these first four books, which were all illustrated with vigorous humor by Paul Galdone. Because MacGregor left behind notes for many more books and because author Doris Pantell, 10 years later, showed the same ability for combining fact and fantasy that marked MacGregor's efforts, the series was resumed by Pantell in 1965.

Another heroine, less adventurous than Miss Pickerell but just as perceptive, was introduced in the character of Mrs. Piggle-Wiggle, who understands children better than anyone else. Although the Mrs. Piggle-Wiggle series was actually started in 1947, each of the original books was illustrated by a different artist—one by Richard Bennett, one by Kurt Wiese, and one by Maurice Sendak—until Hilary Knight, who portrayed the irrepressible Eloise in Kay Thompson's delightful romp through the Plaza Hotel in New York City, created a portrait of Mrs. Piggle-Wiggle that matched the appeal of Mary Shepard's drawings for *Mary Poppins* (1934). In 1957, all the Mrs. Piggle-Wiggle books were re-illustrated by Knight to create a more consistent and recognizable portrait of the perpetually cheerful, always understanding Mrs. Piggle-Wiggle.

Learning to Read with Make Believe

Trade publishers wanted to capture a share of the education market along with their bookstore and library sales and knew that, in America, fantasy would never be part of the school curriculum unless it was disguised as an educational tool. Enter Dr. Seuss! *The Cat in the Hat* (1957) was created by him expressly to get rid of the homogenous Dick and Jane primers after it was suggested by education writer John Hersey in *Life* magazine that perhaps the ailing educational system should be handed over to Dr. Seuss. This led to a request by William Spaulding, textbook chief at Houghton Mifflin, that Dr. Seuss meet the challenge by creating a book from a list of 300 words. The first two words on the list were *cat* and *hat,*[7] and the result was a supplemental reader called *The Cat in the Hat* (1957), published as a textbook by Houghton Mifflin and as a trade book by Random House. So well received was this book that a new genre in children's books, designated "easy reader," was formed, and the market became inundated by a wide variety of picture storybooks in the easy-to-read format, usually 64 pages in length, divided into four or five chapters, with short sentences, simple vocabulary, repetitive words and phrases, and with illustrations on every double spread. Most publishers limited the text to a pre-set list of vocabulary words, but Coward, McCann & Geoghegan, now part of G.P. Putnam Sons, developed an easy-reader line called Break-of-Day, which followed all the prerequisites for the easy-reader format but had no language restrictions, thereby allowing a more complicated storyline and a challenge for readers.

Seuss became the editor in chief of Beginner Books at Random House and either wrote or edited all of the easy readers published by that line. Another successful line of easy readers was the series of I Can Read books at Harper and Row, and it was here that Elsie Minarik introduced the Little Bear series, aimed at a more advanced readership and given depth by the perceptive illustrations of Maurice Sendak.

Good Night, Margaret Wise Brown

The warm relationship between Little Bear and his mother brings to mind the similar emotions expressed in Margaret Wise Brown's *The Runaway Bunny* (1942). By 1952, Brown had a hundred books to her credit with perhaps another hundred in the works. She was engaged to be married, and who could say what new, exciting projects were ahead for her. Unfortunately, an emergency operation to remove her appendix while she was in Europe led to her unexpected death from a blood clot that traveled from her leg to her brain on the day she was to be discharged from the hospital. She was 42 years old.[8]

Brown's simple lively texts have never been duplicated, and one of her last efforts, *Mister Dog: The Dog Who Belonged to Himself* (1952), was a "small comic masterpiece"[9] and a tribute to her own dog, Crispian, as well as an indication of how far she herself had come in the process of maturing. In the story, Crispian invites a boy to live in his house with him, a house modeled by Garth Williams after Margaret's own house, Cobble Court: "And there was plenty of room in his house for the boy to live there with him." Margaret had always been a private person, and almost all of her earlier books focused on a single character, for example, the bunny in *Goodnight Moon* and the small dog Muffin in the Noisy book series, but following her engagement to James Rockefeller, whom she had nicknamed Pebble, she allowed her characters to become more interactive in keeping with her own increasing awareness and emotional acceptance of others. Her artistic as well as her social development had only just begun to flower when she died. She had never been married and never had children, but she did have a direct connection to childhood.

Even though she was not one to give freely of herself, she was generous with her illustrators, always making sure they received an equal share of royalties. Two of her closest friends were Edith Hurd and her husband Clement Hurd, illustrator of *Goodnight Moon*. She and Edith, whom she nicknamed Posie, worked together on the texts of several Little Golden Books, usually without conflict. But in 1952 the two argued over a Golden Books project called *The Early Milkman*. Edith objected to the beginning, finding it dull, and offered some editorial comment, to which Margaret responded with sarcasm. They had always managed to come to an agreement over past texts, settling on a final manuscript, but when Margaret died, this manuscript was still in a state of revision. As Margaret had written in a note to Edith: "Here is my rewrite which I expect you to rewrite which I expect S & S [Simon and Schuster] to rewrite which I expect us to rewrite and so go the pains of collaboration."[10] This vital, witty, extremely attractive young woman left behind a wealth of material and innovative ideas that she never had a chance to develop, but her unique rhythmic verses coupled with some of the best illustrators in picture books for the very young led the way for other talents just starting out in the picture-book field.

Expanding the Genre

Ruth Krauss and Maurice Sendak took picture books in a new direction with *A Hole Is to Dig: A First Book of First Definitions* (1952). Not only was Krauss able to match Brown in the simple direct rhythms that appealed to preschoolers, but also the pattern of her text was carefully developed to create connections throughout that led the reader to anticipate from one page to the next what might follow. Sendak was the perfect illustrator for these books, displaying small mischievous children interacting in groups and with each other. His children were not all blond-haired and blue-eyed but, rather, reflected the immigrant population of America, with its mix of cultures. The lively interaction among the children brought to mind the illustrations of Randolph Caldecott and Kate Greenaway in their early collections of nursery rhymes as children frolicked and cavorted at a dizzy pace for the sheer joy of it.

Both Sendak and Krauss celebrate friendship freely and joyously in their collaborations, especially in *I'll Be You and You Be Me* (1954). With the encouragement and expertise of Ursula Nordstrom, editor of children's books at Harper and Brothers, these two major talents redefined the picture book by incorporating the direct voice and vision of the child into books for children. In their first book, *A Hole Is to Dig*, definitions were collected from small children, and Krauss arranged the collection into a concise whole. Her husband, Dave "Crockett" Johnson, author of the perpetually popular *Harold and the Purple Crayon* (1955), in which simplicity is taken to the heights of imagination, interjected a quiet note into the meetings between Sendak and Krauss. Johnson was calm and Krauss was emotionally volatile, and Sendak, at the age of 23, was somewhat intimidated by both. At the end of their work on *A Hole Is to Dig*, Krauss, who was, as Sendak says, "fiercely liberated," suddenly realized that Sendak had been "assigning the kids middle-class roles: boys doing boy things, and girls (even worse!) doing girl things." And she had no objection to letting her illustrator know how she felt. "God forbid, a boy should jump rope!" she told him.[11] Sendak later went back to his drawing board and made some hasty changes.

Too Many Books

With so many books being published, both good and not-so-good, when the award-winning books may not, in retrospect, have been the best choices for a given year, *Madeline's Rescue* (1953) by Ludwig Bemelmans edged out Krauss's *A Very Special House* (1953), illustrated by Maurice Sendak, for the 1954 Caldecott Medal. The Krauss-Sendak collaboration was highly innovative, however, while Bemelmans wrote a story that purported to be about Madeline but was actually about a dog called Genevieve. *A Tree Is Nice* (1956) by Janet May Udry, illustrated by Mark Simont, was awarded the 1957 Caldecott Medal. Though it is a satisfying effort, it was Margaret Wise Brown and Ruth Krauss who first established the market for this type of poetic essay and *A Tree Is Nice* seems a pale imitation. Caldecott runner-up *Anatole* (1956) by Eve Titus, illustrated by Paul Galdone, has a more developed story line, as it introduces an anthropomorphic and rather sophisticated mouse in Paris who finds a way to give and take in the human world, thereby assuring himself and his fellow mice a lifetime source of food and safety.

The 1952 Newbery Medal was awarded to Eleanor Estes for *Ginger Pye* (1951), although it is not her best effort. The story tends to ramble and to repeat scenes, change viewpoints, and offer predictable solutions when the Pye children's dog, Ginger, is kidnapped. Sidney Taylor's *All-of-a-Kind Family* (1951) is, in retrospect, a more laudable effort and was the first book to explore religious ethnicity in a middle-grade novel. The story relates the day-by-day routine of a Jewish family in New York City at the turn of the century, with emphasis on the individual personalities of the five little girls in the family.

Beverly Cleary, author of *Henry Huggins* (1950), created a cast of characters that have become recognizable throughout the world over the past 40-plus years, but Cleary did not receive a Newbery Medal until 1984. Cleary's Henry, Beatrice Quimby (Beezus) and her younger sister Ramona, Otis Spofford, Ribsy the dog, and Ralph the mouse have a timeless appeal. Where Carolyn Haywood's Betsy books acknowledged the simple daily routine of her middle-grade audience and Estes tried to interject humor into her fiction, Cleary went one step further and allowed her characters to muddle through and make mistakes. Their shortcomings were, however, born of childlike logic and good intentions gone awry through inexperience. The child, in American society, was taken off the pedestal by Beverly Cleary and given honest human attributes.

Much of the charm of Cleary's books is due to the way in which the illustrations by Louis Darling bring Cleary's words to life. With a few strokes of the pen, he created exuberant, realistic representations of the characters, and his efforts have not been duplicated since his death in 1970. Alan Tiegreen went on to create a different look, less energetic and more blunt, though still humorous, but it will always be the Darling illustrations that exemplify Cleary's books.

The artistic development of Cleary's characters by Darling was born of great affection, and he wrote her to say, "Henry Huggins and Ribsy, Beezus, Ramona, and all the others have taken their place in a very special circle of esteemed friends which can be added to, unfortunately, only once in a great while. Thank you for writing about them."[12] Both Darling and his wife were especially enamored of Ramona and expressed this preference as early as 1954, although Cleary didn't write a book especially about her until *Ramona the Pest* in 1968.

Just as Beverly Cleary achieved a breakthrough in capturing the essence of the middle-grade child in a way that all children could appreciate, so Sydney Taylor achieved another breakthrough in acknowledging Jewish family life and religious observances for the first time in children's literature in a series of books about a family living on the East Side of New York City at the turn of the century. The first book, *All-of-a-Kind Family* (1951), eased into Jewish observances gradually, with the first reference on page 37 of Taylor's book, where Yom Kippur is mentioned but not explained. The story continues throughout the year to describe different Jewish ceremonies including Yom Kippur, as part of routine family life.

Joseph Krumgold was awarded not one but two Newbery Medals, the first in 1954 for *And Now Miguel* (1953) and the second in 1960 for *Onion John* (1959), a story about a homeless man and the boy who befriends him. Both were extremely insightful novels deserving of awards, but Dorothy Sterling's *Mary Jane* (1959), a fictional account of the integration effort in the public schools that created so much conflict in the Fifties, wasn't recognized by the Newbery Committee. Her book, unfortunately out of print, remains perceptive even now, and it certainly opened the door for the authors of the Sixties who dared explore taboo subjects.

While the books recognized by the Caldecott and Newbery committees tended to reflect the veneer of complacency that marked the Fifties, beneath the surface chances were being taken in children's book publishing. Not all award-winning books were bland; some reflected the new awareness that would mark the 1960s as being a time of social revolution. Elizabeth Yates acknowledged the unconscionable exploitation of Africans as slaves in this country in the Newbery-winning biography, *Amos Fortune, Free Man* (1950), even though Amos himself is never mistreated and is almost immediately offered his freedom. In Meindert DeJong's *Wheel on the School* (1954) and Elizabeth Speare's *The Witch of Blackbird Pond* (1958), both Newbery Award books, a disabled character is given an important role, and in *The House of Sixty Fathers* (1956), a Newbery Honor book, readers were made aware for the first time of how Americans might appear to another culture, in this case to the Chinese.

Both Jean George, whose *My Side of the Mountain* (1959) was a Newbery Honor book, and Joseph Krumgold explored the complications of trying to lead a simple life in a highly developed society. In George's book, 12-year-old Sam leaves home to live in the wilderness but loses his pioneering spirit when he realizes his self-imposed isolation has been replaced by domestic complacency—he finds himself building a guest house for family and friends.

In *Onion John*, Krumgold introduced homelessness in a children's book long before it became a social issue in America. In it, Andy Rusch, age 12, admires the man known as Onion John, who has made himself a shelter from piled-up stones on Hessian Hill and survives by selling the onions and other vegetables he grows. But a well-meaning effort by Andy's father to bring John into the community simply doesn't work, and, when Andy has to decide whether to believe in Onion John or accept his father's values, which make more sense to him, the decision forever marks his future. Both authors displayed great perception regarding a person's desire to be free from the shackles of civilization in a world that had progressed too far to allow it, a desire that would make itself known throughout the United States in the Sixties, in some cases by whole families trying to leave technology behind.

CHRONOLOGICAL BIBLIOGRAPHY 1950–1959

Cleary, Beverly. *Henry Huggins*, illtd. Louis Darling. New York: Morrow, 1950; New York: Avon, 1990. (Realistic Fiction/Chapter Book/Humor)

Cleary captured the essence of childhood better than any other writer of middle-grade fiction. Henry Huggins is a rather serious youngster who always means well but somehow manages to find himself involved in one dilemma after another. Each chapter of this book builds to a precarious climax, as Henry finds a stray dog, names him Ribsy and tries to bring him home on the bus, decides to buy guppies and watches them multiply beyond reason, loses a friend's football and has to earn money to buy a new one, tries to avoid being chosen for the Christmas play and is given the lead, and, finally, enters Ribsy in a pet show, which leads to the worst dilemma of all.

Duvoisin, Roger. *Petunia*. New York: Knopf, 1950, 1962. Reprinted in Duvoisin's *Petunia the Silly Goose Stories* (New York: Knopf, 1987). (Fantasy/Picture Book/Animal)

Anthropomorphic but never transgressing her goose boundaries, Petunia is a liberated female, born in the Fifties with a vision of the Nineties. She might be somewhat arrogant at times but she also is capable of rising above her mistakes. When she finds a book, she's convinced that just by owning it she is wise, and her positive bearing convinces her friends of her brilliance. Her advice, however, causes more problems than it solves until Petunia finally realizes it's not enough to own a book; she must know how to read it and, even more, to understand what she is reading. No problem for Petunia; she immediately starts learning the alphabet, preparing herself for a lifetime of academia.

Lewis, C. S. The Chronicles of Narnia, published by Macmillan in the United States, include: *The Lion, the Witch and the Wardrobe*, 1950; *Prince Caspian*, 1951; *The Voyage of the Dawn Treader*, 1952; *The Silver Chair*, 1953; *The Horse and His Boy*, 1954; *The Magician's Nephew*, 1955; *The Last Battle*, 1956. (Fantasy)

Although these books can be read and enjoyed in any order, Lewis suggests that *The Magician's Nephew* should be first, followed by *The Lion, the Witch and the Wardrobe* and *The Horse and His Boy*, then *Prince Caspian*, *The Voyage of the Dawn Treader*, *The Silver Chair* and *The Last Battle*.[13] If read in this order, the land of Narnia, as well as references to the faun Mr. Tumnus, to Aslan the lion, to the evil White Witch, and to the lamp post as a beacon, have a familiarity that ties the series together from one book to the next. But each book is satisfying in itself, as four children, Peter, Susan, Edmund, and Lucy Pevensie, become the saviors of Narnia, with good ultimately triumphing over evil.

Lindgren, Astrid. *Pippi Longstocking*, tr. Florence Lamborn. New York: Viking, 1950; New York: Puffin, 1988. Also, *Pippi Goes on Board*, tr. Florence Lamborn. (New York: Viking, 1957; New York: Puffin, 1977); *Pippi in the South Seas*, tr. Gerry Bothmer. (New York: Viking, 1959; New York: Puffin, 1977). (Fantasy/Tall Tales/Sweden)

These books, translated from the Swedish, reflect an all-American sense of fun but without the American propensity for avoiding controversial behavior that might lead to adult disapproval. Pippi Longstocking is a free spirit, a little girl whose mother is dead and whose father is lost at sea. Pippi manages to take care of herself without adult supervision and even convinces the authorities that she is just fine on her own. Her two friends, Tommy and Annika, who live next door, join Pippi in her adventures and are continually amazed at the things she says and does. Even though the translated text in the first two titles is sometimes awkward—*Pippi in the South Seas* is a much smoother translation—Pippi's actions reveal the relaxed mores of her Swedish origin, and she continues generation after generation to appeal to American children who live in a more repressed society.

Milhous, Katherine. *The Egg Tree*. New York: Scribners, 1950. CALDECOTT MEDAL. (Picture Book/Regional/Holiday)

Pennsylvania Dutch folk art illustrates this bland and overwritten story of a little girl looking for colored eggs at Easter time and finding instead those her grandmother had painted years before. This discovery leads to the decoration of a small Easter egg tree, which becomes a much larger tree the following Easter.

Seuss, Dr. (pseud. of Theodor Seuss Geisel). *Yertle the Turtle and Other Stories*. New York: Random House, 1950, 1985. (Fantasy/Picture Book/Humor)

Yertle the turtle wants to rule a kingdom larger than his small pond and decides that the higher he is, the more he can see, and the more he can see, the more powerful he'll be. But the turtles stacked up to be his throne are dependent for balance on the bottom turtle, Mack, whose smallest inadvertent action finally topples Yertle's kingdom.

Yates, Elizabeth. *Amos Fortune, Free Man*, illtd. Nora Unwin. New York: Dutton, 1950. NEWBERY MEDAL. (Informational/Biography/Black American)

At-mun and Ath-mun, son and daughter of the king of the At-mun-shi tribe in Africa, are separated when At-mun is captured by white slavers and transported by ship to America. At-mun, 15 years old when he leaves Africa, is called Amos by his kind owners and then earns the name Amos Fortune. Through all the years, he never stops searching for his sister, who was born lame and would always need care, but he doesn't find her. Instead, he devotes his life to caring for others, and, when he accepts his freedom at the age of 60 and has his own tanning business, spends his savings again and again to free others. This admirable man was born in 1710 and died in 1801. His life was a testament to his royal blood, and this book, awarded a Newbery Medal in 1951, is a testament to the African race at a time in American history when segregation was taken for granted.

Estes, Eleanor. *Ginger Pye*. New York: Harcourt, 1951; San Diego: Harcourt, 1990. NEWBERY MEDAL. (Realistic Fiction/Family)

Unlike English family stories, practical and understated, Estes allows her imagination free rein, even though the story at times spirals out of control and has to be brought back with great effort on the part of the author.

> A tall boy named Sam Doody, who lived a few doors away in their block, came and knocked at the kitchen door. Sam Doody was about fifteen years old and he was so tall that every time any little boy or girl met him they always asked him how the air was up there . . . Sam Doody and Judge Ball and a man named Mr. Tuttle were the three tallest people in the church. Sitting, they all towered above everybody else. Standing, Sam Doody and Judge Ball still towered. But Mr. Tuttle shrank and mingled with the congregation for his tallness was only from the waist up. From the waist down he was very short. Anyway Sam Doody was tall from top to toe . . .[14]

Ginger Pye is the fox terrier puppy that Jerry Pye purchases with the dollar he earns by cleaning the church for Sam Doody. When Ginger follows Jerry's scent to school and climbs the fire escape to Jerry's classroom, holding in his mouth the pencil Jerry dropped on the way to school, Ginger is considered the smartest dog in the world. But then he is kidnapped, and Jerry and his sister Rachel are devastated. For the remainder of the book, they make an effort to find him and try to manage their lives without him, but things just won't ever be the same without Ginger. The reader is made aware of Ginger's location early on and the happy ending is predictable.

MacGregor, Ellen. *Miss Pickerell Goes to Mars*. New York: Whittlesey House, 1951. Also, *Miss Pickerell Goes Undersea* (New York: McGraw-Hill, 1953). Both are illustrated by Paul Galdone. (Science Fiction)

The appeal of these books lies in the use of up-to-date scientific developments in the midst of humorous nonsense and unfettered imagination. In *Miss Pickerell Goes to Mars*, Miss Pickerell, who lives in a small country community with her cow, has no intention of going to Mars but makes the best of it when she ends up in a rocket ship that is traveling there. In *Miss Pickerell Goes Undersea*, she travels under the ocean in an atomic-powered submarine and is introduced to underwater television and sonar equipment as well as deep sea diving.

Will (William Lipkind) and Nicolas (Mordvinoff). *Finders Keepers*. New York: Harcourt, 1951; San Diego: Harcourt, 1989. CALDECOTT MEDAL. (Picture Book)

This simple story of two dogs attempting to take possession of one bone is humorous and has appeal for the preschooler, but the award-winning illustrations, quaint and colorful, might seem old-fashioned to adults.

Taylor, Sydney. *All-of-a-Kind Family*. New York: Follett, 1951; New York: BDD (Dell Yearling), 1989. (Realistic Fiction/Jewish American)

Ella, who is 12, Henny, Charlotte, Sarah, and Gertie, four, are like steps-and-stairs in age and size, and because they are all dressed alike in their crisp, white pinafores, dark dresses, and high-topped shoes, some people call them the all-of-a-kind family. Papa, who loves them all, sometimes wishes there were at least one boy in the family. But the five little girls love to visit Papa, who owns a junk shop in their lower East Side neighborhood, and make their weekly visits to the library and stop at Mrs. Blumberg's candy store on the rare occasions when they have a penny to spend. Each child has a distinctive personality, with Henny the loner, Sarah the most independent, Charlotte and Ella the most practical, and Gertie precocious and eager to do everything her sisters do. With very little money and a great deal of love, these children learn responsibility and family tradition in a close-knit Jewish community.

Brown, Margaret Wise. *Mister Dog: The Dog Who Belonged to Himself*, illtd. Garth Williams. New York: Simon & Schuster (Golden Books), 1952; New York: Western Publishing (Golden Books), 1992 (in *Three Best Loved Tales*). (Fantasy/Picture Book)

This charming story is Brown's tribute to her dog, Crispian, and to her own realization of self-worth, as the self-possessed Mister Dog meets a self-possessed little boy and it is decided that the two are meant to be friends and live together in mutual love. Garth Williams modeled the "two-story dog house" after Brown's own house, Cobble Court.

Clark, Ann Nolan. *Secret of the Andes*, illtd. Jean Charlot. New York: Viking, 1952; New York: Puffin, 1976. NEWBERY MEDAL. (Realistic Fiction/Cultural/Peru/Incan)

This story set in Peru is only one of Clark's many stories about various Indian tribes. Other books are set in Guatemala, Ecuador, North America (Navaho), and Costa Rica. In this award-winning novel, Cusi is a young Incan boy who has never left the valley in which he lives until his uncle, Chuto, takes him on a mysterious journey intended to fulfill the boy's destiny. Once Cusi has been shown the way, he knows he must again make the trip, this time alone. The contrast between the Indian population and the Spanish population in the city of Cuzco is brought into play with Cusi's Incan pride and love of his llamas not at all shared by those Spanish residents who make the rules for the city. Jean Charlot's bold, strong illustrations reflect Indian pride and stature.

Frank, Anne. *Anne Frank: The Diary of a Young Girl.* New York: Doubleday, 1952; New York: BDD, 1995 (Special Anniversary Edition). (Informational/Autobiographical)

Originally published in Holland in 1947, the words of Anne Frank, an adolescent Jewish girl who spent the years 1942 through August of 1944 with her family and others in a secret hideaway, were translated and published in England and the United States eight years after her death at Auschwitz. Anne was 13 when the Nazi threat sent her and her family into hiding, and she put her experiences in a diary she had received for her birthday in June 1942. The diary was found and published because of its honest commentary about a time in history that continues to be under contention.

Krauss, Ruth. *A Hole Is to Dig: A First Book of First Definitions*, illtd. Maurice Sendak. New York: Harper, 1952, 1989. Also, *A Very Special House* (1953, 1990) and *I'll Be You and You Be Me* (1954, 1990). New York: Harper. (Picture Book/Concept)

A Hole Is to Dig, the first collaboration between Krauss and Sendak, offers a fresh, new concept in picture books by creating both text and pictures that directly reflect the way children think and act. In *A Very Special House*, a small boy sings a song to himself—"Oh, it's just a house for me Me ME"—and Sendak, with unrestrained imagination, illustrates the song and the imaginary house. "Oh, it's root in the moodle of my head head head," the little boy sings, and Sendak shows us an active boy in blue overalls who is very, very pleased with himself as "bung," his song ends and he exits the scene. *I'll Be You and You Be Me* is an interactive book about friendship with lively children acting out the scenes.

Ward, Lynd. *The Biggest Bear.* Boston: Houghton Mifflin, 1952, 1973. CALDECOTT MEDAL. (Picture Book/Regional)

When Johnny Orchard brings home a bear, it isn't one he has shot, as is the case for all of his neighbors. Instead, it's a small live bear cub that grows into a very large bear and causes so many problems that it becomes necessary to send him back into the wild. But the bear doesn't want to go and keeps coming back. Just when the only recourse for Johnny is to shoot his bear, a piece of maple sugar saves the day, and Johnny is able to visit his bear in a zoo.

White, E. B. *Charlotte's Web*, illtd. Garth Williams. New York: Harper, 1952, 1974. (Fantasy)

Although this book was not chosen as the 1953 Newbery award-winner, it has become a staple for middle-grade children who want more than the dry vocabulary of the basal reader or even the mediocre vocabulary of some of the more mundane titles of the Fifties. It has also become a favorite of teachers, who read it aloud in the classroom to show the richly patterned tapestry of language in literature. Charlotte is a spider who offers advice to Wilbur the pig and saves him from the axe only to die herself. The saving factor is the legacy she leaves behind.

Bemelmans, Ludwig. *Madeline's Rescue*. New York: Viking, 1953; New York: Puffin, 1993. CALDECOTT MEDAL. (Poetry/Picture Book)

This addition to the Madeline series isn't really about Madeline at all. It's about a dog called Genevieve who becomes a much loved addition to Miss Clavell's school in Paris, where Madeline is only one of 12 little girls who all look alike.

Freeman, Lydia and Don. *Pet of the Met*. New York: Viking, 1953; New York: Puffin, 1988. (Picture Story Book/Fantasy/Animal)

Don Freeman's bright, cheerful chalk drawings complement wife Lydia's sophisticated but simple text in a story that showcases the Metropolitan Opera House and Mozart's *The Magic Flute*. This introduction to classical music is a first in books for children and also the Freemans' first book.

Krumgold, Joseph. *And Now Miguel*, illtd. Jean Charlot. New York: Crowell, 1953; New York: Harper, 1987. NEWBERY MEDAL. (Realistic Fiction/Cultural)

Just as *Secret of the Andes* celebrates the Indian culture of the southern half of this continent, *And Now Miguel* is one of the few books written for children that celebrates the Spanish imprint in the southern part of the United States. Miguel is a middle child who questions his identity. His father never seems to pay attention to him as a person, never seems to understand what Miguel is trying to say, and until he does, Miguel will never fulfill his dream of going to the Sangre de Cristo Mountains to bring their sheep to summer feeding grounds. When he prays to San Ysidro, his wish comes true, but

Miguel finds there is a price to pay. The details of everyday life in a sheep-raising family and the close relationships between members of the family create an indelible portrait of the Chavez family in Taos, New Mexico.

Norton, Mary. *The Borrowers.* New York: Harcourt, 1953; San Diego: Harcourt, 1989. Also, *The Borrowers Afield* (New York: Harcourt, 1955; San Diego: Harcourt, 1990) and *The Borrowers Afloat* (New York: Harcourt, 1959; San Diego: Harcourt, 1990). All three books are illustrated by Beth and Joe Krush. (Fantasy)

The Clock family—Pod, Homily, and little Arrietty—are part of a vanishing breed of little people called "Borrowers," who have been made forever real in this award-winning English fantasy. If anyone has ever lost a needle, a safety pin, a pencil, or a matchbox and has had to replace it, it's very likely there are Borrowers in the house. When young Kate loses her crochet hook, old Mrs. May recalls a strange story about the Borrowers and how her brother had befriended them when he was a small boy. When Mrs. May's brother, to his delight, discovers them, he inadvertently brings them to the attention of the housekeeper, Mrs. Driver, who sets about to exterminate them. The Clock family lives beneath the grandfather's clock, hence their name, and has papered their walls with old letters rescued from the trash, hung pictures of Queen Victoria as a girl, which were actually borrowed postage stamps, and created a chest of drawers from matchboxes. Each generation of Borrowers becomes smaller than the last, and, because of their size, no matter if they are in the house, banished to a field, or set afloat, the dangers they face are greatly magnified and require imaginative ingenuity in order to be overcome.

Rockwell, Thomas. *How to Eat Fried Worms*, illtd. Emily McCully. New York: Franklin Watts, 1953; New York: Dell, 1992. (Chapter Book/Humor)

Thomas Rockwell's humorous approach combined with Emily McCully's clever illustrations offers a whole book about eating worms, in this case as a means of winning a bet. Billy has to eat a worm a day for 15 days to win a $50 bet, and if Alan, who has the money in his savings account but doesn't want to use it, can't find a way to make Billy forfeit the bet, he'll have to admit to his father what he has done. Here is a book that appeals directly to middle-grade readers, who have been known to love grossness more than anything.

Boston, Lucy. *The Children of Green Knowe*. New York: Harcourt, 1954; San Diego: Harcourt, 1989. (Time Fantasy)

There is magic in this story of a boy named Tolly who visits his great-grandmother Granny Oldknow at her home called Green Knowe, an estate steeped in generations of English history, so layered by time that Tolly is able to bring to life the three children who lived there 400 years earlier. Tolly shares with them all the things that mattered to them in a way satisfying to them all, even Granny, and to any reader willing to believe in magic.

Cameron, Eleanor. *The Wonderful Flight to the Mushroom Planet*. Boston: Little, Brown, 1954, 1988. (Science Fiction/Fantasy)

David and his friend Chuck are offered an opportunity to travel through space three years before Sputnik became a reality and long before the Americans landed on the moon. The book was written by Cameron to fulfill a request by her son David, and the research she undertook to validate the story makes believers of us all. Naturally, there is a planet called Basidium-X, and, naturally, the two boys are able to build a space ship, with the help of Mr. Tyco Bass, that will take them there so they can save that planet's population, assisted by a chicken named Mrs. Pennyfeather. This is the first of many books about this unusual planet, which is so real it clearly demanded sequels.

Dalgleish, Alice. *The Courage of Sarah Noble*. New York: Scribner, 1954; New York: Macmillan, 1991. (Realistic Fiction/Historical)

This short novel is easy to read but lacks substance, even though it is based on fact. Sarah accompanies her father to the Connecticut wilderness, where he is to build a house for the family and Sarah is to serve as his cook. Sarah's mother must stay behind in the Massachusetts colony with the baby, who is sickly, and the rest of the children are to stay with her until the house is completed. When Sarah's father finishes the house and goes back to Massachusetts during the winter to pick up the rest of the family, Sarah stays behind, living with an Indian family until her father returns. Because this story is so simply written, this amazing decision on the part of Sarah's father to leave his young daughter in such a primitive setting lacks conviction. In addition, Sarah shows no character development, and the text offers minimal detail about life in an Indian village.

DeJong, Meindert. *The Wheel on the School*, illtd. Maurice Sendak. New York: Harper, 1954, 1972. NEWBERY MEDAL. (Realistic Fiction/

Cultural/Netherlands)

Although this story begins slowly, it builds in suspense as the children in a small Dutch fishing village attempt to bring storks to their village. First, they must determine why there are no longer any storks in Shora, then find a way to bring them back to nest. With the cooperation of their teacher, and later with the help of the villagers, the six boys and one girl who make up the student body of the school are determined to succeed in their quest. While involved in this effort, they become acquainted with the old and the lame of the village and are surprised to discover these people have exceptionally worthwhile attributes. When they determine that a wagon wheel on the pointed roof of the school will attract storks, the apparently simple task of putting one there becomes more and more complicated as the children try without success to find a discarded wagon wheel. The effort slowly builds to a breathtaking climax in the midst of a terrible storm, as the whole village becomes involved in bringing the storks to Shora.

Eager, Edward. *Half Magic*. New York: Harcourt, 1954; San Diego: Harcourt (Odyssey), 1982. (Fantasy)

As Eager introduces the four children in this story, he quickly refers to the fantasies of his idol, E. Nesbit, as favorite books of these children. When Mark, Katherine, Jane, and Martha discover magic of their own with a coin that makes wishes come true, they, like the children in Nesbit's *Five Children and It* (1902), discover that wishes have a way of going awry. In this case, only half of the wish comes true unless the holder of the coin wishes for twice as much. No matter how hard they try, the children will forget and make thoughtless wishes. Things have a way of balancing themselves, however, and after a few perilous adventures, the children find themselves with a stepfather and a new appreciation of family life in the best American tradition.

Perrault, Charles. *Cinderella, or the Little Glass Slipper*, tr. and illtd. Marcia Brown. New York: Scribner, 1954. CALDECOTT MEDAL. (Fantasy/Fairy/Picture Book)

This was the first of the picture books utilizing old, well-known fairy tales in order to showcase an artist's talent, with little importance given to the author's writing style, which was not always equal to the artistic ability displayed. Brown uses a soft, somewhat ethereal artistic style in this picture storybook, and more text than really necessary is used to tell this familiar fairy tale.

Tolkien, J. R. R. *The Lord of the Rings Trilogy*, consisting of: *The Fellowship of the Ring* (Boston: Houghton Mifflin, 1954, 1992); *The Two Towers* (Boston: Houghton Mifflin, 1955, 1992); and *The Return of the King* (Boston: Houghton Mifflin, 1956, 1992). (Fantasy)

Fans of *The Hobbit* eagerly sought *The Fellowship of the Ring* and followed *The Lord of the Rings* trilogy to its completion. In Tolkien's carefully developed otherworld, Hobbit Bilbo Baggins's nephew, Frodo, and his loyal friends, Sam, Pippin, and Merry, set out on a journey to save the Shire from destruction. Frodo must deliver the One Ring, given to him by Bilbo, to a place that will keep it from being used for evil. During the journey, he must also have the strength to resist the ring's spell. *The Hobbit* is an immediate adventure that builds quickly to a climax and offers a satisfying denouement. *The Lord of the Rings* is a more gradual study, sometimes bogged down by detail, more often building in suspense, a trilogy that calls for more than one reading.

Johnson, Crockett. *Harold and the Purple Crayon*. New York: Harper, 1955, 1981. (Picture Book/Concept)

When Harold decides to go for a walk in the moonlight, he needs a moon and something to walk on. With his purple crayon he creates line drawings of a moon and a path and is on his way. Whatever he needs on his travels he creates with his purple crayon. When he inadvertently draws himself into an ocean, he creates a boat. When he falls off a mountain, he makes a hot air balloon, and when he can't find his bedroom window, he remembers it was right around the moon and, sure enough, it is. Harold makes his bed, climbs in, and as Harold goes to sleep, the purple crayon drops on the floor.

Langstaff, John, ed. *Frog Went A-Courtin'*, illtd. Feodor Rojankovsky. New York: Harcourt, 1955. CALDECOTT MEDAL. (Picture Book/Folk Song)

This old Scottish ballad is given an American personality, with a setting in the Appalachian Mountains, in Feodor Rojankovsky's rendition of John Langstaff's version of this song. The book is oversize, colorful, and delightfully busy, especially when the wedding of Mister Frog and Miss Mouse is unexpectedly turned into chaos.

Latham, Jean Lee. *Carry On, Mr. Bowditch*. Boston: Houghton Mifflin, 1955, 1973. NEWBERY MEDAL. (Informational/Historical/Biographical)

This historical biography tells the story of Nathaniel Bowditch, who wrote "The New American Practical Navigator" before he was 30 years old. Latham animatedly portrays Bowditch's colorful adventures and travels, making nonfiction appealing to the young.

Sandburg, Carl. *Prairie-Town Boy*, illtd. Joe Krush. New York: Harcourt, 1955; San Diego: Harcourt, 1990. (Informational/Autobiographical)

Excerpted from Sandburg's autobiography, *Always the Young Strangers*, the young reader is introduced to the author of *Rootabaga Stories* (1922) and *Abe Lincoln Grows Up* (1928). The book covers Sandburg's regional background and the many jobs he held but makes no mention of his literary career. The excerpt ends at the point where Sandburg decides he wants an education and enrolls in college, but his experiences up to that point ultimately found their way into his work: his childhood in Illinois in the late 1800s, his growing interest in history, especially of the United States, his many odd jobs (delivering newspapers, working at a pharmacy, a boathouse, an icehouse, and as jack-of-all-trades at a racetrack), his love of theater, and his fascination with Chicago.

Thompson, Kay. *Eloise*, illtd. Hilary Knight. New York: Simon and Schuster, 1955. (Picture Book/Urban)

Is there anyone who has never heard of Eloise, who lives at the Plaza in New York City and infiltrates every area of the hotel at one time or another? She is a distinctively precocious child who makes the best of a lonely life, and Hilary Knight's animated illustrations of Eloise and her routine would be self-explanatory even without text. Eloise stays at the Plaza because her parents are too busy to take care of her, and she has a nanny, a day maid, a night maid, and a tutor, as well as a dog and a turtle, but she doesn't have any friends her own age. Because Eloise is six years old, this book has ended up on children's lists, but at the time it was written it was far more sophisticated than any other children's book and has turned out to be more educational for adults who have forgotten what children are like than for children who already know.

Butterworth, Oliver. *The Enormous Egg*, illtd. Louis Darling. Boston: Little, Brown, 1956, 1993. (Fantasy/Picture Book/Dinosaur)

Butterworth's story and Louis Darling's illustrations, both unexpectedly believable, managed to devise the ultimate dinosaur fantasy and, until Michael Crichton's computer-oriented *Jurassic Park*, no one was able to match it. Even now, it has humor, pathos, and sufficient technical detail to make it seem real. Nate Twitchell, who nurtures the enormous egg and watches his triceratops, whom he names Uncle Beazley, hatch and grow larger than life, must finally give him up to government authorities in Washington, D.C. Fortunately, Nate is invited to Washington to spend time with his dinosaur; unfortunately, the dinosaur outgrows Washington and can't stay even at the Washington Zoo because the government decides it costs too much to feed him. Senator Granderson proposes legislation to prohibit dinosaurs in America: "no un-American, outmoded creatures from foreign places." But Nate goes on television to plead for Uncle Beazley, and the public, with true American spirit, denies the senator's legislation and contributes enough money to maintain Uncle Beazley at the zoo.

DeJong, Meindert. *The House of Sixty Fathers*, illtd. Maurice Sendak. New York: Harper, 1956, 1987. HANS CHRISTIAN ANDERSEN AWARD, 1962.[15] (Realistic Fiction/World War II/China)

DeJong, who was born in the Netherlands and came to the United States when he was eight years old, was awarded a Newbery Medal in 1955 for *The Wheel on the School* (1954), but it is this moving story set in China that becomes indelibly imprinted on the reader, with Sendak's illustrations unevenly but emotionally rendered. During World War II, DeJong was stationed in China and became devoted to a small Chinese boy who had been "adopted" by DeJong's outfit, the "sixty fathers" in the title. *The House of Sixty Fathers* is a fictionalized account of this boy's very real experiences when he was separated from his family and found himself behind Japanese lines. From the moment Tien Pao awakes to find himself drifting without oars on his family's sampan, all alone except for his pet pig, until he manages to reach neutral territory once more, this story carries the reader with no letup in suspense. The book was not even recognized as an Honor Book by the Newbery Committee, but in 1962 DeJong was the first American to be awarded the Hans Christian Andersen Medal.

Titus, Eve. *Anatole*, illtd. Paul Galdone. New York: McGraw-Hill, 1956; New York: Bantam, 1990. (Fantasy/Picture Book/Animal)

Galdone's button-eyed Parisian mouse, Anatole, travels about the city on his bicycle with his friend Gaston looking for leftovers in people's homes and discovers that mice are not highly regarded by humans. He considers his honor compromised and vows to change people's attitudes toward mice. He does this by setting up a system in the Duval Cheese Factory to judge various cheeses. Then he not only labels the cheeses according to quality but also adds recommendations on how to make them better. This is Titus's first in a series of seven delightful books about Anatole, First Vice-President in Charge of Cheese-Tasting at the Duval Factory.

Udry, Janice May. *A Tree Is Nice*, illtd. Marc Simont. New York: Harper, 1956, 1987. CALDECOTT MEDAL. (Picture Book/Concept)

This essay about different ways of defining a tree is brought into the realm of the child by Marc Simont's colorful illustrations. The text lacks the playfulness of Ruth Krauss's *A Hole Is to Dig*, and Marc Simont's sketches occasionally emulate Maurice Sendak's group scenes, but though this book lacks the innovative qualities of the Krauss-Sendak collaborations and perhaps isn't the best choice for a Caldecott, it does offer a pleasant interlude between parent and child.

Zion, Gene. *Harry the Dirty Dog*, illtd. Margaret Bloy Graham. New York: Harper, 1956. (Picture Book/Animal)

There is something about dirt that greatly appeals to children and dogs. But when Harry the dog gets so dirty his family doesn't recognize him, being dirty and hating baths are all of a sudden not so appealing anymore. It's much nicer to be loved even if it takes a bath to turn things around.

Keith, Harold. *Rifles for Watie*, illtd. Peter Burchard. New York: Crowell, 1957; New York: Harper, 1991. NEWBERY MEDAL. (Realistic Fiction/Historical/Civil War)

This is the first book since *Red Badge of Courage* (1895) to offer a candid portrait of the Civil War. Where *Red Badge* basically covers only one incident and the effect it has on a young boy, *Rifles for Watie* presents a specific area of fighting not usually covered in Civil War history: the Kansas, Arkansas, Oklahoma territories where battles were fought between Stand Watie's Cherokee Indians fighting for the Confederacy and the several tribes in the same area whose loyalties were with the Union forces. The story is told by a 17-year-old, white Union soldier, who grows up quickly as he observes and participates in the carnage of war. There is no attempt here to gloss over the imperfections of human nature or even to take sides. War, Keith shows us, is a dirty business.

McCloskey, Robert. *Time of Wonder*. New York: Viking, 1957. CALDECOTT MEDAL. (Poetry/Picture Book/Regional)

"Where do hummingbirds go in a hurricane," the child wonders in this poem celebrating the coast of Maine and McCloskey's love of land and sea on a special island in summer. Pastel watercolors bring to life the sand, trees, flowers, birds, and children in this simple, comfortable poetic essay. The story builds with the approaching summer storm, which leaves an altered landscape in its wake.

MacDonald, Betty. *Mrs. Piggle-Wiggle*, illtd. Hilary Knight. Philadelphia: Lippincott, 1957; New York: Harper, 1985. (Chapter Book/Tall Tales/Humor)

Mrs. Piggle-Wiggle's cures for the behavior problems of the children in her neighborhood are drastic but effective. All the children love to go to Mrs. Piggle-Wiggle's upside-down house, and she never has any problems with them there, but their parents aren't so fortunate. In a repetitive sequence of events, various parents call other parents to try and solve their child's unexpectedly bad behavior. Each time, their efforts lead to Mrs. Piggle-Wiggle, who always has the answer, whether the problem is not putting toys away, not going to bed or not wanting to take a bath. Mrs. Piggle-Wiggle suggests the radish cure for Patsy, who won't bathe, allowing her to get dirtier and dirtier until, when her parents plant radish seeds in her layers of grime, she actually grows radishes.

Minarik, Else Homelund. *Little Bear*, illtd. Maurice Sendak. New York: Harper, 1957. Also, *Father Bear Comes Home*, illtd. Maurice Sendak. New York: Harper, 1959. New York: Harper, 1992 (Boxed Set). (Chapter Book/Animal/Family)

The charm of these simple stories, with their minimal text, lies in the warm, comfortable portrayal of family life and the subtle communication between child and adult. Sendak's illustrations, so different from the frolicking children in his collaborations with Ruth Krauss, express the security felt by Little Bear as he interacts with members of his family.

Seuss, Dr. (pseud. of Theodor Seuss Geisel). *The Cat in the Hat*. Boston: Houghton Mifflin, 1957; New York: Random House, 1957, 1987. (Fantasy/Easy Reader)

As precarious as the Little Bear stories are comforting, Seuss appeals to children's inner mischievous sensibilities as he introduces two children to the antics of The Cat in the Hat, who comes to their house and creates chaos on a rainy afternoon. In his own inimitable style, he utilizes nonsensical verse to tell the story with a limited number of words.

———. *How the Grinch Stole Christmas*. New York: Random House, 1957. (Fantasy/Picture Book/Holiday)

The Whos, introduced in *Horton Hears a Who* (1954), try to deal with the Scrooge-like Grinch, who hates Christmas and makes up his mind to stop it from coming to Whoville by confiscating all the presents and food and even the Christmas tree. But Christmas, he soon discovers, "doesn't come from a store. Maybe Christmas . . . perhaps . . . means a little bit more!" This is one of Seuss's most popular creations.

Brown, Margaret Wise. *The Dead Bird*, illtd. Remy Charlip. (Originally in *The Fish With the Deep Sea Smile* [1938], a collection by Brown.) New York: Scott, 1958; New York: Harper, 1989. (Picture Book/Animal/Death)

When a group of children find a dead bird, they decide to give it a funeral and bury it. Written without sentimentality, the children do what has to be done to put the bird to rest and then, "every day, until they forgot, they went and sang to their little dead bird and put fresh flowers on his grave." This story is a subtle contradiction of society's efforts to protect children from trauma through avoiding acknowledgment of death. Children are often far more capable of dealing with reality than adults are, as this book clearly indicates.

Cooney, Barbara. *Chanticleer and the Fox*, adapted from *The Canterbury Tales* by Geoffrey Chaucer. New York: Crowell, 1958; New York: Harper, 1982. CALDECOTT MEDAL. (Folk/Myth/Picture Book/Medieval)

A very simple incident from a Chaucer tale has been made a vehicle for Cooney's art. As such, it contains many levels of enjoyment for anyone who appreciates conscientious detail. This is the story of Chanticleer the rooster and his seven hens and how he is tricked by the fox who appeals to his ego. Chanticleer, however, manages to escape from the fox by using the same type of trickery used on him. In order to make the illustrations for this book, Barbara Cooney actually kept chickens in her studio for models and studied 14th-century illuminated manuscripts for inspiration. Every flower and ground cover shown in the book actually grew in Chaucer's time.

Hoff, Syd. *Danny and the Dinosaur*. New York: Harper, 1958, 1985. (Fantasy/Easy Reader/Dinosaur)

The fascination children have for dinosaurs became the theme of Syd Hoff's easy reader, as Danny visits a museum and discovers a dinosaur exhibit. His desire to play with a dinosaur becomes reality, and Danny spends a wonderful day showing off his dinosaur to the people in his town. This is the type of book that, because it looks so simple, makes it seem that anyone can write for children, but both text and illustrations say only as much as necessary to present the story in its simplest terms, an accomplishment that requires careful sculpting.

Speare, Elizabeth George. *The Witch of Blackbird Pond*. Boston: Houghton Mifflin, 1958; New York: Dell, 1978. NEWBERY MEDAL. (Realistic Fiction/Historical)

Rachel Field's *Calico Bush* (1931) was the story of 12-year-old Marguerite Ledoux, an indentured servant brought to America from France, who was suspected of being a witch because of her dark good looks and Catholicism. In *The Witch of Blackbird Pond*, which takes place in 1687, Kit Tyler is equally suspect because she is from Barbados, feels loyalty toward the English king, and has brightly colored clothing. Although her Puritan relatives accept her because they are her only surviving family, they and others in the community are disturbed by her free spirit. Her rebellion against the strict Puritan way of life results in her being accused of witchcraft. She is imprisoned and tried in court, with rescue coming from a most unlikely source. There is romance in this book, unusual in the 1950s, as Kit and her two female cousins look for true love.

George, Jean Craighead. *My Side of the Mountain*. New York: Dutton, 1959; New York: Puffin, 1991. (Realistic Fiction/Nature)

This is the first of Jean George's many books dealing with the environment. Twelve-year-old Sam Gribley loves nature. He reads everything he can find about it and finally decides to leave home, where he is one of nine children, and try to find his grandfather's farm in the Catskill Mountains. Sam, determined to live on the mountain, finds the site of the farm and then goes into the forest where he makes a home in a hollowed-out tree. He captures and trains a peregrine falcon to supply him with game, builds a fireplace in his tree with clay from the riverbank, makes flour by pounding nuts, and avoids people as best he can. It is, however, difficult to live an isolated life in a civilized world, and Sam finally has to give up his way of life after a year of success when he becomes the subject of newspaper articles and discovers he has become as civilized in his mountain home as he would be in any community.

Gregor, Arthur. *Animal Babies by Ylla*, photog. Ylla (pseud. of Camilla Koffler). New York: Harper, 1959. (Picture Book/Photographs/Concept)

The "mother and child" format of *Animal Babies by Ylla* offers a warm portrait of different animals in a series of black-and-white photos. But Arthur Gregor's text, though simple and to the point, lacks the imagination and verve of Margaret Wise Brown's text for Ylla's photographs in *They All Saw It* (1944).

Krumgold, Joseph. *Onion John*, illtd. Symeon Shimin. New York: Crowell, 1959; New York: Harper, 1987. NEWBERY MEDAL. (Realistic Fiction/Homelessness)

The term "young adult novel" was coined to describe the large number of children's books published in the 1970s that dealt with issues previously disregarded in books for the young. *Onion John* was a successful example of this format before it was labeled "young adult." Twelve-year-old Andy Rusch is fascinated with Onion John, a homeless man who lives on Hessian Hill in a shelter made from piled up stones, and the two strike up a warm friendship. John speaks with a strong European accent; most people cannot understand a word he says, but Andy understands him. Then Andy's father encourages John to become part of the community, and although Onion John is perfectly happy with the house he made himself, even organizes a group to build John a house. The result leads to chaos. John tries his best to please Andy's father, but he's just not used to plumbing and electricity, and the new house is inadvertently burned to the ground. He decides he can no longer live on Hessian Hill where he has had a good life growing vegetables and foraging in the town dump, and Andy, feeling responsible for everything that has happened, decides to run away with him. Andy, however, is beginning to grow up, and the acceptance of Onion John's sometimes bizarre ideas becomes harder and harder for him.

Lionni, Leo. *Little Blue and Little Yellow*, an Astor book. New York: Ivan Obolensky, 1959. (Picture Book/Concept)

This is the ultimate in conceptual art, with good friends Little Blue and Little Yellow, portrayed as blobs of color, hugging each other and turning green. At first, Little Blue's parents don't recognize him and Little Yellow's parents say: "You are not our little yellow—you are green." But when the two completely cry themselves into blue and yellow tears, the parents suddenly understand what happened. Lionni was the first to use collage to create picture book art.

Sterling, Dorothy. *Mary Jane*, illtd. Ernest Crichlow. New York: Doubleday, 1959. (Realistic Fiction/Black American)

This book says more about the 1950s than any other book written during those years of growing unrest. Norman Rockwell's poignant portrayal of a child of color entering a school formerly restricted to white students could have been an illustration for Sterling's book. Mary Jane Douglas chooses to enter seventh grade at Wilson High School because she has recently been given the right to do so and wants the best education she can get. But integration, she discovers, is more than giving her white classmates the opportunity to know her and discover she's not so different from them. The students and many of the teachers have stereotypical ideas about what it means to be "black," and Sterling portrays this exceptionally well. Mary Jane is invited to sing in the choir because "everyone knows her people have rhythm," but Mary Jane, like her grandfather, has never been able to carry a tune. Although the threat of violence calls for security measures, violence never materializes, but when Mary Jane makes friends with Sally, a white student, the two of them cannot interact socially—the park is off-limits to people of color, as is the drugstore where the two attempt to order soft drinks. They can be together only in the integrated school, and, even there, the decision to share a table at lunch causes problems for Sally's parents, whose tolerance is put to the test when their social acceptance is threatened. There are no easy answers here, and almost half a century later, this book continues to be relevant.

NOTES

1. Edmund H. Harvey, Jr., ed. *Our Glorious Century*, p. 249.
2. Ibid.
3. Edmund Lindop. *An Album of the Fifties*, p. 57.
4. Ibid., p. 34.
5. Ruth Hill Viguers. "Golden Years and Time of Tumult: 1920–1967," *A Critical History of Children's Literature*, ed. Cornelia Meigs, p. 409.
6. Ibid., p. 410.
7. Jonathan Cott. *Pipers at the Gates of Dawn*, p. 25.
8. Leonard Marcus. *Margaret Wise Brown: Awakened by the Moon*, p. 279.
9. Ibid., p. 263.
10. Ibid., p. 267.

11. Maurice Sendak. "Ruth Krauss and Me; A Very Special Partnership," *The Horn Book Magazine*, May–June, 1994, pp. 287–288.
12. Letter from Louis Darling to Beverly Cleary, dated July 17, 1950 (Beverly Cleary "correspondence" file, Kerlan Collection, University of Minnesota).
13. Eleanor Cameron. *The Green and Burning Tree*, p. 42n.
14. Eleanor Estes. *Ginger Pye*. New York: Harcourt, 1967, pp. 28, 29.
15. This is an international award given for total contributions to children's literature by the International Board on Books for Young People, founded in 1956.

Illustration by Tom Feelings from To Be a Slave *by Julius Lester (Penguin, 1968), copyright © 1968 by Tom Feelings; reprinted with the permission of E.P. Dutton. Feelings's powerful drawings complement this collection of haunting and tragic slave*

7

ENDING THE STATUS QUO 1960–1969

Books are the treasured wealth of the world and the fit inheritance of generations and nations.

—Henry Thoreau
Walden

A Time of Change

In the Sixties, Americans became aware that the ideal of a perfect America, "land of the free and home of the brave," was suffering a breakdown. In 1958, the country had been scandalized to discover that some quiz shows on television were rigged, with a contestant's personality often being judged more important than honest intelligence. Then Rachel Carson's *Silent Spring* (1962) warned of the dangers of pesticides, Francis Gary Powers was indicted and found guilty of spying against the Soviet Union, the U.S. government released a statement warning that cigarette smoking was a health hazard, blacks began to protest against continued inequality by staging sit-ins and finally rioting in the Watts section of Los Angeles, and President John F. Kennedy, civil rights leaders Medgar Evers, and Martin Luther King, Jr., activist Malcolm X, and Robert Kennedy were all assassinated. There were protests against the Vietnam War, demonstrations for and against abortion rights, and demonstrations calling for gay rights. Any of the above might have weakened the concept of America as a world standard; all of them together, brought directly into living rooms across the country by television, caused a major social revolution in the United States.

Nevertheless, Americans continued to believe in the dream, if not in each other, and by the end of the decade, a more mature America faced the future. The adolescents of this economically prosperous but chaotic decade were members of the baby boomer generation.[1] They were the first to grow up with television, later becoming the target of the advertisers, the first to have their own money to spend, and the first to take for granted a college education in a society that was beginning to place new value on higher education.[2] The rather euphoric Kennedy years—1960 to 1963—reflected the American ideal. And the youngest man ever elected to the presidency, John F. Kennedy, along with his wife, Jackie, encouraged the proliferation of arts and music in education and—in an age of space travel—a stronger focus on education in science and math. The education system, in the spotlight of public interest, came under close scrutiny, and experimental changes began to infiltrate its basic structure. As an offshoot of this scrutiny, a look at school texts showed that black history was missing, that all the characters in school readers were white, and that American publishers were issuing very few books by or about blacks, not to mention other minorities and women.[3]

New Visions

In a society embroiled by mid-decade in revolution, books for children avoided direct commentary on change, and authors and illustrators attempted to right past wrongs with quiet subtlety. Virginia Hamilton, whose ancestors were African American and Native American, was raised in an upper-middle-class setting with a strong pride in her mixed ancestry, leaving her with "a deep sense of roots: of rootedness in a family which itself is rooted in a place. And the place . . . America."[4] Her early books transcended the emerging struggle of blacks to gain social acceptance in this country by focusing on racial pride in *Zeely* (1967) and on black history in *The House of Dies Drear* (1968). All her characters are black, and they are fully developed personalities, not merely symbols. As she herself explains, "the experience of a people must come to mean the experience of humankind."[5]

Ezra Jack Keats's first children's book, *My Dog Is Lost!* (1960), with illustrations classified by Barbara Bader as "stylized naturalism,"[6] introduced Juanito, a Puerto Rican boy who moves to New York City, is unable to speak English, and loses his dog, Pepito. The children who help him find his dog are from Chinatown, Little Italy, Park Avenue, and Harlem, creating a microcosm of multicultural America. *My Dog Rinty* (1946) offered urban black children a story that related to them personally, but *My Dog Is Lost!* went a step beyond by entering the urban neighborhood and showing its diversity.

For 22 years, Keats kept four candid photos of a small boy on his studio wall, which ultimately led to his creation of a middle-class black child named Peter in *The Snowy Day* (1962),[7] winner of the 1963 Caldecott Medal and the first of several books about Peter. The art medium used was collage, introduced by Leo Lionni in *Inch by Inch* (1960), and the textured and patterned materials that made up the overall design of the book enhanced Peter's innocent appeal and made him the popular silhouette in this and subsequent stories about him.

When John Steptoe was 19 years old, he wrote and illustrated a book called *Stevie* (1969), written in a rhythmic inner-city voice and told from the viewpoint of a small black child who resents the intrusion of a foster child in his family, then grudgingly admits he misses him when the child is gone. The book is an innovative portrait of black culture in urban America: direct, honest, and still relevant.

Building American Fantasy

While schools dissected stories as teaching tools in their textbooks, and federal funds created an expanding market, there was a major growth in school libraries. Children's book publication burgeoned in an effort to counter television and to meet the demands of the increased youth population. Even though mediocrity marked much of what was published, especially in books chosen for school libraries as they tried to meet curriculum needs, there was also an opportunity for publishers to take some chances.

It was in the 1960s that fantasy written by American authors began to compete seriously with English fantasy. Lloyd Alexander was one of the first American authors to join Lewis and Tolkien in developing a fantasy world made real in *The Book of Three* (1964), the first of the Prydain books. Alexander was greatly influenced by the King Arthur legends while growing up in Philadelphia and was a writer of adult fiction for 17 years before he began writing children's books. In the course of writing his first children's novel, *Time Cat* (1963), he discovered material on Welsh legends. The Celts and King Arthur came together in his mind, and the result was a series of books, built around what appeared to be a Celtic background, called *The Prydain Chronicles* (1964–1968). Alexander did an extensive amount of research on the mythology of ancient Wales—he had spent time in Wales 20 years earlier as a member of the U.S. Army during World War II—but changed his mind about writing a novel that utilized authentic Welsh mythology. "What had been secretly in my heart all the while was to create my own mythology and my own legendary Land of Prydain,"[8] he said. The Prydain series drew on Alexander's longtime interest in Wales, King Arthur, and the *Mabinogion*, from which the Arthur prototype emerged.

The last book in Alexander's five-book series, *The High King* (1968), was awarded a Newbery Medal in 1969. It should be noted that the practice of choosing a single book rather than recognizing all the books in a given series makes each year's choices more difficult for the Newbery Committee and sometimes creates a distorted view of the best in children's books. Teachers and librarians are apt to place the Newbery-winning books in a separate section, and, if a winning book is part of a series, children might be expected to read the Newbery book but not the earlier books. Alexander's *Prydain Chronicles*, Ursula Le Guin's Earthsea Trilogy and Susan Cooper's *The Dark Is Rising* Sequence all are distinctive fantasy series, which propel a reader from one book to the next with growing anticipation, but in each case only partial recognition for the series was given by the Newbery Committee.

Ursula Le Guin elevated the field of science fiction in general literature with *Rocannon's World* (1966) and placed fantasy on America's list of critically acclaimed accomplishments with her Earthsea Trilogy. The Newbery Committee recognized only the second book in her trilogy when they named *Tombs of Atuan* (1971) a Newbery Honor book in 1972. In Susan Cooper's four-book series, only two of the books—*The Dark Is Rising* (1973) and *The Grey King* (1975)—were lauded by the Newbery Committee, even though the other two parts that make up the whole are equally deserving.

Contemporary vs. Traditional

Any story depending on a 1960s contemporary American setting took the chance of quickly becoming outdated as social attitudes changed, taboos were lifted in children's literature, and technology developed faster than the imagination could keep up. *The Bronze Bow* (1961) by Elizabeth George Speare, winner of the 1962 Newbery Medal, is a book that has lasting value, with its focus on Jewish history, but simulates other award-winning historical novels and lacks the individual style that marks a truly distinguished book.

In retrospect, Norton Juster's *The Phantom Tollbooth* (1961) might have been a better choice for a Newbery. The story is a satisfying blend of humor, logic, imagination, and science that will forever guarantee its uniqueness. Milo considers everything a waste of time until he travels through the magic tollbooth and discovers with the help of the watchdog Tock how to schedule time, how to keep from killing time, and how to spend time in the "word" market. Words and their meanings become the focus of Milo's trip beyond Expectations through Unfortunate Conclusions and toward Infinity. Jules Feiffer's cartoon-like illustrations are the perfect accompaniment.

Richard Scarry gained recognition in the mass marketplace with his best-selling encyclopedia for children called *The Best Word Book Ever* (1963), for which he was paid a flat sum rather than an advance and royalties. It wasn't until the Seventies, when he started publishing with Random House under his own copyright, beginning with *Richard*

Scarry's Busiest People Ever (1976), that he began earning royalties. He had been selling his work outright to Golden Books (Western Publishing Company) for years, and his individualized little animals had appeared in several Golden books before his encyclopedia was published. Because of the encyclopedia's broad appeal, he managed to cross the line between books as "products" and books as "educational material." His later books earned a certain prestige as well as a lot of money, and Golden was able to capitalize on his earlier work. One serious flaw in Scarry's books, however, is the assignment of stereotypical roles to men and women. All the salespeople, sports figures, doctors, lawyers, mail carriers, police officers, fire fighters, clergy, and various other workers in *Best Word Book* and in the 1976 edition of *Busiest People* are male, and all the nurses, teachers, librarians, and homemakers are female. Updated editions of his books more realistically portray changes in attitude regarding roles assigned to men and women.

Although Helen Buckley didn't really alter the status quo, she did offer a new way of writing a picture book—in first person, celebrating the special relationship between child and grandparent—with the result an emotionally involving, rhythmic essay called *Grandmother and I* (1961). This was one of the earliest picture books to boast a television tie-in, as it was featured several times on the popular "Captain Kangaroo" series. Buckley's book opened the door for authors to explore social relationships between friends, between siblings, between child and parent, at a much earlier age than had been done before. Judith Viorst made her child characters more sophisticated than Buckley's, yet they were still very young children trying to interact sociably, in, for example, *I'll Fix Anthony* (1969). Charlotte Zolotow explored every conceivable area of contention in the life of a small child, with stories like *Big Sister and Little Sister* (1966) and *The Hating Book* (1969).

Emily Neville's realistic contemporary work, such as the 1964 Newbery Medal book, *It's Like This, Cat* (1963), was innovative at the time it was written, with its first-person adolescent viewpoint and urban setting, but too many of the details that made it appealing have become outmoded, such as record collections, neighborhood movie theaters, and the 10-cent Coke. Its real value now is historical, since it portrays a background and an economy far different from the present. Compare the cost of a major Broadway show then and now. Dave pays $2.89 for a ticket to see *West Side Story*.

Madeline L'Engle's *A Wrinkle in Time* (1962), winner of the 1963 Newbery Medal, continues to intrigue the reader even though character development at times seems contrived—protagonist Meg Murry's little brother, Charles Wallace, is more of a prototype than a real person. The story is, however, an unusual combination of fantasy and science-based fiction.

L'Engle continues to produce popular and highly acclaimed books that overcome flaws in construction because they explore a major theme in literature, the meaning of existence, but Neville became the victim of a fast-changing society by depending on what was popular at the time.

Beyond the Ordinary

Louise Fitzhugh deliberately rejected the status quo and forever altered the course of children's fiction by originating a protagonist in *Harriet the Spy* (1964) who became, and continues to be, the subject of much controversy. In her private notebook, Harriet speaks her mind without concern for what effect that might have on others. When she does the same as editor of the school paper, it is a painful intrusion on the privacy of others. Because she was so real to her readers, some critics felt that her apparent lack of ethics made her a poor model of behavior and others felt that she, like Holden Caulfield in J. D. Salinger's adult novel, *Catcher in the Rye* (1951), was a typical example of a child ignored and neglected by family and unable to fit in socially. This type of child had appeared in other children's books, including *Heidi* (1884) and *The Secret Garden* (1911), but the alienated children in those stories managed to resolve their social difficulties and become accepted, while Harriet remains unloved and basically unrepentant.

Frances, a small badger-type creature introduced in Russell Hoban's easy reader, *Bedtime for Frances* (1960), was given a distinct personality by Hoban and pictorial form by both Garth Williams and Hoban's wife, Lillian, and the Frances books are longtime favorites. Frances, like Harriet, doesn't always behave in an acceptable manner, but, unlike Harriet, she is secure within a loving family. Therefore, her misbehavior is forgiven and Hoban's resolutions are comforting. The same is true of Max in *Where the Wild Things Are* (1963) by Maurice Sendak, even though the book, which won the Caldecott in 1964, was and sometimes still is the subject of controversy, the argument being that children will be frightened by the "wild things." What children have always known and adults have overlooked is that Max is never in danger. He has the ability to control his nightmares and to return home at will where his dinner, withheld from him earlier by his mother when he behaved badly, is not only waiting for him but is "still hot." Children read this book again and again because it speaks to them so directly, a quality found in all of Sendak's work.

Facing Reality

This was the decade in which children's books began to respect the ability of children to face conflict that didn't always have an easy solution. Susie Hinton was only 16 when she wrote *The Outsiders* (1967), a story written from the viewpoint of a teenage member of an urban gang. The book, based on her own experiences, has held up in a changing society, mainly because the social inequities she explored still exist. Hinton used initials rather than her first name to play down the fact that she was female and made the narrator of the book male. The story was also adapted as a movie in 1982 and featured actors who have since become top film stars: Matt Dillon, Ralph Macchio, Patrick Swayze, Rob Lowe, Emilio Estevez, and Tom Cruise. Both Joanne Greenberg's *I Never Promised You a Rose Garden* (1964) and John Neufeld's *Lisa, Bright and Dark* (1969) dealt, for the first time in children's books, with mental illness. Vera and Bill Cleaver wrote *Where the Lilies Bloom* (1969), a story set in the mountains of Appalachia, with the leading character a young woman of great strength who not only takes responsibility for her younger siblings when their father dies, but also keeps his death a secret from neighbors, especially the landlord, in order to keep the family together. Paul Zindel acknowledged in *The Pigman* (1968) that young people don't always meet the expectations of adults and sometimes make the wrong choices. This was the time when books began to be directed at a "young adult" audience, a time when naivete competed daily with the reality and immediacy of television. Children's literature in America, like America itself, was no longer innocent, but it continued, and still continues, to be nourished by innocence and a solid belief in tomorrow's good fortune.

Middle-grade Fiction

While realism vied with fantasy in the more complicated books for older readers, fantasy coupled with humor was offered to middle schoolers looking for a storyline beyond the simple picture-book text. George Selden created a memorable cast of characters in *The Cricket in Times Square* (1960), a story enhanced by Garth Williams's illustrations of Tucker the mouse, Chester the fiddle-playing cricket, and their friends at the newsstand in Times Square.

Also, Beverly Cleary, highly regarded for her realistic fiction, wrote a humorous fantasy about a mouse, in this case one that rode a motorcycle. Louis Darling, who had illustrated all of Cleary's books, delayed his decision on whether to illustrate this book until he had read the manuscript. He wasn't going to illustrate any book about a mouse who "wore clothes and slept in a bed and ate at a little table."[9] He was, however, quite satisfied with Cleary's realistic mouse descriptions and the two began a detailed correspondence about the way he would draw Ralph. *Runaway Ralph* (1969), the last book Darling illustrated before his death from cancer, was a close-knit collaboration between the two, even though by the time it was written Cleary lived in California and Darling in Connecticut. In fact, Darling asked Cleary to send him some bamboo leaves because he didn't know where to get them in Connecticut and they were an important part of the environment in the book.

Louis Darling died in 1970, and Cleary encouraged his wife, Lois Darling, to send original art and materials to the Kerlan Collection at the University of Minnesota because, she told Darling, "they are so careful about preservation, they arrange exhibits and they do so much for children's literature."[10] Fortunately for this study, Lois Darling did send her husband's work to the Kerlan Collection, although she found it difficult to give up these materials that were so much a part of her life and her husband's.

The highly imaginative and humorous books of English author Roald Dahl continue to delight children, with his books maintaining their popularity even though *Charlie and the Chocolate Factory* (1964) was heavily criticized in the Seventies for depicting black "pygmies," called Oompa-Loompas, as low-paid factory workers who had been transported from Africa in packing boxes by Willy Wonka. A revised edition was issued in 1973, in which "the Oompa-Loompas are little men with long hair who come from Loompaland and bear no resemblance to any known racial group."[11]

John D. Fitzgerald's realistic fiction in *The Great Brain* (1967) offers a humorous and insightful version of his own childhood in a small Utah community, a community made up of 2,000 Mormons, 500 Protestants and Catholics, one Jewish storekeeper, and one Greek immigrant family. The story is set in 1896 and confronts various instances of intolerance and misunderstanding in relation to racial, cultural, and physical differences in a small town. But it is the Great Brain himself, older brother of narrator J.D., who manages to overcome all barriers to tolerance in the community and remains a hero in the eyes of his eight-year-old brother.

Picture Book Art Comes of Age

In picture books, illustrators had discovered the potential of the folk tale, and adapted versions of old stories in the public domain offered them a showcase for original art. Nicolas Sidjakov was awarded a Caldecott Medal in 1961 for *Baboushka and the Three Kings* (1960), a Russian folk tale adapted and written by Ruth Robbins. It was Sidjakov's second children's book, and when he received word that he had been awarded the Caldecott, he at first had little idea of the honor bestowed upon him. Unlike Maurice Sendak, who has always felt very comfortable communicating with children because he is so connected to his own childhood, Sidjakov spoke about his struggle to reach a child audience, to move into the child's world, and finally decided to just forget about children and do his best in illustrating the book. The result was critically acclaimed art but perhaps not a book with built-in child appeal.

The illustrated folk tale became a major contribution to the picture storybook market through the Sixties and Seventies. The best of these combined a fine balance of text, pictures, and overall book design and were pleasing to all ages. Marcia Brown brought the ancient art of woodcut printing into children's picture books with an East Indian fable titled *Once a Mouse . . .* (1961) and was awarded her second Caldecott Medal in 1962. Her first had been presented for *Cinderella* (1954), which was rendered in delicate pastels far different from the bold character of woodcut. As an art medium, woodcut was again recognized in 1968 when *Drummer Hoff* (1967), illustrated by Ed Emberley and adapted by Barbara Emberley from a folk verse, was awarded a Caldecott. Claus Stamm's *Three Strong Women* (1962) was illustrated by Japanese artist

Kazue Mizumara, and Blair Lent illustrated the Japanese folktale, *The Wave*, adapted by Margaret Hodges and published in 1964. Stories of Eastern Europe were collected by Isaac Bashevis Singer and illustrated by Maurice Sendak in *Zlateh the Goat and Other Stories* (1966).

Uri Shulevitz was awarded a Caldecott Medal in 1970 for *The Fool of the World and the Flying Ship* (1969), a Russian tale retold by Arthur Ransome, but it was in *One Monday Morning* (1967), for which he supplied both text (based on a French folk song) and illustration, that he demonstrated his talent for understatement and his ability to expand text through pictures. "One Monday morning the king, the queen and the little prince came to visit me." This simple statement extends over three double spreads: In the first, rain pours down on the row of city tenement buildings, in the second, the rain falls on the head of the king, and in the third, on the heads of the queen and the little prince. "But I wasn't home," the text then reads. The list of prospective visitors builds as the week progresses, but the little boy is never home, until finally, on Sunday, he is, and a celebration is in order.

The Art of Language

Into this flood of folk tales came William Steig's *Sylvester and the Magic Pebble* (1969), winner of the 1970 Caldecott Medal and a true celebration of language and art, offering a reflective story with its roots set in the fears and delights of childhood. Steig, who did not start writing children's books until he was 60 years old,[12] was deeply affected as a child by Grimm's fairy tales, Charlie Chaplin movies, Humperdinck's opera *Hansel and Gretel*, the Katzenjammer Kids, and Collodi's *Pinocchio*. He states in his Caldecott acceptance speech, "It is very likely that Sylvester became a rock and then again a live donkey because I had once been so deeply impressed with Pinocchio's longing to have his spirit encased in flesh instead of in wood."[13] There is such a rigid progression in a folk tale, with boundaries structurally set over time, that Steig's originality in the midst of a decade of folktale-based picture books became a breath of fresh air. Steig had been an artist for the *New Yorker* magazine before he began creating children's books and showed with *Sylvester* how words and pictures could merge into a rhythmic whole expressing the clearest logic and candor. He had the ability to find exactly the right word to describe an action, as did E. B. White, also on the *New Yorker* staff. When Sylvester wishes the rain would stop and it does, Steig writes, "It didn't stop gradually as rains usually do. It ceased." The word "ceased" is immediate and absolutely right for the moment.

As a prime example of the type of damaging criticism that too often infiltrates literature, the Illinois Police Association recommended that schools and libraries remove *Sylvester* from circulation because, in a book in which all of the characters are animals, the police happen to be pigs. In the letter sent by the association to its members, attention was brought to a color spread of Sylvester's parents at the police station, depicting "the law enforcement officer as a pig and the public as 'jack asses.'" The letter went on to say that the book "is written for our youngsters in their formative years, ages 5–8 . . . Please check your grade school libraries and public library to see if this book is there. If it is, ask them to remove it."[14] Had the book been published a decade earlier or a decade later, showing a policeman as a pig would not have been considered derogatory, but in the Sixties and early Seventies, those who defied authority labeled policemen as "pigs." Until that defiance faded in the late Seventies, the label stuck.

While traditional folk tales were being adapted throughout the picture-book genre, Jane Yolen's first picture book was an original fairy tale, *The Emperor and the Kite* (1967), illustrated by Ed Young and named a Caldecott Honor book in 1968. Yolen's father was an expert on kites, and she had helped him with his research, later using it as a basis for the story. Her personal relationship with her father was less than satisfactory as reflected in her comment, "My father never read any of my books."[15] In this gentle story, a tiny princess, "not thought very much of—when she was thought of at all," saves her father's life with her kite, and he rewards her with love and respect, which is all she ever wanted. Yolen has continued to be prolific, with close to 200 books to her credit, and during the Seventies, she defined the folk and fairy tale genre with original poetic stories of kingdoms, fairies, and fools, illustrated by some of the greatest artists in the children's book field. At a time when folk and fairy tales were enjoying a renaissance in picture storybooks, Yolen's work stood above the rest, but her books were higher-priced than most and were therefore purchased by a limited audience.

Let's Read and Find Out

In listing books that represent development in children's literature after the mid-20th century, the most difficult area to explore is informational books. The reason for this is the speed with which new developments began to take place in technology, science, and medicine. Much of the research material being written was out of date by the time it was published. One series published by T.Y. Crowell called the "Let's-Read-and-Find-Out" science series, however, became and continues to be an innovative collection of picture books written for very young children to explain the most basic elements of the sciences. These books—one of which was *Fireflies in the Night* (1963), written by Judy Dawes and illustrated by Kazue Mizumura—are so basic that they do not become outdated.

Revising History

Although children's books in the Sixties showcased the familiar fairy and folk tales of Great Britain and Europe, and American writer Jane Yolen offered original fairy tales, the media made an effort to correct the misinformation in the history textbooks by publicizing the imperfections that showed America to be less than ideal. Now children were informed of new truths day by day on the television screen, and it became imperative in the classroom to recognize and acknowledge changes in attitude.

The Seventies became a time of overwhelming production in children's books, as publishers moved to supply schools and libraries with updated reference materials and stories that reflected new cultural awareness. In education and in the libraries, the emphasis was on informational books and realistic fiction, which began to edge out the fairy tales.

Chronological Bibliography 1960–1969

Estes, Eleanor. *The Witch Family*. New York: Harcourt, 1960, 1990. (Fantasy)

Amy and Clarissa are six years old, blonde and blue-eyed, and best of friends. Their favorite pastime is drawing pictures—pictures of witches. First there is Old Witch, then Little Witch Girl, who also happens to be blonde and blue-eyed like them, and the baby, Weenie Witchie. Old Witch has been "banquished" to the glass hill for being bad, and if she promises to be good all year, she can be her regular witch self on Halloween. But it's hard to keep a promise to be good, and Old Witch has more trouble than most. Between the shenanigans of Old Witch, the magic of the bumblebee, Malachi, under a spell that makes him a "spelling bee," and Amy's yearning to fly on Halloween, the story builds to a climax, and reality gets all mixed up with magic.

Hoban, Russell. *Bedtime for Frances*, illtd. Garth Williams. New York: Harper, 1960, 1976. Also, *A Baby Sister for Frances*, illtd. Lillian Hoban (New York: Harper, 1964, 1976), *Bread and Jam for Frances*, illtd. Lillian Hoban (New York: Harper, 1964, 1986). (Easy Reader/Social Behavior)

Frances, like many small children, hates to give in and go to sleep at bedtime, and in *Bedtime for Frances* she keeps finding reasons to avoid sleeping, complaining to her parents until her father shows signs of completely losing patience, at which time she decides she's sleepy after all. In *A Baby Sister for Frances*, the precocious and imaginative Frances feels neglected and somewhat resentful of her new baby sister, Gloria. She decides to run away, under the dining room table, but changes her mind when she hears her parents discussing how important she is to the family. In *Bread and Jam for Frances*, Frances sings a little song about eggs, beginning, "I do not like the way you slide,/I do not like your soft inside,/ . . ." All she will eat is bread and jam, so that's all she gets until she decides she can't possibly eat it anymore—she'd rather eat anything but bread and jam. Illustrator Garth Williams portrayed Frances and her family as badger-like creatures with human attributes, and Russell Hoban's wife, Lillian, continued that portrayal in subsequent books.

Keats, Ezra Jack, and Pat Cherr. *My Dog Is Lost!*, illtd. Ezra Jack Keats. New York: Crowell, 1960. (Picture Book/Social Relationships/Urban)

Juanito has just moved to New York City. He doesn't know anyone, he cannot speak English, and he loses his dog, Pepito. The children who help him find Pepito are all from different ethnic groups and social backgrounds, and together they bring Juanito and his dog into their lives. It is unfortunate that the book is out of print, not only because of its historical value but because of its social value as well.

Lionni, Leo. *Inch by Inch*. New York: Obolensky, 1960; New York: Astor-Honor, 1962. (Picture Book/Concept)

Utilizing a collage of cut-paper designs, Lionni, with minimal text, portrays a tiny but astute inchworm who saves himself by measuring beaks and tails of birds that otherwise would eat him, but when the nightingale asks him to measure her song or she will gobble him up, he has to come up with a new way to save his life.

O'Dell, Scott. *Island of the Blue Dolphins*. Boston: Houghton Mifflin, 1960, 1990. NEWBERY MEDAL. (Realistic Fiction/South Pacific)

When the Russian Captain Orlov and his Aleut workers take otters for their skins from the island of the Blue Dolphins and refuse to pay what they have promised, Karana's father faces them and is killed. The fight that follows decimates the native Indian tribe. Of 42 men, only 15 are left and seven of these are old men. Finally, the tribe leaves the island on a large ship, but Karana, who discovers her six-year-old brother Ramo, is still on the island, jumps off the ship, which cannot turn back. The two young people are left behind, and when Ramo is attacked by wild dogs and killed, Karana must make it alone on the island. Both the story of this female Robinson Crusoe and Jean George's *Julie of the Wolves* (1972) celebrate the heretofore unrecognized strength of women facing nature's adversity and surviving.

Robbins, Ruth. *Baboushka and the Three Kings*, illtd. Nicolas Sidjakov. Berkeley: Parnassus, 1960; Boston: Houghton Mifflin, 1986. CALDECOTT MEDAL. (Folk Myth/Picture Book)

When an old woman passes up an opportunity to travel with three wise men to see the birth of Jesus, she regrets it and spends many years trying to find the child. This adaptation of a Russian folk tale offers a different aspect of a familiar Christmas story.

Selden, George. *The Cricket in Times Square*, illtd. Garth Williams. New York: Farrar, Straus, 1960; New York: Dell, 1990. (Fantasy/Animal/Urban)

Although not as emotionally absorbing as White's *Charlotte's Web* (1952), the author presents readers with a compelling adventure, featuring a musical cricket named Chester, along with Tucker Mouse and Harry Cat, who live at a newsstand on New York's Times Square. Garth Williams, who created illustrations for both White and Selden, made Selden's characters as unforgettable as he did White's. While *Charlotte's Web* took place in a rural setting, *Cricket* offers an authentic Manhattan locale and sets up the obstacles that might be met in an urban setting.

Sendak, Maurice. *The Sign on Rosie's Door*. New York: Harper, 1960. Adapted for television and expanded in book form as part of *Maurice Sendak's Really Rosie Starring the Nutshell Kids* (New York: Harper, 1975). (Realistic Fiction/Picture Book/Urban)

In the 1940s, when Maurice Sendak was 14 years old, he used to sit at the window of his New York City apartment and watch nine-year-old Rosie across the street making up stories and assigning roles to the other neighborhood children. He wrote her story in 1960, casting her both as Alinda the Lovely Lady Singer and as Rosie, and the story, along with *Nutshell Library* (1962), was made into a television musical in 1975. That was when he actually met the real Rosie, who still lived in Brooklyn,[16] for the first time. The television adaptation was then put into book form with Carole King's music.

Ungerer, Tomi. *Emile*. New York: Harper, 1960; New York: Dell, 1992. (Fantasy/Picture Book/Animal/Humor)

It is rather unlikely that an octopus would be accepted in society, but Emile is not your ordinary octopus. He saves the life of a deep-sea diver, and the ship's captain gives him special treatment. The passengers discover that Emile, with his eight arms, is able to play piano, harp, and bass viol, all at the same time. He becomes a lifeguard and is able to save three children all at once. When a coast guard cutter is confiscated by two unsavory characters, he tangles seaweed in the propellor and saves the day. Emile becomes the guest of honor on board ship and spends his spare time playing checkers with the deep-sea diver at the bottom of the sea.

Buckley, Helen E. *Grandmother and I*, illtd. Paul Galdone. New York: Lothrop, Lee and Shepard, 1961, 1994 (with new illustrations).

(Picture Book/Concept/Family/Aging)

A deceptively simple text written in first person, not usual at the time in children's picture books, gives emotional expression to the special place grandparents have in a child's life. Paul Galdone's illustrations portray a grandmother who is just shy of being a complete stereotype, but the little girl fits very nicely in a contemporary setting. Buckley's grandmother offers comfortable acceptance and undemanding love.

Burnford, Sheila. *The Incredible Journey*, illtd. Carl Burger. Boston: Little, Brown, 1961; New York: Bantam, 1990. (Realistic Fiction/Animal)

Three unlikely partners, an English bull terrier, a Labrador retriever, and a Siamese cat, travel westward across the Canadian mountain wilderness toward home, meeting many obstacles and more than once flirting with death. The three pets have been left with a relative while the family travels abroad, and when the relative goes on a trip, the retriever decides it's time to go home and takes it for granted the other two animals will join him. A misunderstanding on the part of the relative causes her to think he has taken the animals with him, and no one knows the animals are missing until Uncle John returns and the pets' owners are on their way back home. Burnford tells the story, which was well presented in a recent film version, in a way that avoids giving the animals human attributes, remains true to their animal natures, and in so doing creates a deeply emotional description of their pilgrimage and its culmination.

Speare, Elizabeth George. *The Bronze Bow*. Boston: Houghton Mifflin, 1961, 1973. NEWBERY MEDAL. (Realistic Fiction/Historical/Israel)

Daniel Bar Jamin is 18 years old and dedicated to driving the Romans, who have been responsible for the deaths of his mother and father and for his sister's inability to lead a normal life, from Israel. The boy's hatred drives him until he meets the carpenter called Jesus and finds himself questioning the value of vengeance. Speare presents historical details of the time in which the story takes place and portrays Jesus as a man who may or may not be the Messiah whose coming has been predicted. But this is Daniel's story, not the story of Jesus, and the young man's struggle toward maturity is the focus of the book.

Brown, Marcia. *Once a Mouse . . .* New York: Scribner, 1961; New York: Macmillan, 1989. CALDECOTT MEDAL. (Folk/Myth/Picture Book/ndia)

Based on an ancient East Indian fable, Brown's dramatic woodcut illustrations accompany the story in which a small mouse threatened by a cat is turned into a cat himself by an old hermit. The hermit continues to protect the animal by making him larger and larger until he becomes a tiger. But the tiger becomes so arrogant in his newfound strength that he ignores the old man's reminder that he was once a humble mouse and plots to kill him. In a cyclical pattern associated with Eastern thought, the tiger finds himself once more a mouse.

Juster, Norton. *The Phantom Tollbooth*, illtd. Jules Feiffer. New York: Random House, 1961; New York: Knopf, 1988. (Fantasy)

A boy named Milo who is never satisfied, never interested in anything, and who considers the seeking of knowledge to be a waste of time, discovers a strange package in his room one afternoon. It's a turnpike tollbooth, and by following the directions, he can travel to a land called Dictionopolis. Having nothing better to do, he travels to the Lands Beyond, beyond expectations and into the land of the imagination, where logic, humor, and curiosity make language come alive and give Milo a never-ending source of excitement.

Clarke, Pauline. *Return of the Twelves*. New York: Coward, 1962; New York: Dell, 1992. (Fantasy/Toys)

When the Morleys move into a country house, young Max decides to explore the attic, and behind a loose board he finds 12 wooden soldiers. His parents are concerned because he wants to spend all his time in the attic, but they don't know Max's secret: The soldiers are alive. Not only that, they talk to him. As Max becomes more familiar with the Twelves, he discovers that they are very old and are accustomed to having someone imagine their adventures, which, once imagined, might very well take place. When Max's sister, Jane, and, finally, his older brother, Philip, share his secret, the children discover that the soldiers used to belong to the Brontes—Branwell, Charlotte, Anne, and Emily—and that Branwell actually wrote up their history in a published volume called *The History of the Young Men*. Because the Brontes were famous, the little soldiers are very valuable, and Max, who loves them dearly, must decide whether to keep them or allow them to return to their home called Haworth, which is now a Bronte museum.

D'Aulaire, Ingri and Edgar. *D'Aulaire's Book of Greek Myths*. New York: Doubleday, 1962; New York: Dell, 1992. (Folk/Myth/Picture Book)

The D'Aulaires maintain the integrity of the original adult

versions of the Greek myths while also manipulating language in an effort to soften the harshness of the gods' actions. Instead, the simplicity of the text tends to delineate the often uncontrolled passions of the gods. Both Nathaniel Hawthorne and Edith Hamilton have set forth the myths without calling undue attention to the gods' baser instincts, probably because, unlike the D'Aulaires, they didn't try to focus on the gods' unorthodox family tree.

L'Engle, Madeleine. *A Wrinkle in Time.* New York: Farrar, Straus, 1962; New York: Dell, 1976. NEWBERY MEDAL. (Fantasy/Science Fiction)

The opening words of this novel—"It was a dark and stormy night"—contradict the story's unusual content, which combines science fiction and fantasy with Christian concepts to focus on 12-year-old Meg Murry's inability to fit into her family's unorthodox lifestyle or into the more normal activities of her classmates at school. With the appearance of three witches straight out of *Macbeth* and the strange disappearance of her father, Meg finds herself embroiled in an adventure that takes her "tessering" through space with her friend Calvin and her five-year-old brother, Charles Wallace, on a journey to save her father's life. The experience allows her a deeper understanding of herself and a new awareness of her untapped capabilities.

Keats, Ezra Jack. *The Snowy Day.* New York: Viking, 1962; New York: Puffin, 1976. CALDECOTT MEDAL. (Realistic Fiction/Picture Book)

With a storyline that introduces a small boy, Peter, and portrays his unrestrained joy at the activities open to him on a snowy day, Keats creates the essence of childlike wonder, deftly combining patterned materials in a collage that goes a step beyond the illustrations of Leo Lionni by developing Peter, who is black, as a flesh-and-blood individual rather than simply a design on the page.

Sendak, Maurice. *Nutshell Library* (*Alligators All Around*; *One Was Johnny*; *Chicken Soup with Rice*; *Pierre*). New York: Harper, 1962. (Picture Book/Concept)

Book one is an alphabet book, book two is a counting book, book three a calendar book, and book four is a cautionary tale about Pierre who doesn't care. The four tiny books, only 2½ by 4 inches and easy to memorize, allow a young child to hold each book and pretend to read once the book has been read aloud a few times.

Stamm, Claus. *Three Strong Women*, illtd. Kazue Mizumura. New York: Viking, 1962, 1990. (Folk/Myth/Picture Book)

Stamm's adaptation of this humorous folk tale tells of sumo wrestler Forever Mountain who has his pride clipped a few notches when a young girl proves to be stronger than he. Her mother and grandmother are even stronger, but they train him until he is able to overcome every other wrestler in Japan. Assured of his own ability, he goes back to the mountain and marries the girl whose family trained him. The illustrations of Kazue Mizumura, wife of Claus Stamm, portray authentic details of early Japan with well-defined characterizations, composed with only a few sweeping brush strokes.

Alexander, Lloyd. *Time Cat*. New York: Holt, Rinehart and Winston, 1963; New York: Dell, 1985. (Fantasy/Time Travel)

A boy, Jason, and his cat, Gareth, travel back to ancient Egypt, then forward in time to specific periods in the history of Great Britain, Asia, Europe, and North and South America. In each location, domestic cats are either unknown or considered deities of some kind. In dealing with the different cultures, details of that culture, sometimes combined with the appearances of well-known figures of that time, enter into the story. Alexander makes general references to different lifestyles, a little too generally to make those periods really come alive, but with enough details to establish a tentative credibility.

Dawes, Judy. *Fireflies in the Night*, illtd. Kazue Mizumura. New York: Crowell, 1963, 1991 (revised). (Informational/Picture Book/Science)

The "Let's-Read-and-Find-Out" science series began in 1960 and continues to offer concise informational picturebooks for young children. This early contribution to the series is a quiet book, written from the first-person viewpoint of a small boy, sitting outdoors at night with his grandparents and learning all about fireflies. The illustrations by Japanese artist Kazue Mizumura are softly rendered, except for the sharp detail of the firefly when presented as a scientific depiction.

Neville, Emily. *It's Like This, Cat*, illtd. Emil Weiss. New York: Harper, 1963, 1975. NEWBERY MEDAL. (Realistic Fiction/Social Behavior)

First-person narrator Dave Mitchell, 14, lives in New York City, and in the course of his daily routine manages to touch on the major landmarks throughout the city—Coney Island, the Staten Island Ferry, Central Park and the Central Park Zoo, the Fulton Street fish market, and the New York Public Library. Dave is offered a cat by a neighbor who takes in stray cats, and he takes it home mainly because his father prefers a dog. He brings the cat with him almost everywhere he goes, and more often than not Cat, Dave's name for his pet, creates complications. The storyline is somewhat disjointed, as Dave clashes with his father; meets a prospective criminal, Tom, who ultimately rejects a life of crime; builds up to a fight with his best friend, Nick; meets a girl, Mary, and makes a date with her; and causes his neighbor, Kate, who gave him Cat, to be in trouble with the authorities because she has too many cats. All of these conflicts are quickly and too easily resolved. The story lacks tension and focuses on details that might be quite unfamiliar to today's children.

Parish, Peggy. *Amelia Bedelia*, illtd. Fritz Seibel. New York: Harper, 1963, 1992. (Chapter Book/Humor/Series)

The charm of this easy reader is in the use, or perhaps the misuse, of the English language. Amelia Bedelia goes to work for the Rogers family and follows Mrs. Rogers' written instructions in her own practical way. When Mrs. Rogers says to change the towels in the green bathroom, she changes them by cutting pieces out of them. She "dusts the furniture" by covering it with dusting powder, and draws the drapes by sketching them on a piece of paper. But because the first thing Amelia Bedelia did when she arrived at work was bake a delicious lemon pie, the Rogers decide she should stay. The popularity of Amelia Bedelia led to several more books, but only the first three were illustrated by Fritz Seibel.

Scarry, Richard. *Best Word Book Ever*. New York: Golden Books, 1963, 1980 (revised). (Picture Book/Concept)

Just one page of this book could entertain many preschoolers for a week, though some might lose interest after a few seconds of trying to sort things out because the pages are so crowded. From kindergarten up, Scarry's busy little animals offer a challenge, especially in trying to find Lowly Worm on each page, even though the text is somewhat condescending and lacks depth.

Sendak, Maurice. *Where the Wild Things Are*. New York: Harper, 1963, 1988. CALDECOTT MEDAL. (Fantasy/Picture Book)

When Max misbehaves and is sent to his room without supper, he creates his own world and journeys to where the wild things are, who make him their king. But once Max has tamed the wild things, he finds that he is homesick and returns home, where his dinner is waiting, still hot. The book is a subtle combination of text and pictures, and each scene in the book takes up more space on the page than the one before it, until three double spreads in the middle show the wild rumpus taking place with no need—and no room—for text. As Max starts back home, the text resumes and the framed illustrations get smaller and smaller.

Sobel, Donald J. *Encyclopedia Brown, Boy Detective*, illtd. Leonard Shortall. New York: Morrow, 1963; New York: Bantam, 1985. (Mystery/Easy Reader)

Leroy Brown, better known as Encyclopedia because of his photographic memory, sets up his own detective agency and not only solves crimes for his friends but even helps out his father, who is chief of police in Idaville. Encyclopedia, at 10, is smarter than any of his friends, and each case he solves offers the child reading the book an opportunity to guess the solution and check the end of the book to see if it's right—10 cases and 10 solutions in each book. This resourceful young hero has been the star detective in many Encyclopedia Brown books over the years, and was introduced by Sobel to emulate the respected Sherlock Holmes mysteries for older readers.

Stockton, Frank R. *The Griffin and the Minor Canon*, illtd. Maurice Sendak. New York: Holt, Rinehart and Winston, 1963; New York: Harper, 1987. (Fantasy/Fairy)

Stockton was an assistant editor and frequent contributor to *St. Nicholas* magazine in the late 1800s. He was one of the few American authors who wrote fairy tales on a regular basis, and this story, despite its European background, reflects a sense of humor that is completely American in its droll treatment of the apparent dilemma faced by villagers convinced their children will be eaten up by the terrible Griffin who has just come to town. As it turns out, the Griffin merely wants to see the statue of himself on the church, and the only person who seems to understand this and accept him is the Minor Canon. Maurice Sendak brings the characters to life in this picture book version of Stockton's story.

Alexander, Lloyd. *The Book of Three*. New York: Holt, Rinehart and Winston, 1964; New York: Dell, 1980. Also, *The Black Cauldron* (New York: Holt, 1965; New York: Dell, 1980); *The Castle of Llyr* (New York: Holt, 1966; New York: Dell, 1980); *Taran Wanderer* (New York: Holt, 1967; New York: Dell, 1980); and *The High King* (New York: Holt, 1968; New York: Dell, 1980). (Fantasy)

In this epic adventure Taran is a young farmboy who becomes Assistant Pig Keeper for the oracular pig Hen Wen, and when the pig, sensing evil close by, digs her way out of her pen and dashes off into the woods, Taran follows. During his search, he accumulates an unlikely group of friends: Gurgi, a whining, always disheveled, but loyal creature; Eilonwy, a princess two years younger than Taran and outspoken to a fault; the heroic Gwydion, who has vowed to protect Taran; and Fflewddur, a bard who carries his harp with him at all times. Threatened by witches, wizards, and sorcerers, Taran and his friends protect Hen Wen from the warlord called the Horned King, whose master, King Arawn of the Land of the Dead, wants her for her powers. The group continually faces danger in their quest for the black cauldron and their vow to save Prydain from evil.

Dahl, Roald. *Charlie and the Chocolate Factory*, illtd. Joseph Schindelman. New York: Knopf, 1964; New York: BDD, 1989. (Fantasy)

Only five children holding golden tickets will be allowed to tour the Wonka factory, a candy factory owned by the mysterious Willy Wonka. Charlie, who lives with his mother and father and four bedridden grandparents, dreams of finding a ticket but knows how unlikely it is. The tickets are hidden in candy bars and only those who can buy candy every day have a good chance of winning. Charlie gets one candy bar a year on his birthday, and his gift candy bar doesn't have a golden ticket. Then, when it seems too late, and four of the five tickets have been found, Charlie finds a whole dollar in the street and, because he is so very hungry, he buys not one but two candy bars and in the second bar is the coveted golden ticket. And so begins Charlie's adventure in the fabulous candy factory, an adventure quite different from what he and the other ticket holders expected.

De Regniers, Beatrice Schenk. *May I Bring a Friend?*, illtd. Beni Montresor. New York: Atheneum, 1964; New York: Macmillan, 1989. CALDECOTT MEDAL. (Picture Book/Concept)

Montresor came to America from Italy in 1960, at which time the only children's book he had ever read was *Pinocchio*. The illustrations in this award-winning book are colorful and sharply detailed. The story is written in rhyme and describes a small child's visit to the king and queen, who have invited him to tea. "May I bring a friend?" he asks, and each day for six days he brings with him a different animal until, on Saturday, he reciprocates by inviting the king and queen to tea where the animals are—at the zoo.

Fitzhugh, Louise. *Harriet the Spy*. New York: Harper, 1964, 1990. (Realistic Fiction/Social Behavior)

Eleven-year-old Harriet Welsch writes down her impressions of people in her notebook, and not only is she painfully honest with her descriptions, she also has an exceptional command of language and is able to make those descriptions quite vivid. When her classmates confiscate her notebook and read her unflattering descriptions, Harriet is ostracized, and her resulting unacceptable behavior at home causes her parents to send her to a psychiatrist, who insists she give up the notebook. Old Golly, the live-in sitter who watches out for Harriet because her parents are seldom around, is the only dependable person in Harriet's life. But Harriet's parents, wealthy and painfully conscious of social standing, dismiss Old Golly when they discover that Harriet has gone to the movies with Old Golly and her gentleman friend, Mr. Waldenstein. Harriet is left with nothing to cling to, and when she is offered the editorship of the school paper, it seems to be the answer to all her problems. But, in an effort to entertain her readers without alienating them, Harriet writes about the private lives of the families she spies on, including comments her parents have made about people in the neighborhood. Old Golly told her once that sometimes the truth hurts too much and small lies are necessary. Harriet has to decide which is more important—her compulsion to write, which means making an insincere public apology, or always telling the truth.

Green, Hannah (pseud. of Joanne Greenberg). *I Never Promised You a Rose Garden*. New York: Holt, Rinehart and Winston, 1964. (Realistic Fiction/Autobiographical)

One subject never discussed in children's books, even in the socially aware Sixties, was mental illness. When this book was published, it not only addressed a subject that needed exploration, especially for a young adult audience, it was also autobiographical, though not revealed as such until some time after publication. The protagonist in the story is 16-year-old Deborah Blau, and Joanne Greenberg, under the pseudonym of Hannah Green, allows the reader to enter Deborah's bizarre world and experience her very gradual emergence from madness to self-control. Greenberg handles her material with consummate skill, and the book is one that will never be outdated, as we can recognize and relate to that introspective aspect of ourselves that is explored in this novel.

Hodges, Margaret (adapted from Lafcadio Hearn). *The Wave*, illtd. Blair Lent. Boston: Houghton Mifflin, 1964. (Folk/Myth/Picture Book/Japan)

Hodges, a children's librarian, discovered this story in a book by Japan expert Lafcadio Hearn and adapted it for children. Blair Lent's cardboard-cut block prints follow Japanese traditional art to create growing suspense as a tidal wave threatens a small village after an earthquake and Ojiisan, an old man, sets fire to his hillside rice fields to bring the villagers up the mountain where they will be safe from the wave.

Hunt, Irene. *Across Five Aprils*. New York: Follett, 1964. (Realistic Fiction/Historical/Civil War)

Hunt extends the Civil War beyond the textbooks and into the human realm, portraying the war's emotional impact as experienced by the Creighton family when they watch two sons set out to fight on the Union side and one son on the Confederate side, brother against brother. They try to understand the convoluted reasoning behind the war and the sometimes controversial actions of military and political leaders. The youngest Creighton boy, Jethro, nine years old and excited about the war at its beginning, takes on the main responsibility at home when his father suffers a heart attack, and over the years comes to a deeper understanding of the tragic circumstances brought about by those who rely too much on violence and revenge instead of looking for a peaceful resolution.

Merrill, Jean. *The Pushcart War*, illtd. Ronni Solbert. New York: Scott, 1964; New York: Dell, 1987. (Science Fiction/Social Adjustment)

This story was set in a distant future, namely 1996, but that future has become a very real present in a New York City overrun with traffic and becoming overwhelmed by big business. The lighthearted setting of the conflict, between pushcart peddlers on the streets of New York and the greedy conglomerates who own the huge trucks that are crowding out the pushcarts, makes war seem like fun in this timeless fantasy, but Merrill's underlying message—that if enough American people join in a common cause, they can win against all odds—makes the story far more serious than seems evident at first. It is the written word, through letters to the editor in the local paper, that turns the tide, limits the number and size of trucks on the city streets, and guarantees the presence of pushcarts selling pretzels, hot dogs and sauerkraut, fruit and vegetables, and peanuts to the people who depend on them every day.

Silverstein, Shel. *The Giving Tree*. New York: Harper, 1964. (Picture Book/Concept)

Silverstein created this simple story of a tree that never stops giving until nothing is left but a stump, and the tree finally gives even that, never asking for anything in return. The boy, who, through the story, ages from a young man to an old man, never stops taking from the tree, and by the same token, never knows the satisfaction that comes from giving. For a child, this may be a story that offers security, but for the parent reading the story to a child, the ethical message is disturbing.

Wojciechowska, Maia. *Shadow of a Bull*, illtd. Alvin Smith. New York: Atheneum, 1964; New York: Macmillan, 1992. NEWBERY MEDAL. (Realistic Fiction/Spain)

Ten-year-old Manolo's father, Juan Olivar, who was the greatest bullfighter in all of Spain, was killed by a bull when Manolo was three. Now, it is expected that Manolo will follow in his father's footsteps, although no one has ever asked Manolo if he is an *aficion*, a lover of the sport of bullfighting. No one has asked if he would rather be something else, perhaps a doctor who cares for those who are injured in the ring. Finally, Manolo has to make his own choice and stand up for himself to the people in the town, who have made sure he and his mother have not needed anything since his father died, and to whom Manolo owes a debt.

Cleary, Beverly. *The Mouse and the Motorcycle*, illtd. Louis Darling. New York: Morrow, 1965; New York: Avon, 1990. (Fantasy/Chapter Book)

Ralph is a personable and adventurous mouse who lives with his family behind a knothole in Room 215 of the Mountain View Inn, a rather old but stately hotel slightly off the beaten track. When a young boy, Keith, occupies Room 215, Ralph watches him play with his toy vehicles, one of which is a bright red motorcycle. Ralph's dream is to be mature enough to go to the first floor of the hotel and to ride a motorcycle. Thanks to the boy's generosity, Ralph not only rides the motorcycle but also is given a little helmet with a rubber band under his chin to keep him safe. And when Keith becomes ill, Ralph has to go to the first floor and even outside to try and find an aspirin for Keith's fever when it seems there are no aspirins readily available.

De Trevino, Elizabeth Borton. *I, Juan De Pareja*. New York: Farrar, Straus and Giroux, 1965, 1987. NEWBERY MEDAL. (Realistic Fiction/Biographical/Spain)

In this tale, based on the life of 17th-century Spanish painter Diego de Silva Velazquez, de Trevino (who was born in California and became a resident of Mexico) writes the story from the viewpoint of a black slave, Juan de Pareja, whose portrait, painted by Velazquez, is one of the artist's most famous works. The various settings in the story offer a clear view of Europe in the 1600s with its hardships, lack of medical knowledge, and social hierarchies, as well as a deep appreciation of fine art. The loyalty of Pareja to his master, his apparent acceptance of the condition of slavery, and his concern for his own soul when he violates the law by giving in to his creative needs seem more the result of the author's creativity than what may have been the true feelings of Pareja himself. Pareja's portrait by Velazquez hangs in the Metropolitan Museum of Art in New York City.

MacGregor, Ellen, and Dora Pantell. *Miss Pickerell on the Moon*. New York: McGraw-Hill, 1965. (Science Fiction/Series)

Miss Lavinia Pickerell, a female Doctor Dolittle, is the first to explore the far side of the moon. In this adventure, the moon community in the book has been settled for quite some time, with an apartment complex, a laboratory, and even a newspaper office. No computers, however. Dora Pantell carries on MacGregor's propensity for combining fact and fiction as Miss Pickerell dines in the Astral Cafeteria on the moon and has dehydrated vegetable salad made edible by squirting water into a bag. During her visit to this well-established community, Miss Pickerell is the only woman there. The effort to create equal opportunities for women in fields heretofore limited to men had only just begun.

Neville, Emily Cheney. *Berries Goodman*. New York: Harper, 1965, 1992. (Realistic Fiction/Social Behavior)

Bertrand Goodman, nicknamed "Berries," is the narrator in this story that attempts to explore anti-Semitism in a suburb of New York City. Unfortunately, Neville makes nine-year-old Berries the narrator, and because of his naive viewpoint the clash between his prejudiced neighbors, specifically Sandy Graham and her mother, and Berries' friend Sidney Fine and his mother, who live in the Jewish section of town, loses its emotional impact. Neville's choice of resolution is for the Goodmans to sell their house, located in a residential section that has always avoided selling to Jewish families, to friends from New York City, also named Goodman, who happen to be Jewish. Laura Hobson had addressed anti-Semitism in America almost two decades earlier with her best-selling adult novel *Gentleman's Agreement.*[17]

Nic Leodhas, Sorche. *Always Room for One More*, illtd. Nonny Hogrogian. New York: Holt, 1965. CALDECOTT MEDAL. (Folk/Myth/Picture Book/Scotland)

The Scottish words in this old song make this book fun to read aloud, and Hogrogian's illustrations utilize pen-and-ink cross-hatching style of art to create the house and the people, all resting on a soft grassy hill of purple heather. Lachie MacLachlan is a hospitable man, and, though he has a wife and 10 children in a two-room house, everyone is welcome because, he says, there is always room for one more. But one day the house can take no more and it dings down (collapses). But generosity brings rewards, and a new house "double as wide and high" takes the place of the old house.

Peet, Bill. *Chester the Worldly Pig*. Boston: Houghton Mifflin, 1965, 1980. (Picture Book/Animal/Humor)

Former Disney artist Peet transfers his cartooning experience to the characters he creates in his well-crafted picture storybooks. Chester is a pig, but not just any pig. He wants more than anything to be discovered by the circus, and every time a train goes by, Chester balances on his nose, just in case it's a circus train. But when the circus train does go by, nobody notices him and he has to follow the circus to show them his talents. Sure enough, they put him in the show, but what he is expected to do is not at all what he thought it would be. Poor Chester has a great many disappointing adventures before his true nature finally becomes evident and his dreams come true.

Sendak, Maurice. *Hector Protector and As I Went Over the Water*. New York: Harper, 1965, 1990. (Poetry/Picture Book)

Sendak interprets two short nursery rhymes in his own original fashion. In the first, the line, "Hector Protector is dressed all in green," is transformed into a continuing series of illustrations, in which Hector, independent and stubborn to a fault, is rejected by the king and queen and is finally sent to bed by his mother without dinner, all because he hates green. In the second rhyme, a small boy is very much in control as captain of his ship and manages to befriend a sea monster and two crows. There is a certain similarity in this half of the book to Sendak's award-winning *Where the Wild Things Are* (1963).

Waber, Bernard. *Lyle, Lyle, Crocodile*. Boston: Houghton Mifflin, 1965. (Fantasy/Picture Book/Series)

Lyle is a pet crocodile who now lives with the Primm family in a house on 88th Street in New York City, after having belonged to the traveling Hector P. Valenti, star of stage and screen. Imagine Lyle's surprise when he runs into Mr. Valenti at a department store on Fifth Avenue. He also meets up with Mr. Grumps, who highly disapproves of Lyle and happens to be Mr. Valenti's new boss. The result is that Mr. Valenti gets fired and Lyle is sent to the Central Park Zoo. But Mr. Valenti decides to resume his acting career—with Lyle—and the two start out, first passing the house on 88th Street and then discovering by chance that Mr. Grumps's house is on fire. Needless to say, Lyle saves the day and is once more living on 88th Street. Familiar New York City settings add to the appeal of the story.

Cooper, Susan. *Over Sea, Under Stone* (*Dark Is Rising Sequence*, vol. 1). New York: Macmillan/McElderry, 1966, 1989. (Fantasy)

When the three Drew children, Simon, Barney, and Jane, travel to Cornwall with their parents for a holiday, they look forward to a nice visit with Great-Uncle Meriwether Lewis—"Gumerry," as they call him. But Gumerry keeps disappearing, and the children soon find themselves embroiled in a mystical quest for what might be the Holy Grail, dating back to the days of King Arthur. Their search is hampered by dark forces, which have taken on human form, and the three children are in great peril as they vow to keep the grail from being taken over by the Dark. So begins Cooper's fantasy sequence, which builds slowly in this first book but carefully sets the scene for the suspense to follow in later volumes.

Hunt, Irene. *Up a Road Slowly*. New York: Follett, 1966; New York: Silver Burdett, 1993. NEWBERY MEDAL. (Realistic Fiction/Family/Social Relationships)

Hunt writes with an old-fashioned flair as Julie Trelling tells her story from age seven through age 17, eventually making all the right choices as she observes the mistakes of others. When her mother dies, no one thinks to explain death to her, and when she is taken into her aunt's house, she discovers that her uncle, who lives with his sister, is an unfulfilled alcoholic author who deludes himself but no one else regarding his efforts. Julie also finds herself angry at her sister, who prefers the company of her new husband to spending time with her. She ignores the boy next door who understands her better than anyone and becomes infatuated with a boy who is more concerned about his own desires than with her needs. The story has a quaint charm, reflecting a time that unfortunately no longer exists. Its appeal at present lies in the security it generates.

Ness, Evaline. *Sam, Bangs & Moonshine*. New York: Holt, Rineheart and Winston, 1966. CALDECOTT MEDAL. (Realistic Fiction/Picture Book)

Samantha has a vivid imagination, but the trouble is that her friend Thomas believes everything she says, and when she sends Thomas off to visit her imaginary mermaid mother in a cave by the sea, the tide comes in early and a fast-rising storm almost drowns Thomas and Sam's cat, Bangs. The story is a little too predictable and the tension too quickly resolved, but the experimental style of the illustrations creates appealing characterizations and unusual backgrounds.

Raskin, Ellen. *Nothing Ever Happens on My Block*. New York: Atheneum, 1966; New York: Macmillan, 1989. (Fantasy/Picture Book/Humor)

In Dr. Seuss's *And To Think I Saw It on Mulberry Street* (1937), the protagonist creates imaginary action in an effort to please his father, while in Raskin's book, real action is totally lost on Chester Filbert as he sits on the curb of the street where he lives and moans about the fact that nothing ever happens on his block. In the meantime, behind him, a house is in flames, a masked burglar is hiding behind a tree, a group of children are ringing doorbells and running away, and a parachutist lands on the sidewalk, but Chester sees none of it. Each double spread is a bonanza of activity with Raskin's detailed, color-accented pen-and-ink drawings creating the busy background.

Singer, Isaac B., and Elizabeth Shub. *Zlateh the Goat*, illtd. Maurice Sendak. New York: Harper, 1966. (Folk/Myth/Jewish)

Polish author Singer was a Yiddish storyteller, and this was his first children's book, in which he and Elizabeth Shub translated seven tales from Yiddish into English and Maurice Sendak relied on his own European Jewish roots to interpret the text with perceptive pictures. The stories are those passed down over many generations. The first story is an explanation of the term "fool's paradise"; the second story introduces the devil and his tricks; the third shows how foolish the people of Chelm are; and the fourth singles out one young man of Chelm who is betrothed but cannot seem to hang on to any of the gifts given to him by the bride's family. When he loses a penknife in the hay, he is told he should have kept it in his pocket. So he puts the next gift, a jar of fried chicken fat, in his pocket, and it breaks. This type of misunderstanding continues until the young man and his betrothed seek the advice of the Elder of Chelm, who has no difficulty being wiser than any other adult in the village. The fifth story explains the term "shlemiel"; the sixth is a story in which the devil meets his match through the cleverness of David, a child; and the seventh is the title story about a boy and his goat.

Emberley, Barbara. *Drummer Hoff*, illtd. Ed Emberley. New York: Prentice-Hall, 1967; New York: Simon & Schuster, 1985. CALDECOTT MEDAL. (Folk/Myth/Picture Book)

The text, adapted from folk verse, is deliberately predictable as cumulative rhymes show exactly what Drummer Hoff plans to do. When he finally does it, the resulting chaos is exactly what a child would want it to be. Highly detailed woodcut block prints in bright colors carry the story to its satisfying climax.

Fitzgerald, John D. *The Great Brain*. New York: Dial, 1967, 1985. (Realistic Fiction/Family/Series)

American ingenuity is the key to 10-year-old Tom D. Fitzgerald's success in the community as he uses his great brain to solve every problem that faces him. He is the middle child in the family and the pride of his younger brother, J.D., narrator of the story. Tom is convinced that his great intelligence will always make him a winner, and no matter how the things he does go against him, he always comes out on top in the end. Even though he believes in being rewarded monetarily for his good deeds, his actions are often heroic, thoughtful, and compassionate. The story ends when Tom decides it's wrong to benefit from his own good deeds, but his antics and his reasons for doing them continue in several more books in this series.

Hamilton, Virginia. *Zeely*. New York: Macmillan, 1967, 1993. (Realistic Fiction/Black American/Africa)

In Hamilton's first book, Elizabeth Perry and her younger brother, John, travel by train to their uncle's farm to spend the summer. Elizabeth, who lives in her imagination most of the time, informs her brother that while they are at the farm she will be known as Geeder and he will be called Toeboy. Toeboy is a sociable child who quickly makes new friends in the community, but Geeder is a loner who prefers her imaginary world, until she discovers Zeely, who is 6 feet tall and as regal as a queen. In fact, Geeder is convinced that Zeely is a queen when she discovers a picture of an imperial Watutsi woman in a magazine and it looks just like Zeely. But Zeely, though descended from the African Watutsi tribe, is not descended from royalty. She helps her father take care of his hogs and does her job with pride and compassion. Zeely has learned to accept who she is, and through her, Elizabeth appreciates her own heritage. "We all came out of Africa," Zeely tells her.

Hinton, S. E. *The Outsiders*. New York: Viking, 1967; New York: Dell (Laurel-Leaf), 1982. (Realistic Fiction/Urban)

When 16-year-old Susie Hinton decided to tell her story by creating a young male protagonist called Ponyboy, whose parents have died and whose older brothers, Darry and Soda, watch out for him, she astounded reviewers with her perception and candor. The story is set in New York City where 14-year-old Ponyboy is a member of the Greasers, made up of hoodlums and dropouts and adolescents identified by their long hair, slicked down with grease. The members of an opposing group are called Socs, and they are overprivileged, have their own cars, a great deal of spare time, and take great pleasure in ganging up on Greasers and beating them mercilessly. In the long run, being a Soc is not a particularly enviable state to be in; dysfunctional family life knows no social barriers, and the Socs in many ways are as desperate for emotional security as the Greasers. The story builds to a major confrontation between the Greasers and the Socs, resulting in murder and self-sacrifice. But it is Ponyboy, bright and articulate, who becomes proof that it is possible to set reachable goals in the midst of inner-city despair.

Konigsburg, E. L. *From the Mixed-Up Files of Mrs. Basil E. Frankweiler*. New York: Atheneum, 1967; New York: Buccaneer Books, 1992. NEWBERY MEDAL. (Realistic Fiction/Urban)

Mrs. Frankweiler, a wealthy dowager, explains to her lawyer why she has decided to make 11-year-old Claudia Kincaid her heir. The story she tells evolves into Claudia's viewpoint: Claudia is convinced her family doesn't appreciate her and makes plans to run away from home. To alleviate boredom, she invites her younger brother Jamie to join her because he always has money. Their destination is the Metropolitan Museum of Art in Manhattan because Claudia considers it different, interesting, and very elegant. Claudia enjoys preparing for her adventure as much as she expects to enjoy the adventure itself. The two young people spend several nights in the museum and actually sleep in the beds of royalty, but, as satisfying as the whole event turns out to be when Claudia solves a mystery it is the final outcome that keeps Claudia from ever being bored again, thanks to Mrs. Frankweiler.

Langton, Jane. *The Swing in the Summerhouse*, illtd. Eric Blegvad. New York: Harper, 1967. (Fantasy)

Eleanor and Edward Hall's Aunt Lily and Uncle Krishna are off to India, and the two children are left under the care of bookish, absentminded Uncle Freddy. Uncle Krishna has built a six-sided summerhouse to entertain the children, but he hasn't quite finished it. He warns them not to use the unfinished doorway, the sixth side, although they can use the other five entrances into the summerhouse. He knows the summerhouse is a gateway to several different adventures for the children, but he hasn't yet put up the swing that will take them into those adventures, and he has boarded up the unfinished and dangerous gateway. Of course Edward puts up a swing, and of course, the barrier is broken and the dangerous gateway is entered. Edward and Eleanor, along with the next-door neighbors, Mrs. Dorian and her five-year-old daughter, Georgie, as well as Edward's friend Oliver and Uncle Freddy, all become involved in the secret of the summerhouse with the result that the children and Mrs. Dorian learn what Uncle Freddy has always known—one must always look at the world with the enthusiasm and curiosity of a child.

Lionni, Leo. *Frederick*. New York: Pantheon, 1967; New York: Knopf, 1973. (Folk/Myth/Picture Book)

A stone wall, a tree, and grass and flowers cut from paper and formed into a collage create the setting for a family of field mice getting ready for winter, all except Frederick, who doesn't seem to be working. But Frederick has a special gift that dispels the gloom of winter and makes it grow bright, the gift of words and colors to create uplifting poetry when it's needed most.

Mayer, Mercer. *A Boy, A Dog and a Frog*. New York: Dial, 1967; New York: Viking, 1992. (Picture Book/Wordless/Humor)

Mayer goes one step beyond simple language in books for preschoolers and leaves out language altogether, telling this story in pictures only, as a small boy and his dog set out to capture a frog, which chooses not to be caught. The concept appealed to children and four more of these books were published: *A Boy, a Dog, a Frog and a Friend*; *One Frog Too Many*; *Frog on His Own*; and *Frog, Where Are You?*

Sandburg, Carl. *The Wedding Procession of the Rag Doll and the Broom Handle and Who Was In It*, illtd. Harriet Pincus. New York: Harcourt, 1967, 1978. A picture book adaptation from *Rootabaga Stories* (1992). (Fantasy)

llustrator Pincus, whose style brings Sendak to mind, takes Sandburg's imaginative text into the realm of the picture book with this adaptation and shows the way in which choice words help to create choice pictures. At the wedding of the Rag Doll and the Broom Handle, the wedding procession is highly unusual and includes Spoon Lickers, each with "something slickery sweet or fat to eat on a spoon"; the Tin Pan Bangers; Chocolate Chins; the Dirty Bibs, who "looked around and laughed and looked around and laughed again"; several more unique beings; and ends with the Sleepyheads, whose heads were "slimpsing down" and who never looked around at all.

Shulevitz, Uri. *One Monday Morning*. New York: Scribner, 1967; New York: Macmillan, 1986. (Picture Book/Fantasy)

On a rainy Monday, the king, the queen, and the little prince decide to visit a small boy, but he's at the corner in his raincoat waiting for a bus. On Tuesday, the king, the queen, the little prince, and the knight decide to visit, but the little boy is riding the subway. They all return on Wednesday, with the addition of the royal guard, but the little boy is at the laundromat watching clothes spin. Each day the line of visitors gets longer, but the little boy is never home. Finally, on Sunday, his visitors find him at home, and the sun comes out.

Snyder, Zilpha Keatley. *The Egypt Game*, illtd. Alton Raible. New York: Atheneum, 1967; New York: Dell, 1986. (Realistic Fiction/Mystery)

When a group of children meet in a deserted shed to play an imaginative game set in Egypt, someone is watching them. After awhile, they realize they're being observed but make that part of the game as well. In the meantime, a child has been murdered in the neighborhood, and the murderer could be nearby. But the very real danger the children face is not played up by the author and in fact the threat is much too easily resolved and never is the focus of the story. The imaginary Egypt Game and the characters of each of the children take on the most importance, while the reader anticipates a far more sinister development that doesn't happen.

Yolen, Jane. *The Emperor and the Kite*, illtd. Ed Young. New York: World, 1967; New York: Philomel, 1988. (Original Folk/Myth/Picture Book/China)

Djeow Seow, Chinese for "the smallest one," is the fourth daughter of the emperor, who pays no attention to her at all. "In fact she was so insignificant, the emperor often forgot he had a fourth daughter at all." Her four brothers and three sisters ignore her as well, and she is a lonely child who has only her kite to keep her company. When her father is overthrown and imprisoned in a high tower, Djeow Seow's brothers and sisters escape to a neighboring kingdom, but the small girl is left behind and manages to use her kite to keep her father alive by tying a basket of food to the kite twice every day. The people of the kingdom are sad because they think their emperor is dead, until, with the help of a monk, Djeow Seow finds a way to use her kite to rescue her father from the tower. Young's East Asian papercut illustrations embellish this story of recognition and love.

Alexander, Lloyd. *The High King* (final book of the *Prydain Chronicles*). New York: Henry Holt, 1968; New York: Dell, 1980. NEWBERY MEDAL. (Fantasy)

In the first book of the *Prydain Chronicles*, Taran is very young and not too sensible, not even living up to the job of Assistant Pig Keeper, but as his adventures continue, Taran Wanderer reaches a maturity that makes him a leader, and in this last book his new maturity helps him not only to overcome evil, but also to know who he really is. Although this volume can be appreciated without reading the four books that precede it, the rich characterizations and continuing suspense of the earlier volumes add much to the adventure.

Carle, Eric. *1,2,3 to the Zoo*. New York: William Collins and World Publishing, 1968; New York: Putnam, 1990. (Picture Book/Concept)

Carle, like Lionni, used collage to create his art, but he added more textures and designs than Lionni and always made sure children could interact with the concept he was presenting. In this counting book, a train is taking animals to the zoo—one elephant, two hippos, etc.—and down in the left corner of each double spread, the train accumulates flatcars with cages containing the proper number of animals until, at the end, a fold-out page shows all the animals in the zoo and, in the corner below, empty cages on a string of flatcars being pulled by an engine.

Freeman, Don. *Corduroy*. New York: Viking, 1968; New York: Puffin, 1993. Also, *A Pocket for Corduroy* (New York: Viking, 1978; New York: Puffin, 1993). (Fantasy/Picture Book/Toys)

The story is slight but the character of Corduroy, a stuffed bear, appealed enough to small children to warrant a sequel. With pastel drawings, Freeman places Corduroy on a shelf in a toy store, where he is seen by a little girl, but because he has lost a button on his overalls, the girl's mother won't buy him. Not to worry, for the little girl, Lisa, has saved up some money and returns to the store to buy Corduroy, much to his delight. The fact that Lisa is black has no real bearing on the story except to finally recognize, as was the case with Ezra Jack Keats's Peter in *The Snowy Day* (1962), that all of society is not white.

Hamilton, Virginia. *The House of Dies Drear*. New York: Macmillan, 1968, 1984. (Realistic Fiction/Mystery)

Thomas Small is the protagonist here and shares his father's interest in black history. The Smalls—mother, father, Thomas, and twin baby brothers—move from Tennessee to Ohio because Thomas's father, a black college professor, wants to research an old house on the slave route. It's a house that was owned by Dies Drear, who assisted slaves heading for Canada through the Underground Railroad system. Drear and two of three escaping slaves were murdered, and it is said the house is haunted. The story touches on the prejudices of small communities, the twins' telepathic awareness, the concept of the underworld, the mystery of a hidden treasure and the solution to murder, any one of which could have been the basis for a book. This story, with its myriad characters and paths of intrigue, doesn't always move in a logical way. It's as if Hamilton had so many things she wanted to explore, she never really followed through on any of them.

Hutchins, Pat. *Rosie's Walk*. New York: Macmillan, 1968, 1984. (Picture Book/Animal)

Hutchins describes, with a minimum number of words, Rosie the chicken's walk around the farm where she lives. In the pictures, however, Rosie is stalked by a fox, although she never notices him, a fox who is thwarted every time he tries to catch Rosie. Rosie matter-of-factly ends her walk and gets back home just in time for dinner. Hutchins' colorful, detailed designs add energy to her illustrations.

Larrick, Nancy, ed. *Piping Down the Valleys Wild*, illtd. Ellen Raskin. New York: Delacorte, 1968, 1985. (Poetry/Anthology)

This anthology presents a broad spectrum of poetry and verse, old and new, as chosen by children. Certain poems have an unforgettable beat that keeps them alive through many generations, for instance: "I must go down to the seas again, to the lonely sea and the sky" (John Masefield); "They're changing the guard at Buckingham Palace—/Christopher Robin went down with Alice" (A. A. Milne); "They fished among all the fish in the sea/For the fish with the deep sea smile" (Margaret Wise Brown); and "I like it when it's mizzly/and just a little drizzly" (Aileen Fisher).

Le Guin, Ursula. *The Wizard of Earthsea*. New York: Parnassus Press, 1968; New York: Macmillan, 1992. (Fantasy)

At age seven, the boy Ged discovers that he can make magic, and by the time he is 15, still limited in what he is allowed to do, he is anxious to use those powers, even if he doesn't understand the full extent of his magical ability. Ged, whose secret name is Sparrowhawk, was born a wizard in the archipelago of Earthsea, but he was impatient with his teachers, who recognized his ability and tried to teach him the importance of restraint. At 15, on a dare from a fellow student of wizardry, he chooses to draw upon powers he is not able to control in order to assuage his wounded pride. In so doing, he lets evil loose on the archipelago, a dark shadow that threatens to control Ged for its own purposes. Followed by *The Tombs of Atuan* (Atheneum, 1971) and *The Farthest Shore* (Atheneum, 1972).

Mosel, Arlene. *Tikki Tikki Tembo*, illtd. Blair Lent. New York: Henry Holt, 1968, 1989. (Folk/Myth/Picture Book/China)

Based on a Chinese folk tale and illustrated with pen-and-ink wash drawings, storyteller Mosel explains why Chinese families never give their children long names. When brother Chang falls in the well, Tikki tikki tembo-no sa rembo-chari bari ruchi-pip peri pembo is able to tell someone quickly and Chang is saved before any real damage is done, but when Tikki tikki tembo falls in the well, it takes so long for Chang to say his name to those who might save him that Tikki tikki tembo's rescue and recuperation is lengthy indeed.

Lester, Julius. *To Be a Slave*, illtd. Tom Feelings. New York: Dial, 1968; New York: Scholastic, 1986. (Informational/Anthology/Historical/Black American)

This collection of slave narratives was put into book form by Lester, who tied the story together by interjecting definitive commentary between accounts. Feelings's powerful illustrations added drama (see illustration p. 160). One hundred years after the end of the Civil War, the black population in America was almost as oppressed as they had been as slaves. Lester and Feelings tried to reach the American public with this painfully honest account of a tragically downtrodden race of people and decipher why it has been so difficult for them to rise above poverty. The book was recognized as a Newbery Honor Book in 1969.

Zindel, Paul. *The Pigman*. New York: Harper, 1968. (Realistic Fiction/Social Behavior)

Written as if narrated by two young people who take turns writing the chapters, this book is a double confession of wrongdoing through thoughtlessness. John Conlan offers a candid description of his teachers and the school librarian in the first chapter, and Lorraine Jensen follows up in the second chapter with excuses for John and an attempt to justify what happened to the man they call "the Pigman." Mr. Pignati (the Pigman) is a truly good person who is very lonely and John and Lorraine take advantage of his ingenuous nature by accepting his charity. Not satisfied with that, they actually invade the old man's house when he is taken to the hospital with a heart attack and invite their classmates in for a party the night before he is scheduled to return home. But Mr. Pignati comes home early, and the result of their escapade is tragically irreversible.

Armstrong, William. *Sounder*. New York: Harper and Row, 1969, 1972. NEWBERY MEDAL. (Realistic Fiction/Animal/Regional)

Sounder is a coon dog, a mixture of Georgia redbone hound and bull dog, and he belongs to a loving family that often has little to eat. But the dog is completely loyal to his master and cares deeply for the family that always shares what they have with him, even when it's nothing more than a few crumbs of stale mush. The father, heartsick because his family has so little, finally goes out one night and steals a pig. For a short and memorable time, the family eats ham and sausage. But the memory of that feast must last the boy, his mother, and the younger children a very long time. The father is dragged off to prison, and when Sounder tries to follow, he is shot down, then disappears into the woods. For many months, the boy searches for Sounder, refusing to accept that he might be dead. Finally, the dog, crippled and deformed by his injury, returns. When, after many years, the father, also crippled and deformed, returns, the reunion is a painful one. As the boy matures in his father's absence, he suffers great humiliation at the hands of cruel whites because he is poor and black. Armstrong's description of the boy's treatment and his great effort to control his almost unbearable anger shows the power of language to create understanding and empathy.

Benchley, Nathaniel. *Sam the Minuteman*, illtd. Arnold Lobel. New York: Harper, 1969, 1987. (Easy Reader/Realistic Fiction/American Revolution)

Benchley made history easy to digest for beginning readers and gave a succint overview of the onset of the Revolutionary War from the viewpoint of a young boy, Sam, who found himself involved in war after someone, on the morning of April 19, 1775, fired a gun just as he, his friend John, and other Minutemen were planning to leave a scene without confronting the English troops. The story is perfectly complemented by Arnold Lobel's concisely rendered illustrations.

Carle, Eric. *The Very Hungry Caterpillar*. New York: Philomel, 1969; New York: Putnam, 1991. (Picture Book/Animal/Interactive)

Carle's books connect very solidly with small children who are encouraged to become involved in the pictures through Carle's collages and unusual format. In this small adventure, a caterpillar eats through everything in sight, and there is a hole in each page to prove it, until he wraps himself up in a chrysalis and emerges as a butterfly.

Cleaver, Vera and Bill. *Where the Lilies Bloom*, illtd. Jim Spanfeller. Philadelphia: Lippincott, 1969; New York: Harper, 1991. (Realistic Fiction/Regional)

In the land "Where the Lilies Bloom So Fair," as the old hymn says, 14-year-old Mary Call Luther finds herself faced with her father's sudden death and cannot let the neighbors know about it because they will divide the family. Mary Call and her three brothers and sisters manage to bury their father and survive through a long, hard winter in the Great Smokies. The strength and independence of Mary Call make her a true heroine in a man's world. She also represents a proud people, the "wildcrafters," who gather medicinal plants on the mountain slopes, a people about whom little is known but who deserve recognition.

Jarrell, Randall. *Fly by Night*, illtd. Maurice Sendak. New York: Farrar, Straus & Giroux, 1969, 1985. (Fantasy/Poetry)

This book is a modern fairy tale, a combination of text and poetry, describing a repetitive dream and a story poem within the dream:

> The boy plays on the lawn with the dog and cat or in the forest with the dog—there aren't any children for him to play with. In the middle of the afternoon he goes and stands by the mailbox, so that the mailman can hand the mail to him instead of putting it in the box . . . Sometimes the mailman hears him calling, "Here Reddy! Here Reddy!" to the dog. The cat's name is Flour, the boy's name is David. At night David can fly.

But during the day David forgets that he was able to fly during the night. After he has the dream about the owl mother, he almost remembers the next morning, but when "the sunlight streams in through the windows, he holds his hand out for the orange juice, and his mother looks at him like his mother."

Konigsburg, E. L. *About the B'Nai Bagels*. New York: Atheneum, 1969. (Realistic Fiction/Humor/Social Adjustment/Jewish American)

Marc Seltzer, a 12-year-old Jewish boy living in a suburb of New York City, is preparing for his bar mitzvah. In the meantime, it is almost Little League time and much to Mark's chagrin, his mother has volunteered as manager of his team and has appointed his 21-year-old brother, Spencer, as coach. Mark's team didn't do well at all the summer before, and he doesn't believe this year will be any different. But it is. Mark learns something new about friendship and about character, faces prejudice for the first time, and has to make an ethical decision. By the time he is 13 and ready for his bar mitzvah, he is also ready for manhood.

Neufeld, John. *Lisa, Bright and Dark*. Chatham, N.Y.: S.G. Phillips, 1969; New York: NAL Dutton, 1970. (Realistic Fiction/Social Behavior)

When Lisa Shilling tells her parents she's hearing voices and fears she may be going crazy, they refuse to believe her. In desperation, she finally confides in her friends, Mary Nell Fickett and Betsy Goodman.

Mary Nell, referred to as M.N. in the story, is convinced that if they all work together, they can help Lisa. But even when they include Elizabeth Frazer, who somehow seems to understand Lisa better than anyone else, these three well-meaning teenagers find themselves facing a situation far more dangerous than they had ever anticipated.

Raskin, Ellen. *Spectacles*. New York: Atheneum 1969; New York: Macmillan, 1988. (Picture Book/Humor)

Iris Fogel is frightened by dragons and giant birds, entertained by an Indian, a horse, and a bull dog, and confronted by a kangaroo, a caterpillar, and an elephant until she gets a pair of glasses and discovers that all those things are really friends and relatives. Raskin's sketches, showing the contrast between seeing and not seeing, are clever and imaginative.

Steig, William. *Sylvester and the Magic Pebble*. New York: Simon and Schuster, 1969, 1988. CALDECOTT MEDAL. (Fantasy/Picture Book/Animal)

Sylvester Duncan happens to be a donkey and lives very happily with his mother and father at Acorn Road in Oatsdale. Sylvester collects pebbles, and one day he finds a unique red pebble and discovers that it is magic and will grant wishes. Unfortunately, Sylvester, who isn't used to magic, wishes himself a rock and has no way of reversing the wish. His parents are greatly concerned when he doesn't come home and spend several weeks trying to find him but finally decide that tragedy has befallen him. In the meantime, night follows day and day follows night again and again. The seasons pass, and on a sunny day in May, Sylvester's parents go on a picnic to Strawberry Hill and set out their food on the rock that is Sylvester. Mr. Duncan finds a red pebble and says, "What a fantastic pebble . . . Sylvester would have loved it for his collection." He places the pebble on the rock, giving Sylvester the ability to make a wish.

Steptoe, John. *Stevie*. New York: Harper, 1969, 1986. (Picture Book/Black American/Urban)

When Bobby's mother offers to baby-sit for a neighbor's little boy, Stevie, Bobby resents the intrusion. He's an only child and he's not used to sharing or having responsibility for someone younger. "Why I gotta put up with him? My momma only had one kid. I used to have a lot of fun before old stupid came to live with us," says Bobby. But then Stevie moves away, and Bobby starts remembering all the good things about him. For some reason, he remembers a lot more good than bad.

Viorst, Judith. *I'll Fix Anthony*, illtd. Arnold Lobel. New York: Harper, 1969; New York: Macmillan, 1988. (Picture Book/Humor)

Anthony's younger brother can't wait until he is six years old, because when he's six he'll fix Anthony, who orders him around all the time and tells him he thinks he stinks, even though his mother insists that Anthony loves him. When he is six, he is convinced he will be bigger than Anthony and will be able to do everything better than his brother. But he's not six yet, and Anthony still says he stinks. Lobel's illustrations add character to this story, the text of which originally appeared in *Good Housekeeping* magazine.

Zolotow, Charlotte. *The Hating Book*, illtd. Ben Shecter. New York: Harper, 1969, 1989. (Picture Book/Concept/Social Relationships)

Zolotow is noted for saying a great deal using only a few words about social challenges in the lives of very small children, and illustrator Shecter portrays with understanding the alienation of two friends who must learn to communicate with one another before they can resume their friendship.

NOTES

1. Children born between 1946 and 1964 are commonly known as baby boomers because of the increased birth rate in this country following World War II.
2. James Haskins and Kathleen Benson. *The 60s Reader*, pp. 2–3.
3. Ibid., p. 60.
4. John Rowe Townsend. *A Sounding of Storytellers*, p. 100.
5. Ibid.
6. Barbara Bader. *American Picturebooks*, p. 368.
7. Lee Kingman, ed. *Newbery and Caldecott Medal Books: 1956–1965*, p. 239.
8. Quote by Lloyd Alexander from Holt, Rinehart and Winston library promotion brochure regarding *The Book of Three*, 1963. Located at Kerlan Collection, University of Minnesota.
9. Beverly Cleary correspondence file, Kerlan Collection, University of Minnesota. Letter from Louis Darling dated January 18, 1965.
10. Ibid., Letter from Beverly Clearly to Lois Darling.
11. Ellen Chamberlain responding to critic Eleanor Cameron in *Horn Book Magazine*, June 1973, p. 227.
12. Jonathan Cott. *Pipers at the Gates of Dawn*, p. 88.

13. William Steig. "Caldecott Acceptance Speech," in Lee Kingman's *Newbery and Caldecott Medal Books 1966–1975*, p. 218.
14. Cott, op. cit., p. 119.
15. Quote from a taped interview with Jane Yolen in 1992.
16. From a speech by Maurice Sendak at Children's Literature New England conference at Mount Holyoke College, South Hadley, Massachusetts, in July 1994.
17. Hobson, Laura. *Gentleman's Agreement*. New York: Simon and Schuster, 1947.

Illustration by author Paul Goble from The Girl Who Loved Wild Horses *(Bradbury, 1978), copyright © 1978 by Paul Goble; reprinted with the permission of Macmillan Books for Young Readers, an imprint of Simon and Schuster's Children's Publishing Division. Authentic detail distinguishes the artwork in this Plains Indian legend told in the traditional style of the oral storyteller.*

8

RIDING THE CREST 1970–1979

In classrooms . . . the child's reading of a lyric poem or fantasy or even a comic short story is immediately followed by some such initial question as, "What does the work teach us?" or "What do we learn about so-and-so?"

—Edward W. Rosenheim, Jr.
"Children's Reading and Adults' Values," *Only Connect*

No More Heroes

During the 1970s, events swirling around and within the country helped plunge America into a psychological depression. At the beginning of the decade, four college students were shot and killed by National Guardsmen at Kent State College in Ohio while at a peaceful gathering to protest the Vietnam War. Drug use accelerated, and in 1970 guitarist Jimi Hendrix and blues singer Janis Joplin, both in their twenties, died of overdoses. Vice President Spiro T. Agnew resigned in 1972 when charged with income tax evasion, and the Watergate scandal led to the resignation of Richard M. Nixon as president of the United States in 1974. The Vietnam War did come to an end during this decade, but for the first time in America's history, the United States did not win a major conflict.

During the Forties, gasoline had been temporarily rationed because it was needed for the war effort, and patriotic Americans accepted the shortage, but in 1973 the Arab-dominated Organization of Petroleum Exporting Countries (OPEC) stopped all shipments to the United States. Not only was there an acute shortage of oil, but also the price escalated at the gas pumps from 35 cents to $1 a gallon. America's domestic supply of oil, for the first time, could not meet the demand. The United States was consuming 30% of the world's available energy, and dependence on the politically motivated OPEC created an untenable situation that America moved to resolve. The effects of the energy crisis continued throughout the decade even though the embargo was lifted in 1974. Americans, realizing that natural resources might not last forever and wanting to end dependence on OPEC, began looking into alternative energy sources.

Becoming Socially Aware

The American people have always shown the ability to bounce back from adversity, and though the American dream occasionally weakens, it never dies, nor does our need to bring the imagination to life, as evidenced by the 1971 opening of Disney World in Orlando, Florida, offering a magical fantasy in the midst of national chaos.

From 1974 through 1976, America continuously celebrated her 200th birthday, which culminated in the 1976 Fourth of July celebration. By that time, the word bicentennial was suffering from overkill, and the reality of a plummeting stock market, climbing interest rates, and accelerating unemployment intruded on America's celebration.

In an effort to overcome the racial, ethnic, and gender discrimination that had been publicly acknowledged in the Sixties, the media started featuring more African Americans and more independent women in advertisements, on television sitcoms, in films, and on magazine covers. The illustrations in textbooks began to show an occasional child with different-colored skin—but the same homogenous features as the rest of the children in the picture. *Parents' Magazine* went out of its way in April 1978 to show the entire Andrew Young family on its cover. Young, an African American, was the new ambassador to the United Nations, but the focus of the article, in keeping with the new recognition of the working woman in America, was on his wife, Jean.

Racial awareness was the goal of the Seventies, and publishers began to rethink marketing children's books that could be considered controversial. One series of books that went out of print was Hugh Lofting's Doctor Dolittle adventures from the 1920s. *Little Black Sambo* (1905) was held to one authorized version available only through bookstores, as critics judged it demeaning in a decade of developing black pride, and librarians removed all copies from their shelves.

In education, government grants had encouraged public and school libraries to purchase informational books on the environment, animals, conservation, health, and fitness. There were so many of these books published and purchased in the 1970s and so much new information being discovered that, when the budget cuts of the late 1970s negated the purchase of updates, many books remaining on library shelves became not only outdated but also incorrect altogether. One example was a book on killer whales in which orcas were called monsters of the ocean, dangerous to people as well as to other sea life. The killer-whale image was refuted by the behavior of the orca Shamu at Sea World in California and other publicized examples of interaction between whales and people. At the same time, books such as Alice Schick's *The Peregrine Falcons* (1975) and *Zoo Year* (1978) offered a new perspective on wildlife. The first book described the work that was being done to bring peregrine falcons back from near extinction; the second, written by Schick and Sara Ann Friedman, presented the efforts to reevaluate the needs of animals and the importance of natural habitats in zoos.

Sex and the Single Girl

While schools attempted to interest students in science, math, and the environment, sex education was tentatively approached as part of health classes. Because of the sexual freedom brought about by birth control pills introduced in the Sixties, young people were openly experimenting with sex before marriage, and upper-elementary-grade students were introduced to the subject as part of health education in some schools. To cite a typical example of the difficulties encountered, a teacher was hired in the mid-Seventies specifically to teach health in a small-town school and didn't even last a whole semester. One of his students went home and described to her mother in detail what she she was learning about sex. The school board immediately fired the teacher, who thought he was following the syllabus.

Anything Goes

In publishing, all restraints were off, and authors of children's books were free to write about any subject they wished. Divorce, drugs, sexuality, mental illness, death and abortion became grist for the children's book writer's mill. For the first time, the category of "young adult" was added to the children's book genre, with books that acknowledged the concerns of young people between the ages of 12 and 18 in a turbulent and changing society. *Catcher in the Rye* (1951) by J. D. Salinger, previously published on an adult list, was given a "young adult" label. Any writer of adult fiction whose protagonist happened to be an adolescent could have an upcoming book categorized as young adult. Journalist-turned-author Robert Cormier, who never planned to write books for young people, found himself the embodiment of the young adult author when *The Chocolate War* (1974) and *I Am the Cheese* (1977), stories exploring psychological and ethical issues, were published as young adult novels. Cormier's books were quickly chosen by teachers as epitomizing the genre, and the teachers made them part of the curriculum and developed teaching guides to go along with the novels themselves.

John Donovan's *I'll Get There, It Better Be Worth the Trip* (1969) deals sensitively and clearly with death, alcoholism, and sexual preference through first-person narration, as two young boys tentatively experiment with sex, are caught and accused of perversion. Another book that explores sexual preference is *The Man Without a Face* (1972)[1] by Isabelle Holland, in which the narrator, 14-year-old Chuck, finds himself physically attracted to his tutor, Justin McLeod. Justin, a recluse and former teacher who has ugly scars on one side of his face, gains Chuck's respect as perhaps the only adult he can trust, and is sensitive enough to understand and empathize with Chuck's confusion.

During the Seventies, libraries began setting aside a separate section of the library called "Young Adult." In an effort to fill the shelves in this new genre, quantity, for a time, became more important than quality. Some of the authors who moved into the young adult field focused on social issues, allowing subject matter to override character development, and the books that resulted were called "problem" novels, stories that tended to rely on sensationalism and lacked depth. One author whose popularity flared during this time was Norma Klein (*Mom, the Wolf Man and Me* [1972]), with the degree of interest in her books measured by their "shock value." She wrote about sex and drugs, about dysfunctional families and communication obstacles, and especially about romance (*Love Is One of the Choices* [1978]), a subject new to children's books. Klein, who died in 1989 at the age of 51, wrote a great many books and was often castigated by critics as relying too much on sensationalism, but her books are still popular and deal with issues that are very much a part of this society.

Mainstream Popularity

By far the most popular author of the Seventies was Judy Blume, who was able to communicate with adolescents better than any other writer. Her first book, *Are You There, God? It's Me, Margaret* (1970), presented a first-person narrator who sounded like a typical, contemporary adolescent. Margaret is concerned about her religious beliefs, or lack thereof, and her physical development, or lack thereof. Being the only child of a Jewish father and a Christian mother, both of whom gave up practicing any kind of religion, creates a quandary for Margaret. Should she join the Y or the Jewish Community Center? Also complicating matters, her breasts have not yet developed and she has not started her menstrual periods. How long will she have to wait to reach puberty?

This was Blume's most fully realized book, with Margaret ultimately resolving the issues with which she is faced. Many of Judy Blume's books presented issues but relied mainly on Blume's ability to speak the language of adolescence, leaving the issues unresolved.

Blume's candid approach to the concerns of adolescence delighted her readers but caused controversy among adults. One of her books, *Deenie* (1973), the story of a prospective teen model who discovers she has scoliosis and must wear a brace, was removed from a Lenox, Massachusetts, library at the request of one parent because of a brief reference in the book to masturbation. The short article in the local newspaper describing the decision started an avalanche of protests from parents who resented having decisions made for them and for their children, and *Deenie* was returned to the library shelves.

After being sent copies of the material regarding the controversy, Judy Blume responded by citing other efforts at censorship of her books. The principal of the school her children attended refused to have *Margaret* on the shelf of his library because it discussed menstruation. And the principal of a school in Montana wrote to Blume saying *Deenie* was being withheld from his library and would she please answer a long list of questions, including, "Where is the medical evidence that states it is all right for a young person to masturbate?" Blume said in her letter that she had considered sending him the Hite Report.[2]

Blume's body of literature encompasses a wide range of age levels. For example, *Tales of a Fourth Grade Nothing* (1972) concerns rivalry between a fourth-grader and his younger brother, Fudge, but by the mid-Seventies Blume was writing for a young-adult audience in *Forever* (1976), the story of a first sexual relationship between two young people. Because she had become the idol of many children still in elementary school, who looked forward to every new title written by her, the Puritan ethic instilled in many American adults kicked in, and they rebelled. *Forever* was not a book that they wanted their children to read, which, of course, made the book all the more appealing to young people. The story, however, has a limited theme. It's a love story and little else, somewhat like reading a person's diary or being told step by step the most satisfactory way to lose one's virginity, with the emphasis on birth control and protection against venereal disease. It's a lecture for 16- and 17-year-olds, and lack of character development and lack of conflict make the book colorless.

Censorship on the Rise

The censorship of books for children was not new in the 1970s. It was an issue when *Huckleberry Finn* (1885) was published, and *The Wonderful Wizard of Oz* (1900) was not available in libraries for many years simply because it was considered by influential librarians to be poorly written. Throughout the first half of this century, the establishment of a separate category of books especially for children brought with it a list of subjects to be avoided in children's books. It was therefore taken for granted that, once the taboos were established, censorship was not going to be necessary in the children's book field. The lifting of taboos in the Seventies suddenly allowed children's book authors and illustrators the same kind of freedom and attention to basic truths that marked the early classics. At the same time, this new freedom created the same controversies and attempts at censorship that marked objections to the early classics. Several pressure groups, advocating censorship of books for children, have insisted that the public funding of most schools and libraries has made them subject to "community censorship." However, the First Amendment (the constitutional protection of free speech) contradicts this challenge.

Katherine Paterson, wife of a minister, child of missionaries, and herself a missionary, found much to her surprise that her *Bridge to Terabithia* (1978), the Newbery Medal winner in 1979, had been placed on the Banned Books List of the American Booksellers Association.[3] Further, in the 1980s, *Terabithia* was removed from classrooms in Mariposa, California, first, because the term "Oh, Lord" and the slang term "Lordy" were considered as taking the name of the Lord in vain; second, because the depiction of a boy stealing a Twinkie was said to promote theft; and third, because the book was said to depict large families in a poor light. One of the parents considered the book inappropriate for children but admitted she had never read it.[4]

Terabithia was written as Paterson's way of dealing both with the pain her son felt when he was faced with the death of a classmate who was a close friend and with the fact of her own mortality after a diagnosis of cancer, which has since responded successfully to treatment. The author's forthright passion and empathy make reading *Terabithia* an emotionally enduring experience.

A Different Viewpoint

Katherine Paterson's first book was an unlikely candidate for publication. The setting of *Sign of the Chrysanthemum* (1972) was 12th-century Japan, and many Americans had continued since the end of World War II to feel animosity toward Japan, especially since her economy was growing while America's was waning. Also, publishers were not looking for historical fiction. But Paterson, born in China and later a resident of postwar Japan, felt compelled to write this book. Virginia Buckley, her first and only editor, recognized and nurtured Katherine Paterson's unique creative abilities. Paterson wrote three more acclaimed historical novels for young adults and two picture books set in East Asia. She was accorded a National Book Award for *The Master Puppeteer* (1975) and another for *The Great Gilly Hopkins* (1979),[5] as well as receiving her second Newbery Medal for *Jacob Have I Loved* (1980).

Maurice Sendak had already faced controversial opinions regarding *Where the Wild Things Are* (1963), but with *In the Night Kitchen* (1970), the second book in his trilogy of dream sequences, he dared to show frontal nudity in a small boy, and this caused so much concern that some librarians actually drew in a diaper to cover the child. Sendak was extremely upset that his work was so trivialized. Selma Lanes, Sendak's biographer, says of *In the Night Kitchen*: "Perhaps none of us sufficiently values the dreams of childhood—our own or our children's. Sendak has given his audience a bona fide child's dream, curiously unmonitored by Maurice the adult."[6]

Correcting an Oversight

Throughout America's history, one of the most ignored areas in society has been physical impairment and the problems facing those trying to overcome not just the impairment but also the social rejection that usually accompanies it. America was built for the able-bodied; anyone less endowed for whatever reason became a cipher in the scheme of things. It was not until the 1980s that any major public effort was made to correct this long-term oversight. In children's books, Harriet May Savitz began writing about the achievements of the physically impaired long before it was a noteworthy thing to do. Her first novel, *Fly, Wheels, Fly* (1970), portrayed the frustrations of a teenage boy in a wheelchair as he tries to become better acquainted with a girl to whom he is attracted. He can't even call her on the phone because he can't get his wheelchair into the phone booth. At the end of the decade, she wrote *Wheelchair Champions: A History of Wheelchair Sports* (1978), in which she chronicled the achievements of physically challenged men and women who had overcome their disabilities and succeeded in their chosen sports. The book not only describes their development as athletes and the chronological development of wheelchair sports through the 1940s, 1950s, 1960s, and 1970s, but also describes public attitudes toward the handicapped during these decades and offers suggestions for improvement, many of which have been instituted since this book was published. There were so many informational books published in so many different fields in the 1970s that this book, like many others, could have been lost; fortunately, it was not and continues to be relevant.

Books dealing with physical impairment were indeed rare, but Jane Yolen sensitively portrayed a story about a blind princess and a wise old man who shows her how to see by touch in an original folktale called *The Seeing Stick* (1977), set in China.

Happy Birthday, America

By 1974, attention also began to shift toward historical timelines and the 200th birthday of America's independence from England. James Lincoln Collier and his brother Christopher were awarded the 1975 Newbery Medal for *My Brother Sam Is Dead* (1974), a story that brings the War for Independence into new focus and allows readers to see history through people, not just through events. Jean Fritz's *And Then What Happened, Paul Revere?* (1973) and *Why Don't You Get a Horse, Sam Adams?* (1974) are only two of her many easy readers in which small details add personality and empathy to history. Patricia Lee Gauch's *This Time, Tempe Wick?* (1974) features a female hero who shows great bravery when Revolutionary War troops stationed near Tempe Wick's house rebel for lack of supplies and Tempe must save her horse, Bonnie, from them. Like Ben Franklin's inventive mouse Amos in *Ben and Me* (1939) (see p. 98), narrator Molly the Crow, in *The Remarkable Ride of Israel Bissell as Related by Molly the Crow* (1976) by Alice Schick and Marjorie N. Allen, is the driving force behind Israel Bissell, post rider, as he carries the call to arms in record time from Watertown, Massachusetts, to Philadelphia, Pennsylvania, spreading the word that the War for Independence has begun. Joel Schick's black-pen illustrations elaborate and extend the purposely minimal text in this fact-based story:

> Watertown, Worcester, Pomfret, Brooklyn,
> Plainfield, Norwich, New London, Lyme—
> Post Rider Bissell persevered,
> Completing his route in record time.

Multicultural America

Authors of the 1970s expanded history by including stories by black Americans about black Americans and their history. Muriel and Tom Feelings offered a counting book, *Moja Means One* (1971), and an alphabet book, *Jambo Means Hello* (1974). Both were set in East Africa and utilized the Kiswahili language spoken in Africa. The Dillons, Leo, who is black, and his wife, Diane, were awarded back-to-back Caldecott Medals, one for their illustrations in Verna Aardema's adaptation of an African folk tale, *Why Mosquitoes Buzz in People's Ears* (1975), and one for Margaret Musgrove's *Ashanti to Zulu: African Traditions* (1976).

Virginia Hamilton, who considers her books an extension of her own black heritage, added *The Planet of Junior Brown* (1971) and *M.C. Higgins the Great* (1974) to her list of critically acclaimed novels. *Junior Brown* explored the underside of New York City and *M.C. Higgins*, a story about survival, garnered the 1975 Newbery Medal. Sam Cornish's poetic essay, *Grandmother's Pictures* (1974), illustrated by Jeanne Johns, connected black children to their ancestral past by depicting a child remembering good times with a well-loved grandparent. In her 1974 Newbery book, *The Slave Dancer* (1973), Paula Fox, though not black, insightfully and uncompromisingly tells the story of a young white boy conscripted to sail in a slave ship and play his fife to accompany the slaves when they are brought up from the hold for exercise. And in *Roll of Thunder, Hear My Cry* (1976), awarded the 1977 Newbery Medal, Mildred D. Taylor drew upon family experience to present a land-owning black family in the midst of a community of sharecroppers and intolerant whites and the family's struggle to stay proud and solvent during the Great Depression of the 1930s.

This new awareness extended to the media when the 1977 adaptation of Alex Haley's novel, *Roots* (1976), as a television miniseries held people in thrall for eight consecutive nights, and American viewers were given a graphic portrayal of what it meant to be a slave.

While children's book authors writing about Asian culture tended to set their stories in Asia, Lawrence Yep's *Dragonwings* (1975) and *Child of the Owl* (1977) were set in San Francisco in a deliberate attempt to acquaint Americans with a specific family of Chinese immigrants settling there at the beginning of the 20th century. In his words: "Of the hundreds of thousands of Chinese who flocked to these shores we know next to nothing. They remain a dull, faceless mass: statistical fodder to be fed to the sociologists, or lifeless abstractions to be manipulated by historians."[7] *Dragonwings*, the story of Moon Shadow, who sails to America to join his father in San Francisco's Chinatown, is set in the early 1900s and is based on a true story. *Child of the Owl* is more contemporary. It takes place in San Francisco's Chinatown in the 1960s and is the story of Casey, who is searching for her roots while trying to cope with her gambler father. Lawrence Yep has attempted in his novels to counter stereotypes that "present an image of Chinese not as they really are but as they exist in the mind of White America . . . [by showing] that Chinese-Americans are human beings upon whom America has had a unique effect."[8] Unfortunately, Asians are still being seen by some as outsiders, even though they may be second- or third-generation Americans.

Gerald McDermott's abstract and colorful paintings for *Arrow to the Sun* (1974), a traditional Pueblo Indian story, earned him a Caldecott Medal in 1975, even though his use of conceptual design to illustrate the book caused some adults to question whether the book would be understood by children. Since children generally do not explore the books they read for complicated levels of symbolism, this book has remained popular with them. In *The Girl Who Loved Wild Horses* (1978) by Paul Goble, winner of the 1979 Caldecott Medal, a young Indian girl loves the wild horses so deeply that she finally goes off to join them. Authentic detail distinguishes the artwork in this Plains Indian legend told in the traditional style of the oral storyteller (see illustration, p. 204).

Beverly Brodsky McDermott, Gerald McDermott's wife, adapted a Jewish legend in *The Golem* (1976) and created powerful, sweeping art to illustrate it, resulting in a clear perception of human weakness in God's realm. Margot Zemach's *It Could Always Be Worse* (1976), told in the matter-of-fact voice of a Jewish storyteller, is a lighter look at life, with a very practical resolution. Milton Meltzer's *Never to Forget: The Jews of the Holocaust* (1976) gives the history of the Jewish people and how they have been persecuted through the years, culminating in the horror of the attempted extermination of Jews in Nazi Germany. In a more contemporary vein, a book for young adults called *I Never Saw Another Butterfly: Children's Drawings and Poems from Terezin Concentration Camp, 1942–1944* (1978) is a collection actually created by Jewish children during World War II. Most of these children died in 1944, and, as reflected in their poems and pictures, most of them knew they were going to die.

Just for Fun

Betsy Byars wrote the Newbery-award-winning *Summer of the Swans* (1970), in which 14-year-old Sara comes to terms with her own weaknesses when she must search for her mentally retarded brother who is lost in the woods. But not all children's books during this time were written to illustrate the imperfections of the human race. Byars also wrote *The Eighteenth Emergency* (1973), a light and humorous work that introduced a pair of creative 12-year-old boys, Benjie (nicknamed "Mouse") and his friend Ezzie, who, after making a list of 17 ways to meet an emergency, find themselves facing an emergency for which they have no immediate solution. The book was adapted as a television special called "Hammerman's After Me," but Byars unfortunately never followed up with a sequel featuring these resourceful boys.

Florence Parry Heide wrote *The Shrinking of Treehorn* (1971), and Edward Gorey's bizarre illustrations were the perfect accompaniment for a low-key story of a boy who begins to shrink into nothingness and can't seem to get any adult to notice his predicament. John Bellairs's *The House With the Clock in the Walls* (1973), also illustrated by Edward Gorey, introduced suspense with a penchant for the supernatural long before R.L. Stine discovered the market in the Nineties. Bellairs's young protagonist actually manages to raise the dead on Halloween night. Harry Allard's picture book, *Miss Nelson Is Missing* (1977), featured James Marshall's comic-book caricatures of sweet Miss Nelson, an elementary-grade teacher who is replaced by the horrid Miss Swamp in a story about appreciating what you have because things could be worse.

The Shifting Tide of Children's Books

The Sixties and Seventies introduced such a wide variety of genres in children's literature that many of the authors and illustrators introduced during that time have become firmly established as pioneers in their own special areas of the children's book field.

For example, Blair Lent's illustrations for *The Funny Little Woman* (1972), a Japanese folktale, were most interpretive and unusual, complementing a story that takes place in the unlikely setting of Japanese Purgatory. This Caldecott Award winner calls for special commentary because, although it is an entertaining story, there is no explanation of its place in Japanese folklore. The illustrations are representative of Japanese scroll art in the Kamakura Period (1185–1333), with the story based on popular, rather than classical literature of the time. The monks who did this type of art relied on a sense of humor and portrayed common people as the subject of their sketches, which were often set in the Underworld and often featured Jizo-sama, the savior of the dead in Hell, and *oni*, or demons. But none of this background material is included in the book.

From 1971 through 1977, the Caldecott Medal books were almost all retellings of traditional folk tales, but even with folk tale adaptations topping the award list, the American public appreciated and lauded the originality of illustrators who created their own stories, such as Maurice Sendak, Arnold Lobel, and David Macaulay. Lobel's Frog and Toad books set a standard for easy-readers that has yet to be surmounted. These stories of friendship are deceptively simple in text and pictures, yet they clearly establish the characters of Frog and Toad and are especially good for reading aloud. Sendak continued to make every book he created different from anything he had done before, and David Macaulay brought architecture into the realm of the child with *Cathedral* (1973).

Poetry reached across all interest levels with Nikki Giovanni's *Spin a Soft Black Song* (1971) celebrating black identity; Shel Silverstein's *Where the Sidewalk Ends* (1974) and Jack Prelutsky's *Nightmares: Poems to Trouble Your Sleep* (1976) creating popular light verse for children. Tana Hoban used photography to create imaginative concept books such as *Push-Pull Empty-Full* (1972).

It would seem that every conceivable subject had been covered in children's books by the end of the Seventies. But the passing of Proposition 13 in 1978 in California, a bill intended to lower taxes, had an impact on the entire nation and caused a noticeable curtailment of public funds.[9] Libraries and schools began to suffer major budget cuts. These cuts forced librarians to buy fewer books and after another bill was passed taxing books stored in warehouses, new children's books were not reprinted when a first printing ran out. Instead of fighting for their libraries, parents began going to bookstores, and publishers began to capitalize by issuing paperback editions of books for children. By 1979 editors who since the 1950s had mainly depended on hardcover sales to public libraries, were no longer asking, "How useful will this book be in a library?" but instead were asking, "How will it sell in a bookstore?"[10]

CHRONOLOGICAL BIBLIOGRAPHY 1970–1979

Blume, Judy. *Are You There, God? It's Me, Margaret*. New York: Bradbury, 1970; New York: Dell, 1991. (Realistic Fiction/Social Adjustment)

The story is written from the viewpoint of Margaret Simon, who, at 11, feels that everyone in the world knows more about life than she does. Blume gives the problems of adolescence the frank attention that makes her books so popular with young people. Margaret wants to wear a bra, wants to get her first period, joins her friends in looking at a nude male body in an anatomy book and a nude female in *Playboy* magazine, wonders if she'll ever need deodorant, and can't decide if she wants to be Jewish like her father or Christian like her mother. The religion question runs through the book and gives it some depth, but it is the contemporary dialogue between pre-pubescent girls that appeals to Blume's many fans.

Byars, Betsy. *Summer of the Swans*, illtd. Ted Coconis. New York: Viking Press, 1970; New York: Puffin, 1981. NEWBERY MEDAL (Realistic Fiction/Social Adjustment)

Fourteen-year-old Sara Godfrey is convinced nobody could possibly care about her, and she spends most of her time enumerating all her faults to herself and to anyone else who will listen. Her older sister, Wanda, is attractive and popular, and her younger brother, Charlie, 10, has been mute since the age of three, when he was ill with a very high fever, and has not developed mentally since that time. Sara loves Charlie though she sometimes loses patience with him. One night, Charlie decides to leave the house and look for the swans on the lake and becomes lost in the woods. As the search for Charlie continues, Sara loses her self-absorption and begins to consider the feelings of others, including her Aunt Willy, who has cared for the family since the death of Sara's mother, and Joe Melby, whom she has denounced without proof because she thinks he stole Charlie's watch a few weeks earlier. By the time Charlie is found, Sara has taken a giant step toward maturity.

Haley, Gail. *A Story, A Story*. New York: Atheneum, 1970; New York: Macmillan, 1988. CALDECOTT MEDAL. (Folk/Myth/Picture Book/African)

Marcia Brown adapted an East Indian folk tale for her woodcuts in *Once a Mouse* . . . (1961). Gail Haley, also a woodcut artist, lived in the Caribbean and kept hearing stories about tigers and leopards, animals not found there. She researched the origins of the stories and discovered they were from Africa. The African storyteller introduces a story by saying: "We do not really mean, we do not really mean that what we are about to say is true. A story, a story; let it come, let it go." And so Haley wrote a story about the Sky God and Ananse, the Spider man, who wanted to buy the Sky God's collection of stories, and to do so had to capture the tiger, the hornet, and the fairy whom-men-never-see. Clever Ananse succeeds and from that time on the stories are called spider stories. The story of Brer Fox and the Tar Baby had its origins in this African folk tale (see pp. 10–11).

Lobel, Arnold. *Frog and Toad Are Friends*. New York: Harper, 1970. Also, *Frog and Toad Together* (New York: Harper, 1972); *Days with Frog and Toad* (New York: Harper, 1979); New York: Harper, 1993 (Boxed Set). (Easy Reader/Social Relationships)

Frog and Toad are distinctly different personalities. Frog is exuberant and ready to meet the day, while Toad is slow to respond and quite deliberate in his actions. But each is ready to compromise for the other when necessary, because Frog and Toad are truly friends. In unadorned language and warm illustrations, Lobel offers a quartet of easy readers about an unlikely but loyal friendship.

Monjo, F. N. *The Drinking Gourd*, illtd. Fred Brenner. New York: Coward, McCann and Geoghegan, 1970; New York: Harper, 1983. (Realistic Fiction/Easy Reader/Historical)

Monjo did not focus on the black characters in this easy reader, even though the subject is the Underground Railroad that helped many slaves reach freedom in the north before the Civil War. The story is about Tommy Fuller, a young white boy who discovers runaway slaves in his barn and, with his father's help, hides them in a haywagon and takes them to the river. Much of the story is an exchange of dialogue between Tommy and his father or between Tommy and the slaves, as Tommy learns about the "drinking gourd," or big dipper that serves as a guide for the slaves and about the unfair law that calls for returning runaway slaves to their masters.

Sendak, Maurice. *In the Night Kitchen*. New York: Harper, 1970, 1985. (Fantasy/Picture Book)

In *Where the Wild Things Are* (1963), Sendak presented the dream world of the very young child as Max explores his need to show his independence from his mother. In this second book, Mickey moves into another dream level, and another level of growth, as he imagines what it would be like if he could stay up all night like the grownups. Sendak calls this book "a kind of homage to New York City,"[11] and his illustrations celebrate some important childhood memories—Disney, comic books, the movies of Laurel and Hardy, and the memory of an advertisement by Sunshine Bakers, which said "We bake while you sleep."

Anonymous. *Go Ask Alice*. Englewood Cliffs, N.J.: Prentice-Hall, 1971; New York: Avon, 1976. (Autobiographical/Social Adjustment)

This is an account of the inner torment of a teenager struggling with drug abuse. From the age of 15, when she unknowingly was given drugs for the first time in a glass of soda, through a period of increasing drug use to when she was found dead in her bedroom from an overdose, this intimate portrait depicts a life spiraling out of control and a girl who believes she has nowhere to turn. The terrible tragedy of her death led her family to share with the public these diaries found after she died so that others might then have a chance to keep such a thing from happening in their lives. In the diaries, she speaks of her inability to confide in her own family; she presents a contrast in emotions and a desperate need for communication; she portrays the personality changes brought about by drugs, and makes comments about the widespread use of drugs in the schools. And though her parents and others in the community are confronted with their children's drug use, they deny the dangers until it is too late.

Feelings, Muriel. *Moja Means One*, illtd. Tom Feelings. New York: Dial, 1971, 1987. (Picture Book/Concept/Africa)

African-American children are made more clearly aware of their heritage as Feelings's counting book introduces the African language called Kiswahili to black children in America, and in so doing offers a great deal of information about the African continent and the East African culture that is most familiar to the author.

Giovanni, Nikki. *Spin a Soft Black Song*. New York: Hill and Wang, 1971; New York: Farrar, Straus & Giroux, 1987. (Poetry/Black American)

These poems, meant to be read aloud, say so much about childhood, so much about living in the city, so much about being black and proud, that both children and adults can appreciate and understand in the best possible way what is being said here:

daddy says this world is
a drum tight and hard
and i told him
i'm gonna beat
out my own rhythm

Hamilton, Virginia. *The Planet of Junior Brown*. New York: Macmillan, 1971, 1993. (Realistic Fiction/Urban)

Junior Brown weighs 300 pounds and is a musical prodigy who is not allowed to realize his dream of making music. His mother has cut the wires in the piano so there is no sound to disturb her, and Junior's piano teacher, Miss Peebs, holds the promise of her grand piano over his head but won't let him play. Junior's only friend, Buddy Clark, depends on Junior for a connection to family, such as it is. Buddy has no real family, just his planet, the planet of Tomorrow Billy, part of a network of shelters in abandoned buildings, where he has inherited the responsibility of an earlier Tomorrow Billy. It is up to Buddy to teach survival to new members of his planet, to boys who have no one else to care about them. Buddy and Junior have one adult friend, Mr. Pool, the school janitor, who has created a solar system in the basement of the school, and Buddy has named one of the planets the Planet of Junior Brown. The story builds to a climax as poor, frustrated, and talented Junior reaches his breaking point, and Buddy finds himself responsible for saving the solar system and all its planets. Without compromise, Hamilton presents the underside of New York City and the secret society of the unloved who have only each other.

Heide, Florence Parry. *The Shrinking of Treehorn*, illtd. Edward Gorey. New York: Holiday House, 1971. Also, *Treehorn x 3* (New York: Dell, 1992). (Picture Book/Humor/Social Adjustment)

The humor in this story is tongue in cheek as Treehorn, a small boy depicted by cartoonist Edward Gorey as a miniature adult, keeps getting smaller and smaller. At first, his parents don't even notice his predicament, and even when they do, they consider it a nuisance to themselves. Treehorn has to be helped onto the school bus, gets sent to the office for jumping up and down while trying to reach the water bubbler out in the hall, and listens to the principal offer a series of platitudes about being there to guide, not punish. Treehorn manages to revert to normal size on his own, and when he turns green in the process, doesn't bother to mention it to his parents.

Hoban, Tana. *Look Again!* New York: Macmillan, 1971. (Picture Book/Concept/Photographs/Wordless)

A small square cutout in the middle of the page reveals a photographic design, and the child has a chance to guess what the design might be. The puzzle is divided into three steps: first, the cutout; next, the full page showing just part of the object; and then, the whole object on the back of that page. Vertical stripes become a striped face and finally a zebra. A spiral design becomes an empty shell and then a shell that contains the roar of the sea when held against a child's ear. Hoban introduced photographs as illustrations for preschool picture books, an innovation that has made her books exceptionally popular with small children. Her books—this one has no text—are intended to be shared by parent and child.

Hutchins, Pat. *Changes, Changes*. New York: Macmillan, 1971, 1987. (Picture Book/Concept/Wordless)

Colorful, balanced illustrations, depicting a small wooden man and woman who create different shapes with blocks each time they are threatened by disaster or need transportation to a different place, negate the need for language to tell the couple's story. This is a book a preschooler can "read" alone.

Miles, Miska. *Annie and the Old One*, illtd. Peter Parnall. Boston: Little, Brown, 1971, 1985. (Picture Book/Death/Navajo)

Helen Buckley's *Grandmother and I* (1961) dealt with a close relationship between a child and an older relative. Miles goes one step beyond that when she writes about the impending death of a grandmother and her granddaughter's effort to stop the inevitable.

Annie's Navajo grandmother tells her family that when the rug on the loom is finished, she will die. Annie tries to keep her mother from finishing the rug by misbehaving at school and at home, and she puts off using the weaving stick her grandmother has given her. But her grandmother takes her for a walk and tells her she cannot hold back time. "The sun comes up from the edge of earth in the morning. It returns to the edge of earth in the evening. Earth, from which good things come for the living creatures on it. Earth, to which all creatures finally go." The two then return to the hogan, and Annie takes her grandmother's weaving stick and begins to weave.

O'Brien, Robert C. *Mrs. Frisby and the Rats of NIMH*, illtd. Zena Bernstein. New York: Atheneum, 1971; New York: Macmillan, 1986. NEWBERY MEDAL. (Fantasy/Animal)

Mrs. Frisby, a widowed field mouse, and her four children have been living comfortably on Mr. Fitzgibbon's farm until she discovers that the family will have to move because the farmer is going to plow her home out of existence. But her younger son, Timothy, is convalescing after having pneumonia and is too weak to be moved. The only way to resolve the problem is to become involved with the rats of NIMH who live under the rose bush and who were, at one time, laboratory rats. When Mrs. Frisby visits the rats, she finds them to be sophisticated, literate, and highly civilized in an underground community with elevators, a library, and running water. In addition, her late husband, Jonathan, who also was highly intelligent, had some kind of connection to these rats, as Mrs. Frisby discovers when they tell her their story. The rats go out of their way to help Mrs. Frisby, and she in turn discovers that they are in terrible danger and goes out of her way to help them.

Viorst, Judith. *The Tenth Good Thing About Barney*, illtd. Eric Blegvad. New York: Atheneum, 1971. (Picture Book/Death/Social Adjustment)

While Margaret Wise Brown's book *The Dead Bird* (1938) matter-of-factly presents a young child's acceptance of death when a group of children find a dead bird and decide to bury it, Viorst explores acceptance of death when a loved one dies, in this case a small boy's cat, Barney. The boy's mother tells him to think of 10 good things about Barney, and they will bury him in the morning. But he can think of only nine—until after the funeral when he is helping his father plant the garden, and his father tells him that Barney will be part of the earth and will help things grow. That's the tenth good thing, the boy says, and that's a pretty nice job for a cat.

Adams, Richard. *Watership Down*. London: Rex Collins, 1972; New York: Penguin, 1972; New York: Avon, 1993. (Fantasy/Animal)

Awarded the Carnegie Medal[12] in 1973, this allegorical adventure story features a community of rabbits involved in a quest to find a new home. It was published in the United States to the highest acclaim, was labeled an "instant classic" by reviewers, and quickly appeared on the adult best seller list. The book, anthropomorphic but not condescending, explores the precarious fates of brave Hazel, psychic Fiver, and the rest of their band as the rabbits travel across the countryside in search of a home. They must confront General Woundwort and his troops and free the imprisoned female rabbits. Through it all, their actions never contradict their animal natures. Adams has created his world so completely that the rabbits even have their own myths.

Blume, Judy. *Tales of a Fourth Grade Nothing*, illtd. Roy Doty. New York: Dutton, 1972. (Realistic Fiction/Chapter/Humor)

Nine-year-old Peter Harcher's problems with his little brother, Fudge, are the basis for this middle-grade novel. Fudge is completely unpredictable and a thorn in Peter's side, an affliction often experienced by older siblings, and this situation creates empathy among those who, like Peter, have to deal with younger siblings. Because Blume doesn't try to explore issues but simply relates incidents, this story is delightfully funny and the characterizations are timeless.

Cobb, Vicki. *Science Experiments You Can Eat*. Philadelphia: Lippincott, 1972; New York: Harper, 1994 (Rev. ed.).

Imagine learning all about solutions, suspensions, carbohydrates, proteins and any number of scientific properties just by going into the kitchen and cooking something. When the experiment is completed, the snack is ready to eat, for instance, recovering solute crystals by making rock candy or discovering what makes popcorn pop. Cobb was the first to introduce science to children as a fun activity instead of a learning chore and has continued to add titles over the years.

George, Jean Craighead. *Julie of the Wolves*, illtd. John Schoenherr. New York: Harper, 1972. NEWBERY MEDAL. (Realistic Fiction/Social Adjustment/Nature)

Miyax is her Eskimo name, but Amy, her pen pal in San Francisco, calls her Julie, and when Miyax is forced into a marriage she doesn't want and is almost raped by her husband, Daniel, she runs away across the tundra, intent on traveling to San Francisco. But Miyax becomes lost and survives only because she learns from a pack of wolves how to live on the tundra. She also remembers lessons taught her in early childhood by her father, Kapugen, who explained nature's secrets and the old ways. It is this mix of old and new that Miyax/Julie must deal with to have any future at all.

Hoban, Tana. *Push-Pull Empty-Full*. New York: Macmillan, 1972. (Picture Book/Concept/Photographs)

Hoban offers, in clear black-and-white photos, the concepts presented in the book's title. A double spread showing a child in a wagon with another child pulling it and a third child pushing makes for a dramatic beginning. A puddle containing a child's rubber-booted foot is labeled "wet," and on the opposite page a child's legs in sneakers walking on dry leaves is labeled "dry." In and out, up and down, thick and thin and, of course, empty and full are only a few of the many concepts portrayed.

Holland, Isabelle. *The Man Without a Face*. Boston: G.K. Hall, 1972; New York: Harper, 1988. (Realistic Fiction/Social Adjustment)

At 14, Charles Norstadt is trying very hard to deal with his mother, with two sisters who don't understand him, and with the fact that he has a new stepfather every time he turns around. His own father was his mother's second husband, his older sister's father was his mother's first husband, and his younger sister's father her third. There have been other stepfathers since then but, fortunately, no more siblings. Charles feels trapped in a family of females; he doesn't like women much, and he wants to go away to boarding school. The only way he can do so is if he gets tutored, and when he discovers that Justin McLeod, the recluse who lives nearby and has a burn scar over half his face, used to be a teacher, he approaches him. The relationship that develops is one of mutual respect until Charles betrays his friend's trust. But he admits to Justin what he has done, and Justin forgives him. For the first time in his life, Charles feels love for another person, and it opens the door to understanding himself and the members of his family even as it closes the door on his relationship with Justin. This novel explores homosexuality with a sensitivity that has kept the story fresh and new.

Marshall, James. *George and Martha*. Boston: Houghton Mifflin, 1972. (Fantasy/Picture Book/Humor)

Two massive hippopotamuses named George and Martha show true friendship in a series of very short stories. George doesn't like the pea soup Martha makes every day and finally tells her so, only to discover she doesn't like it either, she just likes to make it. "Would you like some chocolate chip cookies instead?" she asks. When George decides to go for a ride in a balloon, he is so heavy the balloon won't leave the ground. But when he gets out, the balloon floats away. "That's all right," said Martha. "I'd rather have you down here with me." Using gentle humor and the sincerest emotion, Marshall began his renowned series of George and Martha books and in 1974 wrote and illustrated the first of his delightful Stupids series. The humor in his stories, Marshall says, is visual. He sees the scene in his mind and later puts in the text.[13]

Mosel, Arlene. *The Funny Little Woman*, illtd. Blair Lent. New York: E.P. Dutton, 1972; New York: Puffin, 1993. CALDECOTT MEDAL. (Picture Book/Folk/Myth/Japan)

A little woman drops her rice dumpling. When she tries to retrieve it, the earth gives way beneath her, and she finds herself in the Underworld. She follows a road lined with statues of the deity known as Jizo, and one of the statues warns her against the *oni* at the end of the road, but the little woman wants her dumpling and continues on. Though the Jizo statues try to protect her, she gives herself away by laughing "Tee-he-he-he," and the *oni* take her to be their cook, giving her a magic paddle that multiplies grains of rice. But she becomes lonesome and decides to escape, taking the paddle with her, and though the *oni* try to catch her, it is she who has the last laugh.

Peck, Robert Newton. *The Day No Pigs Would Die*. New York: Knopf, 1972; New York: Dell, 1983. (Realistic Fiction/Social Adjustment)

In graphic terms, Peck offers an autobiographical portrait of daily life on a Vermont farm and softens the harshness by describing a close and caring relationship with his father, Haven Peck, who makes a living slaughtering pigs. Robert, at 12, is allowed to have a pig of his very own to raise. He names her Pinky, and she follows him every chance she gets. But when she grows too big to keep except as a breeder and is found to be barren, she is slaughtered to feed the family during the winter months. Even though Robert knows that his father, a strict Shaker who couldn't allow compassion to overrule duty, had to kill Pinky, Robert finds it difficult to forgive him. But eventually he does, and, when his father dies, the boy finds himself the man of the family. Ironically, the day of the funeral is the day no pigs would die. In a much lighter vein, Peck also wrote a series of books about a boy named Soup, also set in the Vermont of his childhood.

Reiss, Johanna. *The Upstairs Room*. New York: T.Y. Crowell, 1972; New York: Harper, 1990. (Realistic Fiction/World War II/Holland)

In this autobiographical novel set in Holland during the last two years of World War II, 10-year-old Annie de Leeuw and her 20-year-old sister, Sini, are separated from their parents and oldest sister, Rachel, when it becomes evident that because they are Jewish, their lives are in danger. The Germans, who were occupying Holland, were methodically weeding out the Jews by sending them on trains to Germany where—it was later discovered, after many of their Jewish neighbors had already volunteered to go on the trains—they were being taken to concentration camps to be gassed and burned. For two years, Annie lives in the upstairs room of a farmhouse belonging to a Gentile family, one of many families hiding Jews during the war. Annie is reunited with her family at the end of the war, but many are not so fortunate, both Jew and Gentile. The penalty for harboring Jews was execution.

Rodgers, Mary. *Freaky Friday*. New York: Harper, 1972. (Fantasy/Humor)

Written in first person by 13-year-old Annabel Andrews, who wakes up one morning and discovers she has become her mother, Rodgers's story is a delightful romp from beginning to end. While Annabel is in her mother's body, Annabel's mother is Annabel with all of Annabel's bad habits. Annabel as her mother finds it necessary to take on more responsibility than she wants and, as she observes herself through adult eyes, becomes painfully aware of how she appears to others. By the time she becomes herself again, her world is in chaos, but the new Annabel learns how to see things in a whole different way.

Smith, Robert Kimmel. *Chocolate Fever*. New York: Coward, McCann & Geoghegan, 1972; New York: Dell Yearling, 1981. (Fantasy/Chapter Book/Humor)

This is a story about the perils of gluttony. Henry Green doesn't just love chocolate in an ordinary sense—he flavors everything he eats with chocolate. In fact, he consumes so much chocolate that one morning he wakes up and starts breaking out in chocolate-colored spots. This strange malady causes him to become an object of ridicule and to be harassed by his peers. He also becomes a medical curiosity when tests reveal that Henry's spots are pure chocolate. He runs away, becomes involved in a hijacking, and makes a new friend before he discovers a cure for chocolate fever.

Steig, William. *Dominic*. New York: Farrar, Straus, and Giroux, 1972. (Fantasy/Animal)

Although awarded a Caldecott Medal for his illustrations in *Sylvester and the Magic Pebble* (1969), Steig shows his versatile approach to the English language in this, his first novel. Dominic is a dog who decides to go on an adventure and meets several characters along the way, not all of them savory. Dominic, however, is both clever and optimistic, and manages to overcome mishaps and continue on his journey. Hats are an important part of his routine—"He owned an assortment of hats which he liked to wear, not for warmth or for shade or to shield him from rain, but for their various effects—rakish, dashing, solemn, or martial." His hats come in handy when he is threatened throughout the story by the Doomsday Gang, consisting of a fox, a ferret, and a weasel, who are very good at being evil. He also has a magic spear and a growing reputation for bravery among the animals. True to his animal nature throughout, he sniffs his way to romance when he rescues a beautiful female dog from a spell and walks off with her on a new adventure.

Turkle, Brinton. *The Adventures of Obadiah*. New York: Viking, 1972; New York: Puffin, 1987. (Realistic Fiction/Picture Book/Quaker)

Obadiah Starbuck is a Quaker boy who lives on the island of Nantucket, but his behavior contradicts that expected from the child of a Quaker family. It is his uncontrollable imagination that causes him to tell tall tales. He tells his sister a wolf almost ate him up and he tells his teacher he caught a lion. "Thee did no such thing," his teacher says. But then Obadiah has a real adventure, and when he tells his story, nobody believes him. The popularity of the unconventional young Obadiah led to more books about him: *Thy Friend, Obadiah; Obadiah the Bold*; and *Rachel and Obadiah*.

Adoff, Arnold. *Black Is Brown Is Tan*, illtd. Emily Arnold McCully. New York: Harper, 1973; New York: Harper Trophy, 1992. (Poetry/Picture

Book/Mixed Cultures)

"Black is brown is tan/is girl is boy/is nose is face/is all the colors/of the race . . ." Here is an essay poem celebrating a family—mother, father, two children—each a different shade. Father is "light with pinks and tiny tans." Mother is black with brown sugar, "tasty tan and coffee pumpkin pie." And the children, as well as the grandparents and the aunts and uncles on both sides of the family, are somewhere in between. This picture book was published at a time in American culture when a mixed couple was viewed with skepticism by many, but Adoff and his wife, Virginia Hamilton, proved the fallacy of such an attitude.

Bellairs, John. *The House With the Clock in Its Walls*. New York: Dial, 1973; New York: Puffin, 1993. (Fantasy/Mystery)

When 10-year-old Lewis Barnavelt goes to live with his Uncle Jonathan after his parents are killed in an auto accident, strange things happen in his uncle's spooky house, not the least of which is chiming clocks all through the house. Lewis discovers that his uncle is a wizard and that he is looking for a clock hidden in the walls, a clock that has been set by the powers of evil to destroy the world. In the process of trying to save the world, Lewis and his newfound friend, Tarby, visit the cemetery on Halloween night, and Lewis uses one of his uncle's spells to raise the dead. The spell works, but instead of helping his uncle, Lewis finds he has given evil a human form. Now, it is up to Lewis to find the clock in the walls and deactivate it because the magic has been transferred to him alone and only he can save the world from destruction.

Blume, Judy. *Deenie*. New York: Bradbury, 1973; New York: Dell, 1991. (Realistic Fiction/Social Adjustment)

Seventh-grader Deenie Fenner has dreams of being a teenage model by the time she is 17, and because she is so conscious of appearances, she finds deformed people distasteful. But her dreams are suddenly over when she discovers she has scoliosis, a curvature of the spine, and has to wear a brace that will keep her from having her career. She manages to adjust pretty easily to the changes in her life, accepting her condition and giving in to her father's insistence that she wear her brace to a co-ed social function. Had this book not been the subject of continuing controversy, because of one paragraph in which Deenie refers to her special place that makes her feel good when she rubs it, this book would probably have faded in popularity because it isn't Blume's best effort. The resolution to Deenie's problem seems too contrived.

Byars, Betsy. *The Eighteenth Emergency*, illtd. Robert Grossman. New York: Viking, 1973; New York: Puffin, 1982. (Chapter Book/Humor)

Benjy and Ezzie have made a list of all the ways they know to stay alive in an emergency. There are 17 solutions on the list, but when Benjy, nicknamed Mouse, becomes convinced that the class bully Hammerman is after him, it's time to find the 18th solution. Mouse has a compulsion to make written labels for things. When he discovers a loose thread in the couch, he pulls at it for awhile, then writes a note on the wall with an arrow pointing toward the thread: PULL THREAD IN CASE OF BOREDOM. At school when he notices a chart of early man on the wall, he feels compelled to draw a picture of Marv Hammerman with an arrow pointing toward Neanderthal man, an act that will surely bring retribution from Hammerman. Throughout the remainder of the book, Mouse and Ezzie try every way they can think of to avoid Hammerman. But the confrontation is inevitable.

Childress, Alice. *A Hero Ain't Nothin' But a Sandwich*. New York: Coward, McCann and Geoghegan, 1973; New York: BDD, 1989. (Realistic Fiction/Social Adjustment)

One of the early young-adult novels dealing with social issues that marked the Seventies as a time of new freedom in writing for children, this story explores heroin addiction. Benjie is 13 and is using heroin, and several people who know him offer differing perspectives into Benjie's personality, which when put together create an emotional and frightening portrait. Fortunately, what could have turned out to be a disastrous situation does not materialize. Though Benjie's future is still precarious, there is hope at the end.

Clifton, Lucille. *The Boy Who Didn't Believe in Spring*, illtd. Brinton Turkle. New York: Dutton, 1973; New York: Viking, 1992. (Picture Book/Mixed Cultures/Urban)

The charm of this book is in the character of King Shabazz, a small black boy who has very strong opinions, one of which is that spring is not just around the corner at all and he's going to "go round there and see what do [he] see." His friend Tony Polito goes with him, and even though they go farther around the corner than they have ever gone before, they don't find any signs of spring until they make an amazing discovery in a vacant lot. "Man, it's spring," admits King Shabazz to his friend Tony. Black poet Clifton speaks the language of the city, and Brinton Turkle creates children of all colors in King's classroom, where only King, who is as cute as can be, has an attitude.

Cooper, Susan. *The Dark Is Rising*. New York: Atheneum, 1973; New York: Macmillan, 1987. Also, *Greenwitch* (New York: Atheneum, 1974); *The Grey King* (New York: Atheneum, 1975); *Silver on the Tree* (New York: Atheneum, 1977)—all reprinted by Macmillan in 1987. (Fantasy)

There are four Things of Power that must be found to save the world from darkness: the golden chalice known as a grail, the Circle of Signs, the sword of crystal, and a harp of gold. In the first book of Cooper's acclaimed series, *Over Sea, Under Stone* (1966), the grail is found, and in the second, Uncle Meriwether Lewis makes himself known to Will Stanton on Will's 11th birthday as one of the Old Ones. It seems that Will is the seventh son of a seventh son, and he is not only an Old One himself but also has special powers against the forces of Dark, which are rising. This book deals with his effort to use his power to find the Circle of Signs without destroying his family, who are unaware of Will's destiny. In the remaining books of the series, Will continues his quest for the Things of Power and learns much more about himself and his place in the world.

Fox, Paula. *The Slave Dancer*, illtd. Eros Keith. Scarsdale, N.Y.: Bradbury, 1973; New York: Dell, 1991. NEWBERY MEDAL. (Realistic Fiction/Historical/Black American)

In 1840, when Jessie Bollier is 13, he is kidnapped and taken aboard a ship bound for Africa. Because he plays the fife, it becomes his job to accompany the slaves, picked up in Africa, when they are brought up from the hold for exercise and made to dance. There are no compromises in this portrait of inhumanity as Jessie is told he must earn his way by "playing a few tunes to make the niggers jig," and discovers that ethical behavior has no place on a ship such as this. This is brought home when he watches one of the crew bring up a little girl from the hold, dead from suffocation, and throw her over the rail into the sea as if she were a pail of slops. But when Jessie refuses to play his fife, he receives a lashing, and when he is forced into the hold with the Africans to retrieve his fife, it is almost more than his compassionate nature can stand. Jessie escapes from the ship when it sinks in a storm, and his experiences on the slave ship, and on the island where he finds the compassion he thought was lost, are indelibly marked in his memory.

Fritz, Jean. *And Then What Happened, Paul Revere?* illtd. Margaret Tomes. New York: Coward, McCann and Geoghegan, 1973. (Easy Reader/ Biographical/Humor)

Paul Revere was immortalized in Henry Wadsworth Longfellow's poem, "Paul Revere's Ride" (1863), but as Fritz makes eminently clear, the poem is inaccurate. Nevertheless, her book lets us know the real Paul Revere, who was an accomplished silversmith, a participant in the French and Indian War at Lake George in New York state, as well as the man who spread the news about the Boston Tea Party. Revere set out with the message on December 16, 1773, traveling from Boston to Cambridge to Watertown to Worcester to Hartford to New York and Philadelphia, the same route followed by 20-year-old post rider Israel Bissell, beginning April 19, 1775, to herald the beginning of the Revolutionary War (p. 242). But Paul's children and then his grandchildren never stopped asking, "And then what happened . . ."

Hoover, H. M. *The Children of Morrow*. New York: Four Winds, 1973. (Science Fiction)

With very few meaningful science-fiction novels written for children, this one stands out as a well-developed character study as well as a warning for the future, unless humans give as much thought to animals as to people. Set in a distant future, 12-year-old Tia and eight-year-old Rabbit are physically and mentally different from the others in their small community, and because of these differences, the leaders are afraid of them. Tia is accused of witchcraft because she is telepathic. Rabbit, also telepathic, inadvertently uses his mind to kill when Tia's life is threatened, and the two children have no choice but to run away. If they can reach the sea and elude the cruel leaders trying to catch and kill them, other people like themselves will meet them there and care for them.

Macaulay, David. *Cathedral: The Story of Its Construction*. Boston: Houghton Mifflin, 1973, 1981. (Informational/Architecture)

For the first time, a book that equally combines text and illustrations was written for a young adult audience. Utilizing a mechanical drawing style, Macaulay explores the creation of a cathedral in sophisticated, detailed drawings, showing each step of the cathedral's development. The immediate popularity of the book led to *City*

(1974), *Underground* (1976), *Castle* (1977), and several more in a similar format.

Zemach, Harvé. *Duffy and the Devil*, illtd. Margot Zemach. New York: Farrar, Straus and Giroux, 1973. CALDECOTT MEDAL. (Folk/Myth/Picture Book/Cornwall)

Harvé Zemach is a fine teller of tales, and this is the story of Duffy, who has made a deal with the devil after he has helped her to knit socks and shirts for the squire. When Duffy reaches the three-year limit the devil has set before he takes her away with him, Old Jone intercedes and saves Duffy and the squire from the devil's clutches.

Collier, James Lincoln and Christopher Collier. *My Brother Sam Is Dead*. New York: Four Winds, 1974; New York: Macmillan, 1984. (Realistic Fiction/Revolutionary War/Death)

Rather than focusing on battle scenes, the Colliers present the effect of war on a family when the older son, Sam, 16, leaves home to fight for freedom with the Patriots, while his younger brother, Tim, 12, remains loyal to his father's Tory beliefs. Tim, who narrates the story, later becomes confused when his father ends up on a British prison ship and dies from cholera and his brother, Sam, is court-martialed for a crime he didn't commit and sentenced to death by his own commanding officer as an example to others. Tim tries his best to save his brother, but to no avail. "It's just so unfair," he cries out. And the officer who has tried to help says, "I know, Tim . . . war is never fair. Who chooses which men get killed and which ones don't?"

Cormier, Robert. *The Chocolate War*. New York: Pantheon, 1974. (Realistic Fiction/Social Behavior)

Zena Sutherland, former editor of *The Bulletin of the Center for Children's Books* and renowned for her perceptive reviews, has said that "young adults are drawn to Robert Cormier's novels, at least partly, because he explores the nature of evil in society and its source, the individual." This, Cormier's first young adult book, does not follow the folkloric tradition of "happily ever after." Protagonist Jerry Renault refuses to give in to demands by the power structure at his private school when he is ordered to sell a specific number of packaged chocolates. Because his independence makes him a hero to other students, he becomes the target of Archie Costello, leader of a secret school organization, the Vigils. The organization is actually being run by Brother Leon, the head of the school, who tells Archie to make an example of Jerry. Jerry, who is trying to deal with his mother's recent death, finds himself overwhelmed by rage that his mother has died, that he cannot do what he wants with his life, that he can't communicate with his father. The final blow comes when he discovers that he can't fight the power structure and must adjust to the realization that the good guy doesn't always win.

Cornish, Sam. *Grandmother's Pictures*, illtd. Jeanne Johns. Lenox, Mass.: Bookstore Press, 1974. (Poetry/Picture Book/Black American)

With deep love, Cornish speaks of his grandmother in the language of poetry. When he says, "In the room there was a book case, and records of family births, my grandfather's shoes and a marble-top bureau given to her by some white woman the family had worked for," the text flows, and carefully detailed descriptions bring to life three generations of an urban black neighborhood. Jeanne Johns's charcoal sketches evoke the essence of this very special family.

Feelings, Muriel. *Jambo Means Hello: Swahili Alphabet Book*, illtd. Tom Feelings, New York: Dial, 1974, 1985. (Picture Book/Concept/Africa)

This is a follow-up to the Feelingses' first concept book, *Moja Means One* (1971). The American alphabet takes on new meaning as the words used to represent the ABCs (with the exception of Q and X, which are not used in the Swahili alphabet) describe the people and environment of Africa. The illustrations are a lively panorama of African society.

Gauch, Patricia Lee. *This Time, Tempe Wick?*, illtd. Margaret Tomes. New York: Henry Z. Walck, 1974; New York: Putnam, 1992. (Picture Book/Realistic Fiction/Historical/American Revolution)

Tempe Wick is tall for her age and exceptionally strong, and she believes that America should be free from British rule. In the middle of the war, the Pennsylvania soldiers who are stationed on the Wick property decide to mutiny. Though Tempe is on their side and understands they are underfed and forgotten by their superiors, when two of them make her very angry by attempting to take her horse, Bonnie, she uses her ingenuity and her strength to stop them. The story is based on a true incident and offers a personal view of the Revolutionary War.

Hamilton, Virginia. *M.C. Higgins, the Great*. New York: Macmillan, 1974, 1993. NEWBERY MEDAL. (Realistic Fiction/Social Adjustment)

There are many levels of what Virginia Hamilton calls "rememory"[14] in her writing, and in this award-winning novel, she allows layers of time and history to permeate the setting and characterizations that motivate the protagonist, M.C. Higgins, a 13-year-old black boy who begins to question his own identity. M.C. likes to sit on his 40-foot pole, a gift from his father, and survey his world from his home on Sarah's Mountain, a home that is being threatened by strip mining and an ominous slag heap higher up the mountain. But this story gets its emotional power from M.C.'s interaction with his six-fingered friend, Ben, who has "witchy" fingers according to M.C.'s superstitious father, Jones, and also with the strange girl, Lurhetta Outlaw, who captures M.C.'s heart and then breaks it.

Hazen, Barbara Shook. *The Gorilla Did It*, illtd. Ray Cruz. New York: Atheneum, 1974. (Picture Book/Social Development)

In this book, the text alone does not tell the story. Cruz's interpretation, as suggested to him by Hazen,[15] adds to the impact of the book, which depicts a giant gorilla visiting a small child at night and tapping her on the head. "Shhh!" she says. "Go away. I can't play. I'm sleeping." But he doesn't go away, and when the little girl's mother reprimands her for making a mess in her bedroom, she puts the blame where it belongs—"The gorilla did it." Not only does her mother not see the gorilla, she also doesn't believe he exists. But, being a good mother, she accepts the premise and forgives her daughter.

McDermott, Gerald. *Arrow to the Sun: A Pueblo Indian Tale*. New York: Viking, 1974; New York: Puffin, 1977. CALDECOTT MEDAL. (Picture Book/American Indian)

This adaptation of a Pueblo folk tale tells the story of Boy who is searching for his father, the Sun. An arrow maker changes him into an arrow and sends him to the Sun. But the Sun will not acknowledge the Arrow as his son until he succeeds in meeting the trials set for him. Only then will Boy be allowed to return to earth with the spirit of the Sun, his father, and to resume his human shape once again. The abstract designs that McDermott employs to illustrate the story are based on Pueblo art and strongly enhance the overall effect of the story.

MacGregor, Ellen, and Dora Pantell. *Miss Pickerell Meets Mr. H.U.M.* New York: McGraw-Hill, 1974. (Science Fiction/Humor/Series)

In the Seventies, the use of the computer in business was just beginning to threaten the future of people in the work force who hadn't kept up on new technology. Pantell sends Ellen MacGregor's Miss Pickerell on an adventure in which computers seem to have taken over in society with drastic results, but Miss Pickerell's computer-literate nephew manages to save the day. With references to previous books in the series and the presence of familiar characters from Miss Pickerell's village of Square Toe, Pantell remains true to the original series created by Ellen MacGregor.

Raskin, Ellen. *Figgs and Phantoms*. New York: Dutton, 1974. (Realistic Fiction)

Raskin moves from picture books to narrative fiction, and this book is a delightful adventure in word play. Sissie Figg married Newton "Newt" Newton and had a daughter, Mona Figg Newton. The Figg family happens to be a conglomerate of artistic eccentrics: Mona's mother is a tap dancer and Uncle Truman is a human pretzel. Serious, sensible Mona has trouble fitting in. She relates only to her uncle, Florence I. (for Italy) Figg, a former vaudevillian who has become a dealer in old books. When he dies, Mona must make a major adjustment and does so through a rather involved dream sequence.

Silverstein, Shel. *Where the Sidewalk Ends*. New York: Harper, 1974; New York: Dell, 1986. (Poetry)

This collection of poems written and illustrated by Silverstein is unique and humorous and became very popular with an adolescent audience, an unusual occurrence at a time when young people were turned off on poetry. The humor is dependent on the adolescent's level of experience, for instance:

My dad gave me one dollar bill
'Cause I'm his smartest son,
And I swapped it for two shiny quarters
'Cause two is more than one.

The verses continue, with three dimes, four nickels, and when the narrator ends up with five pennies, he shows his father, who gets red in the cheeks, obviously "too proud of [him] to speak."

Anno, Mitsumasa. *Anno's Alphabet*. New York: Crowell, 1975; New York: Harper Trophy, 1988. Also, *Anno's Counting Book* (New York: Crowell, 1975; New York: Harper Trophy, 1986). (Picture Book/Concept/Interactive)

Anno's Alphabet presents the alphabet in such a way that a child can spend hours building alphabet vocabularies. A is an anvil, B is bicycle, and C is a clock. But all of these items utilize wood in some way, and, depending on the imagination, A can instead be an abode, B can be block, C can be cabinet. And D can be desk instead of dice. Although there are no words in the alphabet book, there is so much to read in the illustrations that it doesn't matter. In *Anno's Counting Book* numbers take on a new persona. The book begins with an empty landscape (zero) and ends with a complete village on that landscape (12). Anno takes the reader through four seasons and offers basic mathematical concepts that keep building. Various concepts—one to one, groups and sets, scales and tabulations—are presented in a charming and colorful format.

Babbitt, Natalie. *Tuck Everlasting*. New York: Farrar, Straus and Giroux, 1975, 1985. (Fantasy/Death)

Ten-year-old Winnie Foster considers running away from her family—mother, father, and grandmother—who won't allow her any independence. But the moment she decides she's not ready to do something so drastic after all, she is kidnapped by a woman, Mrs. Tuck, and her two sons when she ventures for the first time into the wood that belongs to her family and accidentally discovers the Tucks. The Tucks tell her their story: Eighty-plus years earlier, they chanced to drink from a spring in the middle of the wood and ultimately discovered that they were endowed with eternal life. It's so important to them that Winnie keep their secret that they take her to their home so that the father can talk to her and convince her not to tell. The strange man in the yellow suit, the unexpected charm of the youngest Tuck boy, forever 17, and the integrity of the Tuck family all help Winnie to make her final decision concerning the secret entrusted to her, and the story becomes one of the most thoughtful studies of life and death ever written for children.

De Paola, Tomie. *Strega Nona*. New York: Prentice-Hall, 1975; New York: Scholastic, 1992. (Folk/Myth/Picture Book/Italy)

Though not the first picture book created by Tomie de Paola, it is one of his most acclaimed. With understated humor, de Paola presents Big Anthony, who works for the woman called Strega Nona, "Grandmother Witch," in the small village where he lives. When Strega Nona conjures a pot of pasta, Big Anthony listens carefully, and when she goes out for the day, he repeats the spell and invites the whole village to share the pasta he has created. However, not only had Strega Nona told Big Anthony not to touch the pasta pot, he also never noticed the three kisses she blew into the pot to stop the pasta, and Big Anthony finds himself nearly smothered in it. When Strega Nona returns, she stops the flow but insists that Big Anthony take on a punishment that fits his crime.

Aardema, Verna. *Why Mosquitoes Buzz in People's Ears*, illtd. by Diane and Leo Dillon. New York: Dial, 1975; New York: Puffin, 1993. CALDECOTT MEDAL. (Folk/Myth/Picture Book/Africa)

The illustrations, which depict the African people wearing masks and becoming the animal characters in the story, are stunning in this folk tale about the punishment Mosquito receives from Lion and the other animals when he tells a lie that keeps the sun from rising. Like many folk tales, this story is well-suited for reading aloud.

Mathis, Sharon Bell. *The Hundred Penny Box*, illtd. Diane and Leo Dillon. New York: Viking, 1975; New York: Puffin, 1986. (Chapter Book/Social Relationships/Aging)

In the Seventies, not many people lived to be a hundred, and Mathis presents the special relationship between Michael and his 100-year-old great-great-aunt, Dew. Michael loves to hear Aunt Dew's stories about the 100 pennies she has managed to collect for every year of her life, with a different story for each year. Michael's mother is adamant about getting rid of Aunt Dew's longtime accumulation of items, including the decrepit old box holding the pennies, and Michael defies her with plans to hide the box. But Aunt Dew says, "No, don't hide my hundred-penny box! . . . Anybody takes my hundred-penny box takes me!" Mathis gives a well-defined portrait of what happens to people who live past their ability to care for themselves, and Diane and Leo Dillon portray the love between an old black woman and her young nephew, twice-removed.

Mayer, Mercer. *Just For You*. New York: Golden Press, 1975. (Picture Book/Social Adjustment)

Representing any small child who wants to be helpful, Mayer creates a protagonist from his imagination, neither human nor any known animal but nonetheless appealing:

> This morning I wanted
> to make breakfast just for you . . .
> but the eggs
> were too slippery.

When children become older and are better able to help at home, they suddenly develop strange diseases, total exhaustion, or homework that must be done immediately. The very young want so much to help, but lack of coordination and concentration sometimes brings disastrous results.

Paterson, Katherine. *The Master Puppeteer*. New York: Lodestar, 1975, 1991. NATIONAL BOOK AWARD. (Realistic Fiction/Historical/Japan)

The story takes place in 19th-century Japan, during the Tokugawa period when the wars had ended and peace brought poverty to many. Thirteen-year-old Jiro leaves home, where his family cannot afford to feed him, and goes into a puppet theater troupe in Osaka, where he becomes an apprentice puppeteer. He meets Kinshi, son of the master puppeteer, who is proud to a fault, and begins to unravel the mystery of Saburo, a Japanese "Robin Hood" who seems to have some connection to the puppet theater. The story does not compromise itself to fit an American ideal of a happy ending. Kinshi, who is meant to follow in his father's footsteps as a master puppeteer, tragically loses his hand.

Schick, Alice. *The Peregrine Falcons*, illtd. Peter Parnall. New York: Dial, 1975. (Informational/Nature)

This book offers information about a species that was found in the Seventies to be endangered and helps the reader to understand, in a personal way, the delicate balance of life that can so easily be interrupted when man interferes. Schick introduces a peregrine couple and follows them through nesting cycles and the difficulties they experience trying to have a family when the eggs have too thin a shell or the chicks are too weak to survive because of pesticides in the food they eat. An experimental project at Cornell University in New York state becomes the peregrines' hope for the future.

Slote, Alfred. *My Robot Buddy*, illtd. Joel Schick. New York: Harper, 1975, 1991. (Chapter Book/Science Fiction)

With actual advances in technology moving faster than most people's imaginations can follow, Slote predicts the Nineties and Schick gives pictorial form to the future in this story of a 10-year-old boy who gets a robot for his birthday. With his red hair and freckles, Jack's robot, called Danny One, looks just like a real boy, and Jack is glad to teach him how to act like one. He goes one step further and shows Danny how he, Jack, is able to act like a robot, a demonstration convincing enough to make Jack the victim of a robotnapping when the abductors think he, not Danny, is the robot. But communication is the key to defeating the criminals, thanks to Danny One.

Yep, Lawrence. *Dragonwings*. New York: Harper, 1975, New York: BDD, 1990. (Realistic Fiction/Historical/Chinese American)

When Moon Shadow's father sends for him to come to the Land of the Golden Mountain (America), he travels with his uncle to San Francisco's Chinatown, where he lives among the Tang (Chinese) people like himself. But his father has a dream and the two leave Chinatown to work for a demon (white) woman, who turns out to be kind and helpful. With the Chinese immigrants lacking understanding of the white culture and the white people not understanding the Chinese, Moon Shadow endures cruelty and poverty in this new land, but it is all worthwhile when his adored father realizes his dream by creating a flying machine. The San Francisco earthquake and fire that took place in the early 1900s has a role in Moon Shadow's introduction to America.

Allen, Marjorie N. and Carl Allen. *Farley, Are You For Real*?, illtd. Joel Schick. New York: Coward, McCann and Geoghegan, 1976. (Easy Reader/Fantasy/Humor)

E. Nesbit's Psammead in *The Five Children and It* (1902) is a curmudgeon, and Farley, a genie, is equally disagreeable when Archie MacDonald, who collects antique bottles, releases him and by doing so earns three wishes. Though Archie is too practical to believe in magic, he gives in to Farley's insistence that he make a wish, and the result offers Archie a whole new vision of the natural world. Farley is only two inches high, and Archie finds himself the same size. The story is a collaboration between mother and son. Carl Allen outlined it after watching an adaptation of Mary Norton's *The Borrowers* (1953) on television when he was 12.

William, Jay. *Everyone Knows What a Dragon Looks Like*, illtd. Mercer Mayer. New York: Four Winds, 1976; New York: Macmillan, 1984. (Picture Book/Folk Tale/China)

A small fat man with a scraggly beard and a bald head claims to be the Great Cloud Dragon come to save the people of the village of Wu when they are threatened by the Wild Horsemen from the North. But no one believes him. They all know what a dragon looks like. One small boy, however, like the good samaritan of Bible fame, shares his meager meal with the old man, and in return the old man saves the city. Then he shows the boy, Han, what a dragon really looks like. The story is given substance by the energetic and colorful drawings of Mercer Mayer.

McDermott, Beverly Brodsky. *The Golem.* Philadelphia: Lippincott, 1976. (Picture Book/Folk Tale/Jewish)

Mary Shelley wrote *Frankenstein* in 1818, and the monster she created has continued to enthrall people for many generations, but even more ancient is the story of the Golem. McDermott presents her version of the legend with the learned Rabbi Lev shaping a monster from clay and bringing it to life for the purpose of protecting the Jews of the Prague ghetto from the Gentiles who threaten them. As shown by McDermott's bold, sweeping watercolors, the monster evolves into a creature more dangerous than the enemy, ultimately becoming the victim of his own power.

Meltzer, Milton. *Never to Forget: The Jews of the Holocaust.* New York: HarperCollins, 1976, 1991. (Informational/Historical/Jewish)

Considered by the Nazi Party an "inferior" people, unfit to share the earth with their "superiors" (the Nazis), six million European Jews, religious and unreligious, were marked and exterminated during World War II. Meltzer takes the history of the Jewish people back to its ancient beginnings and follows their persecution through different civilizations. Semites, he notes, are Eastern Mediterranean Caucasians comprising Jews and Arabs, ancient Babylonians, Assyrians, Phoenicians.

Musgrove, Margaret. *Ashanti to Zulu: African Traditions*, illtd. Leo and Diane Dillon. New York: Dial, 1976; New York: Puffin, 1980. NEWBERY MEDAL. (Picture Book/Alphabet/Africa)

The illustrations for this unusual alphabet book are so striking that the text is the added bonus to the artwork, rather than the other way around. African tribes, from the Ashanti to the Zulu are described, with a different tribe for each letter in the English alphabet. These are only a few of the many tribes in Africa, but each is uniquely different, as indicated by text and pictures.

Peck, Richard. *Are You in the House Alone?* New York: Viking, 1976. (Realistic Fiction/Social Adjustment/Rape)

In children's books, the subject of rape generally has been avoided, but this low-key exploration is well presented. The book doesn't go that deeply or graphically into the subject, but does bring out the fact that rape can happen to anyone and it can happen anywhere. Gail Osburne is an intelligent 16-year-old high school student. She has been dating the same boy, Steve Pastorini, for two years and is beginning to question her true feelings about him. Then she starts receiving anonymous notes: "You know you want it. You'll get it. And you won't have long to wait." The person always seems to know when she is in the house alone, and one night, he makes good on his threat. When she turns in the rapist, a well-known person to her and the community, she discovers that it is she who is on trial, not he.

Prelutsky, Jack. *Nightmares: Poems to Trouble Your Sleep*, illtd. Arnold Lobel. New York: Greenwillow, 1976. (Poetry/Suspense)

Lobel gives form to Prelutsky's eerie verses, and it is obvious that both author and illustrator enjoyed the collaboration. From the bogeyman ("He skulks in the shadows, relentless and wild,/in his search for a tender, delectable child") to vampires, witches, ogres and ending with 13 dancing skeletons, every poem is chillingly dramatic and fun to read aloud and every picture a perfect accompaniment for the text.

Richler, Mordecai. *Jacob Two-Two Meets the Hooded Fang*. Canada: McClelland and Stewart, 1976. (Fantasy/Chapter Book/Humor)

Jacob Two-Two is six years old, two plus two plus two; he also has two older brothers and two older sisters and because he is the youngest, nobody listens to him the first time, and he has to say everything twice. But Jacob Two-Two, in his matter-of-fact way, gets along just fine in this tall-tale fantasy, even though his habit of saying things twice lands him in prison and brings him face to face with the terrible Hooded Fang.

Schick, Alice, and Marjorie N. Allen. *The Remarkable Ride of Israel Bissell as Related by Molly the Crow*, illtd. Joel Schick. Philadelphia: Lippincott, 1976 (Picture Book/Historical Fiction/Revolutionary War)

Post rider Israel Bissell was only 20 when he made the trip from Watertown, Massachusetts, to Philadelphia, Pennsylvania, to carry the call to arms to the people of the colonies when the War for Independence erupted on April 19, 1775. This book relates his itinerary, and Joel Schick's humorous drawings recreate history with a few embellishments. Although Israel Bissell was a very real person who settled in the Berkshire Hills of Massachusetts after the war, this picture book is the only published record of his accomplishments.

Taylor, Mildred. *Roll of Thunder, Hear My Cry*. New York: Dial, 1976; New York: Puffin, 1991. NEWBERY MEDAL. (Realistic Fiction/Social Adjustment/Black American/1930s)

Most members of the Logan family have learned to avoid direct confrontation with the local whites who run things in a 1930s Mississippi community. But Cassie Logan is still young enough not to have been faced with racial intolerance until she accompanies her grandmother on a shopping trip, and her independence creates a conflict she doesn't understand at first. The story builds as it becomes more and more obvious to Cassie that being black creates barriers not faced by whites, and that overcoming these barriers means going around them rather than straight over the top. The characters in this powerful novel are fully realized, clear-cut and uncompromising.

Allen, Marjorie N. and Carl Allen. *The Marble Cake Cat*, illtd. Marylin Hafner. New York: Coward, McCann and Geoghegan, 1977. (Chapter/Animal Fiction)

This chapter book resulted from the inspiration of Carl Allen at age 14 and deals with the difficulties of being different and therefore the object of unwelcome attention. The marble cake cat doesn't enjoy being unique, one of a kind. "Somewhere there must be someone who would care about him as a cat, an ordinary cat." In each chapter, he is taken in by various people, but no one makes an effort to communicate with him, one on one. He doesn't even have a name—until he meets Tommy, who truly cares and shows it.

Bond, Nancy. *A String in the Harp*. New York: Atheneum, 1977; New York: Puffin, 1987. (Fantasy/Time Travel/Death)

After David Morgan is widowed, he accepts an academic post for a year at the University of Wales and brings his children with him. None of the children has really adjusted to the sudden death of their mother in an accident, nor has their father. Twelve-year-old Peter is having the most difficult time and doesn't want to be in Wales at all. But it is Peter who finds the key that takes him back in time from the 20th century to the 6th century, and he becomes involved with the people and the history of an ancient time. By the time he understands the purpose of the key, he has learned to accept the changes in his life and to deal with his mother's death.

De Paola, Tomie. *The Quicksand Book*. New York: Holiday House, 1977. (Informational/Science/Picture Book/Humor)

Using voice balloons, diagrams, and cartoon-like drawings, de

Paola allows Jungle Girl to fall into quicksand, and Jungle Boy offers a long-winded explanation of exactly how quicksand works and the best way to overcome it. Finally, at the last possible moment, Jungle Boy rescues Jungle Girl, but it is she who has the last word in this comical adventure.

Highwater, Jamake. *Anpao: An American Indian Odyssey*. Philadelphia: Lippincott, 1977; New York: HarperCollins, 1992. (Fantasy/Native American)

This fantasy combines the many facets of Native American culture tied to its ancient past and the people's ancient connection to the land and, in so doing, allows the author to explore his own existence as a Native American whose lineage is traced to the Great Plains and Southwest Indian tribes. Anpao and his twin brother, Oapna, who is a contrary, always saying the opposite of what he really means, set out on a quest to find the lodge of the Sun so that Anpao can get permission from the Sun to marry the woman he loves, Ko-ko-mik-e-is. The trip they make is a dangerous one, and Highwater draws from the traditional Native American storytellers to weave an adventure that not only creates suspense but also establishes an American identity with the written word that ties all people of America together into one nation.

Levy, Elizabeth. *Something Queer at the Library*, illtd. Mordicai Gerstein. New York: Delacorte, 1977: New York: Dell, 1989. (Mystery/Easy Reader)

Jill, Gwen, and Fletcher the dog are very good at solving mysteries whenever something queer happens. With lots of lively pictures breaking up the short paragraphs of the text, this is a series that appeals to early readers. This is the first book in the series, and part of the fun of reading it is trying to solve the mystery before the end of the book.

Lobel, Arnold. *Mouse Soup*. New York: Harper, 1977. (Easy Reader/Animal)

This collection of four short stories is humorous and brings to mind the format of Aesop's fables, though the moral here is implied, not stated. In one, Mouse is captured by Weasel who plans to make soup out of him:

> "Wait!" said the Mouse.
> "This soup will not taste good.

It has no stories in it.
Mouse soup must be mixed
with stories
to make it taste really good."

And so Mouse tells Weasel four stories. In order to put the stories into the soup, Weasel must go out and get certain ingredients contained in the stories, leaving Mouse unattended in the pot.

McCaffrey, Anne. *Dragonsong*. New York: Atheneum, 1976; New York: Bantam, 1983. Also, *Dragonsinger* (New York: Atheneum, 1977; New York: Bantam, 1986); *Dragondrums* (New York: Atheneum, 1979; New York: Bantam, 1980). (Fantasy)

McCaffrey has created a fantasy world in which music plays a major role and dragons are bonded to humans, especially in the case of Piemur, who dreams of owning a little fire lizard. But Piemur must accomplish a special task to save the land of Pern, and, since his career as a dragonsinger has been interrupted by his changing voice, he has been apprenticed to the drums and sent southward to settle the imminent rebellion there. The first two books of the Harper Hall trilogy deal mostly with the music and the threat of the dreaded Threadfall on Pern; the third with Piemur's rite of passage.

Paterson, Katherine. *Bridge to Terabithia*. New York: Harper, 1977, 1987. NEWBERY MEDAL. (Realistic Fiction/Death/Social Adjustment)

Jesse Aarons has lots of sisters, but he's the only boy, and sometimes he is lonesome. Then he meets his new neighbor, Leslie Burke, a girl his own age who happens to like all the things he likes. Against his will, he finds himself bound in friendship to this unusual girl, and together they create an imaginary world called Terabithia. Part of Terabithia's charm is its privacy. Their secret kingdom in the woods is reached by swinging across the creek by rope, and sometimes, when the creek is high, Jess is afraid. But Leslie never shows any fear, and this turns out to be her downfall. One rainy day, when Jess decides he doesn't really want to go to Terabithia, he fully intends to let Leslie know, but then his teacher, Miss Edmunds, invites him to go to the Smithsonian Institution in Washington, D.C., for the day, and he doesn't get in touch with Leslie. After a wonderful day, he returns home to discover that Leslie is dead, drowned in the creek. Paterson portrays Jesse's anguish and guilt without compromise, and his loss becomes painfully clear to the reader.

Spier, Peter. *Noah's Ark*. New York: Doubleday, 1977; New York: Dell, 1992. CALDECOTT MEDAL. (Picture Book/Religion)

The text for this story is from a Dutch text by Jacobus Revius (1586–1658), translated by Spier, who was born in Amsterdam and came to New York in 1952. The collection of short, rhymed verses tells the story of Noah from the Bible and the whole poem is printed on the first page of the book. The rest of the book is divided into detailed, wordless panels showing the animals entering the Ark, two by two, after the rest of the population is destroyed by flood. When the waters recede, the animals return to the land and Noah has "planted a vineyard."

Yolen, Jane. *The Seeing Stick*, illtd. Remy Charlip and Demetra Maraslis. New York: Thomas Y. Crowell, 1977. (Picture Book/Original Folk Tale/China)

Hwei Ming, the daughter of a Chinese emperor, is blind, and her father offers a fortune in jewels to anyone who can help her see. But no one effects a cure until an old man who lives in South China takes his long walking stick, made from a single piece of golden wood, and his whittling knife and sets out for Peking to try and help the princess. All along the way, he carves his experiences with others on his piece of wood and when he is brought in to see the princess, he offers her his stick and teaches her how to use it. And when she has learned, Hwei Ming, whose name means "lightless moon becoming luminous," lives up to the promise of her name.

Goble, Paul. *The Girl Who Loved Wild Horses*. New York: Bradbury, 1978; New York: Macmillan, 1993. CALDECOTT MEDAL. (Picture Book/Native American/Plains)

A young Plains Indian girl loves and understands the wild horses and doesn't hesitate to care for them when they are hurt or need food or shelter. One day, she falls asleep in the meadow, and when she awakens, there is a terrible storm and she leads the horses to safety. She finds that she is lost and welcomes the opportunity to live with the wild horses. When she is finally found by the people, she returns home, but is not happy. Only by returning to live with the horses can she be happy. Each year she returns for a visit home and brings a colt for her family. But one year she does not come, and the people are sure she has become one of the wild horses she loves so much.

Greenfield, Eloise. *Honey, I Love and Other Love Poems*, illtd. Diane and Leo Dillon. New York: Harper, 1978, 1986. (Picture Book/Poetry/Black American)

The little girl who is the narrator of these poems creates her world with a rhythmic beat and celebrates her own background, the people she knows, the children she plays with, her relatives, her parents, her brother Reggie, and, especially, herself. She's an individual, sometimes happy, sometimes pensive, always aware of her surroundings, and the illustrations by the Dillons imbue her with life, vibrant and sparkling.

Hazen, Barbara Shook. *Two Homes to Live In*, illtd. Peggy Luks. New York: Human Sciences Press, 1978. (Picture Book/Divorce)

Luk's illustrations reflect the Seventies—Dad's hair is a little long and he sports a shaggy mustache and wears corduroy trousers and an oversized sweater. Mom has very long, very straight brown hair and wears princess-style long dresses. Hazen's text also reflects the Seventies as a time when divorce rates accelerated and parents discovered that their children were more affected by the separation than they had expected. The child who narrates this book is lovingly reassured and released from blame, learns to appreciate having two homes to live in, despite wishing the impossible—that Mom and Dad might get back together—and finally manages to accept a new and different life-style.

I Never Saw Another Butterfly: Children's Drawings and Poems from Terezin Concentration Camp, 1942–1944. New York: Schocken Books, 1978. (Informational/Poetry/Holocaust/Death)

These translated poems and drawings, reflecting the sufferings of children during the World War II Holocaust, were preserved from a concentration camp in Terezin, a Jewish ghetto in Czechoslovakia. They were created by children up to age 16 between 1942 and 1944, when the camp was liberated by the Soviet army. Of the 15,000 children who passed through the camp, only 100 came back. They knew they were going to die as is evidenced by the following verse from a poem by 12-year-old Franta Bass, who died in 1944 at the age of 14.

A little boy, a sweet boy,
Like that growing blossom,
When the blossom comes to bloom,
The little boy will be no more.[16]

Kerr, M. E. *Gentlehands*. New York: Harper, 1978, 1990. (Realistic Fiction/World War II/Holocaust)

Sixteen-year-old Buddy Boyle is enamored of Skye Pennington, one of the rich summer residents in the community where he lives year-round. Their relationship is colored by differences in background, but Buddy's grandfather helps bridge the gap. He lives on Long Island in a beautiful home and, like Skye, is a connoisseur of good food, wine, music, and art. Then Buddy's grandfather is accused of war crimes committed against the Jews at Auschwitz 30 years earlier, and Buddy has to face the fact that the accusations are true. In her many novels, Kerr often brings up moral issues not usually explored in children's books, not even young adult, but unfortunately for young people looking for solutions, she doesn't really follow through on these issues, preferring to leave the questions unanswered.

McKinley, Robin. *Beauty: A Retelling of the Story of Beauty and the Beast*. New York: Harper, 1978. (Fantasy/Fairy Tale/Narrative)

At a time when American children's books were beginning to cater to the romantic notions of an adolescent audience with a large selection of paperback series books labeled "Wildfire" and "Flare," McKinley told this old fairy tale in the form of a romantic novel and made it a sensitive love story appealing to all ages.

Raskin, Ellen. *The Westing Game*. New York: Dutton, 1978; New York: Puffin, 1992. NEWBERY MEDAL. (Realistic Fiction/Mystery)

When Samuel Westing dies, he leaves a will accusing one of his heirs of murdering him, and young Turtle Wexler, the protagonist of this unusual story, sets out to solve the mystery. The book offers clues all the way through and much of the fun of reading this text comes from the development and logic of the final solution. The characters are wildly absurd, and, as noted by Samuel Westing in his will, it's important to find out who the characters really are. "It's not what you have; it's what you don't have that counts," he tells them.

Savitz, Harriet May. *Wheelchair Champions: A History of Wheelchair Sports*. New York: Crowell, 1978. (Informational/Physical Adjustment)

Savitz divides her book into decades and describes the lack of awareness on the part of the public regarding veterans who suffered spinal-cord injuries during World War II and especially the lack of facilities for the physically disabled in this country. She speaks of two innovative men, one bound to a wheelchair, the other an engineer who developed the folding wheelchair that made wheelchair sports possible. In the Fifties, the Korean War increased the number of disabled, and new breakthroughs in rehabilitation offered the disabled an opportunity to improve their lives. Wheelchair sports, which had been limited to basketball and football, expanded to several other sports events, and by the Sixties, the Paralympics extended wheelchair competition worldwide. The Seventies, Savitz notes, had been a time of planning for the future, a time for making the public aware that a sizable percentage of the population had for many years been faced with obstacles at home, at work, while traveling or trying to participate in various functions because they were denied access by reason of being in a wheelchair.

Schick, Alice, and Sara Ann Friedman. *Zoo Year*, illtd. Joel Schick. Philadelphia: Lippincott, 1978. (Informational/Animal)

With Joel Schick's detailed and personable illustrations of different zoo animals adding the visuals, Schick and Friedman portray zoo life from the viewpoint of the animals and their keepers at a time when new awareness of animals' needs and routines and the importance of proper habitat were changing the role of the zoo throughout the world. Anecdotal and interesting to read, this book remains important to the study of nature.

Sharmot, Marjorie W. *Nate the Great*, illtd. Marc Simont. New York: Harper, 1978. (Easy Reader/Mystery/Series)

Young Nate and his dog, Sludge, are available to solve mysteries for their friends in this appealing "Break-of-Day" easy-reader series. Nate the Great follows through on every clue, and with the help of Sludge, whom Nate considers a great detective, he always manages to crack the case.

Van Woerkom, Dorothy. *Alexandra the Rock-Eater*, illtd. Rosekrans Hoffman. New York: Alfred A. Knopf, 1978. (Folk/Myth/Picture Book/Rumania)

Although a retelling of an old folk tale, this story has a twist: Instead of a hero, it has a heroine. Alexandra and her husband Igor, in a moment of levity, wish they had a child for every turnip they pull. A hundred turnips later, they have a hundred children. Like the old couple trying to care for millions of cats in Wanda Gág's classic tale (see p. 67), they find it difficult to keep all those children fed, especially when a young dragon begins threatening the countryside.

Alexandra sets out to find enough food for her children and meets up with the young dragon, whose mother demands that Alexandra perform three tasks. Alexandra easily outsmarts the dragons, and, when she returns home, she has set her family up for life. Hoffman's humorous and colorful illustrations, with Alexandra's bright red head scarf lighting up each page make for a delightful presentation.

Blos, Joan W. *A Gathering of Days: A New England Girl's Journal.* New York: Scribner, 1979; New York: Macmillan, 1990. NEWBERY MEDAL. (Realistic Fiction/Historical/Regional)

The charm of this book is in the way it is written: as a series of diary entries utilizing the quaint literary style of the early 1800s from the viewpoint of a 13-year-old girl. The history of America presented by Rachel Field in *Hitty: Her First Hundred Years* (1929) is narrowed to a single year in this story, and the details of everyday life in a small New England town take on a clarification that allows the reader to understand the lack of modern facilities in the home, the inability to find a cure for certain diseases, the struggle of poor families to educate their children, the inequity of slavery, and the need to accept the deaths of loved ones at an early age.

Brown, Marc. *Arthur's Eyes.* Boston: Little, Brown, 1979. (Fantasy/Picture Book/Physical Adjustment)

Although Arthur is an animal, he represents any young boy who is embarrassed by having to wear glasses. His friends, a variety of anthropomorphic animals as well, tease him until he hides his glasses and walks into the girls' bathroom by mistake. When he discovers his teacher wears glasses too, he decides to wear his own glasses and finds himself much improved in school and sports. In fact, his friend Francine starts wearing glasses without glass because she says they help her concentrate and make her look beautiful.

Hall, Donald. *The Ox-Cart Man,* illtd. Barbara Cooney. New York: Viking, 1979; New York: Puffin, 1983. CALDECOTT MEDAL. (Picture Book/Poetry/Regional)

With Cooney's authentic New England scenery illustrating Hall's rhythmic text, this series of events shows the routine followed by a farmer as he prepares to take his goods to market, sells them one by one and then buys new supplies so that he can return home and begin again throughout the seasons of the year to shear the sheep, make the wool, and build a new ox-cart wagon. Cooney, by utilizing an

Early American style of art, reproduced a quieter, simpler time in American history.

Cormier, Robert. *After the First Death*. New York: Pantheon Books, 1979. (Realistic Fiction/Terrorism)

As in *The Chocolate War* (1974), the story opens in a private school, but that is the end of any similarity. This book explores the mind and logic of a 16-year-old terrorist, Miro, who idolizes his leader, Artkin, and in the name of freedom feels he must commit murder when he and Artkin highjack a bus full of small children. It looks at the effect of terrorism on Ben Marchand, who begins to question his loyalty to a father who has ultimately disappointed him, and introduces Kate, the young bus driver, brave and caring but a victim nonetheless. As usual, Cormier is uncompromising and creates a story that lingers in its impact.

Howe, Deborah and James. *Bunnicula: A Rabbit Tale of Mystery*, illtd. Alan Daniel. New York: Atheneum, 1979. (Chapter Book/Humor/Mystery)

There are three main characters in this book—a cat, a dog, and a bunny rabbit. The cat and dog are convinced the rabbit is a vampire bunny, and the efforts of the two animals to prove this premise through spying in the night are not only unsuccessful but create far more problems for them than for their nemesis.

MacLachlan, Patricia. *The Sick Day*, illtd. William Pene du Bois. New York: Pantheon, 1979. (Easy Reader/Family/Humor)

MacLachlan's first book is about a small girl named Emily, who very much reflects the sophisticated preschooler in 1970s American society, as well as the elevated status of the female and the new role assigned to males. Emily is sick, and because Mama is working, her father puts her to bed. So begins a game in which Emily manipulates her daddy throughout the day, asking for stuffed animals, a new hairdo, a story, a drawing featuring a monster, and a song to be played on her father's recorder. When her father becomes sick the next day, Emily is only too glad to take care of him.

Van Allsburg, Chris. *The Garden of Abdul Gasazi*. Boston: Houghton Mifflin, 1979, 1982. (Picture Book)

In this, Van Allsburg's first picture book, a young boy, Alan Mitz, takes Miss Hester's dog Fritz for a walk while Miss Hester is visiting a neighbor. But Fritz gets away from him and dashes into the garden of Abdul Gasazi, who hates dogs. The man is a magician and says he has changed Fritz into a duck. The duck who is supposed to be Fritz flies off with Alan's hat. But when a dejected Alan returns to Miss Hester's house, Fritz greets him at the door. Miss Hester tells Alan that Mr. Gasazi played a trick; no one can really change dogs into ducks. But what Alan doesn't know is that Fritz has Alan's hat and what Miss Hester, who chides Fritz for stealing Alan's hat, doesn't know is that it was the duck who had stolen it. The illustrations for this book are sophisticated and surreal, much different from the ordinary, and give the sense that magic does happen.

Farber, Norma. *How Does It Feel to Be Old?*, illtd. Trina Scharf Hyman. New York: Dutton, 1979, 1988. (Picture Book/Aging)

Written as an essay poem, Farber offers an emotional portrait of old age, with all its memories, its joys and fears, its lonely hours missing a mate long gone, and its delight in the wonders of an active world. Most of all, it is a message to grandchildren about the special relationship between the old and the young and the transcience of that relationship as one grows up and the other passes away. Hyman's illustrations make the words come alive and bring a tear to the eye.

NOTES

1. In 1993 the book was made into a sensitively written movie starring Mel Gibson, available in video stores for home viewing.
2. Letter to the author from Judy Blume, dated April 6, 1977.
3. Katherine Paterson. *The Spying Heart*, p. 137.
4. From an article in the "Mariposa Guide," located in the censorship files of the Kerlan Collection, Walter Library, University of Minnesota.
5. While the National Book Award was under the auspices of the National Institute of Arts and Letters from 1950 to 1979, there was a children's book category. When the Association of American Publishers took over the award in 1980, the children's book category was canceled.
6. Selma Lanes. *The Art of Maurice Sendak*, p. 189.
7. Laurence Yep. Afterword, *Dragonwings*. New York: Harper Trophy, 1977, p. 247.
8. Ibid., p. 248.
9. Michael Gorman. *School Library Journal*, April 1995, Vol. 41. p. 27.
10. Marjorie N. Allen. "Budget Pinching Affects Book Industry," *The Berkshire Sampler*, Pittsfield, Massachusetts, Jan. 28, 1979.
11. Maurice Sendak. *Caldecott & Co.*, p. 175.
12. Sponsored by the British Library Association, this award is given to the author of the most outstanding children's book first published in English in the United

Kingdom during the preceding year. It is the British counterpart of the Newbery Medal in the United States.

13. Deborah Kovacs and James Preller. *Meet the Authors and Illustrators*, p. 46.
14. Virginia Hamilton. "Rememory," *Horn Book* Magazine, 1981.
15. In an interview, Hazen related that she had submitted her manuscript to the publisher with suggestions for the illustrations, even though this was not the accepted procedure, and that Cruz's illustrations had far surpassed her expectations.
16. *I Never Saw Another Butterfly*, p. 50.

Illustration by Karen Barbour from Flamboyan *by Arnold Adoff, copyright © 1988 by Karen Barbour; reproduced by permission of Harcourt Brace & Company. Set in Adoff's native Puerto Rico, the story celebrates the unique combination of Spanish, Caribbean, and American cultures that constitutes this island commonwealth. Although Puerto Rico has been a United States possession since 1898, it has seldom been the setting for children's books.*

9

WHY CAN'T JOHNNY WRITE? 1980–1989

In their impact on social, economic, political/governmental life and on the attitudes and personal values of Americans, the eighties were the most important years since World War II.

—Haynes Johnson
Sleepwalking Through History

The Dream Personified

Only in the United States could a movie star become the president of a nation. America had experienced two volatile decades and many disappointments in the political arena when Ronald Reagan, best known for his "leading man" roles in movies of the Forties,[1] made his bid for office. The child of alcoholic parents,[2] Reagan was a living example of the American dream, a poor boy who had made good through perseverance and hard work, a true hero. After changing his affiliation from Democrat to Republican, he was elected governor of California in 1966 and served until he became the Republican candidate for president in 1980. He seemed to promise the stability the American people sought, and he told the people what they wanted to hear—that America was not in decline, that inflation would be controlled in his administration, and that the country would regain its status as a leading world power. Reagan was a man who enthusiastically embraced the patriotic ideals that had marked the World War II years, and he seemed to embody what the country identified as American virtues: informality, humor, and patriotism.[3]

Success is very much linked with timing, and Reagan was blessed with good timing. As an actor, he benefited from extensive television coverage at a time in history when television was peaking in the news arena. In his first act as president, he was able to announce the release of American hostages from Iran because the plane bringing the prisoners home didn't take off until after the inauguration ceremony was under way. Although he, like John F. Kennedy, was shot by an assassin, he survived the attempt, which was made just nine days after his inauguration, and throughout the ordeal never lost his sense of humor. Such events served to reconfirm the public's trust in government, and Reagan remained popular throughout the eight years of his presidency.

Undercurrents in Society

While Americans enjoyed the Reagan myth and pretended that the American dream was alive and well, the very structure of society was undergoing a major upheaval and nobody paid very much attention. Japan, Germany, China, and India were becoming stronger as America's economic and educational foundations began to show clear signs of buckling. The U.S. divorce rate had increased fourfold since 1960. The cost of health care had risen sharply. With two-income families the norm and single parents needing to work because of skyrocketing inflation, child care became a necessity, but it was expensive and not easily available.[4]

When Ann Martin, a former editor of children's books, started writing the series called The Baby-sitters Club with *Kristy's Great Idea* (1986), the books were intentionally a reflection of the times, with the emphasis on the need for baby-sitters in a community where split families and working mothers were the rule. In the Eighties, romance and mystery also found their way into light reading for pre-teens. Many publishing companies introduced new series, while Nancy Drew and the Hardy Boys were updated and continued in popularity.

As technical advances streamlined the marketplace, it became more and more evident that education had not kept pace. Rudolph Flesch's *Why Johnny Can't Read*, published in 1955, had caused schools to question their methods of teaching reading, and experimental remedial programs were set up in the Sixties and Seventies. By the Eighties, a new problem surfaced: Johnny couldn't write.

Failed Experiment

In American companies, managers and supervisors were found to be incapable of writing grammatically correct paragraphs, and there was an appalling lack of skill in the fields of math and science. The Eighties brought computers into the limelight, and mechanized systems replaced manpower, first in factory assembly lines, then in the form of personal computers in the offices of large companies. It became imperative to improve education, but the baby boomers were out of school and doing well in the workplace, despite their troubles with spelling and grammar, and the older members of society were enjoying the euphoria of the Reagan years. In the meantime, a lowered birth rate had led to school closings and diminished emphasis on education, even as an increase in the immigrant population was calling for more attention to reading and writing skills in English as a second language.

It was also during this decade that computers became broadly available. The fast-emerging field of microelectronics opened the door for entrepreneurs, and enterprising young people utilized high-tech developments from California's Silicon Valley to start new businesses, quickly becoming millionaires. The rich became richer and the poor became poorer as people seized opportunities for personal gain in a society that lacked regimentation. Power and money seemed to become more important than integrity in dealings with others.

In the meantime, in education, children were left to their own devices. There was more attention given to the programs being set up to increase learning than to the needs of the children who were supposed to benefit from these programs. The effort to fill the education void introduced a flood of added procedures to an already tight curriculum in the schools. Teachers were not included in the planning nor were the children asked for their opinions. With the discovery of personal computers as writing aids, some schools brought computers in but never thought to instruct teachers or students on how to use them.

A New Philosophy

When Jim Trelease, an author from Springfield, Massachusetts, wrote his *Read-Aloud Handbook* (1981), it captured the imagination of those baby-boomer parents who wanted their children to surpass all others in accomplishments, and it became a runaway best-seller. About the same time, educators Kenneth Goodman and Lucy McCormick Calkins had developed a new approach to reading called whole language, a philosophy that included both reading and writing and called for connecting print with meaning. This approach appealed to teachers who were beginning to question their established curriculum and the value of basal readers in teaching children to read and write.

The work of Goodman and Calkins encouraged educators to initiate a growing whole-language movement in this country, although the actual definition of whole language was hard to pin down. Many teachers also tried to make it fit into an already overburdened curriculum instead of seeing it as a new philosophy leading to the student's enjoyment of the reading and writing process. In the meantime, the market demand for children's books began to grow as baby boomers bought books for their children and schools slowly began to develop literature-based curriculums. Teachers were introduced to trade children's books in which story and characters took precedence over vocabulary and spelling lists.

Reality with a Flair

While William Steig, Lawrence Yep, and Beverly Cleary continued to share with children their unique talents for fiction, and teachers began to discover the rich material available in children's books, innovation was finding its way into informational books, which stopped being textual tomes and began to rival fiction as examples of imaginative ingenuity.

Jill Krementz used photography to create books that relied on the reaction of children to adversity in their lives. The results were *How It Feels When a Parent Dies* (1981) and *How It Feels When Parents Divorce* (1984). Each text is made up of interviews with children who have experienced death or divorce and are trying to deal with the trauma. Another photographer who displayed a resourceful use of the camera's eye was Patricia Lauber with her *Seeds: Pop, Stick, Glide* (1981), the first of many unusual and sophisticated informational books in which photographs served as much for their artistic design as for sources of information. Russell Freedman's *Lincoln: A Photobiography* (1987) used period photographs to illustrate the Lincoln presidency and elaborated on the photographs with a captivating text. The book was awarded the 1988 Newbery Medal.

Aliki Brandenburg's *Digging Up Dinosaurs* (1981) combined humor and cartoon-like drawings with facts and put a new face on Crowell's already popular "Let's-Read-and-Find-Out" science series. Vicki Cobb continued to make science great fun with *The Scoop on the Ice Cream* (1985) and many other food-related books. One of the most popular new science writers for children was and is Joanna Cole, whose *How You Were Born* (1984) continues to educate young children curious about the birth process. In the photographs and sketches used to illustrate this book, some of the pictures are unexpectedly graphic, but parents who are open and comfortable with the reproductive process will not be bothered by this. In addition to the ease with which Cole answers children's questions about birth, the photographs include people of all colors and cultural backgrounds, one of the first children's books to portray a cultural mix.

Cole is also credited with *The Magic School Bus: At the Waterworks* (1986), the first book in this popular series. Text by Cole and illustrations by Bruce Degen join to create a comic-book format easy to read and fun to look at. Many books whose purpose is to teach can be tedious to read, but the Magic School Bus series makes learning a pleasure. In

The Magic School Bus: Lost in the Solar System (1989), instead of learning about the solar system in the classroom, Ms. Frizzle and her students go on a field trip into space, where the magic school bus becomes a space ship, and the children observe the planets firsthand. This is the kind of informational book publishers love to see because it sells many, many copies. A successful television series for children and an imaginative collection of CD-ROMs for the computer crowd[5] have been based on the books.

America's Penchant for Humor

Collections of poetry by Myra Cohn Livingston, Eve Merriam, anthologist Lee Bennett Hopkins, and David McCord showed their ability to find humor in everyday occurrences. Poet Nancy Willard's interpretive picture book, *A Visit to William Blake's Inn: Poems for Innocent and Experienced Travelers* (1981), with Alice and Martin Provensen's illustrations, was named a Newbery book in 1982. Jack Prelutsky spoke the language of middle-grade children with *The New Kid on the Block* (1984), a collection of mini-jokes, plays on words, and character sketches written in rhyme.

With the expanding demand for books that would appeal to preschoolers and even toddlers, Audrey and Don Wood joined talents to create what came to be known as predictable picture books.[6] *The Napping House* (1984) is similar in format to the well-known nursery rhyme, "The House that Jack Built," as an increasing number of participants decide to take a nap—granny, a child, a dog, a cat, a mouse—one on top of the next, until a wakeful flea bites the mouse and in a flurry of precarious activity everyone from top to bottom wakes up.

Emotional Involvement

Two books of the Eighties that truly represent the concerns of the decade are Jane Yolen's *Owl Moon* (1987), for which John Schoenherr was awarded the 1988 Caldecott Medal, and the 1986 Newbery Medal winner, *Sarah, Plain and Tall* (1985), by Patricia MacLachlan. Although

Owl Moon is a deceptively simple poem about a child and a father out looking for owls on a cold winter's night, it is also a celebration of nature. It is even more an expression of an abiding love between father and child. The sense of belonging that this book imparts seems to have a special appeal for children without a father figure in the home, a common situation in the 1980s. Schoenherr, known for his nature illustrations, creates in *Owl Moon* the mysterious atmosphere of the woods at night in the moonlight and the drama of coming face to face with an owl when least expected, connecting text and pictures into an integrated whole.

Yolen, who wrote poetry in college, was more interested in traditional fairy and folk tales when she first began writing children's books than in furthering her career as a poet. She became a highly skilled prose stylist, writing original stories that served to showcase a long list of artists, many of whom first entered the picture-book field with a Yolen project. She is a prolific author who has explored every area in the children's book field. As the demand for picture books utilizing classical fantasy and fairy tales diminished in the 1980s, Yolen extended her expertise to humorous word play, easy readers, and books for older readers.

Piggins (1987) was the result of a close collaboration between Yolen and illustrator Jane Dyer. The two created a sophisticated, humorous picture book patterned after the well-known English mysteries in which "the butler did it." The story is filled with various clues that become obvious when the mystery is solved and that encourage children to read the book again just to find those clues. Naturally, the impeccable butler, Piggins, is not the culprit. This is a seamless combination of words and pictures in a picture book aimed at older readers.

When *Owl Moon* was chosen as a Caldecott book, Yolen finally accepted her special talent as a poet. She continues to have books published in all areas of literature—fantasy and science fiction for both adults and children, picture books, short stories, and easy readers, as well as editing her own line of Jane Yolen Books at Harcourt Brace and compiling short story and poetry collections for young adults.

When Patricia MacLachlan's mother was diagnosed with Alzheimer's Disease in the mid-Eighties, it was an illness not well-known or understood by the general public. At the time MacLachlan began writing *Sarah, Plain and Tall*, the only clear memory left to her mother was the story of a 19th-century ancestor who left Maine to become the mail-order bride of a widowed midwestern farmer with two children. In an effort to put her mother's memory into print so she would never lose it, MacLachlan tried writing the story as a picture book, but, as it increased in complexity, it developed into a short novel.[7] The characterizations are well-defined in this emotional story about loss and the healing powers of love and acceptance.

An earlier book by MacLachlan was *Arthur for the Very First Time* (1980), the story of a 10-year-old boy who likes routine, but, when he stays with his aunt and uncle on a farm for the summer, discovers that spontaneity offers new and exciting possibilities for him. MacLachlan said that in her first draft of this book, there were so many characters that the storyline was almost completely lost. She managed to pare the work down to its core with the helpful assistance of writer friends and discovered that most of the discarded characters had their own stories to tell—for instance, in *Through Grandpa's Eyes* (1980) and *Seven Kisses in a Row* (1983).

While Jane Yolen and Patricia MacLachlan set a standard difficult to surpass, their efforts were at least equaled by Mordicai Gerstein's *Mountains of Tibet* (1987), Dennis Nolan's *The Castle Builder* (1987), Chris Van Allsburg's 1986 Caldecott book, *The Polar Express* (1985), and Gary Paulsen's *Dogsong* (1985). In a decade where full-color picture books had become the norm, these books did not depend on color for their appeal. *Mountains of Tibet*, a storybook adaptation of the cycle of life as set forth in the *Tibetan Book of the Dead*, depends as much on text as on the color illustrations to portray the concept. Elizabeth Coatsworth had been the first children's author to inquire into Eastern beliefs, with the connection between man and the animals set forth in *The Cat Who Went to Heaven* (1930). Gerstein's book goes further by exploring the mystery of life and death, their cycles, and the connections among all living things.

Nolan creates a dream within a dream in *The Castle Builder* as a boy builds a castle from sand and makes it real. Still another dream story, *The Polar Express*, is a fantasy journey by train to the North Pole at Christmastime.

Paulsen's *Dogsong* is storytelling at its best with a text that sings. The setting, as in Jack London's *Call of the Wild* (1903), is Alaska, and Russel, an adolescent Eskimo boy, travels by dog team and sled on a long, hard journey toward self-discovery. This book contains a dream sequence connecting Russel to the past. Following the old ways as his ancestors did, he is finally able to bond with his dogs, his surroundings, and even his prey.

Balancing the Scales

Jean George portrayed a female protagonist struggling for survival on the Alaskan tundra in *Julie of the Wolves* (1972), introducing a portrait of wolves that negated the commonly held opinion at the time her book was written that they were an enemy. John Schoenherr was the illustrator for George's Newbery Medal winner but received little acknowledgment for his contribution at the presentation ceremony. When he in turn was awarded the Caldecott Medal for *Owl Moon*, author Jane Yolen remained similarly unacknowledged as a deserving partner. This is a flaw in the selection process for Newbery and Caldecott awards. When author and illustrator are not the same person, only one of the pair receives the award. In the case of *Ashanti to Zulu* (1976), for which Diane and Leo Dillon received their second Caldecott, author Margaret Musgrove was not even invited to the award ceremony.[8] *A Visit to William Blake's Inn* (1981), illustrated by Alice and Martin Provensen, was a Caldecott honor book but not a Caldecott Medal winner, while Nancy Willard, the author, was awarded a Newbery Medal for the same book.

With the great number of picture books published in this country, only those that display a seamless integration of words and pictures should be considered for the highest prize, and therefore, in a case where author and illustrator are two different people merging their talents, both should be recognized equally. By the same token, for a Newbery Medal book that would be incomplete without the pictures—*Hitty* (1929), *The Cat Who Went to Heaven* (1930), and *A Visit to William Blake's Inn* (1981)—equal recognition should be given to the illustrator.

Brer Rabbit Reborn

With much of the nation lulled by the assurances of the Reagan administration, less effort was being made to represent the different races and cultures that made up the population of the United States. The search for multi-ethnic authors and illustrators that had begun in the 1970s showed signs of lessening, with only those already recognized being encouraged to continue.

However, the works of author Virginia Hamilton, illustrators Diane and Leo Dillon, and author/illustrator John Steptoe continued to celebrate African-American heritage. Hamilton and the Dillons worked together to present African-American folktales in a collection called *The*

People Could Fly (1985). Handed down from oral tradition predating the Civil War, when African slaves were made to speak American English but were not allowed to be educated, these tales had already been collected by writers like Joel Chandler Harris (see p. 10), who wrote the stories down in the dialect in which they were told. In Hamilton's contemporary collection, she speaks in her own voice, mingled with the original dialect, as part of her personal connection to the slaves and fugitives of early America.

When composer Van Dyke Parks chose to put the Joel Chandler Harris stories to music in 1984 in an album called *Jump*, artist Barry Moser offered to illustrate them in book form. The result was *Jump! The Adventures of Brer Rabbit* (1986) and *Jump On Over* (1989). Black author Julius Lester and black illustrator Jerry Pinkney also put together their interpretation of these folktales in *The Tales of Uncle Remus: The Adventures of Brer Rabbit* by Joel Chandler Harris (1987).

The work of illustrator Ed Young and author Lawrence Yep continued to represent Asia, with Young being awarded a 1990 Caldecott Medal for *Lon Po Po: A Red Riding Hood Story from China* (1989). Paul Goble continued to create in words and pictures the world of the American Indian with *Beyond the Ridge* (1989), in which death becomes not an end but a beginning, similar in concept to *Mountains of Tibet*. Arnold Adoff, husband of Virginia Hamilton, wrote a rolicking picture book, *Flamboyan* (1988), with Karen Barbour's bright, lively illustrations adding to the story's energy (see illustration p. 254). Set in Adoff's native Puerto Rico, the story celebrates the unique combination of Spanish, Caribbean, and American cultures that constitutes this island commonwealth. Although Puerto Rico has been a United States possession since 1898, it has seldom been the setting for children's books.

Even though publishers seemed to be relying on the tried and true, new black talent emerged toward the end of the decade with Jeanette Winter's *Follow the Drinking Gourd* (1988), the story of slaves who were aided in their pre-Civil War escape efforts by Peg Leg Joe telling them how to follow the Big Dipper to the Underground Railroad and freedom. A different version of the story was written by F. N. Monjo in *The Drinking Gourd* (1970) as an easy reader, but neither the point of view nor the pictures in Monjo's book create the high degree of drama and cohesion seen in Winter's endeavor. Illustrator Jerry Pinkney and author Patricia McKissack merged their talents in a modern African-American folktale called *Mirandy and Brother Wind* (1988), which was named a Caldecott honor book in 1989. Rhoda Blumberg added much to America's understanding of Asian history and culture in *Commander Perry in the Land of the Shogun* (1985).

It was also in this decade that tongue-in-cheek retellings of traditional fairy tales inaugurated a new approach to well-known stories that transcended the age limits of the picture-book set. The brazen excuses of the wolf in *The True Story of The Three Little Pigs! by A. Wolf* (1989) were set forth by Jon Szieszka and complemented by the droll, off-key drawings of Lane Smith. This book opened the door for fractured fairy tales, which have become popular with young adult readers.

It is, of course, impossible to list all the significant books from the vast array of children's books published in the 1980s. It isn't enough to speak of choosing books that are still in print because so many noteworthy books are not reprinted, as a result of less than spectacular sales, and others less noteworthy, such as some of the series books, keep appearing in new volumes. A law passed at the end of the Seventies taxing publishers on books stored in their warehouses has caused publishers to reprint only the books that sell out fast. Quantity many times overrides quality.

One positive result of the publishers' efforts to economize was the reissuance of many titles that had not been stocked in bookstores for years, though they had never stopped circulating in library collections where they had become dog-eared from use. Another reason for the reprints was the unexpected popularity of Jim Trelease's *Read-Aloud Handbook*, which listed many older titles as being especially suitable for reading aloud to children. The emergence throughout the country of bookstores selling only children's books and the increasing demand by parents for recommended titles led to new editions of works by E. Nesbit, L. Frank Baum, Frances Hodgson Burnett, Margaret Wise Brown, Hugh Lofting, and many others. The public television program "Reading Rainbow" brought children's books to the attention of the consumer, and many paperback editions of titles discussed on the program became popular.

Lowered Expectations

Those involved with literature for children—writers and illustrators, librarians, teachers and parents—have always wished to see good children's books given the attention they deserve. Even though teachers during the Eighties tried to make up for years of neglecting trade children's books in the classroom and parents were starting earlier than ever to build libraries for their children, the child was seldom consulted. No one seemed to consider children capable of independent thought. The aphorism that low expectation leads to low achievement appeared to be reflected in the education system: No matter how innovative it tried to be, little improvement could be seen.

During the Eighties, children also were faced with violence presented on television news and watched maladjusted families on talk shows. They learned about AIDS and drugs and firearms and abortion. They were aware of the homeless, of alcohol abuse, of the dangers of smoking. They learned that many children were victims of abuse, and that a stranger might be a rapist or a child-killer. In the meantime, censorship was growing in the field of children's books. Some parents were trying to ban certain books from library shelves because of a swear word or a reference to sexual curiosity. Children were learning far more about the basic realities of life from television than from any book, but without the balanced optimism that many good children's books offer.

By the time President Reagan had spent two terms in office, there were stirrings of unrest throughout the nation. Trouble was brewing in the Middle East, and the economy in the United States began to weaken. Unemployment was growing as businesses started to cut their staffs. The number of people reaching retirement age was expanding geometrically as high-priced advanced medical care and new treatments began to keep the elderly alive and active much longer. At a time when women were finally being recognized as capable of leadership, many couples put off having children, while the number of single teenage mothers on welfare kept increasing. But, when Reagan's vice president, George Bush, was elected president in 1988, it seemed the administration that had carried us on its flying carpet through the Eighties was going to continue well into the Nineties.

CHRONOLOGICAL BIBLIOGRAPHY 1980–1989

Allen, Marjorie N. *One, Two, Three—AhChoo!*, illtd. Dick Gackenbach. New York: Coward, McCann and Geoghegan, 1980; Scarborough, Ontario: Ginn Publishing Canada, 1994. (Easy Reader/Allergies)

When Wally Springer has to give up his new puppy because it

makes him sneeze, his parents supply him with pets that don't have fur and feathers. But his frogs jump into his mother's cold cream and his pet snake causes havoc in the kitchen by unexpectedly waking up from a winter sleep. Then Wally discovers the perfect pet—almost.

Blume, Judy. *Superfudge*. New York: Dutton, 1980. (Chapter Book/Humor)

Peter Hatcher had been introduced a decade earlier in *Tales of a Fourth Grade Nothing* (1972), and though he is now a couple of years older, so is his little brother, Fudge, who has infiltrated Peter's routine at school by starting kindergarten. Fudge immediately begins acting out several of his many fantasies and alienates himself from one teacher, which necessitates a move to another kindergarten class on his very first day of school.

Feeney, Stephanie. *A Is for Aloha*. Honolulu: University of Hawaii Press, 1980. (Picture Book/Concept/Hawaii)

The clear-cut examples for each letter in this alphabet book are presented not only in sharply defined black-and-white photos, but also reflect the language and the setting of the Hawaiian Islands and the various cultures living in this 49th state. At the end of the book, there is an explanation for each example that uses the Hawaiian language. "Aloha" means "hello," "goodbye," or "I love you." "Tutu" is the Hawaiian word for grandmother or grandfather. It is important for American children to relate not only to the region in which they live but to neighboring states as well, even as far away as Hawaii and Alaska.

Hill, Eric. *Where's Spot?* New York: Putnam, 1980. (Picture Book/Interactive)

At a time when parents were just beginning to look for books that might appeal to their toddlers, Eric Hill created this "lift-the-flap" book about a mother dog looking for her baby dog—behind the door, in the clock, under the bed, etc. In each place, a strange animal is behind the flap, not Spot, until finally . . . there is Spot. This very simple concept has been utilized in a long string of Spot books that remain popular.

Maruki, Toshi. *Hiroshima no Pika (The Flash of Hiroshima)*. New York: Lothrop, Lee and Shepard, 1980, 1982. (Picture Book/World War II/Japan)

The Japanese people, deeply concerned that the horrors of Hiroshima and Nagasaki, both ravaged by the atomic bomb in 1945, would be forgotten, resolved never to let that happen. Maruki, a Japanese artist noted for his "A-bomb paintings," created this picture book for children and makes a powerful statement to all people, not just children, about the inhumanity of nuclear weapons and the horror of war. The illustrations are stunningly explicit, bringing to mind ancient Japanese art scrolls of a Buddhist hell. The story is about a little girl, Mii, who loses most of her family when the bomb falls. The reader sees the event through the eyes of this child, and the use of strong colors in the pictures deliberately creates an even greater impact.

Paterson, Katherine. *Jacob Have I Loved*. New York: Crowell, 1980; New York: Harper, 1990. NEWBERY AWARD. (Realistic Fiction/Regional/Social Adjustment)

The biblical story of Jacob and Esau is the foundation for this story of twin sisters, one beautiful, one plain. Much of the charm of this award-winning novel is in its characterization of the plain sister and her gradual realization that she, too, has personal worth, even though the adjustment is painful. The details of life in the Chesapeake Bay area of Maryland offer a clear portrait of a specific group of people in a particular region of the United States.

Schick, Alice and Joel, adapt. and illtd. *Bram Stoker's Dracula* and *Mary Shelley's Frankenstein*. New York: Delacorte, 1980. (Fantasy/Suspense)

These fantasy classics have been adapted for children by the Schicks with cartoon-style illustrations, voice boxes, and minimal text. On one side, one title appears, introducing Stoker's story of Dracula, who can never die naturally, and by turning the book over and upside down, the title of the other can be seen, introducing Shelley's story of Dr. Frankenstein, who experiments with life and creates a monster. Both adaptations remain true to the original storylines, rather than following the movie versions of these two books. Although the original authors never intended their books for children, the mysteries of human existence are explored in a way that intrigues children who may have discovered the movie versions and want to see how the book compares. The Schicks have offered an abbreviated but well-developed opportunity for young people to do just that.

Yolen, Jane. *Commander Toad in Space*, illtd. Bruce Degen. New York: Coward, McCann and Geoghegan, 1980. (Easy Reader/Science

Fiction/Series)

Yolen was able to indulge her penchant for puns in this delightful easy reader patterned after the popular "Star Wars" movies of this decade. Commander Toad is the heroic leader on the spaceship called "Star Warts," and his crew consists of Mr. Hop, Young Jake Skyjumper, Doc Peeper, and Lieutenant Lily. They travel across the galaxy to rescue those in peril, and one adventure leads to another in this series.

Brandenburg, Aliki. *Digging Up Dinosaurs*. New York: Crowell, 1981; New York: Harper, 1988. (Informational/Picture Book/Archaeology/Dinosaur)

Offering skeletons of various prehistoric animals, with museum visitors making comments in voice balloons as they view them, Aliki then shows sketches of these now extinct animals and gives information on the archaeological studies that have helped us know more about them. This book, one of the "Let's-Read-and-Find-Out" science series, gives children the information they want in an easy-to-read format.

Brown, Ruth. *A Dark, Dark Tale*. New York: Dial, 1981. (Picture Book/Suspense)

With dark, sweeping scenes of a moor, shrouded in mist, a wood at night, a castle, and a cobwebbed hall, this simple tale about a small black cat prowling at night builds in breathless suspense until the climax is reached and the dark, dark tale is over. This is a story that very small children love and want to hear over and over, even when they know how it ends. Brown, who lives in London, utilizes settings familiar to her to create drama.

Krementz, Jill. *How It Feels When a Parent Dies*. New York: Alfred A. Knopf, 1981. (Informational/Photographs/Death)

Through individual interviews and accompanying photographs of the young people interviewed, Krementz offers a collection of stories and pictures detailing how each child adjusts to the death of a parent. The same format is used in *How It Feels to be Adopted* (1982) and *How It Feels When Parents Divorce* (1984). In her earlier Very Young series (1976–79), aimed at a younger audience, Krementz follows the routine of a dancer, a gymnast, a skater, a rider, and a circus flyer.

Lauber, Patricia. *Seeds: Pop, Stick, Glide*. New York: Crown, 1981, 1991. (Informational/Photographs/Science)

Lauber also utilizes photographs to illustrate her texts, but scientific concepts are the subject of her books for children, as in this exploration of how seeds travel and make new things grow throughout different areas.

Sendak, Maurice. *Outside Over There*. New York: Harper, 1981. (Fantasy/Picture Book)

This book completes the trilogy that includes *Where the Wild Things Are* (1963) and *In the Night Kitchen* (1970) and is the story of how the goblins stole Ida's baby sister and how Ida brought her home again. It sounds simple enough, but the book is an exhilarating combination of poetry, music, and art, and it speaks to the individual:

> When Papa was away at sea,
> and Mama in the arbor,
> Ida played her wonder horn
> to rock the baby still—
> but never watched.

So begins the text and so begins one of Sendak's finest works for anyone willing to accept the Sendak magic without asking for impossible explanations.

Uchida, Yoshiko. *A Jar of Dreams*. New York: Macmillan, 1981. (Realistic Fiction/Social Adjustment/Japanese American)

In 1949, Uchida put together a collection of folktales popular in Japan (see p. 126), retold in an American style, and in this perceptive novel, she tells of 12-year-old Rinko, born and brought up in San Francisco, a child of Japanese immigrant parents. She has two brothers, one older and one younger, and her older brother, Cal, is a college student who wants to be an engineer but is becoming discouraged about his chances of getting a job after graduation—because he is Japanese. Rinko wants to be a teacher, but listening to her brother makes her wonder about her chances. After all, she sometimes has to deal with disparaging remarks from her white upperclass peers at school, where she is the only Japanese student. But when her Aunt Waka comes from Japan for a visit, many things change. Waka is proud of being Japanese and ready to stand up for her heritage—and she helps not only Rinko but also all the members of the family to understand and appreciate their ancestral ties and to stand up for themselves as Americans.

Willard, Nancy. *A Visit to William Blake's Inn: Poems for Innocent and Experienced Travelers,* illtd. Alice and Martin Provensen. New York: Harcourt, 1981. NEWBERY MEDAL. (Picture Book/Poetry)

This collection of poems by Willard, with poet William Blake and the world she has created for him the subject of the verses, is perfectly complemented by the Provensens' picturesque art style in this award-winning book. Willard became enamored of Blake when she was in bed with the measles and her baby-sitter, Miss Pratt, read the poem that began: "Tyger, Tyger, burning bright/In the forests of the night," and then sent her copies of *Songs of Innocence* and *Songs of Experience.*

Adler, David. *Cam Jansen and the Mystery of the Babe Ruth Baseball.* New York: Viking, 1982; New York: Puffin, 1991. (Chapter Book/Mystery/Series)

Fifth-grader Cam Jansen's photographic memory makes her a natural detective. When Cam looks at something and says "click," it's as if she has just taken a picture of it, and when Henry Baker's baseball, signed by Babe Ruth, disappears from the hobby show at the community center, Cam uses her special mental talent to determine who the thief might be. Written in a style easy to read, this series appeals to beginning readers, most of whom will solve the mystery before Cam Jansen does.

Louis, Ai-Ling. *Yeh Shen: A Chinese Cinderella,* illtd. Ed Young. New York: Philomel, 1982; New York: Putnam, 1988. (Picture Book/Traditional Fairy Tale/China)

The Cinderella story was written during the T'ang dynasty (618–907 A.D.), long before there was a Western version, and was adapted by Louis, who heard the story from her grandmother. The illustrations by Young are presented as panels in a folded painted screen, with both words and pictures creating the panel designs. Yeh-Shen is an orphan. She lives in the home of her stepmother, who is jealous of her and treats her badly. But Yeh-Shen befriends a magic fish who makes her dreams come true. After she goes to the king's festival, dances with the king and loses her golden slipper, it seems that she has forfeited the magic—until the king discovers her and notes how tiny her feet are. The slipper fits and the two are wed.

Spinelli, Jerry. *Space Station Seventh Grade.* Boston: Little, Brown, 1982, 1991. (Chapter Book/Science Fiction)

What Blume did for adolescent girls, Spinelli does for adolescent boys, but without adding complicated issues to be resolved. Jason

Herkimer has a mother, father, and stepfather along with assorted grandparents, and he accepts the situation with aplomb. He spends some time trying to figure out his buddy, Peter Kim, whose parents are Korean, though Peter says he himself is American. Jason's father, who also occupies his thoughts, and who has decided to be Jewish, is strange but not half as strange as his stepfather. But Jason's biggest problem is being 13 and suddenly having to deal with changes in himself and in his world—his first pimple, his first love, and especially the trauma of plummeting from the top of the ladder in sixth grade to being lower than low in the seventh.

Voigt, Cynthia. *Dicey's Song*. New York: Atheneum, 1982. NEWBERY MEDAL. (Realistic Fiction/Social Adjustment)

Dicey at 13 is used to caring for her three younger brothers and sisters, but when her mother gives up the struggle to raise four children without a father and has to be hospitalized, they all are taken in by their grandmother. The adjustment is difficult for Dicey, but she is able to write down her feelings in essay form and in a school essay she tells about her mother. Unfortunately, her English teacher dismisses her talent, convinced that she must have plagiarized the material. No 13-year-old, he publicly announces, can write that well. None of this matters to Dicey, who has stopped caring what people think. But when she and her grandmother go to visit her mother, who is dying, she sees a side of her grandmother she has never seen before, and her own life begins to take on new meaning.

Cleary, Beverly. *Dear Mr. Henshaw*. New York: Morrow, 1983; New York: Dell, 1992. NEWBERY MEDAL. (Realistic Fiction/Humor)

Writing to a children's book author as a class assignment became popular in the 1980s, and Cleary wrote this award-winning story as a series of letters exchanged between Leigh Botts and his favorite author, Mr. Henshaw, beginning when Leigh is in second grade and following him through each stage of his development as a potential author.

Prelutsky, Jack, ed. *The Random House Book of Poetry for Children*, illtd. Arnold Lobel. New York: Random House, 1983. (Poetry/Humor)

Prelutsky's choices reflect the highest quality in poetry for children, and the book is enhanced by the illustrations of the late Arnold Lobel. The collection is divided into sections—nature, seasons, animals, people—with clear language visuals. Lillian Moore writes: "Until I saw the sea/I did not know/that wind/could wrinkle water so." The audience for this book is mainly elementary rather than preschoolers. From James Whitcomb Riley to Margaret Wise Brown and Sylvia Plath to Shel Silverstein, the collection explores the potential of language in new and different ways, and the illustrations present well-rounded characters engaged in various activities.

Berger, Barbara Helen. *Grandfather Twilight*. New York: Philomel, 1984. (Fantasy/Picture Book/Concept)

Grandfather Twilight glows with a misty light as he carries the moon to its silence above the sea, then puts himself to bed. The text of this appealing book is as minimal as it can be and still be called text, and the pictures are softly rendered and calmly comfortable for preschoolers first being introduced to books. It has the same quiet charm as Margaret Wise Brown's *Goodnight Moon* (1947).

Carle, Eric. *The Very Busy Spider*. New York: Philomel, 1984. (Fantasy/Picture Book/Concept/Interactive)

From the first page of this charming adventure, the spider's web captures the child reader. It's a tactile web, raised slightly on the page so that the child can feel it, and as one animal after another asks the spider to leave her spinning and have fun, the spider doesn't answer but keeps spinning the web, which becomes more detailed on each progressive page until it is finished, and a rooster asks the spider if she would like to catch a pesky fly.

Cole, Joanna. *How You Were Born*. New York: Morrow, 1984, 1993 (rev.). (Informational/Science)

Cole presents a matter-of-fact text that is designed to answer the questions children might ask about where babies come from, including one page illustrated by a sketch that shows male and female genitalia—"When a sperm and an egg join together, a special cell is formed. This one cell can grow into a baby." The growth of the baby from a tiny cell to a full-term baby at birth and on to the toddler stage is covered in this satisfying presentation that utilizes photographs and an occasional sketch to portray the development.

Hodges, Margaret. *St. George and the Dragon*, illtd. Trina Schart Hyman. Boston: Little, Brown, 1984, 1990. CALDECOTT MEDAL. (Fantasy/Picture Book)

This legend from *The Faerie Queene* by Edmund Spenser is taken into the realm of the child in this ornately designed picture book. When Una leaves the safety of her castle to find a champion who will kill the terrible dragon and save the kingdom, she finds the Red Cross

Knight, and they set forth in the company of a small dwarf to accomplish the deed. The knight, George, was born to be a savior, and although he comes close to death several times during the battle, he miraculously becomes rejuvenated each time and slays the dragon, earning the hand of the beautiful Una in marriage. The pictures bring to mind the richly illustrated manuscripts of medieval times.

Lord, Betty Bao. *In the Year of the Boar and Jackie Robinson*, illtd. Marc Simont. New York: Harper, 1984. (Chapter Book/Chinese American)

While Lawrence Yep educates the American public about the hopes and desires of Chinese Americans, Lord approaches cultural misunderstandings from a lighter point of view. When Sixth Cousin, known as Bandit, travels to America with her mother, she takes on an American name. The choice of name is hers, and the only one she can think of is Shirley Temple. So nine-year-old Shirley Temple Wong, who is 10 in Chinese years, begins a new life in a new home in Brooklyn, New York. In school, because her mother tells them she is 10, she finds herself in a higher grade, and to compound the situation, she speaks no English. But Shirley has a special charm that helps her get by, and, best of all, she is athletic enough to become a stickball hero, which leads her into following baseball, the Brooklyn Dodgers, and especially Jackie Robinson, the first black major league player, whom she has the good fortune to meet personally.

McCully, Emily Arnold. *Picnic*. New York: Harper, 1984, 1992. (Picture Book/Wordless)

When the Mouse family takes their nine children on a picnic, the smallest falls out of the back of the pickup truck, and no one misses him at first. When they do, they search everwhere, unaware the smallest mouse has found a way to have a picnic of his own.

Pienkowski, Jan. *Christmas*. New York: Knopf, 1984, 1989. (Informational/Picture Book/Holiday)

Creating scenes in black silhouette against a background of red, blue, and green with gold highlights, Pienkowski tells of events leading to the birth of Jesus. The text is taken from the King James version of the Bible. Although this is a story familiar to many adults, this direct and simple approach to the true meaning of Christmas is one children will enjoy.

Prelutsky, Jack. *The New Kid on the Block*, illtd. James Stevenson. New York: Greenwillow, 1984. (Poetry/Humor)

"Cocoa Mocha Macaroni/Tapioca Smoked Baloney/Checkerberry

Cheddar Chew/Chicken Cherry Honeydew" are only a few of the ice cream flavors at Bleezer's Ice Cream Store. In this broad selection of humorous verses with child appeal, Prelutsky cancels the longtime objection of children to poetry and defines it in a new way:

> Homework! Oh, homework!
> You're last on my list,
> I simply can't see
> why you even exist.

Wood, Audrey. *The Napping House*, illtd. Don Wood. New York: Harcourt, 1984. (Picture Book/Predictable)

"There is a house, a napping house, where everyone is sleeping." So begins this sing-song repetitive recitation of exactly who is sleeping in the napping house until the appearance of a wakeful flea, "who bites the mouse, who wakes the cat" and on down to granny, "who breaks the bed, in the napping house, where no one now is sleeping." Don Wood's slightly distorted illustrations of the snoring granny in her nightcap and gown, the tousle-headed boy, and the growing accumulation of various animals create the type of precarious, breathtaking balance that Dr. Seuss brings to his art, especially in *The Cat in the Hat* (1957).

Blumberg, Rhoda. *Commodore Perry in the Land of the Shogun*. New York: Lothrop, Lee and Shepard, 1985. (Informational/Historical Japan)

The history of America's relationship with Japan as it was first inaugurated by Commodore Perry in 1853 is presented in a well-written, authentically illustrated format that is captivating to study. The book is written in two parts, each containing several chapters, and the back matter contains appendices, end notes, information regarding the illustrations, a research bibliography, and an index. The illustrations are a combination of Japanese block prints and sketches from scrolls, photographs, and drawings made by official artists of the Perry Expedition. The book shows great insight into Japanese culture and the way in which Americans were viewed by the Japanese.

Dubanevich, Arlene. *Pig William*. New York: Bradbury, 1985. (Picture Book/Wordless/Humor)

In a comic book format with dialogue in balloons and no printed text, Dubanevich features the one pig brother who follows his own path, seldom joining his older siblings in ordinary pursuits. Though he exists in his own time frame, Pig William manages to enjoy himself and in the long run doesn't miss out on anything. The active, colorful details in the simple drawings bring out the personalities of the pig characters, and the humor is perfectly suited for young children. Other "pig" books are *Pigs in Hiding* (1983), *Pigs at Christmas* (1986), and *The Piggest Show on Earth* (1989).

Hamilton, Virginia. *The People Could Fly*, illtd. Diane and Leo Dillon. New York: Knopf, 1985. (Folk/Myth/Black American)

Here is a collection of familiar and not-so-familiar folktales told to the children of American blacks, passed down through many generations. The story of Brer Rabbit and the Tar Baby becomes in this version "Doc Rabbit, Bruh Fox, and Tar Baby," as Bruh Fox shapes a baby rabbit from tar and sets it in the brook to trap Doc Rabbit when he tries to steal a drink from Bruh Fox's crock. A subject of other tales is the black hero known as John de Conquer, "said to have come to America from Africa on a slave ship following the wind like an albatross."[9] Less familiar to the general population are stories of how slaves managed to run away to freedom. Hamilton explored one segment of this subject in her novel, *The House of Dies Drear* (1968).

MacLachlan, Patricia. *Sarah, Plain and Tall*. New York: Harper, 1985. NEWBERY MEDAL. (Realistic Fiction/Historical/Social Adjustment)

This book is written from the viewpoint of Anna, who is trying to deal with the death of her mother and has had difficulty accepting the brother whose birth brought about her mother's death. Her brother, Caleb, welcomes Sarah, who has responded to his father's ad for a wife, but Anna's feelings are more ambiguous. She likes Sarah, but along with the guilt she feels at accepting a replacement for her mother, she isn't sure how Sarah feels about them, and she's afraid to express her own emotional need. MacLachlan's television script based on the book was nominated for an Emmy award, but the change in viewpoint from Anna to Sarah created a more sophisticated storyline, still successful but less emotional.

McKinley, Robin. *The Hero and the Crown*. New York: Greenwillow, 1985. (Fantasy/Feminism)

The hero in this tale is a young woman, Aerin, who fulfills her rite of passage by confronting evil with as much courage and integrity as any man but with never a doubt that she is a woman. She saves the Kingdom of Damar by redeeming the Hero's Crown for its people and the king. McKinley draws upon mythology and classical Western literature to build a believable world in which a woman is strong, not in spite of her gender but because of it.

Numeroff, Laura Joffe. *If You Give a Mouse a Cookie*, illtd. Felicia Bond. New York: Harper, 1985. (Picture Book/Predictable)

When a little boy gives a mouse a cookie, he discovers that the mouse wants a glass of milk—and a straw—and a napkin—and a mirror—and on and on until the mouse gets thirsty for another glass of milk—and another cookie. The predictable nature of this book captures the interest of small children, but the humor relies on the way in which events are kept within the limited experience of preschoolers.

Paulsen, Gary. *Dogsong*. New York: Bradbury, 1985. (Realistic Fiction/ Alaska)

Russel is an Eskimo boy who inherits a dog team and sled from the old man who has been teaching him the old ways. As the result of a dream, Russel sets out with the team to follow his destiny, meeting obstacles along the way and saving the life of a young woman who was first a part of his dream world and then part of his real world.

Turner, Ann. *Dakota Dugout*, illtd. Ronald Himler. New York: Macmillan, 1985. (Picture Book/Historical/Regional)

With Himler's black-and-white sketches illustrating the spare poetic text, Turner tells of the hardships met by settlers living on the prairie through the narration of a mother to her child. Unlike the idealistic portrait of the West set forth in Laura Ingalls Wilder's Little House books, Turner offers a stark picture, but softens it with the final scenes of a developing city and a secure family setting.

Van Allsburg, Chris. *The Polar Express*. Boston: Houghton Mifflin, 1985. CALDECOTT MEDAL. (Fantasy/Picture Book/Holiday)

Using dark and light in his illustrations to create a sense of mystery, Van Allsburg takes his readers on a journey to the North Pole and makes believers of us all. The Polar Express carries the children through the forests, over the mountains, and across the Great Polar Ice Cap to the North Pole where Santa Claus chooses one child to receive a gift, but the boy loses the bell Santa gives him. He is desolate until Christmas morning when he finds the bell in a package, a bell that rings for him and his sister, but not for his parents.

Wood, Audrey. *King Bidgood's in the Bathtub*, illtd. Don Wood. New York: Harcourt, 1985. (Picture Book/Predictable)

Written in the exuberant style that marks the work of Audrey Wood, King Bidgood, looking very much like Bacchus, the god of wine, refuses to leave the bathtub, although the Knight and the Queen and the Duke and the Court all try to talk him into it. But it is the small Page who finally convinces the King in this delightful Renaissance romp illustrated with charming detail and humor by Don Wood.

Cole, Joanna. *The Magic School Bus: At the Waterworks*, illtd. Bruce Degen. New York: Scholastic, 1986. Also, *The Magic School Bus: Inside the Earth*, illtd. Bruce Degen (New York: Scholastic, 1987); *The Magic School Bus: Inside the Human Body*, illtd. Bruce Degen (New York: Scholastic, 1988); *The Magic School Bus: Lost in the Solar System*, illtd. Bruce Degen (New York: Scholastic, 1989). (Informational/Science/Series)

The text in this perceptive series is written in simple language from the viewpoint of a student in Ms. Frizzle's science class. The pictures portray redheaded, wild-haired Ms. Frizzle and an ethnically representative group of lively children. Comments in voice balloons, maps, informational essays printed on lined paper, and a bus that becomes whatever it needs to be for scientific purposes make learning great fun in this popular series.

Martin, Ann M. *Kristy's Great Idea* (a Baby-sitters Club book). New York: Scholastic, 1986. (Chapter Book/Series)

Twelve-year-old Kristy, whose mother is divorced and has to work, has a much younger brother and shares baby-sitting responsibilities at home with her two older brothers and a paid baby-sitter. She also baby-sits in the neighborhood to earn money. When the paid baby-sitter becomes ill one day, Kristy's mother has trouble replacing her, and Kristy has the idea to start a Baby-sitters Club with her friends. Occasionally didactic, decidedly contemporary, with characters never at risk, Martin's series spread like wildfire through the pre-adolescent population, with several more series written by her to meet a sudden public demand.

Parks, Van Dyke, and Malcolm Jones, adapt. *Jump! The Adventures of Brer Rabbit*, illtd. M. Barry Moser. New York: Harcourt, 1986. Also, *Jump on Over!* illtd. M. Barry Moser (San Diego: Harcourt, 1989). (Folk/Myth/Black American)

Barry Moser's lifelike watercolors present the jaunty Brer Rabbit, slick Brer Fox, and greedy Brer Wolf, along with a varied cast of characters, in active scenes portraying the lyrical storytelling of Parks and Jones. Neither Joel Chandler Harris's Uncle Remus, as storyteller, nor the little white boy to whom he tells his stories, is present in this collection of five stories. In *Jump on Over!* the stories are less familiar than those of the first collection, but children will relate to them strongly because it's Brer Rabbit's family, his Little Rabs, who are featured more often than not.

Kellogg, Stephen. *Pecos Bill.* New York: Morrow, 1986, 1992. (Folk/Myth/Tall Tales/Picture Book)

The American folk tales about Pecos Bill and his horse Lightning take on richer texture in the picture-book format as Kellogg tells Bill's story as the tall tale it is, with pictures that speak louder than words. Pecos Bill is kidnapped as a baby, raised by coyotes, battles monsters and giant rattlesnakes, invents the first western rodeo, and tames his horse Lightning before being reunited with his family and leading them to Texas.

Brown, Laurene Krasny, and Marc Brown. *Dinosaur's Divorce: A Guide to Changing Families.* Boston: Little, Brown, 1986. (Informational/Picture Book/Social Adjustment/Humor)

In a comic-book format, featuring a family of dinosaurs, the Browns share their own experience with divorce through the viewpoint of Marc Brown's children, Tolon and Tucker, and the viewpoint of Laurie Brown as a child of divorced parents. In a collection of chapters, the vocabulary of divorce is presented and the process explained from the initial decision to the effect on the children and to the adjustments necessary, then on to meeting new friends on both sides and accepting stepparents as well as stepsisters and stepbrothers. This was one of the first books to go beyond the initial decision of the parents to get a divorce.

Lauber, Patricia. *Volcano: The Eruption and Healing of Mount St. Helens.* New York: Bradbury, 1986. (Informational/Science/Photographs)

Instead of covering incidents from the distant past, Lauber uses photographs to tell of a recent occurrence, the eruption of Mount St. Helens on May 18, 1980. By using photographs taken before, during, and after the explosion, in which 57 people were killed, Lauber shows the destruction and the slow but sure recovery from this natural disaster as nature heals itself. With some photographs showing scenes as desolate as a moon landscape and others highlighted by bright colors as new growth occurs, the workings of nature are made clear for young scientists.

Roberts, Willo Davis. *The Magic Book*. New York: Macmillan, 1986; New York: Aladdin, 1988. (Chapter Book/Fantasy)

Middle-grade fiction is always in demand. There just aren't that many books that appeal to this age group, but Roberts shows that he has a direct line in this humorous and logical fantasy. Alex goes to a used-book sale with his father, and not only does a book keep falling off a table at his feet no matter how many times he puts it back, but also the book, he discovers, has his name in it. It's a book of magic spells and Alex buys it for 50 cents. But when he tries a spell, he's not sure if the things that happen are coincidental or related to the book. Finally, however, he and his friends Bucky and Jeff are convinced the book is a powerful weapon that can be used to get even with the school bully. The result of their efforts makes them far more knowledgeable about Norm, the bully, than they ever expected.

Yorinks, Arthur. *Hey, Al*, illtd. Richard Egielski. New York: Farrar, Straus & Giroux, 1986. CALDECOTT MEDAL. (Fantasy/Picture Book/Social Adjustment)

This modern fable seems an unlikely subject for a picture book, but the contrast between Al the janitor's dilapidated one-room apartment and the island paradise in the sky that he and Eddie, his dog, discover when they leave home is aimed at an older audience than most picture books. The story seems to represent the difference between making the best of what you have and trying to live a dream. Eddie talks Al into leaving his job and taking advantage of an opportunity to fly off to a place guaranteed to end worry and care, but there is a major price to pay, one that neither, in the long run, chooses to accept. In their escape, Eddie is lost, and Al realizes when he gets back home how much his dog means to him. His reunion with Eddie causes the two of them to brighten up their comfortable one-room apartment and appreciate what they have had all along.

Freedman, Russell. *Lincoln: A Photobiography*. New York: Clarion, 1987. (Informational/Photographs/Biographical)

Freedman gathered the photographs to illustrate this book from archives in Washington, D.C., Springfield, Illinois, Chicago, New York, and other cities. The text, filled with personal anecdotes and punctuated by letters to, from, and about Lincoln, is truly captivating, presenting a portrait of Lincoln, from his birth through his assassination, that enriches the man and his life. This biography is a fit companion to Carl Sandburg's *Abe Lincoln Grows Up* (1928), continuing Lincoln's story where Sandburg left off.

Gerstein, Mordicai. *Mountains of Tibet*. New York: Harper, 1987. (Picture Book/Far East/Death)

Gerstein's exquisitely designed book represents a classic theme not often developed in children's picture books—life, death, and rebirth. A little boy is born. He loves to fly kites and wants to see much of the world, but eventually grows old and dies without ever leaving his home in the mountains of Tibet. Then, in an embryonic rebirth, he is offered the chance to be whatever he wants to be and to go wherever in the universe he wants to go. On one side of the page the text is printed accompanied by the old man in his yellow robe inside a blue circle, and, on the facing page, the circle contains multi-colored choices on a blue background. The old man's final decision reflects a belief in predestination.

Lester, Julius, adapt. *The Tales of Uncle Remus: The Adventures of Brer Rabbit*, illtd. Jerry Pinkney. New York: Dial, 1987. (Folk/Myth/Black American)

Pinkney's traditional and appealing illustrations of Joel Chandler Harris's recognizable characters help bridge the years between the original stories and Lester's authentic and more contemporary retellings. This black author and black illustrator have carved a special niche in the culture of America.

McCully, Emily. *School*. New York: Harper, 1987; New York: Harper Trophy, 1990. (Picture Book/Wordless)

Wordless, but with an obvious storyline, McCully presents eight little mice going off to school, leaving the ninth mouse, who is too young, at home. But he doesn't want to stay home and, when his mother isn't looking, he leaves the house and visits the school. His brothers and sisters are glad to see him, and the teacher lets him help her at the blackboard. Before long, Mother comes to the school looking for her missing child, and all's well that ends well.

Nolan, Dennis. *The Castle Builder*. New York: Macmillan, 1987. (Picture Book/Fantasy)

Nolan's first book is a remarkable accomplishment, with the black-and-white artwork drawn dot by dot with pen and ink, using photographs as reference, and the story an imaginative fantasy that defies disbelief. A small boy at the beach builds a sand castle that grows to life size. As Sir Christopher, he fights a dragon, protects the castle against the marauding Black Knights, and finally has to save himself when the ocean begins to disintegrate the castle.

Richler, Mordecai. *Jacob Two-Two and the Dinosaur*, illtd. Norman Eyolfson. New York: Knopf, 1987. (Fantasy/Chapter Book/Canada/Humor)

Jacob Two-Two has added another two to his age in this sequel to *Jacob Two-Two Meets the Hooded Fang* (1976). He is now eight years old and the proud owner of a real dinosaur. Richler allows the situation to reach preposterous levels, and the action builds until Dippy the dinosaur becomes pulverized, according to the pompous paleontologist, Professor Wacko Kilowatt, and a disagreeable television announcer named Perry Pleaser. But then Jacob Two-Two discovers things aren't quite the way they seem when he reads about strange things happening in isolated sections of the Rockies and puts two and two together. Perhaps Dippy has not been pulverized after all.

Steptoe, John. *Mufaro's Beautiful Daughters*. New York: Lothrop, Lee and Shepard, 1987. (Folk/Myth/Picture Book/Africa)

With illustrations that show the handsome black faces of America in an African setting, Steptoe surpasses himself in this modern fable based on an old folktale. Manyara and Nyasha are daughters of Mufaro and they are exceptionally beautiful. When the king is looking for a wife, Mufaro decides to send both his daughters and let the king choose. But Manyara, though beautiful, is selfish and willful, and Nyasha is understanding and kind. In true folktale tradition, the king chooses the more compassionate sister for his wife, knowing her from past kindnesses when he had appeared to her in other forms. He had done the same with Manyara, who chose to ignore him, and it becomes her fate to be servant to her sister, the queen.

Yolen, Jane. *Owl Moon*, illtd. John Schoenherr. New York: Philomel, 1987. CALDECOTT MEDAL. (Poetry/Picture Book/Nature)

Adult and child are offered a breathtaking and wondrous journey into the natural world from the very first picture—a bird's-eye view of the farmhouse and barn with two small figures setting out across the snow as:

Somewhere behind us,
a train whistle blew,

long and low,
like a sad, sad song.

—to the moment when Pa calls the owl, and father and child face the reader, waiting, waiting, and then move on to the startling confrontation with the owl:

For one minute,
three minutes,
maybe even a hundred minutes,
we stared at one another.

Yolen, Jane. *Piggins*, illtd. Jane Dyer. New York: Harcourt, 1987; San Diego: Harcourt, 1992. (Fantasy/Mystery/Animal)

This is a true meeting of the minds between author and artist in which words and pictures are carefully woven into a storytelling tapestry that titillates the senses and transports the observer. The illustrations employ colored pencil and watercolor, along with silhouettes in black balancing some of the text on the page. Piggins (a pig, of course) is the butler for the Reynards (foxes, of course), and he takes his responsibilities so seriously that when, at a dinner party, Mrs. Reynard's diamond lavaliere disappears, Piggins matter-of-factly and efficiently solves the mystery. Some of the guests at the party are Professor T. Ortoise, Lord and Lady Ratsby, and Pierre Lapin (Peter Rabbit in French). Yolen indulges her love of language and wordplay.

Ackerman, Karen. *Song and Dance Man*, illtd. Stephen Gammell. New York: Alfred A. Knopf, 1988. CALDECOTT MEDAL. (Picture Book/Aging)

This anecdotal picture book offers an aspect of American history not usually explored in books for children. A grandfather, characterized with heart by Gammell, shares his vaudeville past with his three grandchildren. He takes them into the attic, puts on his dancing shoes and performs a soft shoe, tells jokes, and does magic tricks. And after he puts everything away and they all leave the attic, he holds onto the railing as he goes down the stairs and looks back toward the attic with a certain longing.

Adoff, Arnold. *Flamboyan*, illtd. Karen Barbour. San Diego: Harcourt, 1988. (Picture Book/Puerto Rico)

Little Flamboyan has hair the color of the flame-red blossoms on the Flamboyan tree. As she grows older, she helps her mother by feeding the chickens and gathering the eggs, but what she wants to do is fly. One morning, she sits by the Flamboyan tree and dreams about flying. She begins to move. "Her arms lift into the warm breeze. She stretches strong arms and shoulders upward . . . She moves–rises–flies. Flamboyan flies." Author Arnold Adoff, husband of Virginia Hamilton, is a poet and brings into this Puerto Rican setting, colorfully painted by Karen Barbour, the magic of the land of his birth.

Etra, Jonathan, and Stephanie Spinner. *Aliens for Breakfast*, illtd. Steve Bjorkman. New York: Random House, 1988. (Chapter Book/Science Fiction/Humor)

Richard Bickerstaff meets an alien in his breakfast cereal, discovers that the most popular boy in his class at school is also an alien, a Drane that will divide until he takes over the world, and that he has the task of finding a way out of this dilemma, with the help of the alien, Aric, of course. The subject is of high interest, the text is simple.

Fleischman, Paul. *Joyful Noise: Poems for Two Voices*, illtd. Eric Beddoes. New York: Harper, 1988. NEWBERY MEDAL. (Poetry/Interactive)

This is a case in which librarians so enjoyed the opportunity to perform this poetry aloud that they awarded the book a Newbery Medal. The poetry is a sophisticated study of the insect world, but reading it aloud in a way that celebrates its music requires a talent most people don't possess. Certainly, most adolescents would avoid performing something like this publicly, and it isn't the kind of book anyone would want to curl up with on a rainy afternoon. Eric Beddoes's illustrations are delicate and alive, a fitting tribute to Fleischman's poetry.

We don't live in meadows	
crick-et	crick-et
or in groves	
	We're house crickets
	living beneath this gas stove
crick-et	crick-et

Hamilton, Virginia. *In the Beginning: Creation Stories from Around the World*, illtd. Barry Moser. San Diego: Harcourt, 1988. (Folk/Myth/Mixed Cultures)

In this collection of short stories, Moser's imaginative and realistic depictions of the characters from various cultures who make up the created worlds in Hamilton's stories add drama to the overall presentation. From the Americas to China to Africa and India, to the Hebrides, Guinea, Russia, and Australia, Moser's startling illustrations and Hamilton's textured language offer an unusual viewpoint of the world's creation myths.

McKissack, Patricia. *Mirandy and Brother Wind*, illtd. Jerry Pinkney. New York: Knopf, 1988. (Folk/Myth/Picture Book/Black American)

This rhythmic text has a movement of its own, enhanced by Jerry Pinkney's colorful and joyous illustrations, as it tells the story of young Mirandy, who is convinced she can catch the wind and dance the cakewalk with him. The cakewalk, with its origins in African-American slave culture, is a dance for which the winning couple at a jubilee is awarded a cake, and Mirandy wants to win. She even goes to Mis Poinsettia, the conjure woman, to get a spell so she can catch Brother Wind, but the way things turn out isn't quite what she expected, even though she wins the contest.

Myers, Walter Dean. *Scorpions*. New York: Harper, 1988. (Realistic Fiction/Urban/Mixed Cultures)

Myers speaks with the authentic voice of adolescents in an inner-city world that seems to hold them back at every turn. Jamal Hick's brother Randy is in prison for manslaughter, and Jamal, at 12, feels responsible for his mother, who works too many hours, and his eight-year-old sister, Sassy. In school, Jamal is the victim of his teacher's low expectations, and then becomes involved in his brother's gang, the Scorpions, in an effort to get his brother out of jail. His possession of a handgun brings him more trouble than he can deal with when his best friend, Tito, is forced to use the gun to save Jamal's life.

Snyder, Diane. *The Boy of the Three-Year Nap*, illtd. Allen Say. Boston: Houghton Mifflin, 1988. (Folk/Myth/Picture Book/Japan)

In a style reminiscent of Ando Hiroshige, a famed 19th-century Japanese landscape artist, illustrator Allen Say presents a scene on the banks of the Nagara River in Japan as the introduction to Diane Snyder's clever adaptation of a Japanese folk tale. Lazy Taro uses mind over body to win his lady love and assure his future, but Taro is not the only one who plans ahead, and his future takes an unexpected turn. In design and attention to detail, the illustrations reflect Say's Japanese heritage and add depth to Snyder's humorous text.

Winter, Jeanette. *Follow the Drinking Gourd.* New York: Knopf, 1988, 1992. (Picture Book/Cultural/Black American)

Unlike F. N. Monjo's easy reader called *The Drinking Gourd* (1970), the focus in Winter's book is on the slaves themselves, with Peg Leg Joe the only white character. He travels from plantation to plantation and teaches the slaves a song of freedom, and they learn to follow the drinking gourd (a code name for the Big Dipper) north by way of the Underground Railroad.

> When the sun comes back, and the first quail calls,
> Follow the drinking gourd.
> For the old man is a-waiting for to carry you to freedom
> If you follow the drinking gourd.

Although the complete song is printed at the beginning of Monjo's book, the rhythm is changed by neglecting to add one vowel: The word "a-waiting" in Winter's book is simply "waiting" in Monjo's version, and that makes all the difference in the rhythm of the song. Winter tells the story of one particular family that follows the stars to freedom, and each scene is illustrated in shades of bright purple, orange, and green against a background of gray and brown, including the brown skin of the slaves, which creates a richer contrast overall.

Yolen, Jane. *The Devil's Arithmetic.* New York: Viking Penguin, 1988. (Fantasy/Time Travel/Holocaust)

To Hannah, World War II is something from the distant past that makes her Grandfather Will wildly distraught any time it is mentioned. It's embarrassing, and Hannah can't help but wonder why he and the rest of the family can't just forget about things that happened so long ago. But on the eve of Passover Seder, when Hannah is asked to open the door to symbolically welcome the prophet Elijah, she suddenly finds herself transported back in time to the 1940s. In a new identity as Chaya, she experiences the terrible persecution of the Jews by the Nazis. She, Hannah, is finally allowed to pass through the door back into the present, while the girl whose identity she has carried is doomed to die, simply for being Jewish.

Block, Francesca Lia. *Weetzie Bat.* New York: Harper, 1989. (Realistic Fiction/Regional/Urban)

Weetzie's father is named Charlie Bat, and her mother, who is a movie actress, is called Brandy-Lynn. Weetzie's parents are separated, with her father living in New York City and her mother in Los Angeles. Weetzie's on her own and lives in a colorful section of Los Angeles with her two best friends, Dirk and Duck, both of whom are gay. Even though a genie appears and gives Weetzie three wishes, one of which comes true when she meets My Secret Agent Lover Man, the reality in this bittersweet story of love and heartache, miracles and tragedy goes beyond anything one might imagine. The book is compelling but disturbing as a portrait of children who are more responsible than their parents.

Ehlert, Lois. *Eating the Alphabet: Fruits and Vegetables from A to Z*. San Diego: Harcourt, 1989. (Informational/Picture Book/Concept)

Ehlert's unusual collages present equally unusual fruits and vegetables grown in different cultures, and in addition to the appealing designs formed by different foods, Ehlert adds a series of paragraphs at the end of the book explaining different facts about each of the fruits and vegetables pictured. Along with learning the alphabet, children can gather information about a wide variety of foods.

Goble, Paul. *Beyond the Ridge*. New York: Bradbury, 1989; New York: Macmillan, 1993. (Picture Book/Native American/Plains/Death)

Paul Goble, utilizing Plains Indian prayers and cultural traditions concerning death, presents a simple text that describes to the reader an old woman's final journey on Earth, with a series of dreamlike illustrations that culminate in her family's careful preparation of her body for the journey.

> No man knows where the Spirit World is.
> The ancient people said that it is beyond the pines.
> The pine trees are at the edge of the world
> and beyond them is the path of the winds.

There is comfort in this matter-of-fact acceptance of death as a new beginning. In the accompanying illustrations, the clear outlines of the natural landscape, the bright colors of flowers, birds, and butterflies, and the varied designs woven into colorful blankets add texture to words of the spirit.

Kimmel, Eric. *Hershel and the Hanukkah Goblins*, illtd. Trina Schart Hyman. New York: Holiday House, 1989. (Folk/Myth/Picture

Book/Jewish/Humor)

With Hyman's charmingly gruesome goblins trying to outsmart Hershel of Ostropol during the eight nights of Hanukkah, this story, which first appeared in *Cricket* magazine in 1985, blends text and pictures to bring humor to the explanation of Hanukkah as a Jewish tradition. When the goblins keep the people of a neighboring village from celebrating Hanukkah by blowing out the candles, breaking dreidels, and throwing potato latkes on the floor, Hershel offers to spend eight nights in the haunted synagogue and restore the holiday to the people of the village. Each night the confrontations with the goblins build in intensity until the King of the Goblins himself finally arrives.

Lisle, Janet Taylor. *Afternoon of the Elves*. Boston: Orchard Books, 1989. (Realistic Fiction/Social Adjustment)

When Hillary, nine, gives in to curiosity and approaches 11-year-old Sara-Kate Connolly, who lives in a dilapidated house down the hill, she is introduced to Sara-Kate's imaginary world of small stick houses made, Sara tells her, for elves. It is a time of wonder for Hillary even though she has been forbidden to have anything to do with Sara-Kate. But when the harsh reality that marks Sara's existence draws Hillary into a bleak world of poverty and tragedy, Hillary emerges with new insight and lost candor.

Livingston, Myra Cohn. *Remembering and Other Poems*, a Margaret K. McElderry book. New York: Macmillan, 1989. (Poetry)

"I'm the waltz/of white lace/on a pink/toe-shoe girl." Livingston writes of ballet lessons in childhood and, with simple but colorful language, offers a collection of poems to which young people can relate strongly. Many of these poems bring to mind the southwest region of the United States, but all have a common thread, no matter what region is being described. The author of many collections of poetry and an anthologist for many more, Livingston speaks directly to young people, and the simplicity of her verses encourages them to try writing their own verses.

Lowry, Lois. *Number the Stars*. Boston: Houghton Mifflin, 1989. NEWBERY MEDAL. (Realistic Fiction/Historical/World War II/Holocaust)

The World War II persecution of the Jews is portrayed in this story, written from the viewpoint of Annemarie, a fair-haired Danish girl whose best friend, Ellen Rosen, is Jewish and has to be protected from the Germans when her parents leave the area to keep from being arrested. Annemarie had an older sister Lise who was struck by a car and killed many years earlier, and when the German soldiers come to their house looking for the Rosens, Annemarie's mother shows them a picture of her children as babies, including Lise, who happened to have dark hair as a toddler. Ellen must play the part of Lise, even if it means taking off her Star of David necklace, which she has never before removed. Not until the war is over is Annemarie able to give Ellen back her Star of David. In the meantime, Annemarie's parents help Ellen and her parents escape from occupied Denmark, and Annemarie matures quickly when she must deliver a packet through the German patrols to her Uncle Henrik's boat, which will take the Rosens to safety.

Macaulay, David. *The Way Things Work*. Boston: Houghton Mifflin, 1989. (Informational)

This illustrated encyclopedia-type book covers everything from how to capture a mammoth to an explanation of electronically controlled robots. Macauley has utilized the woolly mammoth captured at the beginning of the book as a guide to the material in the book. Although published on a children's book list, this volume became a No. 1 best-seller on *The New York Times* list and continues to be a popular choice for all ages.

Scieszka, Jon. *The True Story of the Three Little Pigs! by A. Wolf*, illtd. Lane Smith. New York: Penguin, 1989. (Picture Book/Fractured Fairy Tale)

Directed at a young adult audience, this is a picture book in which the much maligned wolf of fairy-tale fame offers his version of *The Three Little Pigs*. He says it wasn't his fault the first house blew down—he had a cold and sneezed. Then he needed a cup of sugar for his old granny's birthday cake, and the second pig's house, made of straw, fell down when he tapped lightly on the door. This version will appeal to anyone who is familiar with the original, as it adds sophisticated humor to a traditional offering.

Staples, Suzanne Fisher. *Shabanu: Daughter of the Wind*. New York: Knopf, 1989. (Realistic Fiction/Pakistan)

In the Cholistan Desert of Pakistan, neither 11-year-old Shabanu nor her sister, Phulan, is allowed free choice. Phulan, 13, is about to be married to Hamir, a young man her father has chosen for her, and Shabanu is promised to the young man's brother, Murad, with her wedding planned for the following year. But while Phulan is docile and accepting, Shabanu is not, and she rebels against having her future predetermined. As the time of Phulan's wedding comes near, tragedy strikes when Shabanu and her sister are nearly kidnapped and raped, and in the ensuing confrontation, Hamir is killed. Because Phulan is older and must be married first, it is decided that she will marry Murad, especially after the wealthy Rahim sahib catches sight of Shabanu and asks her father for her hand, assuring security for the family. Shabanu, though a victim of tribal laws and destined to marry a man old enough to be her grandfather, manages to keep a part of herself intact.

Swope, Sam. *The Araboolies of Liberty Street*, illtd. Barry Root. New York: Clarkson N. Potter, 1989. (Fantasy/Picture Book)

The Grinch took it upon himself to steal Christmas in Dr. Seuss's well-known holiday story. In *The Araboolies of Liberty Street*, first-time children's book author Sam Swope goes a step beyond as the Pinches of Liberty Street try to maintain the status quo in their neighborhood by keeping out anyone or anything that is different. Every house looks like every other house on Liberty Street, and all the people are the same color—until the Araboolies move into town. There are several of them and they each change color every day. The Pinches find the situation intolerable and call out the troops to remove the house on Liberty Street that's different, a request that unexpectedly boomerangs, thanks to the ingenuity of a little girl. Barry Root's zany illustrations add visual excitement to this low-key lesson in tolerance.

Young, Ed. *Lon Po Po: A Red Riding Hood Story from China*. New York: Philomel, 1989. CALDECOTT MEDAL. (Picture Book/Fairy Tale/China)

The illustrations for this story, which was translated from the Chinese by Young, are mostly in panels that reflect ancient Chinese art while the paintings themselves are soft, shadowy watercolor pastels utilizing dark and light to create tension. Young's text is analogous to the illustrations, never too wordy or with too much detail, and satisfying in its presentation. In this version of the familiar fairy tale, it is the children, rather than any adult, who are clever enough to thwart the wolf.

NOTES

1. Edmund H. Harvey Jr. *Our Glorious Century*, p. 389.
2. Haynes Johnson. *Sleepwalking Through History*, p. 43.
3. Ibid., p. 41.
4. Ibid., p. 451.
5. In fall 1994, PBS offered "The Magic School Bus" as an animated educational series for children between the ages of six and nine, with actress Lily Tomlin portraying the teacher, Ms. Frizzle.
6. The storyline in a predictable book is one that a child can anticipate and recite ahead of the storyteller as the list of events is repeated each time a new event is added.
7. As related by Patricia MacLachlan during a children's literature seminar, Smith College, 1986.
8. *Horn Book* magazine, October–November 1977.
9. Virginia Hamilton. *The People Could Fly*, p. 114.

Illustration by Bruce Degen from The Magic School Bus on the Ocean Floor *by Joanna Cole, illustrations copyright © 1992 by Bruce Degen; reprinted by permission of Scholastic, Inc. The illustrations in this book show the students in Ms. Frizzle's class to be culturally diverse without calling undue attention to this aspect of American culture.*

WHOLE LANGUAGE AND THE WHOLE CHILD 1990–1995

The whole point of being an artist is to be able to get up every morning and reinvent the world.

—Kathryn Lasky
"Creativity in a Boom Industry"
Horn Book, November–December 1991

High Tech

Looking back on the development of the United States since the end of the Civil War, it becomes clear that the nation has moved through the decades at a dizzying pace, evolving into an industrial giant and ultimately into a world power. Over this 20th century, America has encountered several more wars, produced an economy based mainly on defense, become youth oriented, rebelled against the status quo, lost position in the world market, and finally, in the Nineties, has turned toward innovative technology as a way to regain status. An adolescent country is heading toward maturity.

A Time for Change

During the early Nineties, President George Bush seemed bewildered by the many concerns facing this country, rallying only during the Persian Gulf War at the beginning of 1991 to gain short-lived popularity as a decisive leader. But Governor Bill Clinton of Arkansas seemed to show more understanding than Bush about what the public wanted. His sincerity and belief in himself gave the American people renewed hope for the future. Clinton was elected president in 1992, and even though his lack of experience (Bill and Hillary Rodham Clinton are post–World War II baby boomers) caused a great deal of media criticism in the first years of his presidency, by mid-decade, the economy was showing signs of improvement.

Throughout the rest of the world, a major upheaval had taken place: In 1990, the formal end of the Cold War was declared, communist regimes had crumbled in Eastern Europe, and West and East Germany were reunited after 45 years; in 1991, the Soviet Union broke up, after its republics declared independence, and apartheid was dismantled in South Africa; in 1993, Israel and the PLO signed peace accords.[1]

Immediate Concerns

In this last decade of the 20th century, American children, through television, have already watched a real war erupt in the Persian Gulf, people suffer and die in beatings and shootings in America, and people die from starvation throughout the world. No longer shielded from violence in a nation fragmented by racial tensions, children are confused about what it means to be American. Jules Archer observes the effects of mob violence in the United States in *Rage in the Streets* (1994), and notes that Americans like to think of themselves as peaceful and logical, but poverty, despair, racial prejudice, unfair labor practices, unwelcome government intervention, and police brutality have led to explosive behavior throughout the history of America. Archer says, "It is never enough simply to punish rioters. We also need to examine the basic reasons that compel them to riot. When we do, we will understand what needs to be done in order to prevent riots in the future."

Educators seem to be fighting a losing battle, on the one hand trying to find new ways of reaching students, on the other hand trying to defuse violence. At the same time, teachers, who don't have enough supplies or enough books, are trying to implement the new "literature-based curriculum"[2] with its increased emphasis on using trade children's books in the classroom. Some teachers are even paying for these books out of their own pockets. As a result, publishers have been holding back from publishing their higher-priced hardcover picture books in more affordable trade paperback editions; they have their market cornered.

It is a credit to the children's publishing industry in the 1990s that today's children's books often address immediate concerns in society. And those few books that did so earlier, such as *The Moved-Outers* (1945) by Florence Crannell Means, which presents the treatment of Japanese-Americans during World War II (see Chapter 5), have recently been reissued. It makes perfect sense to share America's problems with her children and adolescents. They are the ones who will have to find the answers a few years from now, and children's book authors can help by giving children the benefit of their experience.

Censorship

The broad scope of subject matter in the children's books of the last two decades, in combination with the overwhelming number of children's books published, has made it more important than ever for parents to be familiar with what their children might choose to read. Herbert Foerstel's *Banned in the U.S.A.* (1994) offers a comprehensive discussion of several controversial titles, first presenting a synopsis of the story, then listing the objections of various organizations. In a 1991–92 study by the People for the American Way, the three most common reasons for the challenging of schools' materials were: Materials were "anti-Christian," "Satanic," "New Age," or generally contrary to challengers' religious views; materials contained profane or other objectionable language; and materials' treatment of sexuality was considered offensive.[3]

No child should be refused access to a book except when a child's parent makes that decision. And no one adult should make that decision for others. As of this writing, a book can be removed from circulation to everyone at the request of just one person, who takes it upon herself or himself to determine the suitability of a certain title. The request for removal is more often than not based on an objectionable word or phrase rather than on story content.

As an example of individual preference influencing public opinion, in the mid-1990s, when Satanism was thought for awhile to be flourishing in America, some of the books labeled as symbolizing Satanic rituals were Bram Stoker's *Dracula* (1897), Lloyd Alexander's *The High King* (1968), Alvin Schwartz's *Scary Stories to Tell in the Dark* (1981), and Eve Merriam's *Halloween ABC* (1987),[4]—four very different books with different themes, none of them in any way advocating Satanism.

Choices

Though homelessness was acknowledged in Joseph Krumgold's *Onion John* (1959) and homosexuality in Isabelle Holland's *The Man Without a Face* (1972), these were novels. Only recently have these subjects been explored in children's picture books, with Eve Bunting's *Fly Away Home* (1991) about a boy and his father who live at the airport; *Daddy's Roommate* (1990) by Michael Willhoite, which tells of a young boy whose parents are divorced and whose father lives with another man; and *Heather Has Two Mommies* (1989) by Leslea Newman, illustrated by Diana Souza, a story about the three-year-old child of a lesbian couple. The latter two titles have been excluded from circulation by various pressure groups who feel they promote, encourage, and facilitate homosexuality. Back in the 1930s and 1940s, Lucy Sprague Mitchell advocated realism in books for young children, while Ann Carroll Moore believed children should be shielded from reality. Fifty-plus years later, those opposite factions still exist. Parents who feel they must protect their children will limit reading choices, and those who want their children to better understand what the future holds will give them the freedom to make their own choices.

Respecting Children

Much progress has been made in this century in children's book creation, topically, technically, and artistically. Children's picture books being printed in the Nineties show a high degree of special care and attention to detail, accounting for their expense and lack of availability in trade paperback editions. The pages often have a silken quality, book jackets are sturdy and colorful, and the type has been carefully selected to enhance the illustrations. Not all of these books on the inside live up to the slick package on the outside. But some do and are worth the price of purchase. Respect for children and their books is evident in the work of Barry Moser, whether illustrating Van Dyke Parks's adaptation of Joel Chandler Harris's Brer Rabbit stories or Cynthia Rylant's crisp and pertinent text in *Appalachia: The Voices of Sleeping Birds* (1991). In this picture book, an author and illustrator celebrate a specific region of the United States. Rylant describes the people of Appalachia—"Inside their homes you will see photographs on the walls, mostly of their children or their families from long ago."—and Moser shows the faces of Appalachia in different shapes and sizes and colors.

Who Decides?

While most children's books in the Nineties reflect the cultural differences that exist in the United States and show respect for diversity, many of the books for children published earlier in the century have since been criticized for a lack of social awareness. A case in point is the *Doctor Dolittle* series by Hugh Lofting (1920s), and its books were allowed to go out of print in the 1970s. In 1988, they were reissued but without, in the words of Hugh Lofting's son Christopher, those "certain incidents . . . considered by some to be disrespectful to ethnic minorities and, therefore, perhaps inappropriate for today's young reader."[5] The term "ethnic minorities" is in itself inappropriate since, according to the dictionary, to be a minority is to be insignificant or inferior. Another example is *Charlie and the Chocolate Factory* (1964), in which the Oompa-Loompas were changed during the 1970s from "African pygmies" to light-haired non-human characters after the book was criticized as racist. Since libraries continue to circulate the copies they have and do not purchase new editions just because minor revisions have been made, children may continue to read about the original Oompa-Loompas.

The Need for Truth

In the present age of expanded communications and new awareness, there is little excuse for a book that manipulates the facts simply to make a social statement. Because ecological concerns have escalated in the Nineties, many children's book authors and illustrators express those concerns in picture books. When children's book illustrator Susan Jeffers created *Brother Eagle, Sister Sky* (1991), she attributed the words of the text to Chief Seattle, a 19th-century chief of the Suquamish, Duwamish, and allied Indian tribes of Puget Sound. She adapted his speech in a way that gave him great insight into ecological concerns, and illustrated this speech with beautiful paintings celebrating the Native Americans and their surroundings.

At first, the book was lauded in the media; then, criticisms began to appear. The speech on which Jeffers based her book was not a translation of the original but a highly edited rewrite by a screenwriter, Ted Perry, who used it in 1972 as Jeffers did in 1991—to publicize ecological concerns.[6] Jeffers used Perry's rewrite, not Seattle's words, when she wrote: "Chief Seattle said . . . What will happen when the buffalo are all slaughtered?" The chief, who lived in the Pacific Northwest, had never seen a buffalo. He certainly didn't write, as Perry says he did, "I have seen a thousand rotting buffaloes on the prairie, left by the white man who shot them from a passing train." Perry admits he made up much of his text without researching the authenticity of his material.[7]

Jeffers does give an ambiguous source for her text, but it is the errors in her illustrations, as pointed out by Native American writer Joseph Bruchac,[8] that cause the book to fail in its attempt to portray ecological concerns through a specific Native American culture. The birchbark canoe was not used in the Northwest, the "perfumed flowers" are California poppies that kill needed food plants, and the clothing represents an amalgam of cultures embodying different tribes rather than the people of the Northwest. Despite the controversy, or perhaps because of it, *Brother Eagle, Sister Sky* has been a major best-seller, with little concern shown for its inaccuracies.

Any book in which the message becomes more important than the story is inclined to lose impact. Chris Van Allsburg, whose book *The Polar Express* (1985) is a subtle celebration of nature's magic and a deserving recipient of the 1986 Caldecott Medal, followed this success with *The Wretched Stone* (1991) and *The Sweetest Fig* (1993), in which the illustrations are technically and artistically superior, while the stories lack dramatic impact. In the first, a stone taken aboard a ship has hypnotic power, with the crew released from their spell only after the captain reads them stories. Those who already know how to read, Van Allsburg tells us, recover more quickly than those who do not. The second book tells of a self-absorbed man who treats others badly, including his dog, and, in the folktale tradition, is punished for his greed after trying to manipulate two magic figs that are supposed to make his dreams come true. After eating the first fig, he dreams he is out on the street in his underwear, and the next day that dream comes true. The second fig is eaten by his dog before the man can arrange his dreams so that he can eat it himself and get what he wants. It is disappointing not to be shown how he is personally affected when he finds he has changed places with his pet. But the story abruptly ends at that point.

One book in which character and story development override the subtle message that lack of respect for nature brings tragic results is *The Wave of the Sea-Wolf* (1994) by David Wisniewski, a story set in the Pacific Northwest and based on a Tlingit myth.

Celebrate the Differences

One of the current problems facing this country is the influx of illegal aliens. To many, the United States is a haven, a golden land of opportunity. In several South American countries, oppression and poverty threaten the people and escaping to the United States seems to them a viable solution, even though it is illegal for them to be here. Fran Leeper Buss and Daisy Cubias wrote *Journey of the Sparrows* (1991), which tells of 15-year-old Maria, who, with her older sister Julia and six-year-old brother Oscar, arrives in Chicago from El Salvador after a cruel trip north. The hardships they face in the city as illegal aliens, with the small triumphs that keep them hopeful, create an emotionally wrenching story. *Grab Hands and Run* (1993) by Frances Temple focuses on the actual escape of one family from El Salvador and the details of the long, hard journey that culminates in a family's successful efforts to reach Canada.

In an effort to offer children new insight into World War II, both author Margaret Chang and her husband, Raymond, and author Sook Nyui Choi wrote about a country invaded by Japan. The Chang book is set in China and the Choi book in Korea. *In the Eye of War* (1990) is Raymond Chang's true story reflected in the person of Shao-shao, a 10-year-old boy who lives in Shanghai, which has been occupied by Japan. Although Shao-shao is able to follow almost the same routine he followed before the occupation, American bombers fly over periodically, striking at targets in the city, and Japanese soldiers police the streets. But Shao-shao feels more oppressed by his father than by the Japanese until he discovers that his father is active in the underground resistance movement, and the story then deals with the developing respect and understanding between these two against the shadow of war. Margaret Chang, who is not Chinese and was born in California, is able to tell her husband's story with an objectivity not characteristic of Choi's book, *Year of Impossible Goodbyes* (1991).

Choi's story is related in first person by 10-year-old Sookan, who, with her mother and younger brother, lives in northern Korea. By the last years of World War II, when this story takes place, her village had already been occupied by the Japanese for 30 years. Sookan's father is a resistance fighter, hiding in Manchuria, and her older brothers have been taken to Japanese labor camps.

Choi lived in Korea during the time she describes in her book, suffering through the Japanese occupation, and the story reflects her emotional journey, marked by bitterness and the momentary joy of liberation by the Americans, only to be faced with a devastating loss of freedom once again when the Communist regime took over. Where Chang's book offers an omniscient point of view that presents the enemy as vulnerable, capable of human emotion, Choi gives us an unforgiving portrait of the Japanese through the actions of the unsympathetic Captain Narita, who goes out of his way to keep Sookan's family from observing Korean traditions or finding any kind of pleasure in their day-to-day existence.

Children's Books: Past, Present and Future

In the early days of the children's book industry, a small group of librarians, editors, and booksellers diligently worked together to bring children's books to the attention of the general public. However, children's books, for most of this century, have been a specialized genre, separate from mainstream publishing. The children's book departments of major publishers were expected, for income tax purposes, to show a loss, and editors were encouraged to try out new ideas without concern for profit lines. Authors and illustrators knew they could count on long-term, steady sales of their books.

But new tax laws and library budget cuts in the Seventies changed the practice of allowing children's books to remain in print for many years, while the enormous strides made in publishing technology in the past 20 years have greatly increased the number of new children's books published each year. At the end of the century, the desire to see children's books as mainstream has been realized, but the price being paid is in the lack of time to allow good books to be noticed before they go out of print.

The new connection for children's books in the 21st century is the computer, with CD-ROM and virtual reality inviting children to participate directly with the books they read. The possibilities inherent in this new technology are overwhelming, with joy of learning topping the list. The Magic School Bus series written by Joanna Cole and illustrated by Bruce Degen has been incorporated into a CD-ROM that takes the user into the Solar System and allows participants to play games while they learn. But no matter how many different ways books can be communicated to children, nothing can replace the human element—the storyteller or artist who has infused the work with his or her life's blood, the editor who adds objectivity to such a personal process, the teacher who brings personal enthusiasm to reading. In addition to being familiar with traditional books, librarians will have to be involved, and many already are, with CD-ROMs and personal computers. Changes are ahead in the education system, and the information network is growing fast.

Books for children will continue to reflect the social climate throughout the coming decades. They will continue to be a prophecy of change, a blueprint of contemporary society, and a window on history. Children who are allowed input into their learning process will enthusiastically choose what interests them, and it is up to parents, educators, and compilers of children's books to know what is available and to offer a wide variety of choices.

In the 19th century, children were treated as small adults; in the early decades of the 20th century, a protective attitude developed. As America moves into the 21st century, the focus is on the needs of children in a society that has become less family-oriented, that seems to take violence for granted, and that acknowledges problems in the education system but doesn't seem to consider them a priority. Many of the children growing up in this chaotic decade will become parents in the 21st century. Some will be forged into leadership roles, some will buckle under pressure, and others will follow the leader. Parents of today's children still have a chance to instill proper values, and children's books continue to be a time-honored way to do so.

CHRONOLOGICAL BIBLIOGRAPHY 1990–1995

Avi. *The True Confessions of Charlotte Doyle.* New York: Orchard, 1990. (Realistic Fiction/Historical/Nineteenth Century)

Because Charlotte Doyle's father has made arrangements for her to sail to America, Charlotte has no choice but to make the trip, even though she turns out to be the only passenger. She befriends a black sailor, Zachariah, but, because she refuses to believe the accusations against Captain Jaggery, she betrays both Zachariah and members of the crew. When it becomes evident that the captain is unstable and she was wrong to believe in him, Charlotte attempts to redeem herself by becoming part of the crew—cutting her hair, dressing as a sailor, and putting in a hard day's work on board the ship. When the captain accuses her of murder, she is sentenced to hang, but with the help of the crew the real murderer is unearthed and Charlotte is saved. Her experiences, however, open her eyes to a way of life far different from her sheltered existence in her father's house and cause her to change her future forever.

Blume, Judy. *Fudge-A-Mania.* New York: Dutton, 1990. (Realistic Fiction/Chapter/Humor)

Fudge is back, as usual harassing his older brother, Peter, who is trying to deal with the fact that Fudge has announced that he is going to marry Peter's worst enemy, Sheila Tubman. The family travels to

Maine for vacation, and so does Sheila. She even offers to baby-sit for Fudge so the Hatchers can enjoy vacation time, and Fudge performs as expected. Familiar characters appear throughout the story—Uncle Feather, Fudge's myna bird; Peter's dog Turtle and his best friend, Jimmy; and Grandma Muriel, who's a gymnast. The appeal of this series has been extended to television with a weekly sitcom featuring Blume's delightful characters and starring Fudge.

Chang, Margaret and Raymond. *In the Eye of War*, a Margaret K. McElderry book. New York: Macmillan, 1990. (Realistic Fiction/World War II/China)

Raymond Chang lived in Shanghai during World War II and experienced both the Japanese occupation and a Communist regime. This is his story recalled in the person of 10-year-old Shao-shao who can't seem to satisfy his father's expectations and who increasingly resents the unfair demands his father places on him until he discovers he hasn't really known his father very well at all. The details of everyday life in an occupied city and the Chinese traditions the family follows give depth and clarity to a way of life very different from that experienced in America.

Christian, Mary Blount. *Sebastian (Super Sleuth) and the Baffling Bigfoot*, illtd. Lisa McCue. New York: Macmillan, 1990. (Chapter Book/Mystery/Animal/Series)

Sebastian is a dog, a shaggy, appealing mutt who helps his human, Det. John Quincy Jones, solve cases, even though no one acknowledges his efforts. The series, of which this book is the 11th, is written from Sebastian's viewpoint, and not only is he unappreciated, he is also often misunderstood and blamed for actions that seem destructive but, as far as he is concerned, are necessary to solve crimes.

Goldin, Barbara Diamond. *The World's Birthday: A Rosh Hashanah Story*, illtd. Jeanette Winter. San Diego: Harcourt, 1990. (Picture Book/Jewish)

With Winter's perceptive illustrations, Goldin celebrates Rosh Hashanah, the Jewish New Year, as young Daniel suggests that his family have a birthday party for the whole world to acknowledge the day of its creation. With a huge birthday cake and a great many candles, Daniel shows his family how to let the world know it is being recognized on its birthday.

Janeczko, Paul, ed. *The Place My Words Are Looking For*. New York: Bradbury, 1990. (Poetry Collection/Biographical)

Janeczko's choices do more than entertain children. These poems by various writers—Eve Merriam, Jack Prelutsky, Karla Kuskin, Myra Cohn Livingston and others—come directly from the vision of a child—the child who is, the child the poet remembers being, and, finally, the memory of childhood lost. These are selections that show in poetry and in autobiographical text the evolution of the poet who has learned to find just the right words to make a poem take on its own life. For the prospective poet of 12 and up, this book offers much inspiration and understanding.

LeGuin, Ursula K. *Tehanu: The Last Book of Earthsea.* New York: Atheneum, 1990. (Fantasy)

This book presents the ending to the saga of Ged and his battle with the dark force that has shadowed him since he foolishly released it many years earlier. But it's really a story about the awakening of woman's power in a man's world, a story just beginning. Tenar of Atuan, who gave up her powers to marry Flint, a farmer of the Middle Valley, and have children, is widowed and her children are grown. She is summoned by the great mage Ogion, who taught Ged and for a time taught her. He is dying and must tell her his true name before he dies. Along the way she rescues a child from a fire and nurses her burns. The child, Therru, ultimately realizes her true potential, and Tenar and Ged are allowed to live together in peace, finally released from magic.

Macaulay, David. *Black and White.* Boston: Houghton Mifflin, 1990. CALDECOTT MEDAL. (Picture Book/Mystery)

In this unusual book, popular with young adults, four panels illustrate four different scenes and art styles, seemingly unrelated but in the long run connected and used together to solve this sophisticated mystery.

Nolan, Dennis. *Dinosaur Dream.* New York: Macmillan, 1990. (Fantasy/Picture Book/Archaeology/Dinosaur)

Nolan employs the simple logic of a child as he takes young Wilbur back through layers of time from the present, with domestic cows, pigs, and chickens, to the Ice Age, with woolly mammoths and saber-toothed cats, to the Cretaceous period, with pteranodons and finally to the Jurassic period, with *Triceratops* and *Tyrannosaurus rex.* When Wilbur finds a baby apatosaur outside his bedroom window, he knows he can't keep it and decides to return it to its own period, the Jurassic. Above the text on each page are three small silhouettes of the animals of a particular period and opposite are stunning full-page action scenes. Through it all, Wilbur reacts in a matter-of-fact manner, and when he returns home after delivering the dinosaur to its relatives, he feels no regret at leaving the Jurassic because he can visit anytime. "It will be easy next time, he [thinks], because now I know the way."

Spinelli, Jerry. *Maniac Magee*. Boston: Little, Brown, 1990. NEWBERY MEDAL. (Realistic Fiction)

Jeffrey "Maniac" Magee is the stuff from which legends are made. His actions are larger than life. While others are protecting themselves against imagined threats, Maniac is facing up to real challenges and coming out on top every time. But Maniac, whose parents were killed in a trolley accident when he was three years old, didn't become a legend overnight. It all started when he left his estranged aunt and uncle at age 11. He lives in the deer pen at the zoo in Two Mills, Pennsylvania. He runs and he reads; he's not afraid of anything but the trestle where his parents were killed, and all he really wants is to belong somewhere. The Beales live in the East End; they're black, and they're good people. The Pickwells live in the West End; they're white, and they're good people. Maniac spends time with both families, but his very presence causes problems for the people who matter most to him in a city firmly split between black and white.

Wilhelm, Hans. *A Cool Kid—Like Me*. New York: Crown, 1990. (Picture Book/Realistic Fiction)

Children have an inner vision of themselves that doesn't always live up to grownup expectations, or at least what they think are grownup expectations. Here is a book that addresses their concerns during those years when independence seems to be taken for granted even though the need for security still exists at times. Wilhelm presents a small boy as narrator whose grandmother is able to see him inside as well as out and accepts his weaknesses as well as his strengths. When she leaves town for a time, she gives him a teddy bear to talk to. His parents dismiss the gift as something he has outgrown, but the boy finds it comforting, and it allows him to be, on the outside at least, the "cool kid" everyone thinks he is.

Willhoite, Michael. *Daddy's Roommate*. Boston: Alyson Publications, 1990. (Picture Book/Social Relationships)

The Alyson Wonderland series focuses on books for and about the children of gay and lesbian parents. This book shows in colorful but simple detail the routine of a child whose parents are divorced and whose father lives with another man. During the week, the little boy in the story lives with his mother and on weekends joins his father and his father's friend Frank. They go to the beach and to the zoo, Frank acts the part of stepparent, and illustrations discreetly show the emotional ties of the two men. The emphasis is on the security the boy feels both with his mother and with his father.

Allen, Marjorie N. *Changes*, photog. Shelley Rotner. New York: Macmillan, 1991; New York: Aladdin, 1995. (Picture Book/Poetry/Nature)

Photographer Shelley Rotner wanted to create a picture book that would celebrate nature, and Marjorie Allen wanted to write about the connection between nature and people. The result is a collection of photographs showing change as portrayed in an abstract sunrise, in growing plants, in animals, and finally in people, accompanied by the simple text of an essay poem.

Bunting, Eve. *Fly Away Home*, illtd. Ronald Himler. New York: Clarion Books, 1991. (Picture Book/Social Adjustment)

In every decade, a social problem previously not highlighted becomes a major concern. In the 1990s homelessness has become one of the issues addressed for the first time in children's picture books, and Eve Bunting tells the story of a small boy, Andrew, and his father who live at the airport. From his young-old viewpoint, Andrew describes their daily routine, the care they take not to be noticed, his father's search for a full-time job and an apartment they can afford, Andrew's making extra money by returning luggage carts and carrying suitcases, and, most of all, Andrew's continuing hope to be released from a binding lifestyle, a release similar to that of a small bird who was also trapped inside the airport but managed to get free and fly away home.

Buss, Fran Leeper, with Daisy Cubias. *Journey of the Sparrows*. New York: Dutton, 1991. (Realistic Fiction/Cultural Adjustment/El Salvador)

Maria, 15, her older sister Julia, who is pregnant and widowed, and her younger brother Oscar manage to make it across the U.S. border and go on to Chicago, where the dream of plenty in this rich land is quickly shattered. But where there is nothing, the smallest victories keep hope alive. Maria's warm friendship with Tomás, a boy her own age, her sister's pregnancy ending in the birth of a healthy baby, her discovery that her mother is still alive and out of El Salvador, and the rescue of Maria's youngest sister, Teresa, from Mexico where her mother had left her, are enough to sustain the family's faith in the future.

Choi, Sook Nyui. *Year of Impossible Goodbyes*. Boston: Houghton Mifflin, 1991. (Realistic Fiction/World War II/Korea)

Ten-year-old Sookan lives in North Korea in the village of Kirimni, Pyongyang, which has long been under Japanese occupation. Through the actions of Captain Narita and his men, the lack of respect that some Japanese have for Koreans is made evident, and Sookan and her family are denied permission to follow the Korean traditions in which they take great pride. They are instead forced to follow Japanese beliefs, outwardly at least, and learn the Japanese language. They are even given Japanese names. When liberation comes at the end of World War II, everyone is overjoyed, but the joy doesn't last as Russian Communists take control of North Korea and a new set of rules is imposed, again denying Korean tradition.

Ehlert, Lois. *Red Leaf, Yellow Leaf*. San Diego: Harcourt, 1991. (Picture Book/Nature)

The fall colors of leaves on the sugar maple tree are so vivid it seems impossible to capture them on paper without using real leaves, which would quickly fade. But Ehlert did reproduce these brilliant colors in a lasting collage made with crunched up paper and a variety of articles, such as seeds, roots, watercolors, and oil pastels. The maple tree is explained in detail by Ehlert right down to how to make a treat for the birds to hang on a branch of the tree.

Frasier, Debra. *On the Day You Were Born*. San Diego: Harcourt, 1991. (Picture Book/Concept)

Connecting human life to nature, Frasier introduces a child to his or her beginnings as part of the planet Earth. "On the day you were born the Moon pulled on the ocean below, and, wave by wave, a rising tide washed the beaches clean for your footprints . . ." And so it goes with the Sun and the Moon and the clouds and the trees and finally the people welcoming the newborn child. With bright, clear-cut visual designs, words and pictures join in a cohesive and natural whole.

Gackenbach, Dick. *Alice's Special Room*. New York: Clarion, 1991. (Picture Book/Social Adjustment/Death)

Even in this age of candor there are too few books that deal with death. Gackenbach does so in a way that offers great solace to a child. Alice's cat Louie is dead, but, she tells her mother, she has a special room where she can play with Louie whenever she wants and also be with her dead grandfather. She can also go to the beach in December and slide down snowbanks in July. Alice follows her mother, who is on a tour of the house to find the special room, but her mother can't find it until Alice tells her the things that happen in that room are all the things she remembers before Louie died and before her grandfather died. The special room is her memory.

Jeffers, Susan. *Brother Eagle, Sister Sky: A Message from Chief Seattle.* New York: Dial, 1991. (Picture Book/Nature)

This is a book that is often read in elementary classrooms as informational instead of the fictional work that it is. It is a book that encourages people to be concerned about ecology, which is good, but it credits an Indian chief with words that he never said and illustrates those words with pictures that contradict the facts of Chief Seattle's Northwest existence. Even though Jeffers adds a disclaimer at the end of the book, saying that her version is an adaptation of a speech "partly obscured by the mists of time," the book presents itself as a direct quote, introduced by the words: "With a commanding presence and eyes that mirrored the great soul that lived within, the Chief rose to speak to the gathering in a resounding voice." The text that follows is that voice, according to Jeffers.

Naylor, Phyllis Reynolds. *Shiloh.* New York: Atheneum, 1991. (Realistic Fiction/Animal)

Marty Preston, at 11, enjoys roaming the hills behind his home in Friendly, West Virginia, even though the family doesn't always have enough to eat and each day is a struggle to survive. Having a pet is out of the question, but when Marty finds a runaway dog that is being mistreated by neighbor Judd Travers, he is strangely drawn to the beagle and gives him a name, Shiloh. He has to return the dog to Judd, but when Shiloh again runs away, Marty hides him in the hills, making a pen for him and sharing his own meager portion of food with the dog. But his secret is difficult to keep and becomes impossible when the dog is attacked by a German shepherd and is badly injured. Naylor creates a story with great emotional impact that joins *Lassie Come-Home* (1940) and *Sounder* (1969) as one of the great animal stories of the century.

Paterson, Katherine. *Lyddie.* New York: Lodestar, 1991. (Realistic Fiction/Historical/New England)

In 1843 America, children of poverty-stricken farm families were often sent out to work in other people's homes, living a virtual slave existence. Paterson tells the story of 13-year-old Lyddie, who is hired out but finds the situation intolerable and looks for a way out. She leaves Vermont to find work in a factory in Lowell, Massachusetts. When her mother is committed to an asylum, Lyddie must also care for her little sister, Rachel. Both Lyddie and Rachel work at the factory, but Rachel is small for her age and picks up the wracking cough that afflicts many of the workers. Details of the backbreaking factory routine, the sexual harassment of female workers, the abuse of power at the administrative level, and the struggles of women to be all they can be permeate this perceptive portrait of early America.

———. *The Tale of the Mandarin Ducks*, illtd. Diane and Leo Dillon. New York: Lodestar, 1991. (Picture Book/Folk Tale/Japan)

The Dillons show great respect for cultures they illustrate by researching backgrounds carefully. This book, illustrated in the manner of 19th-century ukiyo-e, which showed the common people of Japan and their settings rather than utilizing the conventional Chinese-influenced style of art, tells of Yasuko, a kitchen maid, who, along with the lord's one-eyed servant, Shozo, releases the beautiful drake captured by her greedy lord. The two are captured and scheduled for punishment but, unexpectedly, are abandoned in the woods and taken in by imperial messengers supposedly sent from the capital. The next morning, Yasuko, Shozo, and the messengers are gone and on the path are a pair of mandarin ducks, who spend many good years together in the knowledge that "trouble can always be borne when it is shared."

Rylant, Cynthia. *Appalachia: The Voices of Sleeping Birds*, illtd. Barry Moser. San Diego: Harcourt, 1991. (Picture Book/Regional/America)

It is in Barry Moser's almost lifelike illustrations of the hound dogs that the visual essence of Appalachia comes through the clearest, but each illustration throughout the book brings life to Rylant's words, whether she is describing the children, their hardworking parents, the houses they live in, or the relatives whose pictures grace the walls. In text and pictures, the book, understated but emotionally charged, shows what it means to be connected to place in America. Both author and illustrator grew up in the Appalachian Mountains.

Say, Allen. *Tree of Cranes*. Boston: Houghton Mifflin, 1991. (Picture Book/Cultural/Japanese American/Holiday)

Allen Say was born and raised in Japan, but his mother was born in California. At the boy's birth, a small pine tree was planted for him. When his mother becomes homesick for America, she digs up the little pine and creates a Christmas tree in their Japanese house with silver folded paper cranes for decoration.

Walsh, Ellen Stoll. *Mouse Count.* San Diego: Harcourt, 1991. (Picture Book/Concept)

A brightly colored snake finds 10 mice in various shades of brown and puts them in a jar for his dinner. But the snake is greedy and wants just one more mouse, which gives the mice a chance to get away. The snake counts, the mice uncount, and Walsh's charming illustrations make learning fun.

Wiesner, David. *Tuesday*. New York: Clarion Books, 1991. CALDECOTT MEDAL. (Picture Book/Wordless)

The flying saucers that people often report seeing could be frogs on lily pads, according to Wiesner's premise that one night, one Tuesday night, to be exact, frogs took to the skies. After passing through an open window, one spent time watching television with a lady who was sleeping in her chair, while others chased a dog down the street, and when the sun began to rise, the frogs returned to their pond, leaving behind only lily pads. And the next Tuesday night, well, how about flying pigs? Wiesner's text is almost non-existent, but the pictures tell the story very well.

Willard, Nancy. *Pish, Posh, said Hieronymous Bosch*, illtd. Diane and Leo Dillon. San Diego: Harcourt, 1991. (Poetry/Biographical/15th Century)

This unusual poem written by Willard captures in words the unusual style found in a Bosch painting. The Dillons, who not only know this strange painter's work but incorporate it into their own illustrations, join with Willard to present a delightful collection of bizarre creatures that are driving Bosch's housekeeper crazy, but are taken for granted by the painter himself. This oversized book (11 inches by 12 inches) is richly detailed in design and calls for an oral reading as the housekeeper finally resolves her problems.

Wisniewski, David. *Rain Player*. New York: Clarion, 1991. (Picture Book/Traditional Tale/Mayan Indian)

Wisniewski developed the cut-paper craft of illustrating picture books when he and his wife, Donna, started their own shadow puppet theater and he created the plays, puppets, and projected scenery. His unusual illustrations are made by folding and cutting colored paper to produce designs, similar to cutting out snowflake designs, and then putting the different cut-paper designs together on the pages to create scenes. *Rain Player* was his first picture book, and Wisniewski uses his storytelling experience to develop an original tale about a Mayan boy who must use his skill as a ball player to challenge Chac, the god of rain, when the land is threatened by drought. In bright colors and dramatic cut-paper scenes, Wisniewski combines pictures and text to bring his unusual talent to the children's book field.

Wolff, Virginia Euwer. *The Mozart Season*. New York: Henry Holt, 1991. (Realistic Fiction/Social Adjustment/Music)

Allegra Shapiro, like Virginia Hamilton's Junior Brown, is a musical prodigy, but unlike Junior, Allegra is encouraged in the fulfillment of her need. It is Allegra herself who must decide what her goals are when she is chosen to be a contestant in the Ernest Bloch Young Musicians' competition. The violin concerto selected for the competitors is one she has already practiced, Mozart's Fourth. Now she must memorize it until playing it is second nature. But is competence enough? All of the contestants will be competent, but what is the secret of winning in such an equal competition?

Yolen, Jane. *Letting Swift River Go*, illtd. Barbara Cooney. Boston: Little, Brown, 1991. (Realistic Fiction/Picture Book/Regional)

Yolen's simple, moving text, detailing the loss of an entire village when the Quabbin Reservoir is built in Western Massachusetts, and Barbara Cooney's re-creation of the quaint New England village and its demise create a book that shows the importance of place in the scheme of things. Written as an autobiographical reflection, Yolen speaks of the Swift River area before it became a reservoir and of walks through the countryside and picnics in the old cemetery. She talks of catching fireflies during sleepouts under the backyard maples in summertime and tapping maples for sap in early spring. But when plans are made for the Quabbin Reservoir, the cemetery has to be moved and the maples are toppled. The Old Stone Mill is razed and houses are moved. An entire existence is obliterated as:

> The waters from the dammed rivers
> moved in slowly and silently.
> They rose like unfriendly neighbors
> halfway up the sides of hills,
> covering Dana and Enfield,

Prescott and Greenwich,
all the little Swift River towns.
It took seven long years.

Cole, Joanna. *The Magic School Bus: On the Ocean Floor*, illtd. Bruce Degen. New York: Scholastic, 1992. (Informational/Science/Series)

In this welcome addition to the series, Ms. Frizzle's class goes on a field trip to the ocean in the magic school bus. The bus itself becomes a submarine and then a submersible as it takes the children beneath the sea. They find themselves in diving gear and meet up with sharks and are able to study a coral reef. The comic-book format allows for extensive details to be shown about ocean life and makes learning fun. The illustrations show the students in Ms. Frizzle's class to be culturally diverse without calling undue attention to this aspect of American culture (see illustration p. 292).

Cormier, Robert. *Tunes for Bears to Dance To*. New York: BDD, 1992.

Henry works for Mr. Hairston in his grocery store, but, although Mr. Hairston is pleasant to his customers, he has nothing good to say about them after they leave. Henry also discovers that Mr. Hairston physically abuses his daughter and verbally abuses his wife. But it is the favor that Mr. Hairston asks of Henry that clearly shows the man's true nature. Henry has befriended a Jewish neighbor, Mr. Levine, who is a survivor of the Holocaust. Mr. Levine is a wood carver and is reproducing in miniature his village, destroyed during the war, and the people in the village, who were his friends and neighbors. In fact, he has won a prize for his work. But Mr. Hairston wants Henry to destroy the village, and the reason is so terrible that Henry may never resolve the trauma of knowing.

McCully, Emily Arnold. *Mirette on the High Wire*. New York: Putnam, 1992. CALDECOTT MEDAL. (Picture Book/Realistic Fiction/Paris)

McCully shows her more painterly side in this picture storybook about a young girl in 19th-century Paris whose parents run a boarding house. When a mysterious stranger comes to stay, Mirette discovers he is Bellini, a famous high-wire walker, and she begs him to teach her and to take her with him in his act. But he tells her he has become fearful and cannot continue his act. Mirette won't accept his fear, and he agrees for her sake to perform on the wire. But the fear remains, and he freezes midway on the wire during his big performance. It takes the confidence of a small, brave girl to bring him success.

McCully's watercolor illustrations add personality and color to an already rich text.

Meddaugh, Susan. *Martha Speaks*. Boston: Houghton Mifflin, 1992. (Picture Book/Humor)

When Helen, who doesn't like alphabet soup, gives her soup to Martha the dog, the family has an unexpected surprise: "The letters in the soup went up to Martha's brain instead of down to her stomach," and "that evening, Martha spoke." Martha knows how to speak, but she doesn't know enough to stop. She becomes such a nuisance that the family stops giving her alphabet soup. Unfortunately, one night when the family is out, a thief breaks into the house, and when Martha dials 911, all she can do is bark. To keep her quiet, the thief gives her leftover alphabet soup from a pot on the stove. When the family returns, the police are at the house. "We got a call at the station," says a policeman. "Some lady named Martha." With expressive illustrations and commentary in voice balloons supplementing the low-key text, Meddaugh's Martha is an unlikely but very likable heroine.

Rylant, Cynthia. *Missing May*. New York: Orchard Books, 1992. NEWBERY MEDAL. (Realistic Fiction/Social Adjustment/Death)

When Summer's mother dies and the six-year-old girl is taken to live with Aunt May and Uncle Ob, their love for her helps her remain secure. But six years later, May dies, and this small, exquisite novel explores the process of how Summer and Ob deal with their grief and eventually accept the loss, even though they will never stop missing May.

Temple, Frances. *A Taste of Salt: A Story of Modern Haiti*. New York: HarperCollins, 1992. (Realistic Fiction/Culture/Haiti)

Djo is a young man who is seriously injured when the military junta burns down the orphanage where he stays, and who, along with Jeremie, a beautiful young woman, has been attempting to change conditions in Haiti by helping to elect the Reverend Jean-Bertrand Aristide as president. The stories of both young people are filled with tragedy, but their loyalty and love of country carry them through and keep them hopeful in the face of opposition and failed attempts at freeing their country from oppression.

Bosse, Malcolm. *Deep Dream of the Rain Forest*. New York: Farrar, Straus and Giroux, 1993. (Realistic Fiction/Cultural/South America)

Bayan and Tambong are members of the Iban tribe of Borneo,

where dreams must be heeded no matter where the dreamers have to go to gain understanding. In their quest, the two decide they must interact with a white English boy, Harry Windsor, traveling through the rain forest with his uncle, and Harry becomes the catalyst that makes the dream come true in a coming-of-age adventure for all three young people. Bosse is uncompromising in this portrait of life in the rain forest.

Cooper, Susan. *The Boggart*, a Margaret K. McElderry book. New York: Macmillan, 1993. (Fantasy)

Combining the ancient magic of the Scottish Highlands with the technical magic of computers, Cooper writes about a charming and mischievous creature called a Boggart, who travels from Castle Keep in Scotland to Toronto, Canada, trapped in a rolltop desk, and ends up inside a computer. The Volnik family visits the castle in Scotland's Western Highlands that has been left to them. When they return home to Toronto, they unwittingly bring with them the invisible creature known as the Boggart. Young Tommy, who is familiar with the Boggart, uses his computer in Scotland to communicate with Emily and her brother, Jessup, in Canada after the Boggart makes itself known to them. The three young people manage finally to return the elusive creature to the castle by transporting him in a computer game. The appeal of the Boggart calls for more books about him.

Gackenbach, Dick. *Claude Has a Picnic*. New York: Clarion, 1993. (Picture Book)

Claude is a personable hound who goes out of his way to help his human neighbors by quietly arranging a swap of toys between two bored boys and by providing a new kitten for the lonely Mrs. Shane. When Claude discovers that Mrs. Duncan has too many hot dogs and Mrs. Bunker has too much corn on the cob, he makes sure the two women get together, and the result is a picnic for the whole neighborhood, including Claude.

Hendrick, Mary Jean. *If Anything Ever Goes Wrong at the Zoo*, illtd. Jane Dyer. San Diego: Harcourt, 1993. (Picture Book)

In a sweeping rainbow of watercolors, Dyer makes a picture tour of a zoo with the animals in natural habitats, and in a low-key text, Hendrick tells of a little girl, Leslie, who offers her house "if anything ever goes wrong at the zoo." Imagine her mother's surprise when something does go wrong at the zoo—a flood during a heavy rainstorm—and Leslie's house on a hill is the safest place for the animals.

Kerr, M. E. *Linger*. New York: HarperCollins, 1993. (Realistic Fiction/Gulf War/Social Relationships)

This author is inclined to employ a contemporary setting as she writes her novels and to connect her stories to a recent past. *Gentlehands* (1978) explored the moral issues involved when the father of a teenager is accused of war crimes committed in a World War II concentration camp. *Linger* takes place during the Persian Gulf War, but the ethical dilemma that occurs has little to do with war and a great deal to do with social discrimination and with the "haves" setting up barriers against the "have-nots." Within the larger context of the Gulf War, Robert Peel, who is serving in Kuwait, is more disturbed over happenings at home than he is about taking part in a battle. When he is wounded and sent home, his worst concerns are realized.

Lowry, Lois. *The Giver*. Boston: Houghton Mifflin, 1993. NEWBERY MEDAL. (Science Fiction/Social Adjustment)

In a world where memories don't exist and people never question and never try anything new, and where at the age of 12, each child is assigned his or her future career, Jonas is singled out at 12 to be trained as the Receiver. There is only one Receiver in this community, and it is quickly evident to Jonas that he is to be separated from his family and friends. He will receive memories accumulated by the Giver, who possesses all the memories from the ancient past to the present. Every memory transferred to Jonas slightly relieves the Giver of his burden. Then Jonas begins to question as he discovers pain, suffering, joy, ecstasy, and something entirely alien to him—love. But it is when he discovers the existence of death that he comes up with a plan to change things.

McDermott, Gerald. *Raven: A Trickster Tale from the Pacific Northwest*. San Diego: Harcourt, 1993. (Folk/Myth/Picture Book/Native American/Pacific Northwest)

When McDermott was awarded a Caldecott Medal in 1975 for *Arrow to the Sun* (1974), a Pueblo Indian folk tale, there was some concern about whether the book was too abstract for children. But children understood perfectly, and the book has not lost its appeal. Here, McDermott utilizes his abstract artistic style to illustrate a Native American trickster tale from the Pacific Northwest. And again, he manages to communicate directly with his child audience, as he tells the story of how Raven brings light to the world when he is reborn as a boy child, grandson of the Sky Chief, and tricks the Sky Chief and his daughter into giving him the sun.

Meltzer, Milton, ed. *A. Lincoln: In His Own Words*, illtd. Stephen Alcorn. San Diego: Harcourt, 1993. (Biography)

In each decade, there are new insights into the life and times of Abraham Lincoln. In this book, Meltzer creates the text entirely from the words of Lincoln himself, quoted and collected over time, and the inner compassion of the man comes through. Some public figures from the past have been found to have feet of clay, but in Lincoln's case, his greatness is reaffirmed.

Mori, Kyoko. *Shizuko's Daughter*. New York; Henry Holt, 1993. (Realistic Fiction/Social Adjustment/Japan)

The setting of this thoughtful novel is Kobe, a Japanese industrial city southwest of Tokyo, and the story covers a seven-year period in the life of Yuki, 12 years old when the story begins. Yuki's mother, Shizuko, takes her own life and Yuki must deal with this tragedy. When her father remarries, Yuki wants to stay in Tokyo with her aunt, but because people might think her father and stepmother are neglecting her, she is not allowed to do so. The importance of doing what is expected is stressed in this story, and the traditions of an ancient society become part of everyday activities as Yuki adjusts to her altered lifestyle with the help of her grandmother, Masa, mother of Shizuko.

Perrault, Charles. *The Complete Fairy Tales of Charles Perrault*, tr. Neil Philip and Nicoletta Simborowski; illtd. Sally Holmes. New York: Clarion, 1993. (Fantasy/Fairy)

These new translations of well-known, pre-Grimm fairy tales cut through the many versions set forth over the years in an effort to capture the voice of Perrault himself and his style of storytelling. This collection goes to the heart of the story and for the first time offers Perrault's tongue-in-cheek moral rhymes at the end of each story. Here is little Red Riding-Hood who is eaten by the wolf and stays eaten; Cinderella who speaks up for herself when the prince's helper comes to the house trying to find out who owns the slipper. Direct and to the point, with softly detailed artwork by Holmes, these stories, 11 in all, will appeal to the children who listen to them and the adults who read them aloud to the children.

Pilkey, Dav. *Kat Kong*. San Diego: Harcourt, 1993. (Picture Book/Fractured Fairy Tale/Humor)

In a combination of photos and paintings, high drama occurs as three small mice are confronted by a monster cat. The mighty Kat Kong is captured by the three mouse scientists and tied in a burlap bag for the trip home. "As they sailed back to the great city of Mousopolis, they took special care not to let the cat out of the bag." And so it continues, a punster's delight, as Kat Kong escapes and threatens to destroy the city until Captain Limburger manages to save the day with a mysterious package.

———. *Dogzilla*. San Diego: Harcourt, 1993. (Picture Book/Fractured Fairy Tale/Humor)

This book features Pilkey's dog, Leia, and the three mice from *Kat Kong*. "Without warning, the monstrous mutt breathed her horrible breath onto the mice. 'Doggy breath,' screamed the soldiers. 'Run for your lives!'" It's up to the Big Cheese to find a way to save the city from the fire-breathing "hot" dog, and so he does—for the time being, at least. Pilkey prefaces each of his books by saying: "All the animals used in these photographs are the author's pets, and no harm came to them in the making of this book."

Say, Allen. *Grandfather's Journey*. Boston: Houghton Mifflin, 1993. CALDECOTT MEDAL. (Picture Book/Cultural/Japan/America)

This book speaks volumes with few words and exceptional art. It's more than a journey from Japan to America; it begins as a travelogue across the United States from New York to California at the turn of the century. Then it becomes a series of Japanese scenes when grandfather becomes homesick and returns to Japan with his wife and daughter before World War II. Grandfather yearns to visit California one more time before he dies, but he doesn't get there. His grandson, Allen Say, makes the trip for his grandfather, traveling to San Francisco when he is 16. Say makes a perceptive contribution to a multicultural America in this outstanding effort.

Sleator, William. *Oddballs*. New York: Dutton, 1993. (Realistic Fiction/Autobiographical)

Sleator and his sister, Vicky, are the older of four siblings, and they thoroughly enjoy their two younger brothers, Danny and the unnamed new baby, who eventually becomes known as Newby. They don't particularly enjoy the added chore of changing diapers, though, and their favorite game, which has to do with BMs, loses its charm when reality interferes with the imagination. Sleator's somewhat skewed viewpoint of his childhood and of his rather unorthodox parents and siblings creates the humor in this story of a family who really care a great deal about each other, even though their need for experimentation more often than not creates chaos, for instance, when Danny's friend Jack attempts to hypnotize younger brother Tycho and when Danny conducts a Halloween seance.

Stine, R. L. *The Ghost Next Door*, a Goosebumps book. New York: Scholastic Books, 1993. (Fantasy/Suspense)

Like Nancy Drew and the Hardy Boys, written to fill a void for children in the mystery genre, Stine's lightweight suspense stories appeal to children who can't get enough chills and thrills. However, there is a lack of any real depth in these stories, with each book a series of passages promising future scenes of horror that never quite materialize. The concern is in the lack of proper values expressed by some of the characters. In *The Ghost Next Door*, the boy next door and two of his friends steal from a local shop, show disrespect for neighbors, and set a fire in a house, yet they seem to show no remorse for their actions.

Temple, Frances. *Grab Hands and Run*, a Richard Jackson book. New York: Orchard Books, 1993. (Realistic Fiction/El Salvador)

El Salvador is under control of a military regime, and resistance to that regime means death. Young men are forced to go into the military, even at the age of 12, Felipe's age. Felipe's father, Jacinto, disappears. His abandoned motorcycle is found at the edge of town, and Felipe tells the story of how he, his mother Paloma, and his sister Romy, leave El Salvador and become refugees, traveling to Canada and safety, hoping that Jacinto will be able to keep his promise and meet them there. Jacinto had told them: "If they come for me, grab hands and run . . . all the way to Canada. If I ever get free, I'll come there." The family has no papers, and every border crossing can mean their arrest and return to El Salvador, where they would probably be killed. Temple makes no compromises in this stark portrait of what it is like to live with danger, and her story allows the American reader, who has always taken democracy for granted, to better understand the advantages of growing up in a free country.

Archer, Jules. *Rage in the Streets: Mob Violence in America*, illtd. Lydia J. Hess. San Diego: Harcourt, 1994. (Informational/Social Adjustment).

Archer shares the discontent of Americans who have been denied a chance to share the American dream because of long-standing racial prejudice and lack of opportunity in a country that tends to gloss over underlying structural weakness until the "bridge" falls down. The book goes back to the Shays Rebellion and follows through to the most recent riots in Watts and the inner-city turmoil that is accelerating throughout the United States.

Bachrach, Susan D. *Tell Them We Remember: The Story of the Holocaust*. New York: Little, Brown, 1994. (Informational/Historical/World War II/Holocaust)

The United States Holocaust Memorial Museum that opened in Washington, D.C., in 1994 instituted the writing of this book. By reproducing materials from the museum's extensive collection, the story of the Holocaust, a word that originally meant dying by fire and has come to mean the slaughter of human beings on a large scale, is told. The text focuses on the children and is divided into paragraphs telling about individual children, with a real I.D. photograph of each child prefacing the section that speaks of that child. The chronological development of Nazi persecution of Jews and others considered inferior is told by the few survivors and shows the gradual breakup of families, the mass executions in the camps, and the inhuman treatment of children as well as adults. It becomes a most fitting memorial to the millions who died.

Buckley (Simkewicz), Helen. *Grandmother and I*, illtd. Jan Ormerod. New York: Lothrop, Lee and Shepard, 1994. Also, *Grandfather and I*, illtd. Jan Ormerod (New York: Lothrop, Lee and Shepard, 1994). Reprints of 1961 and 1959 Lothrop editions. (Picture Book/Social Relationship/Aging)

With the original, somewhat stereotypical illustrations of Paul Galdone replaced in both books with Ormerod's portraits of an appealing black grandchild and the child's grandparents, Buckley's simple essay text about the relationship between young and old takes on new charm.

Gilden, Mel. *The Pumpkins of Time*. San Diego: Browndeer Press, 1994. (Fantasy/Science Fiction/Humor)

Myron's Uncle Hugo is experimenting with time, trying to discover a way to keep food fresh indefinitely by not allowing time to make it spoil. Myron and his friend Princess become involved in his experiments and find themselves a presence in the past, the present, and the future, all at the same time. The arrival out of nowhere of a stray cat in their lives as well as two villains, one called A.L. and the other Marsy Batter, who arrives in a pumpkin, complicates the situation. This unusual adventure transcends ordinary space travel and aliens in this last decade of the century in which everything seems possible.

Goodman, Joan Elizabeth. *Songs From Home*. San Diego: Harcourt, 1994. (Realistic Fiction/Social Adjustment/Italy)

Eleven-year-old Anna and her father have been wandering through Europe since she was two or three years old. The two of them sing in the streets for money, and they have been in Rome longer than anywhere else. But America is really their home, even though Anna knows very little about it. Her father had left America with her after her mother died. When Anna meets a woman from her father's hometown who knew her mother and father well and tells Anna all about America, Anna decides it's time to go home.

Hoff, Syd. *Duncan the Dancing Duck*. New York: Clarion, 1994. (Fantasy/Picture Book/Animal)

Duncan loves to dance, and because he is so good, the farmer and his wife take him to town. He appears on stage, then on TV, and finally becomes famous throughout the land. But he is so popular people want him to dance and dance. Duncan becomes so tired of dancing he just wants to go back home to his pond and swim. And that's exactly what he does, with just one more dance for his mother.

Krull, Kathleen. *Lives of the Writers: Comedies, Tragedies (and What the Neighbors Thought)*, illtd. Kathryn Hewitt. San Diego: Harcourt, 1994. (Informational/Biographical)

From Shakespeare to Langston Hughes, Mark Twain to E. B. White, and on to 16 more poets, biographers, and novelists who have carved a niche in literary history, this collection offers anecdotes and personal revelations that make the famous more human. Mark Twain's first story was published under the name of "Mike Swain," because the editor couldn't read his writing; Murasaki Shikibu was a female novelist in 10th-century Japan and wrote what is sometimes considered the world's oldest novel, *Tale of Genji*; Emily Dickinson's favorite game was hide-and-seek; and at the age of 29, Jack London was the most highly paid author in America. That's only a sampling of what Krull's book offers, embellished by Hewitt's portraits.

Lasky, Kathryn. *Cloud Eyes*, illtd. Barry Moser. San Diego: Harcourt, 1994. (Folk/Myth/Original/Picture Book)

In an original story set in a time when people and animals shared equal status, Lasky introduces Cloud Eyes, a dreamer who can read the clouds. Cloud Eyes manages, with the help of Great-grandmother Bee, to keep the bears from eating all the honey and destroying the bee trees as they have done before. The resulting agreement between the species means enough honey for all. Moser's dramatic black-and-white drawings bring the story to life.

MacDonald, Suse. *Sea Shapes*. San Diego: Harcourt, 1994. (Picture Book/Concept)

In shades of purple and gold and orange and green, MacDonald's paper cutouts of sea creatures look as if they can be lifted off the page. On the left side of a double spread, a star begins to evolve until at the right it's a starfish under the sea. A circle becomes the eye of a whale, the semicircle a jellyfish trailing tentacles, and the square is angled to become a skate. At the end of the book, short descriptions of each sea creature are accompanied by a small illustration, a practice that began with Lois Ehlert's *Eating the Alphabet* (1989).

Maguire, Gregory. *Seven Spiders Spinning*, illtd. Dirk Zimmer. New York: Clarion Books, 1994. (Realistic Fiction/Humor)

Here is a story that starts out with subtle humor: "Countless thousands of years ago, give or take a couple of days, a mama spider laid some eggs. She admired them and she rested a little. Then she killed the papa spider, to whom she wasn't deeply attached, and sat down to a satisfying meal." But as the story continues, the suspense grows until, at the end of the book, the reader is not quite sure whether this story will have a happy ending or not. Seven motherless spiders, newly hatched, become frozen during the ice age and thaw out several thousand years later in the back of a truck while being transported to a science lab at Harvard University. They get bounced from the truck, find a grove of trees in which to make their webs and discover seven little girls having a club meeting, and each adopts a girl as a mother figure. But these spiders are an ancient breed of tarantula, and unlike the modern tarantula they happen to have a fatally poisonous bite. As the girls plan a Halloween skit guaranteed to win over the skit planned by the boys, the spiders one by one find their way to the school, and the plot thickens, building to a dreaded climax.

Mathews, Sally Schofer. *The Sad Night: The Story of an Aztec Victory and a Spanish Loss*. New York: Clarion, 1994. (Picture Book/Mexico/Aztec)

With illustrations based on a limited collection of authentic Aztec codex art, Mathews, who studied for her master's degree in San

Miguel de Allende, Mexico, makes history accessible. This story tells of Cortés's arrival in Mexico and the loss of many Spanish lives during their escape from Tenochtitlán, now called Mexico City, in the last battle the Aztecs would win before the Spanish conquest of Mexico.

Pinkney, Andrea Davis. *Dear Benjamin Banneker*, illtd. Brian Pinkney. San Diego: Harcourt, 1994. (Picture Book/Biography/Black History)

Not all black people in 18th-century America were doomed to be slaves. Benjamin Banneker's father was able to gain his freedom before 1731 when Benjamin was born, and his mother grew up free. When Benjamin grew up, he took over his father's tobacco farm but at night studied astronomy; the almanac he created was the first compiled by a black man. It bothered him that so many of his race were not only slaves but were also not allowed to be literate; he wrote to Thomas Jefferson, who owned slaves but had signed a declaration that all men were created equal, in protest of slavery and enclosed a copy of his almanac. Jefferson wrote back, agreeing that blacks should be given the opportunity to learn. In 1791 Banneker was hired by President Washington and Secretary of State Jefferson to help survey the capital, later named Washington, D.C. Brian Pinkney's illustrations on scratchboard are richly unique.

Schertle, Alice. *How Now, Brown Cow?*, illtd. Amanda Schaffer. San Diego: Harcourt, 1994. (Picture Book/Poetry)

"How/now,/brown/cow?/How's it going?/Just stopped by—/heard you lowing . . ./Lovely view/Lovely weather./Good to have/this moo /together." And so it goes, with this charming collection of verses all about cows of different sizes, colors, and dispositions, written in a warm and funny style and with the subject animals affectionately portrayed in Schaffer's paintings.

Yolen, Jane. *Animal Fare*, illtd. Jane Street. San Diego: Harcourt, 1994. (Poetry/Nonsense)

With bumple bees and telephants, grizzly bares and blimpanzees, Yolen celebrates language and the way in which it can be manipulated to create new, bizarre creatures, and Jane Street reinvents the nonsensical menagerie in colorful new shapes and designs:

The anteloops go round and round
The prairie paths without a sound.
For their beginnings can't be found
and neither can their ends.

Hinojosa, Maria. *Crews: Gang Members Talk to Maria Hinojosa*, photog. German Perez. San Diego: Harcourt, 1995. (Informational/Social Adjustment/Urban)

Because Hinojosa is Latina and feels at ease with the young men and women she interviews in this book, the result, based on a story she did for National Public Radio, is a compassionate exploration of the children in America's cities. With violence a major concern in the nation, Hinojosa addresses the anger felt by most of these teenagers and their search for someone who cares. By joining a crew, a neighborhood gang, they feel they belong somewhere. In many cases, there is violence within the family and either too much punishment by abusive parents or no punishment at all by apathetic parents. Their stories are told in their own voices as Hinojosa interviews them in their quest for identity and meaning in their lives.

NOTES

1. Edmund H. Harvey Jr. *Our Glorious Century*, p. 501.
2. A curriculum in which trade books are used in classrooms to make learning interesting and memorable throughout the curriculum in reading, social studies and history, science, health, and math.
3. Herbert N. Foerstel. *Banned in the U.S.A.*, p. xviii.
4. As listed by Laurie Goodstein in an article originally from *The Washington Post* that appeared in *The Berkshire Eagle*, October 31, 1994, Section C8.
5. Christopher Lofting. Afterword to Hugh Lofting's *The Story of Doctor Dolittle*. New York: Dell Yearling Centenary Edition, 1988, p. 152.
6. T. Eagan. *The New York Times*, April 21, 1992.
7. Ted Perry. From "Home," a 1972 ABC television film about ecology.
8. From notes taken at Society of Children's Book Writers and Illustrators Conference, May 1993, during a speech by a Native American writer and storyteller, Joseph Bruchac, who is a member of the Abenaki Nation of Vermont.

APPENDIX A: Children's Literature Collections

Universities, Colleges, and Libraries

(Entries are in alphabetical order by state)

Bancroft Library
University of California at Berkeley
Berkeley, CA 94720

Mary Schofield Collection
Cecil H. Green Library
Stanford University
Stanford, CA 94305

The Epstein Collection
University of Colorado Libraries
Boulder, CO 80302

The Carolyn Sherwin Bailey Historical Collection of Children's Books
Southern Connecticut State College
New Haven, CT 06515

Juvenile Collection
Library of Congress
Rare Book Division
Washington, DC 20540

The Lois Lenski Collection
Robert Manning Strozier Library
Florida State University
Tallahassee, FL 32306

The Ethelina Castle Collection
University of Hawaii
Honolulu, HI 96822

Center for Research Libraries
6050 S. Kenwood Avenue
Chicago, IL 60637

Historical Children's Book Collection
Southern Illinois University
Carbondale, IL 62901

May Massee Collection
William Allen White Library
Kansas State University
Emporia, KS 66801

Alice M. Jordan Collection
Research Library
Boston Public Library
Copley Square
Boston, MA 02117

Knapp Collection
Simmons College
300 The Fenway
Boston, MA 02115

The Ruth Hill Viguers Memorial Collection
Wellesley Free Library
Wellesley, MA 02181

Kerlan Collection
University of Minnesota
Walter Library
Minneapolis, MN 55455

de Grummond Children's Literature Collection
University of Southern Mississippi
Southern Station, Box 5148
Hattiesburg, MS 39406

Bank Street College of Education Library
610 West 112th Street
New York, NY 10025

Children's Book Council Library
175 Fifth Avenue
New York, NY 10010

Donnell Library Center
New York Public Library
20 West 53rd Street
New York, NY 10027

The Lois Lenski Collection
Walter Clinton Jackson Library
University of North Carolina
Greensboro, NC 27412

Edgar W. and Faith King Juvenile Collection
King Library
Miami University
Oxford, OH 45056

Sendak Collection
Rosenback Museum and Library
2010 Delancey Place
Philadelphia, PA 19103

Carnegie Library of Pittsburgh
440 Forbes Avenue
Pittsburgh, PA 15213

The Edith Wetmore Collection of Books for Children
Providence Public Library
Providence, RI 02903

Historical Children's Literature Collection
Suzillo Library
University of Washington
Seattle, WA 98195

APPENDIX B: Newbery and Caldecott Awards

Chronological List of Winners and Runners-Up

Newbery Award Books

1922

The Story of Mankind by Hendrik Willem Van Loon

HONOR BOOKS

The Great Quest by Charles Boardman Hawes

Cedric the Forester by Bernard G. Marshall

The Old Tobacco Shop by William Bowen

The Golden Fleece and the Heroes Who Lived Before Achilles by Padraic Colum

Windy Hill by Cornelia Meigs

1923

The Voyages of Doctor Dolittle by Hugh Lofting

(NO RECORD OF HONOR BOOKS)

1924

The Dark Frigate by Charles Boardman Hawes

(NO RECORD OF HONOR BOOKS)

1925

Tales from Silver Lands by Charles J. Finger

HONOR BOOKS

Nicolas by Anne Carroll Moore
Dream Coach by Anne and Dillwyn Parish

1926

Shen of the Sea by Arthur Bowie Chrisman; illustrated by Else Hasselriis

HONOR BOOK

The Voyagers by Padraic Colum

1927

Smoky, the Cowhorse by Will James

(NO RECORD OF HONOR BOOKS)

1928

Gay-Neck, the Story of a Pigeon by Dhan Gopal Mukerji; illustrated by Boris Artzybasheff

HONOR BOOKS

The Wonder Smith and His Son by Ella Young
Downright Dencey by Caroline Dale Snedeker

1929

The Trumpeter of Krakow by Eric P. Kelly; illustrated by Angela Pruszynska

HONOR BOOKS

The Pigtail of Ah Lee Ben Loo by John Bennett
Millions of Cats by Wanda Gág
The Boy Who Was by Grace T. Hallock
Clearing Weather by Cornelia Meigs

The Runaway Papoose by Grace P. Moon
Tod of the Fens by Eleanor Whitney

1930

Hitty: Her First Hundred Years by Rachel Field; illustrated by Dorothy P. Lathrop

HONOR BOOKS

The Tangle-Coated Horse and Other Tales: Episodes from the Fionn Saga by Ella Young; illustrated by Vera Brock
Vaino: A Boy of New Finland by Julia Davis Adams; illustrated by Lempi Ostman
Pran of Albania by Elizabeth C. Miller
The Jumping-Off Place by Marion Hurd McNeely
A Daughter of the Seine by Jeanette Eaton

1931

The Cat Who Went to Heaven by Elizabeth Coatsworth; illustrated by Lynd Ward

HONOR BOOKS

Floating Island by Anne Parrish
The Dark Star of Itza by Alida Malkus
Queer Person by Ralph Hubbard
Mountains Are Free by Julia Davis Adams
Spice and the Devil's Cave by Agnes D. Hewes
Meggy McIntosh by Elizabeth Janet Gray
Garram the Hunter: A Boy of the Hill Tribes by Herbert Best; illustrated by Allena Best (Erik Berry)
Ood-Le-Uk, the Wanderer by Alice Lide and Margaret Johansen; illustrated by Raymond Lufkin

1932

Waterless Mountain by Laura Adams Armer; illustrated by Sidney Armer and Laura Adams Armer

HONOR BOOKS

The Fairy Circus by Dorothy Lathrop
Calico Bush by Rachel Field
Boy of the South Seas by Eunice Tietjens
Out of the Flame by Eloise Lownsbery

Jane's Island by Marjorie Hill Alee
The Truce of the Wolf and Other Tales of Old Italy by Mary Gould Davis

1933

Young Fu of the Upper Yangtze by Elizabeth Foresman Lewis; illustrated by Kurt Wiese

HONOR BOOKS

Swift Rivers by Cornelia Meigs
The Railroad to Freedom by Hildegarde Swift
Children of the Soil by Nora Burglon

1934

Invincible Louisa: The Story of the Author of "Little Women" by Cornelia Meigs

HONOR BOOKS

The Forgotten Daughter by Caroline Dale Snedeker
Swords of Steel by Elsie Singmaster
ABC Bunny by Wanda Gág
Winged Girl of Knossos by Erik Berry
New Land by Sarah L. Schmidt
The Apprentice of Florence by Anne Kyle
The Big Tree of Bunlahy: Stories of My Own Country by Padraic Colum; illustrated by Jack Yeats
Glory of the Seas by Agnes D. Hewes; illustrated by N. C. Wyeth

1935

Dobry by Monica Shannon; illustrated by Atanas Katchamakoff

HONOR BOOKS

The Pageant of Chinese History by Elizabeth Seeger
Davy Crockett by Constance Rourke
A Day on Skates: The Story of a Dutch Picnic by Hilda Van Stockum

1936

Caddie Woodlawn by Carol Ryrie Brink; illustrated by Kate Seredy

HONOR BOOKS

Honk: The Moose by Phil Stong; illustrated by Kurt Wiese

The Good Master by Kate Seredy
Young Walter Scott by Elizabeth Janet Gray
All Sail Set by Armstrong Sperry

1937

Roller Skates by Ruth Sawyer; illustrated by Valenti Angelo

HONOR BOOKS

Phoebe Fairchild: Her Book by Lois Lenski
Whistler's Van by Idwal Jones
The Golden Basket by Ludwig Bemelmans
Winterbound by Margery Bianco
Audubon by Constance Rourke
The Codfish Musket by Agnes D. Hewes

1938

The White Stag by Kate Seredy

HONOR BOOKS

Bright Island by Mabel L. Robinson
Pecos Bill by James Cloyd Bowman
On the Banks of Plum Creek by Laura Ingalls Wilder

1939

Thimble Summer by Elizabeth Enright

HONOR BOOKS

Leader by Destiny: George Washington, Man and Patriot by Jeanette Eaton
Penn by Elizabeth Janet Gray
Nino by Valenti Angelo
"Hello, the Boat!" by Phyllis Crawford
Mr. Popper's Penguins by Richard and Florence Atwater

1940

Daniel Boone by James H. Daugherty

HONOR BOOKS

The Singing Tree by Kate Seredy
Runner of the Mountain Tops by Mabel L. Robinson
By the Shores of Silver Lake by Laura Ingalls Wilder

Boy With a Pack by Stephen W. Meader

1941

Call It Courage by Armstrong Sperry

HONOR BOOKS

Blue Willow by Doris Gates
Young Mac of Fort Vancouver by Mary Jane Carr
The Long Winter by Laura Ingalls Wilder
Nansen by Anna Gertrude Hall

1942

The Matchlock Gun by Walter D. Edmonds; illustrated by Paul Lantz

HONOR BOOKS

Little Town on the Prairie by Laura Ingalls Wilder
George Washington's World by Genevieve Foster
Indian Captive: The Story of Mary Jemison by Lois Lenski
Down Ryton Water by Eva Roe Gaggin; illustrated by Elmer Hader

1943

Adam of the Road by Elizabeth Janet Gray; illustrated by Robert Lawson

HONOR BOOKS

The Middle Moffat by Eleanor Estes
"Have You Seen Tom Thumb?" by Mabel Leigh Hunt

1944

Johnny Tremain by Esther Forbes; illustrated by Lynd Ward

HONOR BOOKS

These Happy Golden Years by Laura Ingalls Wilder
Fog Magic by Julia L. Sauer
Rufus M. by Eleanor Estes
Mountain Born by Elizabeth Yates

1945

Rabbit Hill by Robert Lawson

HONOR BOOKS

The Hundred Dresses by Eleanor Estes

The Silver Pencil by Alice Dalgliesh

Abraham Lincoln's World by Genevieve Foster

Lone Journey: The Life of Roger Williams by Jeanette Eaton; illustrated by Woodi Ishmael

1946

Strawberry Girl by Lois Lenski

HONOR BOOKS

Justin Morgan Had a Horse by Marguerite Henry

The Moved-Outers by Florence Crannell Means

Bhimsa, the Dancing Bear by Christine Weston

New Found World by Katherine B. Shippen

1947

Miss Hickory by Carolyn Sherwin Bailey

HONOR BOOKS

The Wonderful Year by Nancy Barnes

The Big Tree by Mary and Conrad Buff

The Heavenly Tenants by William Maxwell

The Avion My Uncle Flew by Cyrus Fisher

The Hidden Treasure of Glaston by Eleanore M. Jewett

1948

The Twenty-One Balloons by William Pene du Bois

HONOR BOOKS

Pancake-Paris by Claire Huchet Bishop

Li Lun, Lad of Courage by Carolyn Treffinger

The Quaint and Curious Quest of Johnny Longfoot, the Shoe-King's Son by Catherine Besterman

The Cow-Tail Switch, And Other West African Stories by Harold Courlander and George Herzog

Misty of Chincoteague by Marguerite Henry; illustrated by Wesley Dennis

1949

King of the Wind by Marguerite Henry; illustrated by Wesley Dennis

HONOR BOOKS

Seabird by Holling Clancy Holling

Daughter of the Mountains by Louise Rankin

My Father's Dragon by Ruth S. Gannett

Story of the Negro by Arna Bontemps

1950

The Door in the Wall by Marguerite de Angeli

HONOR BOOKS

Tree of Freedom by Rebecca Caudill

The Blue Cat of Castle Town by Catherine Coblentz

Kildee House by Rutherford Montgomery

George Washington by Genevieve Foster

Song of the Pines by Walter and Marion Havighurst

1951

Amos Fortune, Free Man by Elizabeth Yates; illustrated by Nora Unwin

HONOR BOOKS

Better Known as Johnny Appleseed by Mabel Leigh Hunt

Ghandi, Fighter Without a Sword by Jeanette Eaton

Abraham Lincoln, Friend of the People by Clara I. Judson

The Story of Appleby Capple by Anne Parrish

1952

Ginger Pye by Eleanor Estes

HONOR BOOKS

Americans Before Columbus by Elizabeth Chesley Baity

Minn of the Mississippi by Holling Clancy Holling

The Defender by Nicholas Kalashnikoff

The Light at Tern Rock by Julia L. Sauer

The Apple and the Arrow by Mary and Conrad Buff

1953

Secret of the Andes by Ann Nolan Clark; illustrated by Jean Charlot

HONOR BOOKS

Charlotte's Web by E. B. White; illustrated by Garth Williams
Moccasin Trail by Eloise J. McGraw
Red Sails to Capri by Ann Weil
The Bears on Hemlock Mountain by Alice Dalgliesh
Birthdays of Freedom, vol. 1 by Genevieve Foster

1954

And Now Miguel by Joseph Krumgold; illustrated by Jean Charlot

HONOR BOOKS

All Alone by Claire Hutchet Bishop
Shadrach by Meindert DeJong
Hurry Home, Candy by Meindert DeJong
Theodore Roosevelt, Fighting Patriot by Clara I. Judson
Magic Maize by Mary and Conrad Buff

1955

The Wheel on the School by Meindert DeJong; illustrated by Maurice Sendak

HONOR BOOKS

The Courage of Sarah Noble by Alice Dalgliesh
Banner in the Sky by James Ramsey Ullman

1956

Carry On, Mr. Bowditch by Jean Lee Latham

HONOR BOOKS

The Golden Name Day by Jennie D. Lindquist
The Secret River by Marjorie Kinnan Rawlings
Men, Microscopes and Living Things by Katherine B. Shippen

1957

Miracles on Maple Street by Virginia Sorensen; illustrated by Beth and Joe Krush

HONOR BOOKS

Old Yeller by Fred Gipson
The House of Sixty Fathers by Meindert DeJong
Mr. Justice Holmes by Clara I. Judson
The Corn Grows Ripe by Dorothy Rhoads
The Black Fox of Lorne by Marguerite de Angeli

1958

Rifles for Watie by Harold Keith; illustrated by Peter Burchard

HONOR BOOKS

The Horsecatcher by Mari Sandoz
Gone-Away Lake by Elizabeth Enright
The Great Wheel by Robert Lawson
Tom Paine, Freedom's Apostle by Leo Gurko

1959

The Witch of Blackbird Pond by Elizabeth George Speare

HONOR BOOKS

The Family Under the Bridge by Natalie S. Carlson
Along Came a Dog by Meindert DeJong
Chucaro: Wild Pony of the Pampa by Francis Kalnay
The Perilous Road by William O. Steele

1960

Onion John by Joseph Krumgold; illustrated by Symeon Shimin

HONOR BOOKS

My Side of the Mountain by Jean George
America Is Born by Gerald Johnson
The Gammage Cup by Carol Kendall

1961

Island of the Blue Dolphins by Scott O'Dell

HONOR BOOKS

America Moves Forward by Gerald W. Johnson
Old Ramon by Jack Schaeffer
Cricket in Times Square by George Selden

1962

The Bronze Bow by Elizabeth George Speare

HONOR BOOKS

Frontier Living by Edwin Tunis

The Golden Goblet by Eloise Jarvis McGraw

Belling the Tiger by Mary Stolz

1963

A Wrinkle in Time by Madeleine L'Engle

HONOR BOOKS

Thistle and Thyme: Tales and Legends from Scotland by Sorche Nic Leodhas

Men of Athens by Olivia Coolidge

1964

It's Like This, Cat by Emily Cheney Neville

HONOR BOOKS

Rascal by Sterling North

The Loner by Esther Wier

1965

Shadow of a Bull by Maia Wojciechowska

HONOR BOOK

Across Five Aprils by Irene Hunt

1966

I, Juan de Pareja by Elizabeth Borton de Trevino

HONOR BOOKS

The Black Cauldron by Lloyd Alexander

The Animal Family by Randall Jarrell; illustrated by Maurice Sendak

The Noonday Friends by Mary Stolz

1967

Up a Road Slowly by Irene Hunt

HONOR BOOKS

The King's Fifth by Scott O'Dell

Zlateh the Goat and Other Stories by Isaac Bashevis Singer

The Jazz Man by Mary H. Weik

1968

From the Mixed-Up Files of Mrs. Basil E. Frankweiler by E. L. Konigsburg

HONOR BOOKS

Jennifer, Hecate, Macbeth, William McKinley and Me, Elizabeth by E. L. Konigsburg

The Black Pearl by Scott O'Dell

The Fearsome Inn by Isaac Bashevis Singer

The Egypt Game by Zilpha Keatley Snyder

1969

The High King by Lloyd Alexander

HONOR BOOKS

To Be a Slave by Julius Lester

When Shlemiel Went to Warsaw and Other Stories by Isaac Bashevis Singer

1970

Sounder by William H. Armstrong

HONOR BOOKS

Our Eddie by Sulamith Ish-Kishor

The Many Ways of Seeing: An Introduction to the Pleasure of Art by Janet Gaylord Moore

Journey Outside by Mary Q. Steele

1971

Summer of the Swans by Betsy Byars

HONOR BOOKS

Kneeknock Rise by Natalie Babbitt

Enchantress from the Stars by Sylvia Louise Engdahl

Sing Down the Moon by Scott O'Dell

1972

Mrs. Frisby and the Rats of NIMH by Robert C. O'Brien

HONOR BOOKS

Incident at Hawk's Hill by Allen W. Eckert
The Planet of Junior Brown by Virginia Hamilton
The Tombs of Atuan by Ursula K. Leguin
Annie and the Old One by Miska Miles; illustrated by Peter Parnall
The Headless Cupid by Zilpha Keatley Snyder

1973

Julie of the Wolves by Jean Craighead George; illustrated by John Schoenherr

HONOR BOOKS

Frog and Toad Together by Arnold Lobel
The Upstairs Room by Joanna Reiss
The Witches of Worm by Zilpha Keatley Snyder

1974

The Slave Dancer by Paula Fox

HONOR BOOK

The Dark Is Rising by Susan Cooper

1975

M.C. Higgins, the Great by Virginia Hamilton

HONOR BOOKS

Figgs and Phantoms by Ellen Raskin
My Brother Sam Is Dead by James Lincoln Collier and Christopher Collier
The Perilous Gard by Elizabeth Marie Pope
Philip Hall Likes Me. I Reckon Maybe by Bette Greene

1976

The Grey King by Susan Cooper

HONOR BOOKS

The Hundred Penny Box by Sharon Bell Mathis
Dragonwings by Lawrence Yep

1977

Roll of Thunder, Hear My Cry by Mildred D. Taylor

HONOR BOOKS

Abel's Island by William Steig

A String in the Harp by Nancy Bond

1978

The Bridge to Terabithia by Katherine Peterson

HONOR BOOKS

Anpao: An American Indian Odyssey by Jamake Highwater

Ramona and Her Father by Beverly Cleary

1979

The Westing Game by Ellen Raskin

HONOR BOOK

The Great Gilly Hopkins by Katherine Paterson

1980

A Gathering of Days: A New England Girl's Journal, 1830–32 by Joan Blos

HONOR BOOK

The Road from Home: A Story of an Armenian Girl by David Kherdian

1981

Jacob Have I Loved by Katherine Paterson

HONOR BOOKS

The Fledgling by Jane Langton

A Ring of Endless Light by Madeline L'Engle

1982

A Vist to William Blake's Inn: Poems for Innocent and Experienced Travelers by Nancy Willard; illustrated by Alice and Martin Provensen

HONOR BOOKS

Ramona Quimby, Age 8 by Beverly Cleary
Upon the Head of a Goat: A Childhood in Hungary by Aranka Siegal

1983

Dicey's Song by Cynthia Voigt

HONOR BOOKS

The Blue Sword by Robin McKinley
Dr. DeSoto by William Steig
Graven Images by Paul Fleischman
Homesick: My Own Story by Jean Fritz
Sweet Whispers, Brother Rush by Virginia Hamilton

1984

Dear Mr. Henshaw by Beverly Cleary

HONOR BOOKS

The Sign of the Beaver by Elizabeth George Speare
A Solitary Blue by Cynthia Voigt
Sugaring Time by Katherine Lasky; photographs by Christopher Knight
The Wish Giver by Bill Brittain

1985

The Hero and the Crown by Robin McKinley

HONOR BOOKS

Like Jake and Me by Mavis Jukes; illustrated by Lloyd Bloom
The Moves Make the Man by Bruce Brooks
One-Eyed Cat by Paula Fox

1986

Sarah, Plain and Tall by Patricia MacLachlan

HONOR BOOKS

Commodore Perry in the Land of the Shogun by Rhoda Blumberg
Dogsong by Gary Paulsen

1987

The Whipping Boy by Sid Fleischman

HONOR BOOKS

On My Honor by Marion Dane Bauer

Volcano: The Eruption and Healing of Mount St. Helens by Patricia Lauber

A Fine White Dust by Cynthia Rylant

1988

Lincoln: A Photobiography by Russell Freedman

HONOR BOOKS

After the Rain by Norma Fox Mazer

Hatchet by Gary Paulsen

1989

Joyful Noise: Poems for Two Voices by Paul Fleischman

HONOR BOOKS

In the Beginning: Creation Stories from Around the World by Virginia Hamilton; illustrated by Barry Moser

Scorpions by Walter Dean Myers

1990

Number the Stars by Lois Lowry

HONOR BOOKS

Afternoon of the Elves by Janet Taylor Lisle

Shabanu, Daughter of the Wind by Suzanne Fisher Staples

The Winter Room by Gary Paulsen

1991

Maniac Magee by Jerry Spinelli

HONOR BOOK

The True Confessions of Charlotte Doyle by Avi

1992

Shiloh by Phyllis Reynolds Naylor

HONOR BOOKS

Nothing But the Truth by Avi

The Wright Brothers: How They Invented the Airplane by Russell Freedman

1993

Missing May by Cynthia Rylant

HONOR BOOKS

Somewhere in the Darkness by Walter Dean Myers

What Hearts by Bruce Brooks

The Dark-Thirty: Southern Tales of the Supernatural by Patricia C. McKissack; illustrated by Brian Pinkney

1994

The Giver by Lois Lowry

HONOR BOOKS

Crazy Lady by Jane Leslie Conley

Eleanor Roosevelt: A Life of Discovery by Russell Freedman

Dragon's Gate by Lawrence Yep

1995

Walk Two Moons by Sharon Creech

HONOR BOOKS

Catherine, Called Birdy by Karen Cushman

The Ear, the Eye and the Arm by Nancy Farmer

Caldecott Award Books

1938

Animals of the Bible; edited by Helen Dean Fish; illustrated by Dorothy P. Lathrop

HONOR BOOKS

Seven Simeons: A Russian Tale by Boris Artzybasheff

Four and Twenty Blackbirds; edited by Helen Dean Fish; illustrated by Robert Lawson

1939

Mei Lei by Thomas Handforth

HONOR BOOKS

The Forest Pool by Laura Adams Armer
Wee Gillis by Munro Leaf; illustrated by Robert Lawson
Snow White and the Seven Dwarfs; translated and illustrated by Wanda Gág
Barkis by Clare Turlay Newberry
Andy and the Lion by James Daugherty

1940

Abraham Lincoln by Ingri d'Aulaire and Edgar Parin d'Aulaire

HONOR BOOKS

Cock-a-Doodle-Doo by Berta and Elmer Hader
Madeline by Ludwig Bemelmans
The Ageless Story by Lauren Ford

1941

They Were Strong and Good by Robert Lawson

HONOR BOOK

April's Kittens by Clare Turlay Newberry

1942

Make Way for Ducklings by Robert McCloskey

HONOR BOOKS

An American ABC by Maud and Miska Petersham
In My Mother's House by Ann Nolan Clark; illustrated by Velino Herrera
Paddle-to-the-Sea by Holling C. Holling
Nothing at All by Wanda Gág

1943

The Little House by Virginia Lee Burton

HONOR BOOKS

Dash and Dart by Mary and Conrad Buff
Marshmallow by Clare Turlay Newberry

1944

Many Moons by James Thurber

HONOR BOOKS

Small Rain: Verses From the Bible; edited by Jessie Orton Jones; illustrated by Elizabeth Orton Jones

Pierre Pigeon by Lee Kingman; illustrated by Arnold Edwin Bare

The Mighty Hunter by Berta and Elmer Hader

A Child's Good Night Book by Margaret Wise Brown; illustrated by Remy Charlip

Good Luck Horse by Chih-Yi Chan; illustrated by Plato Chan

1945

Prayer for a Child by Rachel Field; illustrated by Elizabeth Orton Jones

HONOR BOOKS

Mother Goose: Seventy-Seven Verses with Pictures; illustrated by Tasha Tudor

In the Forest by Marie Hall Ets

Yonie Wondernose by Marguerite de Angeli

The Christmas Anna Angel by Ruth Sawyer; illustrated by Kate Seredy

1946

The Rooster Crows; edited and illustrated by Maud and Miska Petersham

HONOR BOOKS

Little Lost Lamb by Golden MacDonald (pseudonym of Margaret Wise Brown); illustrated by Leondard Weisgard

Sing Mother Goose by Opal Wheeler; illustrated by Marjorie Torrey

My Mother Is the Most Beautiful Woman in the World by Becky Reyher; illustrated by Ruth Gannett

You Can Write Chinese by Kurt Wiese

1947

The Little Island by Golden MacDonald; illustrated by Leonard Wiesgard

HONOR BOOKS

Rain Drop Splash by Alvin Tresselt; illustrated by Leonard Wiesgard

Boats on the River by Marjorie Flack; illustrated by Jay Hyde Barnum

Timothy Turtle by Al Graham; illustrated by Tony Palazzo

Pedro, the Angel of Olvera Street by Leo Politi

Sing in Praise: A Collection of Best Loved Hymns by Opal Wheeler; illustrated by Marjorie Torrey

1948

White Snow, Bright Snow by Alvin Tresselt; illustrated by Roger Duvoisin

HONOR BOOKS

Stone Soup: An Old Tale by Marcia Brown

McElligot's Pool by Dr. Seuss (pseudonym of Theodor Seuss Geisel)

Bambino the Clown by George Schreiber

Roger and the Fox by Lavinia Davis; illustrated by Hildegard Woodward

Song of Robin Hood; edited by Ann Malcolmson; illustrated by Virginia Lee Burton

1949

The Big Snow by Berta and Elmer Hader

HONOR BOOKS

Blueberries for Sal by Robert McCloskey

All Around Town by Phyllis McGinley; illustrated by Helen Stone

Juanita by Leo Politi

Fish in the Air by Kurt Wiese

1950

Song of the Swallows by Leo Politi

HONOR BOOKS

America's Ethan Allen by Stewart Holbrook; illustrated by Lynd Ward

The Wild Birthday Cake by Lavinia R. Davis; illustrated by Hildegard Woodward

The Happy Day by Ruth Krauss; illustrated by Marc Simont

Henry-Fisherman by Marcia Brown
Bartholomew and the Oobleck by Dr. Seuss (pseudonym of Theodor Seuss Geisel)

1951

The Egg Tree by Katherine Milhous

HONOR BOOKS

Dick Whittington and His Cat; translated and illustrated by Marcia Brown
The Two Reds by Will (pseudonym of William Lipkind) and Nicolas (pseudonym of Nicolas Mordvinoff) (Note: This book suffered from the persecution of anything remotely connected with communism, symbolically identified by the color red.
If I Ran the Zoo by Dr. Seuss (pseudonym of Theodor Seuss Geisel)
T-Bone, the Baby-Sitter by Clare Turlay Newberry
The Most Wonderful Doll in the World by Phyllis McGinley; illustrated by Helen Stone

1952

Finders Keepers by Will (pseudonym of William Lipkind) and Nicolas (pseudonym of Nicolas Mordvinoff)

HONOR BOOKS

Mr. T. Anthony Woo by Marie Hall Ets
Skipper John's Cook by Marcia Brown
All Falling Down by Gene Zion; illustrated by Margaret Bloy Graham
Bear Party by William Pene du Bois
Feather Mountain by Elizabeth Olds

1953

The Biggest Bear by Lynd Ward

HONOR BOOKS

Puss in Boots; translated and illustrated by Marcia Brown
One Morning in Maine by Robert McCloskey
Ape in a Cape: An Alphabet of Odd Animals by Fritz Eichenberg
The Storm Book by Charlotte Zolotow; illustrated by Margaret Bloy Graham
Five Little Monkeys by Juliet Kepes

1954

Madeline's Rescue by Ludwig Bemelmans

HONOR BOOKS

Journey Cake, Ho! by Ruth Sawyer; illustrated by Robert McCloskey

When Will the World Be Mine? by Miriam Schlein; illustrated by Jean Charlot

The Steadfast Tin Soldier by Hans Christian Andersen; translated by M. R. James and illustrated by Marcia Brown

A Very Special House by Ruth Krauss; illustrated by Maurice Sendak

Green Eyes by Abe Birnbaum

1955

Cinderella, or the Little Glass Slipper by Charles Perrault; translated and illustrated by Marcia Brown

HONOR BOOKS

Book of Nursery and Mother Goose Rhymes; edited and illustrated by Marguerite de Angeli

Wheel on the Chimney by Margaret Wise Brown; illustrated by Tibor Gergley

The Thanksgiving Story by Alice Dalgliesh; illustrated by Helen Sewell

1956

Frog Went A-Courtin' by John Langstaff; illustrated by Feodor Rojankovsky

HONOR BOOKS

Play With Me by Marie Hall Ets

Crow Boy by Taro Yashima

1957

A Tree Is Nice by Janice May Udry; illustrated by Marc Simont

HONOR BOOKS

Mr. Penny's Race Horse by Marie Hall Ets

1 Is One by Tasha Tudor

Anatole by Eve Titus; illustrated by Paul Galdone

Gillespie and the Guards by Benjamin Elkin; illustrated by James Daugherty
Lion by William Pene du Bois

1958

Time of Wonder by Robert McCloskey

HONOR BOOKS

Fly High, Fly Low by Don Freeman
Anatole and the Cat by Eve Titus; illustrated by Paul Galdone

1959

Chanticleer and the Fox; adapted from Chaucer and illustrated by Barbara Cooney

HONOR BOOKS

The House That Jack Built ("La Maison Que Jacques a Batie"): A Picture Book in Two Languages by Antonio Frasconi
What Do You Say, Dear? A Book of Manners for All Occasions by Sesyle Joslin; illustrated by Maurice Sendak
Umbrella by Taro Yashima

1960

Nine Days to Christmas by Marie Hall Ets and Aurora Labastida; illustrated by Marie Hall Ets

HONOR BOOKS

Houses from the Sea by Alice E. Goudey; illustrated by Adrienne Adams
The Moon Jumpers by Janice May Udry; illustrated by Maurice Sendak

1961

Baboushka and the Three Kings by Ruth Robbins; illustrated by Nicolas Sidjakov

HONOR BOOK

Inch by Inch by Leo Lionni

1962

Once a Mouse by Marcia Brown

HONOR BOOKS

The Fox Went Out on a Chilly Night: An Old Song by Peter Spier

Little Bear's Visit by Else Minarik; illustrated by Maurice Sendak

The Day We Saw the Sun Come Up by Alice Goudey; illustrated by Adrienne Adams

1963

The Snowy Day by Ezra Jack Keats

HONOR BOOKS

The Sun Is a Golden Earring by Natalia Belting; illustrated by Bernarda Bryson

Mr. Rabbit and the Lovely Present by Charlotte Zolotow; illustrated by Maurice Sendak

1964

Where the Wild Things Are by Maurice Sendak

HONOR BOOKS

Swimmy by Leo Lionni

All in the Morning Early by Sorche Nic Leodhas (pseudonym of Leclaire Alger); illustrated by Evaline Ness

Mother Goose and Nursery Rhymes by Philip Reed

1965

May I Bring a Friend? by Beatrice Schenk de Regniers; illustrated by Beni Montresor

HONOR BOOKS

Rain Makes Applesauce by Julian Scheer; illustrated by Marvin Bileck

The Wave; adapted from Lafcadio Hearn by Margaret Hodges; illustrated by Blair Lent

A Pocketful of Cricket by Rebecca Caudill; illustrated by Evaline Ness

1966

Always Room for One More by Sorche Nic Leodhas (pseudonym of Leclaire Alger); illustrated by Nonny Hogrogian

HONOR BOOKS

Hide and Seek Fog by Alvin Tresselt; illustrated by Roger Duvoisin

Just Me by Marie Hall Ets

Tom Tit Tot by Joseph Jacobs; illustrated by Evaline Ness

1967

Sam, Bangs and Moonshine by Evaline Ness

HONOR BOOK

One Wide River to Cross by Barbara Emberley; illustrated by Ed Emberley

1968

Drummer Hoff by Barbara Emberley; illustrated by Ed Emberley

HONOR BOOKS

Frederick by Leo Leonni

Seashore Story by Taro Yashima

The Emperor and the Kite by Jane Yolen; illustrated by Ed Young

1969

The Fool of the World and the Flying Ship by Arthur Ransome; illustrated by Uri Shulevitz

HONOR BOOK

Why the Sun and the Moon Live in the Sky by Elphinstone Dayrell; illustrated by Blair Lent

1970

Sylvester and the Magic Pebble by William Steig

HONOR BOOKS

Goggles! by Ezra Jack Keats

Alexander and the Wind-Up Mouse by Leo Leonni

Pop Corn and Ma Goodness by Edna Mitchell Preston; illustrated by Robert Andrew Parker

Thy Friend, Obadiah by Brinton Turkle

The Judge: An Untrue Tale by Harve Zemach; illustrated by Margot Zemach

1971

A Story, A Story: An African Tale by Gail E. Haley

HONOR BOOKS

The Angry Moon by William Sleator; illustrated by Blair Lent

Frog and Toad Are Friends by Arnold Lobel

In the Night Kitchen by Maurice Sendak

1972

One Fine Day by Nonny Hogrogian

HONOR BOOKS

If All the Seas Were One Sea by Janina Domanska

Moja Means One: Swahili Counting Book by Muriel Feelings; illustrated by Tom Feelings

Hildilid's Night by Cheli Duran Ryan; illustrated by Arnold Lobel

1973

The Funny Little Woman by Arlene Mosel; illustrated by Blair Lent

HONOR BOOKS

Hosie's Alphabet by Hosea Baskin, Tobias Baskin, and Lisa Baskin; illustrated by Leonard Baskin

When Clay Sings by Byrd Baylor; illustrated by Tom Bahti

Snow-White and the Seven Dwarfs by the Brothers Grimm; translated by Randall Jarrell and illustrated by Nancy Elkholm Burkert

Anansi the Spider: A Tale from the Ashanti by Gerald McDermott

1974

Duffy and the Devil by Harve Zemach; illustrated by Margot Zemach

HONOR BOOKS

Three Jovial Huntsmen by Susan Jeffers

Cathedral: The Story of Its Construction by David Macaulay

1975

Arrow to the Sun: A Pueblo Indian Tale by Gerald McDermott

HONOR BOOK

Jambo Means Hello: Alphabet Book by Muriel Feelings; illustrated by Tom Feelings

1976

Why Mosquitoes Buzz in People's Ears by Verna Aardema; illustrated by Diane and Leo Dillon

HONOR BOOKS

The Desert Is Theirs by Byrd Baylor; illustrated by Peter Parnall

Strega Nona by Tomie de Paola

1977

Ashanti to Zulu: African Traditions by Margaret Musgrove; illustrated by Diane and Leo Dillon

HONOR BOOKS

The Amazing Bone by William Steig

The Contest by Nonny Hogrogian

Fish for Supper by M. B. Goffstein

The Golem: A Jewish Legend by Beverly Brodsky McDermott

Hawk, I'm Your Brother by Byrd Baylor; illustrated by Peter Parnall

1978

Noah's Ark by Peter Spier

HONOR BOOKS

Castle by David Macaulay

It Could Always Be Worse by Margot Zemach

1979

The Girl Who Loved Wild Horses by Paul Goble

HONOR BOOKS

Freight Train by Donald Crews

The Way to Start a Day by Byrd Baylor; illustrated by Peter Parnall

1980

Ox-Cart Man by Donald Hall; illustrated by Barbara Cooney

HONOR BOOKS

Ben's Trumpet by Rachel Isadora

The Treasure by Uri Shulevitz

The Garden of Abdul Gasazi by Chris Van Allsburg

1981

Fables by Arnold Lobel

HONOR BOOKS

The Bremen-Town Musicians by Ilse Plume

The Grey Lady and the Strawberry Snatcher by Molly Bang

Mice Twice by Joseph Low

Truck by Donald Crews

1982

Jumanji by Chris Van Allsburg

HONOR BOOKS

A Visit to William Blake's Inn: Poems for Innocent and Experienced Travelers by Nancy Willard; illustrated by Alice and Martin Provensen

Where the Buffaloes Begin by Olaf Baker; illustrated by Stephen Gammell

On Market Street by Arnold Lobel; illustrated by Anita Lobel

Outside Over There by Maurice Sendak

1983

Shadow by Blaise Cendrars; illustrated by Marcia Brown

HONOR BOOKS

When I Was Young in the Mountains by Cynthia Rylant; illustrated by Diane Goode

A Chair for My Mother by Vera Williams

1984

The Glorious Flight: Across the Channel with Louis Blériot by Alice and Martin Provensen

HONOR BOOKS

Ten, Nine, Eight by Molly Bang

Little Red Riding Hood by the Brothers Grimm; retold and illustrated by Trina Schart Hyman

1985

Saint George and the Dragon by Margaret Hodges; illustrated by Trina Schart Hyman

HONOR BOOKS

Hansel and Gretel by Rika Lesser; illustrated by Paul O. Zelinsky

The Story of the Jumping Mouse by John Steptoe

Have You Seen My Duckling? by Nancy Tafuri

1986

The Polar Express by Chris Van Allsburg

HONOR BOOKS

The Relatives Came by Cynthia Rylant; illustrated by Stephen Gammell

King Bidgood's in the Bathtub by Audrey Wood; illustrated by Don Wood

1987

Hey, Al by Arthur Yorinks; illustrated by Richard Egielski

HONOR BOOKS

The Village of Round and Square Houses by Ann Grifalconi

Alphabatics by Suse MacDonald

Rumpelstiltskin by the Brothers Grimm; retold and illustrated by Paul O. Zelinsky

1988

Owl Moon by Jane Yolen; illustrated by John Schoenherr

HONOR BOOK

Mufaro's Beautiful Daughters by John Steptoe

1989

Song and Dance Man by Karen Ackerman; illustrated by Stephen Gammell

HONOR BOOKS

Free Fall by David Wiesner

Goldilocks and the Three Bears by James Marshall

Mirandy and Brother Wind by Patricia McKissack; illustrated by Jerry Pinkney

The Boy of the Three-Year Nap by Diane Snyder; illustrated by Allen Say

1990

Lon Po Po: A Red-Riding Hood Story from China; translated and illustrated by Ed Young

HONOR BOOKS

Hershel and the Hanukkah Goblins by Eric Kimmel; illustrated by Trina Schart Hyman

The Talking Eggs by Robert D. San Souci; illustrated by Jerry Pinkney

Bill Peet: An Autobiography by Bill Peet

Color Zoo by Lois Ehlert

1991

Black and White by David Macaulay

HONOR BOOKS

Puss 'n Boots by Charles Perrault; illustrated by Fred Marcellino

"More, More, More," Said the Baby: 3 Love Stories by Vera Williams

1992

Tuesday by David Wiesner

HONOR BOOK

Tar Beach by Faith Ringgold

1993

Mirette on the High Wire by Emily Arnold McCully

HONOR BOOKS

The Stinky Cheese Man and Other Fairly Stupid Tales by Jon Scieszka; illustrated by Lane Smith

Seven Blind Mice by Ed Young

Working Cotton by Sherley Anne Williams; illustrated by Carole Byard

1994

Grandfather's Journey by Allen Say

HONOR BOOKS

In the Small, Small Pond by Denise Fleming
Owen by Kevin Henkes
Peppe the Lamplighter by Elisa Bartone; illustrated by Ted Lewin
Raven: A Trickster Tale from the Pacific Northwest by Gerald McDermott
Yo! Yes? by Chris Raschka

1995

Smoky Night by Eve Bunting; illustrated by David Diaz

HONOR BOOKS

Swamp Angel by Anne Isaacs; illustrated by Paul O. Zelinsky
John Henry by Julius Lester; illustrated by Jerry Pinkney
Time Flies by Eric Rohmann

APPENDIX C: Bibliography

Preschool/Nursery

Adoff, Arnold. *Black Is Brown Is Tan*, illtd. Emily Arnold McCully. New York: Harper, 1973; New York: Harper Trophy, 1992. (Poetry/Picture Book/Mixed Cultures)

Anno, Mitsumasa. *Anno's Alphabet*. New York: Crowell, 1975; New York: Harper Trophy, 1988. Also, *Anno's Counting Book* (New York: Crowell, 1975; New York: Harper Trophy, 1986). (Picture Books/Concept/Interactive)

Berger, Barbara Helen. *Grandfather Twilight*. New York: Philomel, 1984. (Picture Book/Concept/Fantasy)

Bianco, Margery Williams. *The Velveteen Rabbit*, illtd. William Nicholson. New York: Doubleday, 1926; San Diego: Harcourt, 1987. (Fantasy/Toys)

Brown, Margaret Wise. *The Noisy Book*, illtd. Leonard Weisgard. New York: Scott, 1939; New York: Harper Trophy, 1993. (Picture Book/Animal/Concept/Series)

———. *The Country Noisy Book*, illtd. Leonard Weisgard. New York: Harper, 1940, 1994. (Picture Book/Animal/Concept/Series)

———. *The Seashore Noisy Book*, illtd. Leonard Weisgard. New York: Scott, 1941; New York: Harper, 1994. (Picture Book/Animal/Concept/Series)

———. *The Indoor Noisy Book*, illtd. Leonard Weisgard. New York: Scott, 1942; New York: Harper, 1994. (Picture Book/Animal/Concept/Series)

———. *The Runaway Bunny*, illtd. Clement Hurd. New York: Harper, 1942, 1977. (Fantasy/Picture Book)

———. *A Child's Good Night Book*, illtd. Remy Charlip. New York: Scott, 1943; New York: Harper, 1992. (Picture Book/Concept)

———. *They All Saw It*, photog. Ylla (pseudonym of Camilla Koffler). New York: Harper, 1944. (Picture Book/Concept/Photographs/Animal)

———. *The Winter Noisy Book*, illtd. Charles Shaw. New York: Scott, 1947; New York: Harper, 1994. (Picture Book/Animal/Concept/Series)

———. *Goodnight Moon*, illtd. Clement Hurd. New York: Harper, 1947, 1977. (Picture Book/Concept)

Buckley (Simkewicz), Helen E. *Grandmother and I*, illtd. Paul Galdone. New York: Lothrop, Lee and Shepard, 1961. Also, *Grandfather and I*, illtd. Paul Galdone (New York: Lothrop, Lee and Shepard, 1959). Both titles reprinted in 1994 with new illustrations by Jan Ormerod. (Picture Book/Family Relationships)

Carle, Eric. *1,2,3 to the Zoo*. New York: William Collins and World Publishing, 1968; New York: Putnam, 1990. (Picture Book/Concept/Interactive)

———. *The Very Hungry Caterpillar*. New York: Philomel, 1969; New York: Putnam, 1991. (Picture Book/Animal/Interactive)

———. *The Very Busy Spider*. New York: Crowell, 1984. (Picture Book/Concept/Interactive)

De Regniers, Beatrice Schenk. *May I Bring a Friend?* illtd. Beni Montresor. New York: Atheneum, 1964; New York: Macmillan, 1989. CALDECOTT MEDAL. (Picture Book/Concept)

Dubanevich, Arlene. *Pig William*. New York: Bradbury, 1985. (Picture Book/Wordless/Humor)

Ehlert, Lois. *Red Leaf, Yellow Leaf*. San Diego: Harcourt, 1991. (Picture Book/Nature)

Feelings, Muriel. *Jambo Means Hello: Swahili Alphabet Book*, illtd. Tom Feelings. New York: Dial, 1974, 1985. (Picture Book/Concept/African)

Fish, Helen Dean, ed. *Animals of the Bible*, illtd. Dorothy P. Lathrop. Philadelphia: Lippincott, 1937; New York: Harper (no date listed). CALDECOTT MEDAL. (Picture Book/Animal)

Flack, Marjorie. *Angus and the Ducks*. New York: Doubleday, 1930. (Picture Book/Animal)

———. *Angus and the Cat*. New York: Doubleday, 1931, 1989. (Picture Book/Animal)

———. *Angus Lost*. New York: Doubleday, 1932, 1989. (Picture Book/Animal)

Frasier, Debra. *On the Day You Were Born*. San Diego: Harcourt, 1991. (Picture Book/Concept)

Gág, Wanda. *Snippy and Snappy*. New York: Coward, 1931. (Picture Book/Animal)
———. *ABC Bunny*. New York: Coward, 1933, 1978. (Picture Book/Concept/Alphabet)
Giovanni, Nikki. *Spin a Soft Black Song*. New York: Hill and Wang, 1971; New York: Farrar, Straus & Giroux, 1987. (Poetry/African-American)
Gregor, Arthur. *Animal Babies by Ylla*, photog. Ylla (pseudonym for Camilla Koffler). New York: Harper, 1959. (Picture Book/Concept/Photographs)
Hill, Eric. *Where's Spot?* New York: Putnam, 1980. (Picture Book/Animal/Predictable)
Hoban, Tana. *Push-Pull Empty-Full*. New York: Macmillan, 1972. (Picture Book/Concept/Photography)
Hutchins, Pat. *Rosie's Walk*. New York: Macmillan, 1968, 1984. (Picture Book/Animal)
———. *Changes, Changes*. New York: Macmillan, 1971, 1987. (Picture Book/Concept/Wordless)
Johnson, Crockett. *Harold and the Purple Crayon*. New York: Harper, 1955, 1981. (Picture Book/Concept)
Keats, Ezra Jack. *The Snowy Day*. New York: Viking, 1962; New York: Puffin, 1976. CALDECOTT MEDAL. (Picture Book/Realistic Fiction/Urban)
Keats, Ezra Jack, and Pat Cherr. *My Dog Is Lost!*, illtd. Ezra Jack Keats. New York: Crowell, 1960. (Picture Book/Social Relationship/Urban)
Krauss, Ruth. *A Hole Is to Dig*, illtd. Maurice Sendak. New York: Harper, 1952, 1989. Also, *A Very Special House*, illtd. Maurice Sendak (New York: Harper, 1953, 1990); *I'll Be You and You Be Me*, illtd. Maurice Sendak (New York: Harper, 1954, 1990). (Picture Book/Concept)
Kunhardt Dorothy. *Junket Is Nice*. New York: Harcourt, 1933. Reissued as *Pudding Is Nice* (Lenox, Mass.: Bookstore Press, 1979). (Picture Book/Concept)
———. *Pat the Bunny*. New York: Simon & Schuster, 1940; New York: Golden Press, 1970. (Picture Book/Concept/Interactive)
Langstaff, John, ed. *Frog Went A-Courtin'*, illtd. Feodor Rojankovsky. New York: Harcourt, 1955. CALDECOTT MEDAL. (Picture Book/Folk Song)
Lenski, Lois. *The Little Auto*. New York: H.Z. Walck, 1934. New York: McKay, 1980. (Picture Book/Concept)
———. *The Little Airplane*. New York: H.Z. Walck, 1938. New York: McKay, 1980. (Picture Book/Concept)

Lionni, Leo. *Little Blue and Little Yellow*, an Astor Book. New York: Ivan Obolensky, New York: 1959. (Picture Book/Concept)
———. *Inch by Inch*. New York: Obolensky, 1960; (Picture Book/Concept)
———. *Frederick*. New York: Pantheon, 1967; New York: Knopf, 1973. (Picture Book/Fable)
MacDonald, Golden (pseud. of Margaret Wise Brown). *The Little Island*, illtd. Leonard Weisgard. New York: Doubleday, 1946; New York: Dell, 1993. CALDECOTT MEDAL. (Picture Book/Regional)
MacDonald, Suse. *Sea Shapes*. San Diego: Harcourt, 1994. (Picture Book/Concept)
Mayer, Mercer. *A Boy, A Dog and a Frog*. New York: Dial, 1967; New York: Viking, 1992. (Picture Book/Wordless/Humor/Series)
———. *Just For You*. New York: Golden Press, 1975. (Picture Book/Social Adjustment)
McCloskey, Robert. *Make Way for Ducklings*. New York: Viking, 1941; New York: Puffin, 1976. CALDECOTT MEDAL. (Picture Book/Regional/Animal)
McCully, Emily Arnold. *Picnic*. New York: Harper, 1984, 1992. (Picture Book/Wordless)
———. *School*. New York: Harper, 1987; New York: Harper Trophy, 1990. (Picture Book/Wordless)
Nolan, Dennis. *The Castle Builder*. New York: Macmillan, 1987. (Fantasy/Picture Book)
Numeroff, Laura Joffe. *If You Give a Mouse a Cookie*, illtd. Felicia Bond. New York: Harper, 1985. (Picture Book/Predictable)
Perrault, Charles. *Cinderella, or the Little Glass Slipper*, tr. and illtd. Marcia Brown. New York: Scribner, 1954. CALDECOTT MEDAL. (Picture Book/Fairy Tale)
Petersham, Maud and Miska. *The Rooster Crows: A Book of American Rhymes and Jingles*. New York: Macmillan, 1945, 1987. CALDECOTT MEDAL. (Poetry/Picture Book)
Piper, Watty (pseud. of Mabel Caroline Bragg). *The Little Engine That Could*. New York: Platt and Munk, 1930; New York: Putnam, 1990. (Fantasy/Picture Book)
Scarry, Richard. *Best Word Book Ever*. New York: Golden Books, 1963 (rev. 1980). (Picture Book/Concept)
Schertle, Alice. *How Now, Brown Cow?*, illtd. Amanda Schaffer. San Diego: Harcourt, 1994. (Poetry/Picture Book)
Sendak, Maurice. *Where the Wild Things Are*. New York: Harper, 1963, 1988. CALDECOTT MEDAL. (Fantasy/Picture Book)

Shulevitz, Uri. *One Monday Morning*. New York: Scribners, 1967; New York: Macmillan, 1986. (Fantasy/Picture Book)

Smith, E. Boyd. *The Farm Book*. Boston: Houghton Mifflin, 1910, 1990. (Informational/Picture Book)

Spier, Peter. *Noah's Ark*. New York: Doubleday, 1977; New York: Dell, 1992. CALDECOTT MEDAL. (Picture Book/Wordless)

Stevenson, Robert Louis. *A Child's Garden of Verses*, illtd. Jesse Willcox Smith. New York: Crown, 1985. (Poetry Collection)

Tresselt, Alvin. *White Snow Bright Snow*, illtd. Roger Duvoisin. New York: Lothrop, 1947; New York: Morrow, 1988. CALDECOTT MEDAL. (Picture Book/Concept)

Udry, Janice May. *A Tree Is Nice*, illtd. Marc Simont. New York: Harper, 1956, 1987. CALDECOTT MEDAL. (Picture Book/Concept)

Ungerer, Tomi. *Emile*. New York: Harper, 1960; New York: Dell, 1992. (Picture Book/Animal/Humor)

Van Allsburg, Chris. *The Polar Express*. Boston: Houghton Mifflin, 1985. CALDECOTT MEDAL. (Picture Book/Holiday)

Walsh, Ellen Stoll. *Mouse Count*. San Diego: Harcourt, 1991. (Picture Book/Concept)

Wells, Rosemary. *Max's Christmas*. New York: Dial, 1986. (Picture Book/Wordless/Holiday)

Wood, Audrey. *The Napping House*, illtd. Don Wood. San Diego: Harcourt, 1984. (Picture Book/Predictable)

———. *King Bidgood's in the Bathtub*, illtd. Don Wood. San Diego: Harcourt, 1985. (Picture Book/Predictable)

Yolen, Jane. *Owl Moon*, illtd. John Schoenherr. New York: Philomel, 1987. CALDECOTT MEDAL. (Poetry/Picture Book/Nature)

Zion, Gene. *Harry the Dirty Dog*, illtd. Margaret Bloy Graham. New York: Harper, 1956. (Picture Book/Animal)

Kindergarten/Lower Elementary

Aardema, Verna. *Why Mosquitoes Buzz in People's Ears*, illtd. Diane and Leo Dillon. New York: Dial, 1975; New York: Puffin, 1993. CALDECOTT MEDAL. (Picture Book/Folk Tale/African)

Ackerman, Karen. *Song and Dance Man*, illtd. Stephen Gammell. New York: Alfred A. Knopf, 1988. CALDECOTT MEDAL. (Picture Book/Realistic Fiction/Historical)

Adoff, Arnold. *Flamboyan*, illtd. Karen Barbour. San Diego: Harcourt, 1988. (Picture Book/Cultural/Puerto Rican)

Allen, Marjorie N. *One, Two, Three—AhChoo!*, illtd. Dick Gackenbach. New York: Coward, McCann and Geoghegan, 1980; Scarborough, Ontario: Ginn Publishing Canada, 1994. (Easy Reader/Realistic Fiction/Allergies)

Allen, Marjorie N. *Changes*, photog. Shelley Rotner. New York: Macmillan, 1991. (Picture Book/Photographs/Poetry/Nature)

Allen, Marjorie N. and Carl Allen. *Farley, Are You For Real?*, illtd. Joel Schick. New York: Coward, McCann and Geoghegan, 1976. (Easy Reader/Fantasy/Humor)

Bannerman, Helen. *The Story of Little Black Sambo*. New York: Harper, 1905; New York: HarperCollins, 1993 (reproduction of 1905 Harper edition). (Fantasy/Picture Book/India)

Bemelmans, Ludwig. *Madeline*. New York: Simon & Schuster, 1939; New York: Viking, 1993. (Picture Book/Realistic Fiction)

———. *Madeline's Rescue*. New York: Viking, 1953; New York: Puffin, 1993. CALDECOTT MEDAL. (Poetry/Picture Book)

Beskow, Elsa. *Pelle's New Suit*. New York: Harper, 1928; Mount Rainier, Maryland: Gryphon House, 1979. (Picture Book/Informational)

Bishop, Clare Huchet. *The Five Chinese Brothers*, illtd. Kurt Wiese. New York: Coward, 1938; New York: Putnam, 1989. (Picture Book/Folk Tale/China)

Brandenburg, Aliki. *Digging Up Dinosaurs*, Let's-Read-and-Find-Out series. New York: Crowell, 1981; New York: Harper, 1988. (Informational/Picture Book/Archaeology)

Brown, Laurene Krasny, and Marc Brown. *Dinosaur's Divorce: A Guide to Changing Families*. Boston: Little, Brown, 1986. (Informational/Social Adjustment/Humor)

Brown, Marcia. *Once a Mouse . . .* New York: Scribners, 1961; New York: Macmillan, 1989. CALDECOTT MEDAL. (Picture Book/Fable/India)

Brown, Margaret Wise. *Brer Rabbit: Stories from Uncle Remus*, illtd. Victor Dowling. New York: Harper, 1941. (Picture Book/Folk/Black American)

———. *Mister Dog: The Dog Who Belonged to Himself*, illtd. Garth Williams. New York: Simon & Schuster, 1952; New York: Western Publishing, 1992 (in *Three Best Loved Tales*). (Fantasy/Picture Book)

———. *The Dead Bird*, illtd. Remy Charlip. (Originally in *The Fish With the Deep Sea Smile*, a collection by Margaret Wise Brown, 1938.) New

York: Scott, 1958; New York: Harper, 1989. (Picture Book/Short Story Collection/Animal)

Brown, Ruth. *A Dark, Dark Tale.* New York: Dial, 1981. (Picture Book/Suspense)

Bunting, Eve. *Fly Away Home*, illtd. Ronald Himler. New York: Clarion Books, 1991. (Picture Book/Social Adjustment/Homelessness)

———. *Smoky Nights*, illtd. David Diaz. San Diego: Harcourt, 1994. CALDECOTT MEDAL. (Picture Book/Social Adjustment/Regional)

Burgess, Thornton. *Old Mother West Wind.* Boston: Little, Brown, 1910; Cutchogue, N.Y.: Buccaneer, 1992. (Fantasy/Short Story Collection/Animals)

Burton, Virginia Lee. *Mike Mulligan and His Steam Shovel.* Boston: Houghton Mifflin, 1939, 1993. (Fantasy/Picture Book)

———. *The Little House.* Boston: Houghton Mifflin, 1942, 1978. CALDECOTT MEDAL. (Fantasy/Picture Book)

Clark, Margery. *The Poppy Seed Cakes*, illtd. Maud and Miska Petersham. New York: Doubleday, 1924. (Realistic Fiction/Cultural/Humor)

Clifton, Lucille. *The Boy Who Didn't Believe in Spring.* New York: Dutton, 1973; New York: Viking, 1992. (Picture Book/Urban/Mixed Culture)

Cole, Joanna. *How You Were Born*, photographs. New York: Morrow, 1984, 1993 (rev. ed.). (Informational/Science)

———. *The Magic School Bus*, illtd. Bruce Degen. New York: Scholastic, 1986. (Informational/Science/Series)

———. *The Magic School Bus: At the Waterworks*, illtd. Bruce Degen. New York: Scholastic, 1986. (Informational/Science/Series)

———. *The Magic School Bus: Inside the Earth*, illtd. Bruce Degen. New York: Scholastic, 1987. (Informational/Science/Series)

———. *The Magic School Bus: Inside the Human Body*, illtd. Bruce Degen. New York: Scholastic, 1988. (Informational/Science/Series)

———. *The Magic School Bus: Lost in the Solar System*, illtd. Bruce Degen. New York: Scholastic, 1989. (Informational/Science/Series)

———. *The Magic School Bus: On the Ocean Floor*, illtd. Bruce Degen. New York: Scholastic, 1992. (Informational/Science Series)

Cooney, Barbara. *Chanticleer and the Fox*, adapted from *The Canterbury Tales* by Geoffrey Chaucer. New York: Crowell, 1958; New York: Harper, 1982. CALDECOTT MEDAL (Picture Book/Folk Tale/Medieval)

Cornish, Sam. *Grandmother's Pictures*, Scarsdale, N.Y.: Bradbury, 1974. (Poetry/Picture Book/Black American)

Daugherty, James. *Andy and the Lion.* New York: Viking, 1938; New York: Puffin, 1989. (Picture Book/Folk Tale)

D'Aulaire, Ingri and Edgar. *Abraham Lincoln*. New York: Doubleday, 1939, 1987. CALDECOTT MEDAL. (Picture Book/Biography)

———. *D'Aulaire's Book of Greek Myths*. New York: Doubleday, 1962; New York: Dell, 1992. (Picture Book/Myth/Greece)

Dawes, Judy. *Fireflies in the Night*, illtd. Kazue Mizumura. New York: Crowell, 1963, 1991 (rev.). (Informational/Picture Book/Nature)

de Paola, Tomie. *Strega Nona*. New York: Prentice-Hall, 1975; New York: Scholastic, 1992. (Picture Book/Folk/Cultural)

———. *The Quicksand Book*. New York: Holiday House, 1977. (Informational/Picture Book/Science/Humor)

Duvoisin, Roger. *Petunia*. New York: Knopf, 1950, 1962. Reprinted in *Petunia the Silly Goose Stories* (New York: Knopf, 1987). (Picture Story Book/Fantasy/Animal)

Ehlert, Lois. *Eating the Alphabet: Fruits and Vegetables from A to Z*. San Diego: Harcourt, 1989. (Picture Book/Concept/Informational)

Farber, Norma. *How Does It Feel to Be Old?* New York: Dutton, 1979, 1988. (Picture Book/Aging)

Feelings, Muriel. *Moja Means One: Swahili Counting Book*, illtd. Tom Feelings. New York: Dial, 1974, 1987. (Picture Book/Concept/African)

Feeney, Stephanie. *A Is for Aloha*. Honolulu: University of Hawaii Press, 1980. (Informational/Concept/Hawaii)

Field, Rachel. *Prayer for a Child*, illtd. Elizabeth Orton Jones. New York: Macmillan, 1944, 1984. CALDECOTT MEDAL. (Poetry/Picture Book/Concept)

Flack, Marjorie. *The Restless Robin*. New York: Doubleday, 1937. (Informational/Picture Book/Nature)

Freeman, Lydia and Don. *Pet of the Met*. New York: Viking, 1953; New York: Puffin, 1988. (Picture Story Book/Fantasy/Animal)

Gackenbach, Dick. *Alice's Special Room*. New York: Clarion, 1991. (Picture Book/Social Adjustment/Death)

———. *Claude Has a Picnic*. New York: Clarion, 1993. (Fantasy/Picture Book/Animal)

Gág, Wanda. *Millions of Cats*. New York: Coward, 1928; New York: Putnam, 1977. (Picture Book/Folk/Modern)

———. *Funny Thing*. New York: Coward, 1929; New York: Putnam, 1991. (Fantasy/Picture Book)

———. *Gone Is Gone*. New York: Coward, 1935. (Picture Book/Folk/Fairy Tale)

Gauch, Patricia Lee. *This Time, Temple Wick?*, illtd. Margaret Tomes. New York: Henry Z. Walck, 1974; New York: Putnam, 1992. (Picture Book/Historical Fiction/Revolutionary War)

Goble, Paul. *The Girl Who Loved Wild Horses*. New York: Bradbury, 1978; New York: Macmillan, 1993. CALDECOTT MEDAL. (Picture Book/American Indian)

———. *Beyond the Ridge*. New York: Bradbury, 1989; New York: Macmillan, 1993. (Picture Book/American Indian/Death)

Goldin, Barbara Diamond. *The World's Birthday: A Rosh Hashanah Story*, illtd. Jeanette Winter. San Diego: Harcourt, 1990. (Picture Book/Jewish Tradition)

Gramatky, Hardie. *Little Toot*. New York: Putnam, 1939, 1992. (Fantasy/Picture Book)

Greenfield, Eloise. *Honey, I Love and Other Love Poems*, illtd. Diane and Leo Dillon. New York: Harper, 1978, 1986. (Poetry/Picture Book/Black American)

Gruelle, Johnny. *Raggedy Ann Stories*. Chicago: P.F. Volland, 1918; New York: Outlet, 1991. (Fantasy/Toys)

———. *The Original Adventures of Raggedy Andy*. Chicago: P.F. Volland, 1920; New York: Outlet, 1991. (Fantasy/Toys)

———. *Eddie Elephant*. Chicago: P.F. Volland, 1921. (Fantasy/Picture Book/Animal)

Haley, Gail. *A Story, A Story*. New York: Atheneum, 1970; New York: Macmillan, 1988. CALDECOTT MEDAL. (Picture Book/Folk Tale/African)

Hall, Donald. *The Ox-Cart Man*, illtd. Barbara Cooney. New York: Viking, 1979; New York: Puffin, 1983. CALDECOTT MEDAL. (Poetry/Picture Book/New England)

Hazen, Barbara Shook. *The Gorilla Did It*, illtd. Ray Cruz. New York: Atheneum, 1974. (Picture Book/Social Development)

———. *Two Homes to Live In*, illtd. Peggy Luks. New York: Human Sciences Press, 1978. (Picture Book/Social Adjustment/Divorce)

Heide, Florence Parry. *The Shrinking of Treehorn*, illtd. Edward Gorey. New York: Holiday House, 1971. Also, *Treehorn x 3* (New York: Dell, 1992). (Fantasy/Picture Book/Social Adjustment)

Hendrick, Mary Jean. *If Anything Ever Goes Wrong at the Zoo*, illtd. Jane Dyer. San Diego: Harcourt, 1993. (Fantasy/Picture Book)

Hoban, Russell. *Bedtime for Frances*, illtd. Garth Williams. New York: Harper, 1960, 1976. Also, *A Baby Sister for Frances*, illtd. Lillian Hoban (New York: Harper, 1964, 1976); *Bread and Jam for Frances*, illtd. Lillian Hoban (New York: Harper, 1964, 1986). (Easy Reader/Social Behavior)

Hoban, Tana. *Look Again!* New York: Macmillan, 1971. (Picture Book/Concept/Wordless/Photography)

Hodges, Margaret. *The Wave*, adapted from Lafcadio Hearn, illtd. Blair Lent. Boston: Houghton Mifflin, 1964. (Picture Book/Folk Tale/Japan)

———. *St. George and the Dragon*, illtd. by Trina Schart Hyman. Boston: Little, Brown, 1984, 1990. CALDECOTT MEDAL. (Picture Book/Traditional Fairy Tale)

Hoff, Syd. *Danny and the Dinosaur*. New York: Harper, 1958, 1985. (Easy Reader/Fantasy)

———. *Duncan the Dancing Duck*. New York: Clarion, 1994. (Fantasy/Picture Book/Animal)

Kellogg, Steven. *A Rose for Pinkerton*. New York: Dial, 1981. (Picture Book/Animal)

———. *Pecos Bill*. New York: Morrow, 1986, 1992. (Picture Book/Tall Tales)

Kipling, Rudyard. *Jungle Book*. New York: Viking, 1990. (Fantasy/Animal)

———. *The Second Jungle Book*. New York: Viking, 1990. (Fantasy/Short Story Collection/Animal)

———. *Just So Stories*, illtd. author. New York: Puffin Books, 1987. (Fantasy/Short Story Collection/Animal)

Krementz, Jill. *How It Feels When a Parent Dies*. New York: Knopf, 1981. (Informational/Photographs/Death)

———. *How It Feels to Be Adopted*. New York: Knopf, 1982. (Information/Social Adjustment)

———. *How It Feels When Parents Divorce*. New York: Knopf, 1984. (Informational/Social Adjustment)

Leaf, Munro. *The Story of Ferdinand*, illtd. Robert Lawson. New York: Viking, 1936; New York: Puffin, 1991. (Picture Book/Humor/Spain)

———. *Wee Gillis*, illtd. Robert Lawson. New York: Viking, 1938, 1967. (Picture Book/Humor/Scotland)

Lobel, Arnold. *Frog and Toad Are Friends*. New York: Harper, 1970. A Frog and Toad boxed set was published in 1993. Also, *Frog and Toad Together* (New York: Harper, 1972, 1993); *Frog and Toad All Year* (New York: Harper, 1976, 1993); *Days with Frog and Toad* (New York: Harper, 1979, 1993). (Easy Reader/Social Relationships/Animal)

———. *Mouse Soup*. New York: Harper, 1977. (Easy Reader/Animal)

Louis, Ai-Ling. *Yeh Shen: A Chinese Cinderella*, illtd. Ed Young. New York: Philomel, 1982; New York: Putnam, 1988. (Picture Book/Traditional Fairy Tale/China)

MacLachlan, Patricia. *The Sick Day*, illtd. William Pene du Bois. New York: Pantheon, 1979. (Easy Reader/Realistic Fiction/Humor)

———. *Through Grandpa's Eyes*, illtd. Deborah Kogan Ray. New York: Harper, 1980. (Picture Book/Realistic Fiction)

Marshall, James. *George and Martha*. Boston: Houghton Mifflin, 1972. (Fantasy/Picture Book/Humor)

McCloskey, Robert. *Lentil*. New York: Viking, 1940; New York: Puffin, 1978. (Picture Book/Realistic Fiction/Humor)

———. *Time of Wonder*. New York: Viking, 1957. CALDECOTT MEDAL. (Poetry/Picture Book/Regional)

McCully, Emily Arnold. *Mirette on the High Wire*. New York: Putnam, 1992. CALDECOTT MEDAL (Picture Book/Realistic Fiction/Paris)

McDermott, Beverly Brodsky. *The Golem*. Philadelphia: Lippincott, 1976. (Picture Book/Folk Tale/Jewish)

McDermott, Gerald. *Arrow to the Sun: A Pueblo Indian Tale*. New York: Viking, 1974; New York: Puffin, 1977. CALDECOTT MEDAL. (Picture Book/Native American)

———. *Raven: A Trickster Tale from the Pacific Northwest*. San Diego: Harcourt, 1993. (Picture Book/Traditional Tale/Native American)

McKissack, Patricia. *Mirandy and Brother Wind*, illtd. Jerry Pinkney. New York: Knopf, 1989. (Picture Book/Folk Tale/Black American)

Meddaugh, Susan. *Martha Speaks*. Boston: Houghton Mifflin, 1992. (Picture Book/Humor)

Miles, Miska. *Annie and the Old One*, illtd. Peter Parnall. Boston: Little, Brown, 1971, 1985. (Picture Book/Navajo/Death)

Milhous, Katherine. *The Egg Tree*. New York: Scribner, 1950. CALDECOTT MEDAL. (Picture Book/Regional Customs)

Milne, A. A. *When We Were Very Young*, illtd. Ernest H. Shepard. New York: Dutton, 1924, 1992. (Poetry)

———. *Winnie the Pooh*, illtd. Ernest H. Shepard. New York: Dutton, 1926; New York: Puffin, 1992. (Fantasy/Toys)

———. *Now We Are Six*, illtd. Ernest H. Shepard. New York: Dutton, 1927; New York: Puffin, 1992. (Poetry)

———. *The House at Pooh Corner*, illtd. Ernest H. Shepard. New York: Dutton, 1928, 1991. (Fantasy/Toys)

Minarik, Else Holmelund. *Little Bear*, illtd. Maurice Sendak. New York: Harper, 1957. Also, *Father Bear Comes Home*, illtd. Maurice Sendak (New York: Harper, 1959). A boxed set was published in 1992.

Mosel, Arlene. *Tikki Tikki Tembo*, illtd. Blair Lent. New York: Henry Holt, 1968. (Picture Book/Folk Tale/Japan)

———. *The Funny Little Woman*, illtd. Blair Lent. New York: Dutton, 1972; New York: Puffin, 1993. CALDECOTT MEDAL. (Picture Book/Folk Tale/Japan)

Musgrove, Margaret. *Ashanti to Zulu: African Traditions*, illtd. Diane and Leo Dillon. New York: Dial, 1976; New York: Puffin, 1980. CALDECOTT MEDAL. (Picture Book/Concept/Africa)

Ness, Evaline. *Sam, Bangs & Moonshine*. New York: Holt, Rinehart and Winston, 1966. CALDECOTT MEDAL. (Picture Book/Realistic Fiction)

Nicholson, William. *Clever Bill*. New York: Doubleday, 1927. (Fantasy/Picture Book/Toys)

Nic Leodhas, Sorche. *Always Room for One More*, illtd. Nonny Hogrogian. New York: Holt, 1965. CALDECOTT MEDAL. (Folk/Myth/Picture Book/Scottish)

Nolan, Dennis. *Dinosaur Dream*. New York: Macmillan, 1990. (Fantasy/Picture Book/Archaeology)

Paterson, Katherine. *The Tale of the Mandarin Ducks*, illtd. Diane and Leo Dillon. New York: Lodestar, 1991. (Picture Book/Folk Tale/Japan)

Peet, Bill. *Chester the Worldly Pig*. Boston: Houghton Mifflin, 1965, 1980. (Picture Book/Humor)

Perrault, Charles. *The Complete Fairy Tales of Charles Perrault*, tr. Neil Philip and Nicoletta Simborowski; illtd. Sally Holmes. New York: Clarion, 1993. (Fantasy/Fairy Tale/Short Story Collection)

Pienowski, Jan. *Christmas*. New York: Knopf, 1984, 1989. (Informational/Picture Book/Holiday)

Pinkney, Andrea Davis. *Dear Benjamin Banneker*, illtd. Brian Pinkney. San Diego: Harcourt, 1994. (Picture Book/Biography/Black History)

Potter, Beatrix. *The Tale of Peter Rabbit*. New York: Frederick Warne, 1902, 1987. (Fantasy/Picture Book/Animal)

———. *The Tale of Squirrel Nutkin*. New York: Frederick Warne, 1901, 1987. (Picture Book/Animal Fantasy)

———. *The Tale of Two Bad Mice*. New York: Frederick Warne, 1904, 1987. (Fantasy/Picture Book/Animal)

———. *The Tale of Mr. Jeremy Fisher*. New York: Frederick Warne, 1906, 1987. (Fantasy/Picture Book/Animal)

———. *The Tale of Mrs. Tittlemouse*. New York: Frederick Warne, 1910, 1987. (Fantasy/Picture Book/Animal)

Pyle, Howard. *Pepper & Salt*. New York: Harper, 1886; New York: Dover, 1990. (Fantasy/Fairy/Poetry)

Raskin, Ellen. *Nothing Ever Happens on My Block*. New York: Atheneum, 1966; New York: Macmillan, 1989. (Fantasy/Picture Book/Humor)

———. *Spectacles*. New York: Atheneum, 1969; New York: Macmillan, 1988. (Picture Book/Humor)

Rey, H. A. *Curious George*. Boston: Houghton Mifflin, 1941, 1973. (Fantasy/Picture Book/Animal)

Robbins, Ruth. *Baboushka and the Three Kings*, illtd. Nicolas Sidjakov. Berkeley: Parnassus, 1960; Boston: Houghton Mifflin, 1986. CALDECOTT MEDAL. (Picture Book/Folk Tale/Holiday)

Rylant, Cynthia. *Appalachia: The Voices of Sleeping Birds*, illtd. Barry Moser. San Diego: Harcourt, 1991. (Picture Book/Regional/America)

Sandburg, Carl. *Rootabaga Stories*, illtd. Maud and Miska Petersham. New York: Harcourt, 1922; San Diego: Harcourt, 1990 (illtd. Michael Hague *Rootabaga Stories: Part One*). (Fantasy)

———. *Rootabaga Pigeons*, illtd. Maud and Miska Petersham. New York: Harcourt, 1923; San Diego: Harcourt, 1990 (illtd. Michael Hague *Rootabaga Stories: Part Two*). (Fantasy)

———. *The Wedding Procession of the Rag Doll and the Broom Handle and Who Was In It*, illtd. Harriet Pincus. New York: Harcourt, 1967, 1978. (Picture Book/Adaptation from *Rootabaga Stories*)

Say, Allen. *Tree of Cranes*. Boston: Houghton Mifflin, 1991. (Picture Book/Cultural/Japanese-American)

———. *Grandfather's Journey*. Boston: Houghton Mifflin, 1993. CALDECOTT MEDAL. (Picture Book/Cultural/Japan/America)

Schick, Alice, and Marjorie N. Allen. *The Remarkable Ride of Israel Bissell as Related by Molly the Crow*, illtd. Joel Schick. Philadelphia: Lippincott, 1976. (Picture Book/Historical Fiction/Revolutionary War)

Sendak, Maurice. *The Sign on Rosie's Door*. New York: Harper, 1960. Adapted for television and expanded in book form as part of *Maurice Sendak's Really Rosie starring the Nutshell Kids* (New York: Harper, 1975). (Picture Book/Realistic Fiction)

———. *Nutshell Library* (*Alligators All Around*; *One Was Johnny*; *Chicken Soup with Rice*; *Pierre*). New York: Harper, 1962. (Picture Book/Concept)

———. *Hector Protector and As I Went Over the Water*. New York: Harper, 1965, 1990. (Picture Book/Nursery Rhymes)

———. *In the Night Kitchen*. New York: Harper, 1970, 1985. (Fantasy/Picture Book)

———. *Outside Over There*. New York: Harper, 1981. (Fantasy/Picture Book)

Seuss, Dr. (pseud. of Theodore Seuss Geisel). *And to Think That I Saw It on Mulberry Street*. New York: Vanguard; 1937; New York: Random House (Books for Young Readers), 1989. (Fantasy/Picture Book)

———. *The 500 Hats of Bartholomew Cubbins*. New York: Random House, 1938, 1989. (Fantasy/Picture Book)

———. *Horton Hatches the Egg*. New York: Random House, 1940, 1991. (Picture Book/Fantasy/Humor)

———. *Yertle the Turtle and Other Stories*. New York: Random House, 1950, 1985. (Picture Book/Short Story Collection/Humor)

———. *Horton Hears a Who*. New York: Random House, 1954. (Picture Book/Fantasy)

———. *How the Grinch Stole Christmas*. New York: Random House, 1957. (Fantasy/Picture Book/Holiday)

———. *The Cat in the Hat*. Boston: Houghton Mifflin, 1957; New York: Random House, 1957, 1987. (Easy Reader/Fantasy)

Silverstein, Shel. *The Giving Tree*. New York: Harper, 1964. (Picture Book/Concept)

Synder, Diane. *The Boy of the Three-Year Nap*, illtd. Allen Say. Boston: Houghton Mifflin, 1988. (Picture Book/Folk Tale/Japan)

Stamm, Claus. *Three Strong Women*, illtd. Kazue Mizumura. New York: Viking, 1962, 1990. (Picture Book/Folk Tale/Japan)

Steig, William. *Sylvester and the Magic Pebble*. New York: Simon and Schuster, 1969, 1988. CALDECOTT MEDAL. (Fantasy/Picture Book/Animal)

Steptoe, John. *Stevie*. New York: Harper, 1969, 1986. (Picture Book/Urban/Black American)

———. *Mufaro's Beautiful Daughters*. New York: Lothrop, Lee and Shepard, 1987. (Picture Book/Cultural/African)

Stockton, Frank. *The Bee-Man of Orn*. New York: Scribner, 1881; New York: Harper, 1987. (Fantasy/Fairy)

Swope, Sam. *The Araboolies of Liberty Street*, illtd. Barry Root. New York: Clarkson N. Potter, 1989. (Fantasy/Picture Book)

Tarry, Ellen, and Marie Hall Ets. *My Dog Rinty*, photog. Alexander and Alexandra Alland. New York: Viking, 1946. (Realistic Fiction/Black American).

Thompson, Kay. *Eloise*, illtd. Hilary Knight. New York: Simon and Schuster, 1955. (Picture Book/Urban/Dysfunctional Family)

Thurber, James. *Many Moons*, illtd. Louis Slobodkin. New York: Harcourt, 1943, 1990 (illtd. Marc Simont). CALDECOTT MEDAL. (Picture Book/Fairy Tale)

Titus, Eve. *Anatole*, illtd. Paul Galdone. New York: McGraw-Hill, 1956; New York: Bantam, 1990. (Fantasy/Picture Book/Animal)

Turkle, Brinton. *The Adventures of Obadiah*. New York: Viking, 1972; New York: Puffin, 1987. (Picture Book/Historical Fiction/Quaker)

Turner, Ann. *Dakota Dugout*, illtd. Ronald Himler. New York: Macmillan, 1985. (Picture Book/Historical Fiction/American)

Van Allsburg, Chris. *The Garden of Abdul Gasazi*. Boston: Houghton Mifflin, 1979, 1982. (Fantasy/ Picture Book)

Van Woerkom, Dorothy. *Alexandra the Rock-Eater*, illtd. Rosekrans Hoffman. New York: Knopf, 1978. (Folk/Picture Book/Rumania)

Viorst, Judith. *The Tenth Good Thing About Barney*, illtd. Eric Blegvad. New York: Atheneum, 1971. (Picture Book/Social Adjustment/ Death)

———. *I'll Fix Anthony*, illtd. Arnold Lobel. New York: Harper, 1969; New York: Macmillan, 1988. (Picture Book/Humor)

Waber, Bernard. *Lyle, Lyle, Crocodile*. Boston: Houghton Mifflin, 1965. (Picture Book/Series/Fantasy/Animal)

Wiesner, David. *Tuesday*. New York: Clarion Books, 1991. CALDECOTT MEDAL. (Picture Book/Wordless)

Wilhelm, Hans. *A Cool Kid—Like Me*. New York: Crown, 1990. (Picture Book/Realistic Fiction)

Will (William Lipkind) and Nicolas (Mordvinoff). *Finders Keepers*. New York: Harcourt, 1951; San Diego: Harcourt, 1989. CALDECOTT MEDAL. (Picture Book)

Willhoite, Michael. *Daddy's Roommate*. Boston: Alyson Publications, 1990. (Picture Book/Social Relationships/Homosexuality)

Williams, Jay. *Everyone Knows What a Dragon Looks Like*, illtd. Mercer Mayer. New York: Four Winds, 1976; New York: Macmillan, 1984.

Winter, Jeanette. *Follow the Drinking Gourd*. New York: Knopf, 1988, 1992. (Picture Book/Cultural/Black American)

Wisniewski, David. *Rain Player*. New York: Clarion, 1991. (Picture Book/Traditional Tale/Mayan Indian)

Yolen Jane. *The Emperor and the Kite*, illtd. Ed Young. New York: World Publishing Company, 1967; New York: Philomel, 1988. (Picture Book/Folk Tale/Modern)

———. *The Seeing Stick*, illtd. Remy Charlip and Demetra Maraslis. New York: Crowell, 1977. (Picture Book/Original Folk Tale/Chinese)

———. *Commander Toad in Space*. New York: Coward, McCann and Geoghegan, 1980. (Easy Reader/Science Fiction/Fantasy)

———. *Letting Swift River Go*, illtd. Barbara Cooney. Boston: Little, Brown, 1992. (Realistic Fiction/Picture Book/Nature)

Yorinks, Arthur, and Richard Egieliski. *Hey, Al*. New York: Farrar, Straus & Giroux, 1986. CALDECOTT MEDAL. (Picture Book/Social)

Young, Ed. *Lon Po Po: A Red Riding Hood Story from China*. New York: Philomel, 1989. CALDECOTT MEDAL. (Picture Book/Fairy Tale/China)

Zemach, Harve. *Duffy and the Devil*, illtd. Margot Zemach. New York: Farrar, Straus and Giroux, 1973. CALDECOTT MEDAL. (Picture Book/Folk Tale/Cornish)

Zolotow, Charlotte. *The Hating Book*, illtd. Ben Shecter. New York: Harper, 1969, 1989. (Picture Book/Concept Rhyme)

Middle Elementary

Adler, David. *Cam Jansen and the Mystery of the Babe Ruth Baseball*. New York: Viking, 1981; New York: Puffin, 1991. (Easy Reader/Mystery/Series)

Alexander, Lloyd. *Time Cat*. New York: Holt, Rinehart and Winston, 1963; New York: Dell, 1985. (Fantasy/Time Travel)

Allen, Marjorie N., and Carl Allen. *The Marble Cake Cat*, illtd. Marylin Hafner. New York: Coward, McCann and Geoghegan, 1977. (Chapter Book/Social Relationships/Animal)

Atwater, Richard and Florence. *Mr. Popper's Penguins*. Boston: Little, Brown, 1938; New York: Dell, 1986. (Chapter Book/Humor)

Bailey, Carolyn Sherwin. *Miss Hickory*, illtd. Ruth Gannett. New York: Viking, 1946; New York: Puffin, 1977. NEWBERY MEDAL. (Fantasy/Toys)

Baum, L. Frank. *The Wonderful Wizard of Oz*, illtd. W. W. Denslow. Chicago: George M. Hill, 1900; New York: New American Library, 1984. (Fantasy)

———. *The Marvelous Land of Oz*, illtd. John R. Neill. Chicago: Reilly and Britton, 1904; New York: Puffin, 1985. (Fantasy)

———. *Ozma of Oz*, illtd. John R. Neill. Chicago: Reilly and Britton, 1907; New York: Puffin, 1992. (Fantasy)

———. *The Patchwork Girl of Oz*, illtd. John R. Neill. Chicago: Reilly and Britton, 1913; New York: Dover, 1990. (Fantasy)

———. *Glinda of Oz*, illtd. John R. Neill. Chicago: Reilly and Britton, 1920; New York: Ballantine, 1985. (Fantasy)

———. *The Magic of Oz*, illtd. John R. Neill. Chicago: Reilly and Britton, 1919; New York: Ballantine, 1985. (Fantasy)

Bellairs, John. *The House With the Clock in Its Walls*, illtd. Edward Gorey. New York: Dial, 1973; New York: Puffin, 1993. (Fantasy/Mystery)

Blumberg, Rhoda. *Commodore Perry in the Land of the Shogun*. New York: Lothrop, Lee and Shepard, 1985. (Informational/Cultural/Japan)

Blume, Judy. *Are You There, God? It's Me, Margaret*. New York: Bradbury, 1970; New York: Dell, 1991. (Realistic Fiction/Social Adjustment)

———. *Superfudge*. New York: Dutton, 1980. (Realistic Fiction/Chapter Book/Humor)

———. *Fudge-a-mania*. New York: Dutton, 1990. (Realistic Fiction/Chapter Book/Humor)

Bontemps, Arna, and Langston Hughes. *Popo and Fifina: Children of Haiti*, illtd. E. Simms Campbell. New York: Macmillan, 1932; New York: Oxford University Press, 1993. (Realistic Fiction/Haiti)

Butterworth, Oliver. *The Enormous Egg*, illtd. Louis Darling. Boston: Little, Brown, 1956, 1993. (Chapter Book/Fantasy)

Byars, Betsy. *The Eighteenth Emergency*, illtd. Robert Grossman. New York: Viking, 1973; New York: Puffin, 1982. (Chapter Book/Humor)

Chrisman, Arthur. *Shen of the Sea*. New York: Dutton, 1925, 1968. NEWBERY MEDAL. (Fantasy/Short Story Collection/China)

Cleary, Beverly. *Henry Huggins*, illtd. Louis Darling. New York: Morrow, 1950; New York: Avon, 1990. (Realistic Fiction, Humor/Series)

———. *The Mouse and the Motorcycle*, illtd. Louis Darling. New York: Morrow, 1965; New York: Avon, 1990. (Fantasy)

———. *Dear Mr. Henshaw*. New York: Morrow, 1983; New York: Dell, 1992. NEWBERY MEDAL. (Realistic Fiction/Humor)

Coatsworth, Elizabeth. *The Cat Who Went to Heaven*, illtd. Lynd Ward. New York: Macmillan, 1930, 1990. NEWBERY MEDAL. (Folk/Myth/Buddha)

———. *Away Goes Sally*. New York: Macmillan, 1934. (Realistic Fiction/Historical/Regional)

Cobb, Vicki. *Science Experiments You Can Eat*. Philadelphia: Lippincott, 1972; New York: Harper (no date listed). (Informational/Science)

Collodi, Carlo. (pseud. of Carlo Lorenzini). *The Adventures of Pinocchio*. New York: Puffin, 1985. (Fantasy)

Dalgliesh, Alice. *The Courage of Sarah Noble*. New York: Scribners, 1954. New York: Macmillan, 1991. (Realistic Fiction/Historical/Regional)

Edmonds, Walter V. *The Matchlock Gun*, illtd. Paul Lantz. New York: Dodd, Mead, 1941. NEWBERY MEDAL. (Realistic Fiction/Historical/Regional)

Estes, Eleanor. *The Moffats*. New York: Harcourt, 1941; San Diego: Harcourt, 1989. (Realistic Fiction/Family Relationships/Series)

———. *Ginger Pye*. New York: Harcourt, 1951; San Diego: Harcourt, 1990. NEWBERY MEDAL. (Realistic Fiction/Family Relationships)

Etra, Jonathan, and Stephanie Spinner. *Aliens for Breakfast*, illtd. Steve Bjorkman. New York: Random House, 1988. (Chapter Book/Fantasy-Science Fiction/Humor)

Fisher, Dorothy Canfield. *Understood Betsy*, illtd. Ada C. Williamson. New York: Holt, 1917; New York: Dell, 1993. (Realistic Fiction/Regional)

Fritz, Jean. *And Then What Happened, Paul Revere?*, illtd. Margaret Tomes. New York: Coward, McCann and Geoghegan, 1973. (Easy Reader/ Biographical/Humor)

Gannett, Ruth Stiles. *My Father's Dragon*, illtd. Ruth Chrisman Gannett. New York: Random House, 1948. (Chapter Book/Fantasy/Humor)

Gerstein, Mordicai. *Mountains of Tibet*. New York: Harper, 1987. (Picture Book/Culture/Far East)

Giblin, James Cross. *The Skyscraper Book*. New York: Crowell, 1981. (Informational/Architecture)

Gilden, Mel. *The Pumpkins of Time*. San Diego: Browndeer Press, 1994. (Fantasy/Science Fiction/Humor)

Godden, Rumer. *The Doll's House*. New York: Viking, 1948. (Fantasy/Toys)

Hamilton, Virginia. *Zeely*, illtd. Symeon Shimin. New York: Macmillan, 1967, 1993. (Realistic Fiction/African American)

Handforth, Thomas. *Mei Lei*. New York: Doubleday, 1938, 1955. CALDECOTT MEDAL. (Fantasy/Picture Book/China)

Harris, Joel Chandler. *Uncle Remus: His Songs and Sayings*, illtd. Frederick S. Church and James H. Moser. New York: Appleton, 1880; illtd. A. B. Frost, 1892; New York: Viking Penguin, 1982. (Short Story Collection/Folk Tales/Black American)

Haywood, Carolyn. *"B" Is for Betsy*. New York: Harcourt, 1939; San Diego: Harcourt, 1990. (Realistic Fiction)

Holling, Holling C. *Paddle to the Sea*. Boston: Houghton Mifflin, 1941, 1969. (Picture Book/Historical/Regional)

Howe, Deborah and James. *Bunnicula: A Rabbit Tale of Mystery*, illtd. Alan Daniel. New York: Atheneum, 1979. (Chapter Book/Mystery/Humor)

Jeffers, Susan. *Brother Eagle, Sister Sky: A Message from Chief Seattle.* New York: Dial, 1991. (Picture Book/Fiction/Nature)

Juster, Norton. *The Phantom Tollbooth*, illtd. Jules Feiffer. New York: Random House, 1961; New York: Knopf, 1988. (Fantasy)

Keene, Carolyn (pseud. of Stratemeyer Syndicate). *The Secret of the Old Clock.* New York: Grosset & Dunlap, 1930; Bedford, Mass.: Applewood, 1991 (rev.). (Realistic Fiction/Series/Mystery)

Keith, Harold. *Rifles for Watie.* New York: Crowell, 1957; New York: Harper, 1991. NEWBERY MEDAL. (Realistic Fiction/Historical)

Kimmel, Eric. *Hershel and the Hanukkah Goblins*, illtd. Trina Schart Hyman. New York: Holiday House, 1989. (Picture Book/Jewish/ Humor)

Larrick, Nancy, ed. *Piping Down the Valleys Wild*, illtd. Ellen Raskin. New York: Delacorte, 1968, 1985. (Poetry/Anthology)

Lasky, Kathryn. *Cloud Eyes*, illtd. Barry Moser. San Diego: Harcourt, 1994. (Picture Book/Traditional/American Indian)

Lauber, Patricia. *Seeds: Pop, Stick, Glide.* New York: Crown, 1981, 1991. (Informational/Photographs/Science)

Lawson, Robert. *Ben and Me.* Boston: Little, Brown, 1939, 1988. (Chapter Book/Fantasy/Biography)

———. *They Were Strong and Good.* New York: Viking, 1940. CALDECOTT MEDAL. (Informational/Picture Book/Biography)

———. *Rabbit Hill.* New York: Viking, 1944. NEWBERY MEDAL. (Fantasy/Animal)

Lester, Julius, adapt. from J. C. Harris. *The Tales of Uncle Remus: The Adventures of Brer Rabbit*, illtd. Jerry Pinkney. New York: Dial, 1987. (Folk Tales/Black American)

Levy, Elizabeth. *Something Queer at the Library.* New York: Delacorte, 1977; New York: Dell, 1989. (Chapter Book/Mystery/Series)

Lewis, C. S. *The Chronicles of Narnia*, published by Macmillan in the United States (*The Last Battle* by Lane), include: *The Lion, the Witch and the Wardrobe*, 1950; *Prince Caspian*, 1951; *The Voyage of the Dawn Treader*, 1952; *The Silver Chair*, 1953; *The Horse and His Boy*, 1954; *The Magician's Nephew*, 1955; *The Last Battle*, 1956. (Fantasy)

Lindgren, Astrid. *Pippi Longstocking*, tr. Florence Lamborn. New York: Viking, 1950; New York: Puffin, 1988. Also, *Pippi Goes on Board,* tr. Florence Lamborn (New York: Viking, 1957; New York: Puffin, 1977); *Pippi in the South Seas,* tr. Gerry Bothmer (New York: Viking, 1959; New York: Puffin, 1977). (Tall Tales/Fantasy)

Lovelace, Maud Hart. *Betsy-Tacy*, illtd. Lois Lenski. New York: Crowell, 1940. Also, *Betsy-Tacy and Tib* (1941), *Over the Big Hill* (1942), *Down*

Town (1943). New editions of Lovelace by Harper Trophy in 1994. (Chapter Book/Realistic Fiction/Series)

MacDonald, Betty. *Mrs. Piggle-Wiggle*, illtd. Hilary Knight. Philadelphia: Lippincott, 1957; New York: Harper, 1985. (Chapter Book/Humor /Series)

MacGregor, Ellen. *Miss Pickerell Goes to Mars*, illtd. Paul Galdone. New York: Whittlesey House, 1951. Also, *Miss Pickerell Goes Undersea*, illtd. Paul Galdone (New York: McGraw-Hill, 1953). (Chapter Book/ Science Fiction/Series)

MacGregor, Ellen, and Doris Pantell. *Miss Pickerell on the Moon*. New York: McGraw-Hill, 1965. (Chapter Book/Science Fiction/Series)

———. *Miss Pickerell Meets Mr. H.U.M.* New York: McGraw-Hill, 1974. (Chapter Book/Science Fiction/Series)

MacLachlan, Patricia. *Arthur for the Very First Time*. New York: Harper, 1980. (Picture Book/Social Adjustment)

Maguire, Gregory. *Seven Spiders Spinning*, illtd. Dirk Zimmer. New York: Clarion Books, 1994. (Chapter Book/Fantasy/Humor)

Martin, Ann M. *Kristy's Great Idea* (a Baby-sitters Club book). New York: Scholastic, 1986. (Chapter Book/Series)

Maruki, Toshi. *Hiroshima no Pika (The Flash of Hiroshima)*. New York: Lothrop, Lee and Shepard, 1980. (Picture Book/World War II/Japan)

Mathews, Sally Schofer. *The Sad Night: The Story of an Aztec Victory and a Spanish Loss*. New York: Clarion, 1994. (Picture Book/Mexico/Aztec)

McCloskey, Robert. *Homer Price*. New York: Viking, 1943; New York: Puffin, 1976. (Chapter Book/Realistic Fiction/Humor)

Monjo, F. N. *The Drinking Gourd*, illtd. Fred Brenner. New York: Coward, McCann and Geoghegan, 1970; New York: Harper, 1983. (Picture Book/Easy Reader/Historical Fiction)

Mukerji, Dhan Gopal. *Kari, the Elephant*, illtd. J. E. Allen. New York: Dutton, 1922. (Fantasy/Animal/India)

———. *Hari, the Jungle Lad*, illtd. Morgan Stinemetz. New York: Dutton, 1924. (Realistic Fiction/India)

Parish, Peggy. *Amelia Bedelia*, illtd. Fritz Seibel. New York: Harper, 1963, 1992. (Chapter Book/Humor)

Parks, Van Dyke, and Malcolm Jones, adapt. from J. C. Harris. *Jump! The Adventures of Brer Rabbit*, illtd. M. Barry Moser. New York: Harcourt, 1986. Also, *Jump on Over!*, illtd. M. Barry Moser (San Diego: Harcourt, 1989). (Folk/Myth/Black American)

Pene du Bois, William. *The Twenty-One Balloons*. New York: Lothrop, Lee and Shepard, 1947; New York: Dell, 1982. NEWBERY MEDAL. (Fantasy/Science Fiction)

Petersham, Maud and Miska. *The Story Book of Clothes* and *The Story Book of Houses*. Chicago: John C. Winston, 1933. (Informational/Picture Book/Series)

———. *The Story Book of Trains, The Story Book of Coal, The Story Book of Iron and Steel, The Story Book of Gold, The Story Book of Oil*, and *The Story Book of Sugar*. Chicago: John C. Winston, 1935. (Informational/Picture Book/Series)

Pilkey, Dav. *Dogzilla*. San Diego: Harcourt, 1993. (Picture Book/Humor)

———. *Kat Kong*. San Diego: Harcourt, 1993. (Picture Book/Humor)

Prelutsky, Jack. *Nightmares: Poems to Trouble Your Sleep*, illtd. Arnold Lobel. New York: Random House, 1976. (Poetry/Suspense)

———. *The Random House Book of Poetry for Children*, illtd. Arnold Lobel. New York: Random House, 1983. (Poetry Collection/Humor)

———. *The New Kid on the Block*, illtd. James Stevenson. New York: Greenwillow, 1984. (Poetry Collection/Humor)

Richler, Mordecai. *Jacob Two-Two Meets the Hooded Fang*. Canada: McClelland and Stewart, 1976.

———. *Jacob Two-Two and the Dinosaur*, illtd. Norman Eyolfson. New York: Knopf, 1987. (Fantasy/Chapter Book/Humor/Canada)

Roberts, Willo Davis. *The Magic Book*. New York: Macmillan, 1986; New York: Aladdin, 1988. (Chapter Book/Fantasy)

Rockwell, Thomas. *How to Eat Fried Worms*. New York: Franklin Watts, 1953; New York: Dell, 1992. (Chapter Book/Realistic Fiction/Humor)

Sandburg, Carl. *Abe Lincoln Grows Up*, adapted from Sandburg's adult biography, illtd. James Daugherty. New York: Harcourt, 1928; San Diego: Harcourt, 1985. (Informational/Biographical)

Schick, Alice and Joel, adapt. and illtd. *Bram Stoker's Dracula* and *Mary Shelley's Frankenstein*. New York: Delacorte, 1980. (Fantasy-Science Fiction/Suspense)

Scieszka, Jon. *The True Story of the Three Little Pigs! by A. Wolf*, illtd. Lane Smith. New York: Penguin, 1989. (Picture Book/Fractured Fairy Tale)

Selden, George. *The Cricket in Times Square*, illtd. Garth Williams. New York: Farrar, Straus, 1960; New York: Dell, 1990. (Fantasy/Animal)

Sharmat, Marjorie W. *Nate the Great*, illtd. Marc Simont. New York: Harper, 1977. (Easy Reader/Mystery/Series)

Silverstein, Shel. *Where the Sidewalk Ends*. New York: Harper, 1974; New York: Dell, 1986. (Poetry Collection)

———. *A Light in the Attic*. New York: Harper, 1981. (Poetry Collection)

Singer, Isaac B. *Zlateh the Goat*, illtd. Maurice Sendak. New York: Harper, 1966. (Folk Tale/Jewish)

Slote, Alfred. *My Robot Buddy*, illtd. Joel Schick. New York: Harper, 1975, 1991. (Easy Reader/Science Fiction)

Smith, Robert Kimmel. *Chocolate Fever*. New York: Coward, McCann & Geoghegan, 1972; New York: Dell Yearling, 1981. (Fantasy/ Chapter Book/Humor)

Sobel, Donald J. *Encyclopedia Brown, Boy Detective*, illtd. Leonard Shortall. New York: Morrow, 1963; New York; Bantam, 1985. (Easy Reader/Mystery/Series)

Steig, William. *Dominic*. New York: Farrar, Straus and Giroux, 1972, 1990. (Fantasy/Animal)

Stine, R. L. *The Ghost Next Door* (Goosebumps series). New York: Scholastic Books, 1993. (Fantasy/Suspense)

Stockton, Frank. *The Griffin and the Minor Canon*, illtd. Maurice Sendak. New York: Holt, Rinehart and Winston, 1963; New York: Harper, 1987. (Fantasy/Fairy Tale)

Stratemeyer Syndicate. Series Books, beginning: The Bobbsey Twins (1904), Tom Swift (1910), Hardy Boys (1927), Nancy Drew (1930). New York: Simon & Schuster. (Realistic Fiction/Series)

Ward, Lynd. *The Biggest Bear*. Boston: Houghton Mifflin, 1952, 1973. CALDECOTT MEDAL. (Picture Book/Regional)

White, E. B. *Stuart Little*. New York: Harper, 1945, 1974. (Fantasy)

———. *Charlotte's Web*, illtd. Garth Williams. New York: Harper, 1952, 1974. (Fantasy)

Wilder, Laura Ingalls. *Little House in the Big Woods*. New York: Harper, 1932, 1993. (Realistic Fiction/Historical/Regional/Series)

———. *Farmer Boy*. New York: Harper, 1933, 1993. (Realistic Fiction/ Historical/Regional/Series)

———. *The Long Winter*. New York: Harper, 1940, 1994. Also, *Little Town on the Prairie* (New York: Harper, 1941, 1994); *These Happy Golden Years* (New York: Harper, 1943, HarperCollins, 1994). (Realistic Fiction/Historical/Regional/Series)

Willard, Nancy. *A Visit to William Blake's Inn: Poems for Innocent and Experienced Travelers*, illtd. Alice and Martin Provensen. San Diego: Harcourt, 1981. NEWBERY MEDAL. (Poetry/Picture Book)

Yolen, Jane. *Piggins*, illtd. Jane Dyer. San Diego: Harcourt, 1987, 1992. (Picture Book/Animal/Mystery)

———. *Animal Fare*, illtd. Jane Street. San Diego: Harcourt, 1994. (Poetry/Nonsense)

Upper Elementary

Adams, Richard. *Watership Down*. London: Rex Collins, 1972; New York: Penguin, 1972. New York: Avon, 1993. (Fantasy/Animal)

Alexander, Lloyd. *The Book of Three*. New York: Holt, Rinehart and Winston, 1964; New York: Dell, 1980. Also, *The Black Cauldron* (New York: Holt, 1965; New York: Dell, 1980); *The Castle of Llyr* (New York: Holt, 1966; New York: Dell, 1980); *Taran Wanderer* (New York: Holt, 1967; New York: Dell, 1980). (Fantasy)

———. *The High King* (final book of the *Prydain Chronicles*). New York: Henry Holt, 1968; New York: Dell, 1980. NEWBERY MEDAL. (Fantasy)

Armer, Laura. *Waterless Mountain*. New York: McKay, 1931; New York: Knopf, 1993. NEWBERY MEDAL. (Realistic Fiction/Navaho Indian)

Armstrong, William. *Sounder*. New York: Harper, 1969, 1972. NEWBERY MEDAL. (Realistic Fiction/Regional/Animal)

Babbitt, Natalie. *Tuck Everlasting*. New York: Farrar, Straus and Giroux, 1975, 1985. (Fantasy)

Blos, Joan W. *A Gathering of Days: A New England Girl's Journal*. New York: Scribner, 1979; New York: Macmillan, 1990. NEWBERY MEDAL. (Realistic Fiction/Historical/New England)

Blume, Judy. *Deenie*. New York: Bradbury, 1973; New York: Dell, 1991. (Realistic Fiction/Social Adjustment)

Bond, Nancy. *A String in the Harp*. New York: Atheneum, 1977; New York: Puffin, 1987. (Realistic Fiction/Social Adjustment/Death)

Bontemps, Arna. *Sad-Faced Boy*, illtd. Virginia Burton, Boston: Houghton Mifflin, 1937. (Realistic Fiction/Black American)

Boston, Lucy. *The Children of Green Knowe*. New York: Harcourt, 1954; San Diego: Harcourt, 1989. (Fantasy/Series)

Brink, Carol Ryrie. *Caddie Woodlawn*. New York: Macmillan, 1935, 1990. NEWBERY MEDAL. (Realistic Fiction/Historical/Regional)

Burnett, Frances Hodgson. *Little Lord Fauntleroy*, illtd. Frederick S. Church. New York: Scribner, 1886; New York: Bantam, 1987. (Realistic Fiction)

———. *A Little Princess*. Philadelphia: Lippincott, 1905; New York: Dell Yearling, 1975. (Realistic Fiction)

———. *The Secret Garden*. Philadelphia: Lippincott, 1911; New York: Random House, 1993. (Realistic Fiction)

Burnford, Sheila. *The Incredible Journey*, illtd. Carl Burger. Boston: Little, Brown, 1961; New York: Bantam, 1990. (Realistic Fiction/Animal)

Byars, Betsy. *Summer of the Swans*, illtd. Ted Coconis. New York: Viking Press, 1970; New York: Puffin, 1981. NEWBERY MEDAL. (Realistic Fiction/Social Adjustment)

Cameron, Eleanor. *The Wonderful Flight to the Mushroom Planet*. Boston: Little, Brown, 1954, 1988. (Science Fiction/Fantasy/Series)

Carroll, Lewis (pseud. of Charles L. Dodgson). *Alice's Adventures in Wonderland*, illtd. John Tenniel. New York: St. Martin's Press, 1977. (Fantasy)

———. *Through the Looking Glass*. New York: Macmillan, 1993. (Fantasy)

Childress, Alice. *A Hero Ain't Nothin' But a Sandwich*. New York: Coward, McCann and Geoghegan, 1973; New York: BDD, 1989. (Realistic Fiction/Social Adjustment/Black American)

Clark, Ann Nolan. *Secret of the Andes*. New York: Viking, 1952; New York: Puffin, 1976. NEWBERY MEDAL. (Realistic Fiction/Cultural)

Clarke, Pauline. *Return of the Twelves*. New York: Coward McCann, 1962. New York: Dell, 1992. (Fantasy/Toys)

Colum, Padraic. *The Children of Odin*. New York: Macmillan, 1920, 1984. (Folk/Myth/Norway)

———. *The Golden Fleece and the Heroes Who Lived Before Achilles*. New York: Macmillan, 1922, 1983. (Folk/Myth/Greece)

Cooper, Susan. *Over Sea, Under Stone* (*Dark Is Rising Sequence*, vol. 1). New York: Macmillan/McElderry, 1965, 1989. (Fantasy)

———. *The Dark Is Rising* (New York: Atheneum, 1973); *Greenwitch* (New York: Atheneum, 1974); *The Grey King* (New York: Atheneum, 1975); *Silver on the Tree* (New York: Atheneum, 1977)—all were reprinted by Macmillan in 1987. (Fantasy)

———. *The Boggart*, a Margaret K. McElderry book. New York: Macmillan, 1993. (Fantasy)

Creech, Sharon. *Walk Two Moons*. New York: HarperCollins, 1994. NEWBERY MEDAL. (Realistic Fiction/Native American)

Dahl, Roald. *Charlie and the Chocolate Factory*, illtd. Joseph Schindelman. New York: Knopf, 1964; New York: BDD, 1989. (Fantasy)

Daugherty, James. *Daniel Boone*. New York: Viking, 1939. NEWBERY MEDAL. (Informational/Biography)

De Angeli, Marguerite. *Bright April*. New York: Doubleday, 1946. (Picture Book/Realistic Fiction/Black American)

———. *The Door in the Wall*. New York: Doubleday, 1949; New York: Dell, 1990. NEWBERY MEDAL. (Realistic Fiction/Historical/Medieval)

DeJong, Meindert. *The Wheel on the School*, illtd. Maurice Sendak. New York: Harper, 1954, 1972. NEWBERY MEDAL. (Realistic Fiction/Cultural/Holland)

———. *The House of Sixty Fathers*, illtd. Maurice Sendak. New York: Harper, 1956, 1987. HANS CHRISTIAN ANDERSEN AWARD, 1962. (Realistic Friction/World War II/China)

Dodge, Mary Mapes. *Hans Brinker; or, The Silver Skates*, illtd. F. O. C. Darley and Thomas Nast. New York: James O'Kane, 1865; New York: BDD (Dell), 1985. (Realistic Fiction/Holland)

Eager, Edward. *Half Magic*. New York: Harcourt, 1954; San Diego: Harcourt, 1982. (Fantasy/Series)

Enright, Elizabeth. *The Saturdays*. New York: Henry Holt, 1941, 1988. (Realistic Fiction/Family Relationships/Series)

Estes, Eleanor. *The Hundred Dresses*, illtd. Louis Slobodkin. New York: Harcourt, 1944; San Diego: Harcourt, 1974. (Realistic Fiction/Social Adjustment)

———. *The Witch Family*. New York: Harcourt, 1960, 1990. (Fantasy)

Field, Rachel. *Hitty, Her First Hundred Years*, illtd. Dorothy Lathrop. New York: Macmillan, 1929, 1969. NEWBERY MEDAL. (Fantasy/Historical/Toys)

———. *Calico Bush*. New York: Macmillan, 1931, 1990. (Realistic Fiction/Historical)

Finger, Charles J. *Tales from Silver Lands*. New York: Doubleday, 1924; New York: Scholastic, 1989. NEWBERY MEDAL. (Folk/Myth/Short Story Collection/South American Indian)

Fitzgerald, John D. *The Great Brain*. New York: Dial, 1967, 1985. (Realistic Fiction/Family Relationships/Series)

Fitzhugh, Louise. *Harriet the Spy*. New York: Harper, 1964, 1990. (Realistic Fiction/Social Behavior)

Forbes, Esther. *Johnny Tremain*, illtd. Lynd Ward. Boston: Houghton Mifflin, 1943; New York: Dell Yearling, 1987. NEWBERY MEDAL. (Realistic Fiction/Historical/Revolutionary War)

Frank, Anne. *Anne Frank: The Diary of a Young Girl*, tr. B. M. Mookyaart. New York: Doubleday, 1952; New York: BDD, 1995 (Special Anniversary Edition). (Informational/Autobiographical/World War II)

Freedman, Russell. *Lincoln: A Photobiography*. New York: Clarion, 1987. (Informational/Biographical/Photographs)

Gates, Doris. *Blue Willow*. New York: Viking, 1940; New York: Puffin, 1976. (Realistic Fiction/Social Adjustment)

George, Jean Craighead. *My Side of the Mountain*. New York: Dutton, 1959; New York: Puffin, 1991. (Realistic Fiction/Social Adjustment/Nature)

———. *Julie of the Wolves*, illtd. John Schoenherr. New York: Harper, 1972. NEWBERY MEDAL. (Realistic Fiction/Social Adjustment/Nature)

Grahame, Kenneth. *Wind in the Willows*. New York: Macmillan, 1991. (Fantasy/Animal)

Gray, Elizabeth Janet. *Adam of the Road*, illtd. Robert Lawson. New York: Viking, 1942; New York: Puffin, 1987. NEWBERY MEDAL. (Realistic Fiction/Historical/Medieval)

Hamilton, Edith. *Mythology*. New York: Dutton, 1942, 1989. (Folk/Myth)

Hamilton, Virginia. *The House of Dies Drear*. New York: Macmillan, 1968, 1984. (Realistic Fiction/Black American/Mystery)

———. *M.C. Higgins, the Great*. New York: Macmillan, 1974, 1993. NEWBERY MEDAL. (Realistic Fiction/Social Adjustment/Regional)

———. *The People Could Fly*, illtd. Diane and Leo Dillon. New York: Knopf, 1985. (Folk Tales/Black American)

———. *In the Beginning: Creation Stories from Around the World*, illtd. Barry Moser. San Diego: Harcourt, 1988. (Folk Tales/Short Story Collection)

Hawes, Charles Boardman. *The Dark Frigate*. Boston: Little, Brown, 1923, 1971. NEWBERY MEDAL. (Realistic Fiction/Historical)

Hawthorne, Nathaniel. *A Wonder Book for Girls and Boys*. Boston: Houghton Mifflin, 1852, 1951. (Folk/Myth)

———. *Tanglewood Tales for Girls and Boys*. Boston: Houghton Mifflin, 1853, 1951. (Folk/Myth)

Heinlein, Robert. *Red Planet*. New York: Scribners, 1949; New York: Ballantine, 1986. (Science Fiction)

Henry, Marguerite. *Misty of Chincoteague*. New York: Macmillan, 1947, 1991. (Realistic Fiction/Animal)

———. *King of the Wind*. New York: Macmillan, 1948, 1991. NEWBERY MEDAL. (Realistic Fiction/Animal)

Hoover, H. M. *The Children of Morrow*. New York: Four Winds, 1973. (Science Fiction)

Hunt, Irene. *Across Five Aprils*. New York: Follett, 1964. (Realistic Fiction/Civil War)

———. *Up a Road Slowly*. New York: Follett, 1966; New York: Silver Burdett, 1993. NEWBERY MEDAL. (Realistic Fiction/Family Relationships/Black American)

I Never Saw Another Butterfly: Children's Drawings and Poems from Terezin Concentration Camp, 1942–1944. New York: Schocken Books, 1978. (Informational/Poetry/Holocaust/Death)

James, Will. *Smoky: A Cow Horse.* New York: Scribners, 1926; New York: Macmillan, 1993. NEWBERY MEDAL. (Realistic Fiction/Regional/Animal)

Janeczko, Paul, ed. *The Place My Words Are Looking For.* New York: Bradbury Press, 1990. (Poetry/Anthology)

Jarrell, Randall. *Fly By Night*, illtd. Maurice Sendak. New York: Farrar, Straus & Giroux, 1969, 1985. (Fantasy/Poetry)

Kelly, Eric P. *The Trumpeter of Krakow.* New York: Macmillan, 1928, 1992. NEWBERY MEDAL. (Realistic Fiction/Historical/Poland)

Kingsley, Charles. *The Water Babies: A Fairy Tale for a Land-Baby.* New York: Crown, 1986. (Fantasy/Fairy)

Klein, Norma. *Mom, the Wolf Man and Me.* New York: Pantheon, 1972. (Realistic Fiction/Social Adjustment)

———. *Love Is One of the Choices.* New York: Dial, 1978. (Realistic Fiction/Social Adjustment)

Knight, Eric. *Lassie Come-Home.* New York: Henry Holt, 1940; New York: Dell Yearling, 1992. (Realistic Fiction/Animal)

Konigsburg, E. L. *From the Mixed-up Files of Mrs. Basil E. Frankweiler.* New York: Atheneum, 1967; New York: Buccaneer Books, 1992. NEWBERY MEDAL. (Realistic Fiction/Social Adjustment/Urban)

———. *About the B'Nai Bagels.* New York: Atheneum, 1969. (Realistic Fiction/Social Adjustment/Humor)

Krull, Kathleen. *Lives of the Writers: Comedies, Tragedies (and What the Neighbors Thought)*, illtd. Kathryn Hewitt. San Diego: Harcourt, 1994. (Informational/Short Story Collection/Biographical)

Krumgold, Joseph. *And Now Miguel.* New York: Crowell, 1953; New York: Harper, 1987. NEWBERY MEDAL. (Realistic Fiction/Cultural/Regional)

———. *Onion John.* New York: Crowell, 1959; New York: Harper, 1987. NEWBERY MEDAL. (Realistic Fiction/Homelessness)

Lang, Andrew, ed. *The Blue Fairy Book.* New York: Dover, 1965. (Fantasy/Fairy)

———. *The Red Fairy Book.* Cutchogue, N.Y.: Buccaneer, 1987. (Fantasy/Fairy)

———. *The Green Fairy Book.* New York: Dover, 1965. (Fantasy/Fairy)

———. *The Yellow Fairy Book.* New York: Puffin, 1988. (Fantasy/Fairy)

Langton, Jane. *The Swing in the Summerhouse*, illtd. Eric Blegvad. New York: Harper, 1967. (Fantasy)

Latham, Jean Lee. *Carry On, Mr. Bowditch*. Boston: Houghton Mifflin, 1955, 1973. NEWBERY MEDAL. (Informational/Historical/ Biography)

Lauber, Patricia. *Volcano: The Eruption and Healing of Mount St. Helens*. New York: Bradbury, 1986. (Informational/Photographs/Science)

Leguin, Ursula K. *A Wizard of Earthsea*. New York: Parnassus Press, 1968; New York: Macmillan, 1992. (Fantasy)

———. *The Tombs of Atuan*. New York: Atheneum, 1971; New York: Macmillan, 1992. (Fantasy)

———. *The Farthest Shore*. New York: Atheneum, 1972; New York: Macmillan, 1992. (Fantasy)

———. *Tehanu: The Last Book of Earthsea*. New York: Atheneum, 1990. (Fantasy)

L'Engle, Madeleine. *A Wrinkle in Time*. New York: Farrar, Straus, 1962; New York: Dell, 1976. NEWBERY MEDAL. (Fantasy/Science Fiction)

Lenski, Lois. *Bayou Suzette*. Philadelphia: Lippincott, 1943; Cutchogue, N.Y.: Buccaneer, 1991. (Realistic Fiction/Regional)

———. *Strawberry Girl*. Philadelphia: Lippincott, 1945; Cutchogue, N.Y.: Buccaneer, 1991. NEWBERY MEDAL. (Realistic Fiction/ Regional)

Lester, Julius. *To Be a Slave*, illtd. Tom Feelings. New York: Dial, 1968; New York: Scholastic, 1986. (Informational/Historical Anthology/ Black American)

Lewis, Elizabeth. *Young Fu of the Upper Yangtze*, illtd. Kurt Wiese. New York: Holt, Rinehart and Winston, 1932; New York: BDD (Dell), 1990. NEWBERY MEDAL. (Realistic Fiction/Historical/China)

Lisle, Janet Taylor. *Afternoon of the Elves*. Boston: Orchard Books, 1989. (Realistic Fiction/Social Adjustment)

Livingston, Myra Cohn. *Remembering and Other Poems*, a Margaret K. McElderry book. New York: Macmillan, 1989. (Poetry)

Lofting, Hugh. *The Story of Doctor Dolittle*. Philadelphia: Lippincott, 1920; New York: BDD (Dell Yearling), 1988 (rev. ed.). (Fantasy)

———. *The Voyages of Doctor Dolittle*. Philadelphia: Lippincott, 1922; New York: Dell Yearling, 1988 (rev. ed.). NEWBERY MEDAL. (Fantasy)

———. *Doctor Dolittle in the Moon*. Philadelphia: Lippincott, 1928; New York: BDD (Dell Yearling), 1988 (rev. ed.). (Fantasy)

London, Jack. *The Call of the Wild*. New York: Macmillan, 1903. (Realistic Fiction/Animal)

———. *White Fang*. New York: Macmillan, 1906. (Realistic Fiction/Animal)

Lord, Betty Bao. *In the Year of the Boar and Jackie Robinson*, illtd. Marc Simont. New York: Harper, 1984. (Realistic Fiction/Social Adjustment/Chinese American)

Lowry, Lois. *Number the Stars*. Boston: Houghton Mifflin, 1989. NEWBERY MEDAL. (Historical Fiction/World War II/Holocaust)

Macaulay, David. *Cathedral*. Boston: Houghton Mifflin, 1973, 1981. (Informational/Architecture)

———. *The Way Things Work*. Boston: Houghton Mifflin, 1989. (Informational)

———. *Black and White*. Boston: Houghton Mifflin, 1990. CALDECOTT MEDAL. (Picture Book/Mystery)

MacLachlan, Patricia. *Sarah, Plain and Tall*. New York: Harper, 1985. NEWBERY MEDAL. (Realistic Fiction/Historical/Regional)

Mathis, Sharon Bell. *The Hundred Penny Box*, illtd. Diane and Leo Dillon. New York: Viking, 1975; New York: Puffin, 1986. (Picture Book/Social Relationships/Aging)

McCaffrey, Anne. *Dragonsong*. New York: Atheneum, 1976; New York: Bantam, 1986. Also, *Dragonsinger* (New York: Atheneum, 1977; New York: Bantam, 1986); *Dragondrums* (New York: Atheneum, 1979; New York: Bantam, 1980). (Fantasy)

McKinley, Robin. *Beauty: A Retelling of the Story of Beauty and the Beast*. New York: Harper, 1978. (Fantasy/Fairy Tale)

Means, Florence Crannell. *The Moved-Outers*. Boston: Houghton Mifflin, 1945; New York: Walker, 1992. (Realistic Fiction/World War II)

Meigs, Cornelia. *Invincible Louisa*. Boston: Little, Brown, 1933, 1968. NEWBERY MEDAL. (Informational/Biography)

Meltzer, Milton. *Never to Forget: The Jews of the Holocaust*. New York: Harper, 1976, 1991. (Informational/Jewish History)

Meltzer, Milton, ed. *A. Lincoln: In His Own Words*, illtd. Stephen Alcorn. San Diego: Harcourt, 1993. (Informational/Biography)

Merrill, Jean. *The Pushcart War*, illtd. Ronni Solbert. New York: Scott, 1964; New York: Dell, 1987. (Science Fiction-Fantasy/Social Adjustment)

Montgomery, Lucy Maud. *Anne of Green Gables*, illtd. M. A. and W. A. Claus. Boston: L.C. Page, 1908. New York: Bantam Classic. (Realistic Fiction)

Mukerji, Dhan Gopal. *Gay-Neck: The Story of a Pigeon*, illtd. Boris Artzybasheff. New York: Dutton, 1927, 1968. NEWBERY MEDAL. (Realistic Fiction/Animals)

Myers, Walter Dean. *Scorpions*. New York: Harper, 1988. (Realistic Fiction/Cultural/African American and Hispanic American)

Naylor, Phyllis Reynolds. *Shiloh*. New York: Atheneum, 1991. NEWBERY MEDAL. (Realistic Fiction/Animal)

Nesbit, Edith. *Five Children and It*. New York: Puffin, 1985. Also, *The Phoenix and the Carpet* (New York: Puffin, 1985) and *The Story of the Amulet* (New York: Puffin, 1986). (Fantasy)

Neufeld, John. *Lisa, Bright and Dark*. Chatham, N.Y.: S.G. Phillips, 1969; New York: NAL Dutton, 1970. (Realistic Fiction/Social Behavior)

Neville, Emily. *It's Like This, Cat*, illtd. Emil Weiss. New York: Harper, 1963, 1975. NEWBERY MEDAL. (Realistic Fiction/Social Behavior)

———. *Berries Goodman*. New York: Harper, 1965, 1992. (Realistic Fiction/Social Behavior)

Norton, Mary. *The Borrowers*. New York: Harcourt, 1953; San Diego: Harcourt, 1989. Also, *The Borrowers Afield* (New York: Harcourt, 1955; San Diego: Harcourt, 1990); *The Borrowers Afloat* (New York: Harcourt, 1959; San Diego: Harcourt, 1990). All three books are illustrated by Beth and Joe Krush. (Fantasy/Series)

O'Brien, Robert C. *Mrs. Frisby and the Rats of NIMH*, illtd. Zena Bernstein. New York: Atheneum, 1971; New York: Macmillan, 1986. NEWBERY MEDAL. (Fantasy/Animal)

O'Dell, Scott. *Island of the Blue Dolphins*. Boston: Houghton Mifflin, 1960, 1990. NEWBERY MEDAL. (Realistic Fiction/Cultural/South Pacific)

O'Hara, Mary. *My Friend Flicka*. New York: Harper, 1941, 1988. (Realistic Fiction/Animal)

Paine, Albert B. *Girl in White Armor, the True Story of Joan of Arc*, adapted from adult biography. New York: Macmillan, 1927. (Informational/Biographical)

Paterson, Katherine. *The Master Puppeteer*. New York: Harper, 1975, 1991. NATIONAL BOOK AWARD. (Historical Fiction/Ancient Japan)

———. *Bridge to Terabithia*. New York: Harper, 1977, 1987. NEWBERY MEDAL. (Realistic Fiction/Social Adjustment/Death)

———. *Jacob Have I Loved*. New York: Crowell, 1980; New York: Harper, 1990. NEWBERY AWARD. (Realistic Fiction/Social Adjustment)

———. *Lyddie*. New York: Lodestar, 1991. (Realistic Fiction/ Historical/ New England)

Peck, Robert Newton. *The Day No Pigs Would Die*. New York: Knopf, 1972; New York: Dell, 1983. (Realistic Fiction/Autobiographical/ Social Adjustment/Shaker)

Porter, Eleanor. *Pollyanna*. Boston: L.C. Page, 1913; New York: Puffin, 1988. (Realistic Fiction)

Pyle, Howard. *The Merry Adventures of Robin Hood*. New York: Scribners, 1883; New York: Macmillan, 1977. (Folk/Myth)

Raskin, Ellen. *Figgs and Phantoms*. New York: Dutton, 1974. (Realistic Fiction)

———. *The Westing Game*. New York: Dutton, 1978; New York: Puffin, 1992. NEWBERY MEDAL. (Realistic Fiction/Mystery)

Reiss, Johanna. *The Upstairs Room*. New York: Crowell, 1972; New York: Harper, 1990. (Realistic Fiction/World War II/Holland)

Rodgers, Mary. *Freaky Friday*. New York: Harper, 1972. (Chapter Book/Fantasy/Humor)

Salten, Felix (pseud. of Siegmund Salzmann). *Bambi*, illtd. Kurt Wiese. New York: Simon & Schuster, 1928, 1991. (Realistic Fiction/Animal)

Sandburg, Carl. *Prairie-Town Boy*, illtd. Joe Krush. New York: Harcourt, 1955; San Diego: Harcourt, 1990. (Autobiographical)

Sauer, Julia. *Fog Magic*. New York: Viking, 1943; New York: Puffin, 1986. (Time Fantasy/Regional American History)

Savitz, Harriet May. *Wheelchair Champions: A History of Wheelchair Sports*. New York: Crowell, 1978. (Informational/Physical Adjustment)

Sawyer, Ruth. *Roller Skates*. New York: Viking, 1936; New York: Puffin, 1986. NEWBERY MEDAL. (Realistic Fiction/Historical/Regional)

Schick, Alice. *The Peregrine Falcons*, illtd. Peter Parnall. New York: Dial, 1975. (Informational/Nature)

Schick, Alice, and Sara Ann Friedman. *Zoo Year*, illtd. Joel Schick. New York: Lippincott, 1978. (Informational/Animal)

Sewell, Anna. *Black Beauty: His Grooms and Companions*. New York: Random House, 1989. (Realistic Fiction/Animal)

Shannon, Monica. *Dobry*. New York: Viking, 1934; New York: Puffin, 1993. NEWBERY MEDAL. (Realistic Fiction/Historical)

Sidney, Margaret (pseud. of Harriet Mulford Stone Lothrop). *Five Little Peppers and How They Grew*. New York: Lothrop, 1881; New York: Scholastic, 1989. (Realistic Fiction)

Silverstein, Shel. *The Giving Tree*. New York: Harper, 1964. (Picture Book/Concept)

Sleator, William. *Oddballs*. New York: Dutton, 1993. (Realistic Fiction/Autobiographical/Humor)

Snyder, Zilpha Keatley. *The Egypt Game*, illtd. Alton Raible. New York: Atheneum, 1967; New York: Dell, 1986. (Realistic Fiction/Mystery)

Speare, Elizabeth George. *The Witch of Blackbird Pond.* Boston: Houghton Mifflin, 1958; New York: Dell, 1978. NEWBERY MEDAL. (Realistic Fiction/Regional)

———. *The Bronze Bow.* Boston: Houghton Mifflin, 1961, 1973. NEWBERY MEDAL. (Realistic Fiction/Jewish History)

Sperry, Armstrong. *Call It Courage.* New York: Macmillan, 1940; Aladdin, 1990. NEWBERY MEDAL. (Realistic Fiction/South Pacific)

Spinelli, Jerry. *Space Station Seventh Grade.* Boston: Little, Brown, 1982, 1991. (Chapter/Science Fiction)

———. *Maniac Magee.* Boston: Little, Brown, 1990. NEWBERY MEDAL. (Realistic Fiction)

Spyri, Joanna. *Heidi,* tr. Helen B. Dole. Boston: DeWolfe Fiske, 1884; New York: Dutton, 1992. (Realistic Fiction)

Staples, Suzanne Fisher. *Shabanu: Daughter of the Wind.* New York: Knopf, 1989. (Realistic Fiction/Cultural/Middle East)

Sterling, Dorothy. *Mary Jane,* illtd. Ernest Crichlow. New York: Doubleday, 1959. (Realistic Fiction/Black American)

Taylor, Mildred. *Roll of Thunder, Hear My Cry.* New York: Dial, 1976; New York: Puffin, 1991. NEWBERY MEDAL. (Realistic Fiction/Social Adjustment/Black American/1930s)

Taylor, Sydney. *All-of-a-Kind Family.* New York: Follett, 1951; New York: Bantam-Doubleday-Dell, 1989. (Realistic Fiction/Jewish American)

Thompson, Blanche J., ed., et al. *Silver Pennies.* New York: Macmillan, 1925. Cutchogue, N.Y.: Buccaneer, 1991. (Poetry)

Thompson, Ernest Seton. *Wild Animals I Have Known.* New York: Scribner, 1898; New York: Viking, 1986. (Informational/Animal)

Tolkien, J. R. R. *The Hobbit.* 1937; Boston: Houghton Mifflin, 1938, 1988. (Fantasy)

Travers, P. L. *Mary Poppins,* illtd. Mary Shepard. New York: Harcourt, 1934; New York: Bantam-Doubleday-Dell, 1991. (Fantasy/Series)

———. *Mary Poppins Comes Back.* New York: Harcourt, 1934; New York: Bantam-Doubleday-Dell, 1991. (Fantasy/Series)

Twain, Mark (pseud. of Samuel Clemens). *The Adventures of Tom Sawyer,* illtd. True W. Williams. New York: Harper, 1876; New York: Scholastic, 1993. (Realistic Fiction)

Uchida, Yoshiko. *The Dancing Kettle and Other Japanese Folk Tales.* New York: Harcourt, 1949; Creative Arts, 1986. (Folk Tales/Short Story Collection/Japan)

———. *A Jar of Dreams.* New York: Atheneum, 1981. (Realistic Fiction/Social Adjustment/Japanese American)

Van Loon, Hendrik Willem. *The Story of Mankind*. New York: Liveright, 1921; 1985. NEWBERY MEDAL. (Informational/Historical)

Washington, Booker T. *Up From Slavery*. Boston: Houghton Mifflin, 1917; Cutchogue, N.Y.: Buccaneer, 1990. (Informational/Biography)

Webster, Jean. *Daddy Long-Legs*. New York: Meredith Press, 1912; New York: Knopf, 1993. (Realistic Fiction)

Wiggin, Kate Douglas. *Rebecca of Sunnybrook Farm*. Boston: Houghton Mifflin, 1903; New York: Outlet, 1993. (Realistic Fiction)

Wojciechowska, Maia. *Shadow of a Bull*, illtd. Alvin Smith. New York: Atheneum, 1964; New York: Macmillan, 1992. NEWBERY MEDAL. (Realistic Fiction/Cultural/Spain)

Wolff, Virginia Euwer. *The Mozart Season*. New York: Henry Holt, 1991. (Realistic Fiction/Social Adjustment/Music)

Yates, Elizabeth. *Amos Fortune, Free Man*. New York: Dutton, 1950. NEWBERY MEDAL. (Informational/Biography/Black American)

Yep, Lawrence. *Dragonwings*. New York: Harper, 1974; New York: BDD, 1990. (Realistic Fiction/Historical/Chinese American)

Yolen, Jane. *The Devil's Arithmetic*. New York: Viking Penguin, 1988. (Fantasy/Time Travel/Holocaust)

Young Adult

Alcott, Louisa May. *Little Women*. Boston: Little, Brown, 1868 (first half); 1869 (second half); New York: Scholastic, 1986. (Realistic Fiction)

———. *Little Men*. Boston: Little, Brown, 1871; New York: Scholastic, 1987. (Realistic Fiction)

Anonymous. *Go Ask Alice*. Englewood Cliffs, N.J.: Prentice-Hall, 1971; New York: Avon, 1976. (Informational/Autobiographical/Social Adjustment)

Archer, Jules. *Rage in the Streets: Mob Violence in America*, illtd. Lydia J. Hess. San Diego: Harcourt, 1994. (Informational/Social Adjustment)

Avi. *The True Confessions of Charlotte Doyle*. New York: Orchard, 1990. (Realistic Fiction/Historical/19th Century)

Bachrach, Susan D. *Tell Them We Remember: The Story of the Holocaust*. New York: Little, Brown, 1994. (Informational/Historical/World War II/Holocaust)

Barrie, James M. *Peter and Wendy* [Peter Pan]. New York: Scribner, 1911; New York: Outlet, 1990. (Fantasy)

Block, Francesca Lia. *Weetzie Bat*. New York: Harper, 1989. (Contemporary Fiction/Regional)

Bosse, Malcolm. *Deep Dream of the Rain Forest*. New York: Farrar, Straus and Giroux, 1993. (Realistic Fiction/Cultural/South America)

Buss, Fran Leeper, with the assistance of Daisy Cubias. *Journey of the Sparrows*. New York: Dutton, 1991. (Realistic Fiction/Cultural Adjustment/El Salvador)

Chang, Margaret and Raymond. *In the Eye of War*, a Margaret K. McElderry book. New York: Macmillan, 1990. (Realistic Fiction/World War II/China)

Chase, Richard, ed. *The Jack Tales: Folk Tales from the Southern Appalachians Collected and Retold*, illtd. Berkley Williams Jr. Boston: Houghton Mifflin, 1943, 1993. (Folk Tales/Short Story Collection/Regional)

Choi, Sook Nyul. *Year of Impossible Goodbyes*. Boston: Houghton Mifflin, 1991. (Realistic Fiction/World War II/Korea)

Cleaver, Vera and Bill. *Where the Lilies Bloom*, illtd. Jim Spanfeller. Philadelphia: Lippincott, 1969; New York: Harper, 1991. (Realistic Fiction/Regional)

Collier, James Lincoln, and Christopher Collier. *My Brother Sam Is Dead*. New York: Four Winds, 1974; New York: Macmillan, 1984. (Realistic Fiction/Revolutionary War/Death)

Cormier, Robert. *The Chocolate War*. New York: Pantheon, 1974. (Realistic Fiction/Social Adjustment)

———. *After the First Death*. New York: Pantheon, 1989. (Realistic Fiction/Terrorism)

———. *Tunes for Bears to Dance To*. New York: BDD, 1992. (Realistic Fiction/World War II/Holocaust)

Crane, Stephen. *The Red Badge of Courage*. New York: Appleton, 1895; in *Great Short Works of Stephen Crane* (New York: Random, 1990). (Realistic Fiction/Historical/Civil War)

De Saint Exupery, Antoine. *The Little Prince*. New York: Harcourt, 1943; San Diego: Harcourt, 1993. (Fantasy)

De Trevino, Elizabeth Borton. *I, Juan De Pareja*. New York: Farrar, Straus and Giroux, 1965, 1987. NEWBERY MEDAL. (Realistic Fiction/Biographical/Cultural)

Eastman, Charles A. *Indian Boyhood*. New York: McClure, Philips, 1902; New York: Dover, 1971. (Informational/Biography)

Fleischman, Paul. *Joyful Noise: Poems for Two Voices*. New York: Harper, 1988. NEWBERY MEDAL. (Poetry/Interactive)

Fox, Paula. *The Slave Dancer*, illtd. Eros Keith. Scarsdale, N.Y.: Bradbury, 1973; New York: Dell, 1991. NEWBERY MEDAL. (Historical Fiction/African American)

Goodman, Joan Elizabeth. *Songs From Home*. San Diego: Harcourt, 1994. (Realistic Fiction/Social Adjustment/Italy)

Green, Hannah (pseud. of Joanne Greenberg). *I Never Promised You a Rose Garden*. New York: Holt, Rinehart and Winston, 1964. (Informational/Realistic Fiction/Autobiographical)

Grinnell, George Bird. *Blackfoot Lodge Tales*. New York: Scribner, 1892; Lincoln: University of Nebraska Press, 1962. (Folk/Myth/American Indian)

Hamilton, Virginia. *The Planet of Junior Brown*. New York: Macmillan, 1971, 1993. (Realistic Fiction/Urban)

Highwater, Jamake. *Anpao: An American Indian Odyssey*. Philadelphia: Lippincott, 1977; New York: HarperCollins, 1992. (Fantasy/American Indian)

Hinojosa, Maria. *Crews: Gang Members Talk to Maria Hinojosa*, photog. German Perez. San Diego: Harcourt, 1990. (Informational/Social Adjustment/Inner City)

Hinton, S. E. *The Outsiders*. New York: Viking, 1967; New York: Dell, (Realistic Fiction/Urban/Social Behavior)

Holland, Isabelle. *The Man Without a Face*. Boston: G.K. Hall, 1972; New York: HarperCollins, 1988. (Realistic Fiction/Social Adjustment/Homosexuality)

Kerr, M. E. *Gentlehands*. New York: Harper, 1978, 1990. (Realistic Fiction/World War II/Holocaust)

———. *Linger*. New York: HarperCollins, 1993. (Realistic Fiction/Social Adjustment/Gulf War)

Lowry, Lois. *The Giver*. Boston: Houghton Mifflin, 1993. NEWBERY MEDAL. (Fantasy)

Mori, Kyoko. *Shizuko's Daughter*. New York: Henry Holt, 1993. (Realistic Fiction/Social Adjustment/Japan)

Paulsen, Gary. *Dogsong*. New York: Bradbury, 1985. (Realistic Fiction/Alaska)

Peck, Richard. *Are You in the House Alone?* New York: Viking, 1976. (Realistic Fiction/Social Adjustment)

Rylant, Cynthia. *Missing May*. New York: Orchard Books, 1992. NEWBERY MEDAL. (Realistic Fiction/Social Adjustment/Death)

Temple, Frances. *A Taste of Salt: A Story of Modern Haiti*. New York: Harper, 1992. (Realistic Fiction/Culture/Haiti)

———. *Grab Hands and Run*, a Richard Jackson book. New York: Orchard Books, 1993. (Realistic Fiction/Central America)

Tolkien, J. R. R. *The Lord of the Rings* trilogy, consisting of: *The Fellowship of the Ring* (Boston: Houghton Mifflin, 1954, 1992); *The Two Towers (Boston: Houghton Mifflin, 1955, 1992); The Return of the King* (Boston: Houghton Mifflin, 1956, 1992). (Fantasy)

Twain, Mark (pseud. of Samuel Clemens). *The Prince and the Pauper*. New York: Harper, 1882; New York: Puffin, 1983. (Realistic Fiction)

———. *Adventures of Huckleberry Finn*. New York: Harper, 1885; New York: Random House, 1985. (Realistic Fiction)

———. *A Connecticut Yankee in King Arthur's Court*. New York: Harper, 1889; New York: Bantam, 1983. (Fantasy)

Voigt, Cynthia. *Dicey's Song*. New York: Atheneum, 1982. NEWBERY MEDAL. (Realistic Fiction)

Zindel, Paul. *The Pigman*. New York: Harper, 1968. (Realistic Fiction/Social Adjustment)

RESEARCH BIBLIOGRAPHY

Arbuthnot, May Hill. *Children and Books*, 3rd ed. Chicago: Scott, Foresman, 1964.

Bader, Barbara. *American Picturebooks from Noah's Ark to the Beast Within*. New York: Macmillan, 1976.

Bechtel, Louise Seaman. *Books in Search of Children*. New York: Macmillan, 1969.

Bingham, Jane M., ed. *Writers for Children: Critical Studies of Major Authors Since the Seventeenth Century*. New York: Scribner, 1988.

Bloom, Harold. *The Western Canon: The Books and School of the Ages*. San Diego: Harcourt, 1994.

Bowker, Editors of R.R. *Best Books for Children: Preschool Through Grade 6*, 4th ed. New Providence, N.J.: R.R. Bowker, 1990.

———. *Children's Books in Print*. New Providence, N.J.: R.R. Bowker, 1970– .

Butler, Francelia, and Richard Rotert, eds. *Reflections on Literature for Children*. Hamden, Conn.: Shoe String Press, 1984.

Cameron, Eleanor. *The Green and Burning Tree: On the Writing and Enjoyment of Children's Books*. Boston: Little, Brown, 1969.

———. *The Seed and the Vision: On the Writing and Appreciation of Children's Books*. New York: Dutton, 1993.

Carpenter, Humphrey. *Secret Gardens: The Golden Age of Children's Literature*. Boston: Houghton Mifflin, 1985.

Cianciolo, Patricia J. *Picture Books for Children, 3rd ed.* Chicago: American Library Association, 1990.

Cott, Jonathan. *Pipers at the Gates of Dawn: The Wisdom of Children's Literature*. New York: McGraw Hill, 1985.

Egoff, Sheila A., G. T. Stubbs, and L. F. Ashley, eds. *Only Connect: Readings on Children's Literature*. New York: Oxford University Press, 1969.

Egoff, Sheila A. *Thursday's Child: Trends and Patterns in Contemporary Children's Literature*. Chicago: American Library Association, 1981.

Fenwick, Sara Innis, ed. *A Critical Approach to Children's Literature*. Chicago: University of Chicago Press, 1967.

Foerstel, Herbert N. *Banned in the U.S.A.: A Reference Guide to Book Censorship in Schools and Public Libraries*. Westport, Conn.: Greenwood Press, 1994.

Frederick, Heather. "Authenticity of Chief's Speech Questioned," *Publisher's Weekly*, June 1, 1992, p. 22.

Green, David L. and Dick Martin. *The Oz Scrapbook*. New York: Random House, 1977.

Harrison, Barbara, and Gregory Maguire, eds. *Innocence & Experience: Essays & Conversations on Children's Literature*. New York: Lothrop, Lee & Shepard, 1987.

Haviland, Virginia, ed. *Books in Search of Children: Speeches and Essays by Louise Seaman Bechtel*. New York: Macmillan, 1969.

———. *Children and Literature: Views and Reviews*. Chicago: Scott, Foresman, 1973.

Hearne, Betsy, ed. *Choosing Books for Children: A Commonsense Guide*. New York: Dell, 1982.

———. *The Zena Sutherland Lectures: 1983–1992*. New York: Clarion, 1993.

Isaacson, Richard H., Ferne E. Hillegas, and Juliette Yaakov, eds. *Children's Catalog*, 15th ed. New York: H.W. Wilson, 1986.

Jones, Malcolm, Jr., with Ray Sawhide. "Just Too Good to Be True," *Newsweek*, May 4, 1992, p. 68.

Karl, Jean. *From Childhood to Childhood*. New York: John Day, 1970.

Kingman, Lee, ed. *Newbery and Caldecott Medal Books 1956–1965*. Boston: Horn Book, 1965.

———. *Newbery and Caldecott Medal Books 1966–1975*. Boston: Horn Book, 1975.

Lanes, Selma G. *The Art of Maurice Sendak*. New York: Harry N. Abrams, 1980.

———. *Down the Rabbit Hole: Adventures and Misadventures in the Realm of Children's Literature*. New York: Atheneum, 1971.

Larrick, Nancy. *A Parent's Guide to Children's Reading*, 5th ed. New York: Bantam, 1975.

Lipson, Eden Ross. *The New York Times Parent's Guide to the Best Books for Children*. New York: Times Books, 1988.

Lurie, Alison. *Don't Tell the Grownups Why Kids Like the Books They Do*. New York: Avon, 1990.

Lynch-Brown, Carol, and Carl Tomlinson. *Essentials of Children's Literature*. Boston: Allyn and Bacon, 1993.

Mahony, Bertha E., Louise P. Latimer, and Beulah Folmsbee. *Illustrators of Children's Books, 1744–1945*. Boston: Horn Book, 1947.

Marsa, Linda. "Talk Is Chief: When Seattle Spoke, Were Environmentalists Listening?" *Omni*, December 1992, vo. 15, issue 3, p. 18.

Meigs, Cornelia, ed. *A Critical History of Children's Literature*. New York: Macmillan, 1953, 1969.

Meyer, Susan E. *A Treasury of the Great Children's Book Illustrators*. New York: Harry N. Abrams, 1987.

Miller, Bertha Mahony, and Elinor Whitney Field. *Caldecott Medal Books: 1938–1957*. Boston: Horn Book, 1957.

———. *Newbery Medal Books: 1922–1955, vol. 1*. Boston: Horn Book, 1957.

———. *Realms of Gold in Children's Books*. New York: Doubleday, 1929.

Moore, Anne Carroll. *My Roads to Childhood: Views and Reviews of Children's Books*. Boston: Horn Book, 1961.

Murray, Mary. "The Little Green Lie." *Reader's Digest*, July 1993, vol. 143, issue 855, pp. 100–104.

Pitz, Henry C. *Illustrating Children's Books: History-Technique-Production*. New York: Watson-Guptill, 1963.

Rudman, Masha Kabakow, ed. *Children's Literature: Resource for the Classroom*, 2nd. ed. Norwood, Mass.: Christopher-Gordon, 1993.

Stewig, John Warren. *Children and Literature*, 2nd ed. Boston: Houghton Mifflin, 1988.

Stuart, Dee. "An Exclusive Interview with Newbery Award-winning Author Lloyd Alexander," *Writer's Digest*, April 1973.

Sutherland, Zena, ed. *Children and Books*, 7th ed. Chicago: Scott, Foresman, 1986.

Townsend, John Rowe. *A Sounding of Storytellers: Essays on Contemporary Writers for Children*. New York: Lippincott, 1979.

Trelease, Jim. *The Read-Aloud Handbook*, photog. Joanne Rath. New York: Penguin, 1982.

Tucker, Nicholas. *The Child and the Book: A Psychological and Literary Exploration*. New York: Cambridge University Press, 1990.

Zinsser, William, ed. *Worlds of Childhood: The Art and Craft of Writing for Children*. Boston: Houghton Mifflin, 1990.

Autobiographies and Biographies

Antler, Joyce. *Lucy Sprague Mitchell: The Making of a Modern Woman.* New Haven: Yale University Press, 1987.

Carpenter, Angelica Shirley, and Jean Shirley. *L. Frank Baum: Royal Historian of Oz.* Minneapolis: Lerner, 1992.

Cleary, Beverly. *A Girl From Yamhill.* New York: Morrow, 1988.

Coffman, Ramon P. and Nathan G. Goodman. *Famous Authors for Young People.* New York: Dodd, Mead, 1943.

Commire, Anne, ed. *Something About the Author.* Detroit: Gale Research, 1971– .

———. *Yesterday's Authors of Books for Children*, vols. 1 and 2. Detroit: Gale Research, 1977.

Gág, Wanda. *Growing Pains.* New York: Coward, 1940.

Holtz, William. *The Ghost in the Little House: A Life of Rose Wilder Lane.* Columbia, Missouri: University of Missouri Press, 1993.

Johnston, Norma. *Louisa May: The World and Works of Louisa May Alcott.* New York: Four Winds Press, 1991.

Kovacs, Deborah, and James Preller. *Meet the Authors and Illustrators: 60 Creators of Favorite Children's Books Talk About Their Work.* New York: Scholastic, 1991.

Lane, Margaret. *The Magic Years of Beatrix Potter.* London and New York: Frederick Warne, 1978.

Lee, Betsy. *Judy Blume's Story.* New York: Dillon Press, 1981.

MacDonald, Ruth K., ed. *Dr. Seuss*, in Twayne's United States Authors series (Children's Literature). Boston: Twayne Publishers, 1988.

Mills, Judie. *John F. Kennedy.* New York: Franklin Watts, 1988.

Milne, Christopher. *The Enchanted Places.* New York: Dutton, 1975.

Montgomery, Elizabeth Ryder. *The Story Behind Great Stories.* New York: Dodd, Mead, 1947.

Paterson, Katherine. *The Spying Heart.* New York: Dutton, 1989.

Scharnhorst, Gary, with Jack Bales. *The Lost Life of Horatio Alger, Jr.* Bloomington: Indiana University Press, 1985.

Scott, Alma. *Wanda Gág.* Minneapolis: University of Minnesota Press, 1949.

Sendak, Maurice. *Caldecott and Co.: Notes on Books & Pictures.* New York: Farrar, Straus and Giroux, 1988.

Sonheim, Amy. *Maurice Sendak*, in Twayne's United States Authors series (Children's Literature). Boston: Twayne Publishers, 1991.

Taylor, Judy. *Beatrix Potter: Artist, Storyteller and Countrywoman*. New York: Frederick Warne, 1986.

Thwaite, Ann. *A. A. Milne: The Man Behind Winnie the Pooh*. New York: Random House, 1990.

American History

Andrist, Ralph. *American Century: One Hundred Years of Changing Life Styles in America*. New York: American Heritage Press, 1972.

Archer, Jules. *The Incredible Sixties: The Stormy Years That Changed America*. New York: Harcourt, 1986.

Barzun, Jacques. *Begin Here: The Forgotten Conditions of Teaching and Learning*. Chicago: University of Chicago Press, 1991.

Bettmann, Otto L. *The Good Old Days—They Were Terrible*. New York: Random House, 1977.

Connell, W. F. *A History of Education in the Twentieth Century World*. New York: Teachers College Press, 1980.

Duden, Jane. *1950s Timelines*. New York: Crestwood House, 1989.

———. *1960s Timelines*. New York: Crestwood House, 1989.

———. *1970s Timelines*. New York: Crestwood House, 1989.

Furnas, J. C. *The Americans: A Social History of the United States, 1587–1914*. New York: Putnam, 1969.

Harrington, Michael. *The Next America: The Decline and Rise of the United States*, photog. Bob Adelman. New York: Holt, 1981.

Harvey, Jr., Edmund H., ed. *Our Glorious Century*. Pleasantville, N.Y.: Reader's Digest, 1994.

Haskins, James, and Kathleen Benson. *The 60s Reader*. New York: Viking-Penguin, 1988.

Horsley, Edith. *The 1950s*. London: Bison Books, 1978.

Inge, M. Thomas, ed. *Handbook of American Popular Culture*, 3 vols. Westport, Conn.: Greenwood Press, 1978–1981.

Johnson, Haynes. *Sleepwalking Through History*. New York: W.W. Norton, 1991.

Kidder, Tracy. *Among Schoolchildren*. Boston: Houghton Mifflin, 1989 (Richard Todd Book).

Lindop, Edmund. *An Album of the Fifties*. New York: Franklin Watts, 1978.

McDermott, John J., ed. *The Philosophy of Dewey: The Lived Experience*, vol. 2. New York: Putnam, 1973.

Orem, R. C., ed. *Montessori: Her Method and the Movement, What You Need to Know*. New York: Putnam, 1967.
Phillips, Cabell. *Decade of Triumph and Trouble: The 1940s*. New York: The New York Times, 1975.
Sidel, Ruth. *On Her Own: Growing Up in the Shadow of the American Dream*. New York: Viking, 1990.
Stern, Jane and Michael. *Encyclopedia of Pop Culture*. New York: HarperCollins, 1992.
Time-Life, eds. of *This Fabulous Century: Sixty Years of American Life*, vols. 1–4. New York: Time-Life Books, 1969.
Vidal, Gore. *United States: Essays 1952–1992*. New York: Random House, 1993.

INDEX

Entries are filed letter-by-letter. Book titles are in *italics*. *Italic numbers* indicate illustrations and captions. **Bold numbers** define location of book titles by age category. An entry followed by an asterisk (*) denotes illustrator only.

A

B

C

D

E

F

G

I

J

K

L

M

N

O

P

Q

R

S

T

U

V

W

X Y Z